NATIONAL
GEOGRAPHIC

A DIVER'S
GUIDE
TO THE
WORLD

Australia's Lord Howe Island is an ecological gem above and beneath the
surface, with cloud forests and the
world's southernmost tropical reef.

A DIVER'S
GUIDE
TO THE
WORLD

Remarkable Dive Travel Destinations
Above and Beneath the Surface

CARRIE MILLER & CHRIS TAYLOR
FOREWORD BY BRIAN SKERRY

NATIONAL GEOGRAPHIC
WASHINGTON, D.C.

The ocean holds incalculable marvels, like this mauve stinger in Gozo. Diving makes our world so much bigger and more connected—and highlights how fragile it is.

CONTENTS

Foreword by Brian Skerry   6
Introduction   8

ALONNISOS, GREECE   16
ANDROS AND NASSAU, THE BAHAMAS   22
SYDNEY, AUSTRALIA   28
BAY OF ISLANDS, NEW ZEALAND   34
TOFO BEACH, MOZAMBIQUE   40
HVAR, CROATIA   46
BYRON BAY, AUSTRALIA   52
MALAPASCUA ISLAND, PHILIPPINES   58
BRITISH VIRGIN ISLANDS   64
BELIZE   70
EASTER ISLAND, CHILE   76
EXMOUTH, AUSTRALIA   82
FRÉGATE, SEYCHELLES   88
GRAND CAYMAN, CAYMAN ISLANDS   94
GOZO, MALTA   100
MUNDA AND GIZO, SOLOMON ISLANDS   106
KENTING NATIONAL PARK, TAIWAN   112
BORMES-LES-MIMOSAS, FRANCE   118
GALÁPAGOS ISLANDS, ECUADOR   124
FLORIDA KEYS, UNITED STATES   130
KO SAMUI, THAILAND   136
KOMODO, INDONESIA   142
HAWAI'I, UNITED STATES   148
LAGUNA BEACH, UNITED STATES   154
LIZARD ISLAND, AUSTRALIA   160
SAINT-MALO, FRANCE   166
MARLBOROUGH SOUNDS, NEW ZEALAND   172
MILFORD SOUND, NEW ZEALAND   178

RAJA AMPAT, INDONESIA   184
MOOREA, FRENCH POLYNESIA   190
ZANZIBAR, TANZANIA   196
NHA TRANG, VIETNAM   202
NOSY AMBARIOVATO, MADAGASCAR   208
NIUE   214
OKINAWA, JAPAN   220
ORKNEY ISLANDS, UNITED KINGDOM   226
OUTER BANKS, UNITED STATES   232
PETIT ST. VINCENT, ST. VINCENT AND THE GRENADINES   238
PORT LINCOLN, AUSTRALIA   244
KO LANTA, THAILAND   250
RAROTONGA, COOK ISLANDS   256
SABA   262
LORD HOWE ISLAND, AUSTRALIA   268
TAVEUNI ISLAND, FIJI   274
TULUM, MEXICO   280
UMKOMAAS, SOUTH AFRICA   286
VALDEZ, UNITED STATES   292
ESPIRITU SANTO, VANUATU   298
CURAÇAO   304
COCOS (KEELING) ISLANDS, AUSTRALIA   310

What to Pack   316
A Conversation With Dr. Sylvia Earle   320
Marine Protected Areas   324
New Diver Resources   326
Dedication   332
Acknowledgments   333
Illustrations Credits   334
Index   337

FOREWORD

BRIAN SKERRY, PHOTOJOURNALIST
AND NATIONAL GEOGRAPHIC EXPLORER IN RESIDENCE

What is the most important photograph ever made? This question or some version of it is one that I have been asked from time to time over the years, and my answer remains the same. For me, it is a photograph called "Earthrise" that was made by astronaut Bill Anders aboard the spacecraft Apollo 8 on Christmas Eve, December 24, 1968.

With this image of Earth rising in the darkness of space and the moon's lunar surface in the foreground, humans were able to see, for the first time, two essential things. First, the breathtaking beauty of our planet that was instantly evident from afar—a shining blue jewel floating alone in the darkness of space. Second, that we clearly live on an ocean world. The distant perspective of Earth from space provides an elegant view of the entire planet, but the whole, of course, is a sum of its parts. As we drift down to sea level and below, to explore individual places, the views get even better.

What I find most fascinating when traveling and documenting nature are the endless connections that exist everywhere around us. The fact that no single animal and no single ecosystem can survive on its own. A coral reef needs mangroves and seagrass beds to survive, and the largest whales need tiny krill and copepods to live. Rainforests need deserts and oceans need land. I have often thought of our planet as a fine-tuned machine, with multiple systems interlaced and interdependent, all working in harmony. Seeing places and animals as siloed and unconnected was once somewhat common, but traveling the world with a holistic view brings even greater wonder and enlightenment.

Though I rarely dive without a camera in hand, some of my fondest memories are those that occurred when I simply watched and tried to learn. I've hovered over coral reefs watching animals transition from day to night, observed tiny pteropods flying beneath pack ice through

winter seas, and swum with a newborn hump-back whale calf, knowing that I was the first human he had ever met. These personal experiences have both exhilarated me and brought me peace. They have changed my perception of things that I thought I knew. Beyond the personal enrichment I've gained from exploration, I have also learned that seeing the natural world holistically often leads to the realization that this finely tuned machine called Earth is both resilient and fragile.

As travelers, we are also ambassadors and must seek new and less damaging ways to explore and protect the places we love. Experts in stewardship-style travel and storytelling,

"What I find most fascinating when traveling and documenting nature are the endless connections that exist everywhere around us," says Skerry.

Carrie Miller and Chris Taylor write not only from experience but also from a mindful perspective, encouraging immersive curiosity and conversation. This book is the result of their rare combination of talents. It is a book quite unlike any other.

If you desire explorations of land and sea and to enrich your soul with global experiences from wildlife to fine food, you can have no better guides. Open this book to any page, read a few sentences, and be transported to a magical place. Then go there!

INTRODUCTION

This book was born from love—a love of travel and a love of the ocean, the phantasmagorical blue expanse that covers more than 70 percent of our planet's surface, unexplored and unprotected, mysterious and magical.

Although the land and sea are wonderfully and inextricably interconnected, travelers tend to visit one or the other. Scuba divers seek out underwater realms, impatiently counting down surface intervals until their next dive. Land lovers might venture out for a snorkel or sail, but they're glimpsing only a pixel of the bigger picture. Exploring both underwater and on land is the most holistic way of experiencing a destination and the divine interconnectedness between the green and blue.

This is a book for those explorations—for dive travelers. It's a different kind of guidebook, written for divers who like to travel, travelers with an interest in the underwater world, or divers traveling with non-diving companions.

We take you on adventures with dragons and manta rays in Komodo (page 142). We ride horses in the opal-tinted Indian Ocean off Zanzibar (page 196), and linger in the land and sea gardens of Bormes-les-Mimosas (page 118), home to the first marine park in Europe and a stone's throw from the glittering Côte d'Azur. We dive in with white sharks and whale sharks in Australia (pages 82 and 244), and experience surf-and-turf safariing in South Africa (page 286).

There is a purpose to these extraordinary experiences: conservation through exploration. Jacques-Yves Cousteau was insistent that "we must go and see for ourselves." He understood people are stronger advocates for things they have seen and experienced directly, a thought seconded by Dr. Enric Sala, National Geographic explorer in

Coral Gardens in Gizo, Solomon Islands. There is a purpose to these extraordinary travel experiences: conservation through exploration.

residence and founder of the Pristine Seas project. "It is that sense of awe and wonder that makes people fall in love with the natural world and begin to care in ways they may never have known possible," he said.

To that end, each chapter in this book highlights a global issue, from the necessity of protecting remarkable ecosystems like coral reefs and mangroves, to sea turtle and shark conservation, to the importance of the high seas. We feature scientists and organizations that are striving to make a difference and suggest ways you can get involved—engaging in hands-on experiences, learning more, or donating your time, money, or skill set.

OUR FIELDWORK

We traveled to 50 locations in 35 countries over 14 continuous months, spending more than 250 hours underwater to bring you this book.

The concept began organically. When Chris and I first met, I was a seasoned traveler and storyteller, having written for National Geographic since 1998. Chris was an experienced diver, with more than 1,000 dives under his weight belt and the knowledge and network that comes with that. He preferred being underwater and still does—I believe he should have been born with gills. And although I have always been an ocean lover and water baby (avid swimmer and snorkeler), I was not a scuba diver.

As we shared our love for our respective worlds with each other—the terrestrial and underwater—we quickly realized how much we were missing out on. And that inspired us to embark on this journey to get divers traveling and travelers diving.

This book is the best of both worlds. As an experienced diver, Chris knows what he's looking for and what questions to ask. I've got the travel chops, but—as a new diver—I'm seeing this world with fresh eyes and I'm asking different questions.

We selected locations based on two criteria. First, the place needed to have a mix of land and ocean activities. Second, the destination needed to be *trying* to do the right thing by the environment—think caretaker rather than profiteer—even if it's not getting it exactly right yet.

During our 14 months on the road, we had the privilege of seeing the world in a snapshot of time, and what we saw was staggering. People have asked us if we saw the beginnings of climate change; our answer is no: We saw it in full-flood. It's happening now. Every place we visited has changed drastically in the past five years—weather patterns are shifting, species

One of our favorite things about diving is that it enhances how you see and understand a place. It gifts you a new perspective.

are migrating, and everywhere there is degradation and rivers of plastic.

However, in every place we visited, we also met legions of people who are fighting to make a difference. That gave us hope.

HOW TO USE THIS BOOK

This book can be enjoyed as a collection of travel stories and as a guidebook. In every chapter, you will find ways to enjoy everything that's wondrous about traveling—the connections, discoveries, and surprises—but mindfully, above and beneath the surface.

We believe the gravest sin we can commit as travel writers is to write the joy out of exploration. To that end, each destination provides a general overview and feel of the place, plus a few suggestions, leaving the rest for you to uncover.

Room with a view at Misool Resort in Raja Ampat, Indonesia. Misool is a shining example of the power of protection.

Our goal for the dive information is the same: We want to provide a realistic overview of the area and the types of diving on offer. Dive sites named in chapters, therefore, are *not* the must-dive spots, but rather what is typical of a few days' diving in that location. We spoke extensively with local dive shops and divers to round out our information.

Chris and I lurk in the margins, sharing some of our favorite experiences and travel moments. It's worth noting our travel style leans toward preferring small, guided tours (which support local communities and provide insights you wouldn't get otherwise), followed by self-exploration.

THE IMPORTANCE OF TRAVEL

There's no getting around the fact that travel is a burden to the planet. However, overtourism and undertourism are equally problematic—both exact costs on the environment.

Right now, tourism is the only juggernaut powerful enough to challenge unsustainable, extractive practices like mining, logging, and overfishing. Sustainable tourism (done in the right way) places an economic value on protecting places and species, which is what we need most right now—to guard our precious biodiversity and remaining wild places before they're gone forever.

Travel also connects us and helps us to see things differently. Most important, it reminds us how extraordinary our wonderfully weird planet is. How special and fragile it is. That firsthand experience is a powerful motivator to care, and to keep fighting for its protection.

It's okay to enjoy traveling—we just have to do things differently. We have to understand change and balance will take time, trial, and error. In the meantime, it's up to us to take personal responsibility for our wanderings. One of the most important things travelers can do is choose places, businesses, and operators that are honestly trying to do the right thing. Eventually those choices will weed out bad operators, and best practice will become the new normal.

"EACH OF US HAS A SUPERPOWER"

So says Dr. Sylvia Earle (page 320), and we agree: We can no longer afford to be planet passengers—we need to be stewards. We have an amazing opportunity to do things differently going

A diver takes pictures in Hawai'i. "Divers have a special role because they see what others do not," says Dr. Sylvia Earle. "They're ambassadors."

forward, and every decision each of us makes contributes to what our world is going to be.

Think of that old tale of everyone picking up a stone to move mountains. If there's one certainty in life, it's that the ground underneath of us can shift faster than we can blink. Sometimes we're able to carry boulders; at other times in our lives, we can barely manage a pebble. Do what you can today, in this moment, and do more when you're able. Encourage one another. Let's make it game on, not game over.

We hope this book encourages you to go and see for yourself. Explore the best you can, with eyes and mind open, and marvel at this perfect planet of ours. There is so much that is good here, from science to sharks, kindness to kingfish. From small steps to giant strides, each of us can embark on our own individual journey to become better caretakers—stewards—of this wonderful green-and-blue planet we call home. We all have a superpower, and together we can move mountains.

"A picture is worth a thousand words," says Dr. Sylvia Earle, "but an experience has got to be worth at least a thousand pictures."

Valdez
United States
292

Orkney Islands
United Kingdom
226

Saint-Malo
France
166

Bormes-les-Mimosas
France
118

Outer Banks
United States
232

Laguna Beach
United States
154

Florida Keys
United States
130

Andros and Nassau
The Bahamas
22

British Virgin Islands
64

Tulum
Mexico
280

Hawai'i
United States
148

Belize
70

Saba
262

Grand Cayman
Cayman Islands
94

Curaçao
304

Petit St. Vincent
St. Vincent & the Grenadines
238

EQUATOR

Galápagos Islands
Ecuador
124

Moorea
French Polynesia
190

Rarotonga
Cook Islands
256

Easter Island
Chile
76

NORTH AMERICA

SOUTH AMERICA

ARCTIC

NORTH PACIFIC OCEAN

NORTH ATLANTIC OCEAN

SOUTH PACIFIC OCEAN

SOUTH ATLANTIC OCEAN

SOUTHE

OCEAN

EUROPE

ASIA

NORTH

PACIFIC

OCEAN

Hvar
Croatia
46

Alonnisos
Greece
16

Gozo
Malta
100

Okinawa
Japan
220

Kenting National Park
Taiwan
112

RICA

Ko Samui
Thailand
136

Nha Trang
Vietnam
202

Malapascua Island
Philippines
58

Ko Lanta
Thailand
250

EQUATOR

Frégate
Seychelles
88

Raja Ampat
Indonesia
184

Munda and Gizo
Solomon Islands
106

SOUTH PACIFIC

Zanzibar
Tanzania
196

Komodo
Indonesia
142

OCEAN

Cocos (Keeling) Islands
Australia
310

Lizard Island
Australia
160

Taveuni Island
Fiji
274

Nosy Ambariovato
Madagascar
208

INDIAN

Exmouth
Australia
82

Espiritu Santo
Vanuatu
298

Niue
214

OCEAN

Tofo Beach
Mozambique
40

AUSTRALIA

Byron Bay
Australia
52

Lord Howe Island
Australia
268

Bay of Islands
New Zealand
34

Umkomaas
South Africa
286

Port Lincoln
Australia
244

Sydney
Australia
28

Marlborough Sounds
New Zealand
172

Milford Sound
New Zealand
178

0 km 1000 2000
0 mi 1000 2000

N OCEAN

TARCTICA

ALONNISOS

A Classic

Greece is geographically spoiled for choice. The country is home to more than 6,000 islands and islets (227 of which are inhabited) peppered throughout the Ionian and Aegean Seas. The island of Alonnisos is part of the Sporades group, which legend tells was created by stone-throwing giants.

This elongated, 25-square-mile (65 sq km) island is a place of wild beauty. Undulating hills are populated with pine forests and dense scrub filled with wild olive, oak, sage, and thyme. All roads lead to a beach here, especially on the eastern side, which is dotted with tiny villages and sparkling coastal coves.

Although it bursts at the seams with summer visitors, people come to Alonnisos for noisy meals with friends, hiking, and swims in the cool, clear waters of the Aegean. Most of the 3,000 permanent residents live around the main harbor town of Patitiri, which took on the mantle after a 1965 earthquake leveled Chora, the former capital. Now known as the picturesque "Old Village," it's a 2.5-mile (4 km) walk from Patitiri along an old donkey trail.

Apart from its natural charms, there is another reason Alonnisos outshines the other Greek islands: It is home to the National Marine Park of Alonnisos and Northern Sporades, Greece's first established marine park and one of the largest marine protected areas in Europe. Designated in 1992 to safeguard an area that is both archae-ologically and ecologically important, it is also a diver's paradise, with exciting and exploratory diving. Plan your odyssey now. ■

Steni Vala is one of many picturesque coastal villages tucked along the eastern side of Alonnisos.

Let's dive straight into the **marine park,** a pentagon-shaped, 873-square-mile (2,260 sq km) protected area. The park was established to protect numerous species, including one of the largest and last populations of critically endangered Mediterranean monk seals. It is also a cultural ark boasting Mesolithic-era sites and B.C.-era shipwrecks, one of which is diveable.

The marine park is divided into three zones. The majority falls in Zone A, which is tightly restricted, allowing some organized tours and hiking, but no diving. Within Zone A is the Core Zone, an area encircling Piperi Island that is a breeding environment for the monk seals. No one has been allowed into the Core Zone since the park was founded in 1992.

The park's left side, Zone B, encompasses Alonnisos. Zone B is open for some use, including 14 established dive sites and some fishing.

Consider that diving was outlawed in Greece until 2005 (prior to that it was considered a paramilitary activity), and you'll understand the true siren song of Alonnisos: Every dive here is a discovery, with a fresh and exploratory feel.

Zone B is riddled with underwater caverns and crevices, ideal hiding places for enormous schools of juvenile fish. *(Tip: Don't forget your underwater flashlight!)*

Choose a nice day, buy a map, rent a car, and road-trip along the east coast of the island, exploring the villages and swimming coves that scallop the coastline, like Chrisi Milia (good for kids), Katerina Vala, and Lefto Gialos.

The **North Pinnacle,** near the island of Agios Georgios, holds plenty of chimneys to drop into, exiting into large caverns. It's dramatic terrain, with large, open spaces punctuated by pillars and boulders.

The **Gorgonian Gardens** lives up to its name. This deep dive (115+ ft/35+ m) holds a secluded garden of massive, brightly colored gorgonian fans, swarmed by small fish and the occasional passing pelagic. *(Tip: Alonnisos is a place where a deep-dive certification comes in handy.)*

Every now and again, an exploratory dive is possible. Although every dive holds something new, there is something thrilling about venturing into an area that is rarely—if ever—visited by divers. We took advantage of a flat calm day to dive an area that is often weathered out. It turned out to be the remnants of a large, underwater landslide that swept huge boulders across the seabed, providing natural nooks and crannies to shelter marine life like crustaceans, moray eels, and octopuses. We named this new site **Buried Alive.**

One site we didn't get the chance to dive (it wasn't opened yet) was the ***Peristera,*** a 2,500-year-old shipwreck holding more than 4,000 amphorae, resting around 98 feet (30 m). Archaeologists believe it was a large Athenian barge used to transport wine, and finding it altered years of thinking. Prior to the *Peristera's* discovery, it was believed that ships of this size were first built by

Greece is gradually opening archaeological sites to divers (from the B.C.-era *Peristera* to the *Christoforos,* pictured, which sank in 1983).

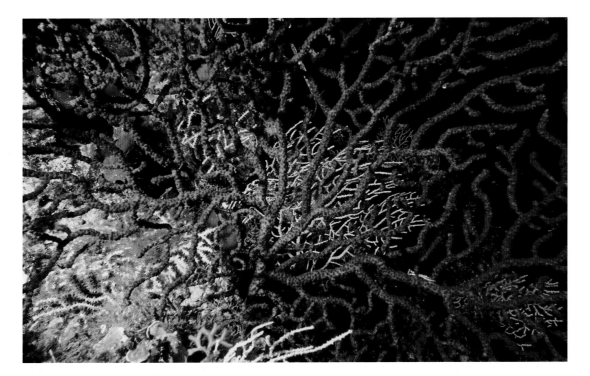

the Romans around the first century B.C.; the *Peristera* was built four centuries earlier.

Alonnisos's plan is to slowly open some of its precious wrecks, like the *Peristera*, to divers, creating underwater museums, complete with signage. And divers should keep a weather eye on Alonnisos: More of the park might be opened in the coming years for additional exploratory diving.

Opening the park does pose risks—unscrupulous treasure-hunters or accidental damage by divers, for example. However, the benefits are an increased number of underwater eyes to help monitor the park (good for measuring the effectiveness of the park's protections against illegal poaching and fishing), as well as generated income (which helps with justifying protections). Alonnisos has a deep love for its marine environment, but it also has a centuries-old fishing culture, and divers can see evidence of that everywhere, from ancient gorgonians wrapped in fishing line, to an absence of medium-size fish.

The National Marine Park of Alonnisos and Northern Sporades, Greece's first marine park, protects archaeological and ecological treasures.

These are conversations to be had. In the meantime, Alonnisos is in possession of something rare and wonderful, and if the community takes slow and measured steps, they will be able to strike a balance between preserving the wealth of the waters and generating economic opportunities.

And it's not just divers who get to enjoy this Aegean jewel: Snorkel safaris and day cruises into the marine park are also on offer.

We chose an all-day outing with **Captain Pakis Athanasiou's Gorgona Cruises.** This comfortable cruise aboard a traditional wooden caïque hugs the coastline, heading north, past pebbled beaches, tiny villages, and pine-tree crested hills. We anchored for the occasional swimming stop or paused to marvel at sleek Eleonora's falcons swooping from steep coastal perches. Captain Pakis frequently settled into his favorite "story spot" on the boat to sit and regale us with the area's history, archaeology, and mythology, an easy marriage of truth and tales. "In Greece, we never tell lies," Captain Pakis said, straight-faced, eyes twinkling. "We tell myths."

The highlight of the cruise is a stop at the **Monastery of Kyra Pangia,** established in A.D. 993. From a breathtakingly beautiful cove, we followed a loose-stoned trail flanked by sage bushes from the dock to the monastery's hillside perch. It's home to three black-robed monks who will live here for the rest of their lives, dedicating one-third of the day to prayer. The monastery is light and airy, shaded by trellises dripping grapes. One room—filled with hanging lamps, gold-leaf portraits, and other objects of opulent beauty—has an ocean-scene floor mural, depicting a dolphin, fish, and flying seabirds. The ocean, it seems, is never far away here.

After a tasty vegetarian lunch back on board, we slid into the bright blue of the Aegean for a couple of afternoon swims before slowly heading back to port. (*Tip: Pack good walking shoes and a respectful shoulder covering for the monastery visit, as well as sun cover, reef-safe sunscreen, swimwear, a towel, and snorkel gear if you have it.*)

No visit to Alonnisos—an island of hiking trails and beaches—is complete without a **walk from Patitiri to the Old Village** along the well-traveled donkey trail. Eventually the trail tips out into narrow cobblestone streets framed by picturesque

Alonnisos's Old Village, restored from a 1965 earthquake, is a walking-only town filled with artisan shops and tavernas.

houses, restored from the 1965 earthquake. This is a walking-only town with eyes over the Aegean. Its cheerfully painted doors and windows beckon visitors into artisan shops and tavernas. Like everything on this island, there's a shade of myth to it, one foot in daylight and the other in lore.

Such is the magic of Alonnisos, and here's hoping it holds tight to what makes it so special.

Make a Difference

The **Hellenic Society for the Study and Protection of the Monk Seal** (MOm) focuses on scientific research and education in an effort to protect Mediterranean monk seals, the rarest of the 33 seal species. There are fewer than 700 of these animals left, and more than half live in Greek waters. Mediterranean monk seals are the ocean's canary in the coal mine: They can live only in clean, unpolluted waters. They are also one of the most threatened mammals in the world due to hunting and habitat degradation. MOm's website (*mom.gr/home*) provides information (a great subject for kids' school projects), as well as opportunities for donations and seal adoptions. Contact MOm in advance and visit their facility when you make it to Alonnisos: They have an office in Patitiri and a rescue center in Steni Vala.

NEED TO KNOW

GETTING HERE: Alonnisos takes a bit of time to get to, but it's worth the effort. The most popular options are to fly from Athens to Skiathos, or take the bus from Athens to Volos or Kymi (roughly three hours), and then catch a ferry/catamaran to Alonnisos.

GETTING AROUND: Car and scooter rentals are available on the island.

PACKING TIPS: Good walking shoes, a hat for shade, and (Mediterranean) casual clothes.

WEATHER: Summer is warm, sunny, and busy—reservations are a must. During spring, the island is covered in flowers and ideal for hiking (expect chilly seas); autumn (September and October) is best for diving: you'll miss the crowds but still have pleasant weather and warmer ocean temperatures. The island is quiet in winter: Many places are closed.

IN ADDITION: Alonnisos is a destination for everyone: solo travelers, couples, families who want to entrust their preteen kids with a little travel freedom. Friendly nepotism makes the island go round—in a good way. Someone's aunt or brother will always help you out, or will know someone who can, so don't be afraid to ask.

Diving

OVERVIEW: The first marine protected area in Greece and one of the largest marine protected areas in Europe is home to B.C.-era shipwrecks, underwater gardens, and endangered Mediterranean monk seals.

- Visibility: 65-plus feet (20+ m)
- Water Temp: 57°F (14°C) in winter / 79°F (26°C) in summer
- Depth Range: On the deeper side—65.6 to 131 feet (20 to 40 m)

MARINE LIFE: Dusky and white grouper, barracuda, amberjacks, scorpionfish, moray eels, octopuses, dentexes, forkbeards, sea hares, nudibranchs, gorgonians, and endangered Mediterranean monk seals

SHOP INFO: We dove with **Alonissos Triton Dive Center.** This locally owned and run shop has a knowledgeable and memorable staff. The team is a lot of fun: Their love of their island is contagious, and they take ocean stewardship seriously. They offer boat dives and courses, as well as exploratory dives in the recently opened sections of the marine park. Guided snorkeling trips are also available. (Book in advance.)

Accommodations

HIGH-END: Located on the southernmost spur of the island, **Marpunta** is elegance encompassed in the style of a traditional fishing village. This serene getaway has three private beaches, wellness facilities, swimming pools, a taverna, and 100 rooms and suites. ~$100 USD

MID-RANGE: Paradise Hotel is aptly named. Perched on a bluff overlooking (and an easy walk down to) Patitiri, Paradise offers 31 comfortable, simple rooms wrapped around a wide terrace with to-die-for views of the Aegean Sea. The terrace features a pool, patio, and path leading down to one of the best ocean swim spots we've ever encountered. ~$80 USD

BUDGET: Kavos Hotel is located next to Patitiri, with picturesque views of the harbor. This family-run spot has a selection of rooms, studios, and apartments, all within a short walk (along a quaint footpath) from town. ~$34 USD

Food & Drink

Astrofegia Restaurant & Bar is a romantic Greek taverna in the Old Village overlooking the sea. Its humble beginnings are the real deal: The owner's friends kept turning up hungry, and so began a restaurant. Traditional meals are served in an outdoor stone courtyard under a canopy of ancient grape vines. (Open during the summer.)

To Votsalo is a family-run seaside restaurant in the harbor next to Patitiri. Their specialty is seafood barbecue, but the salads are also delicious.

Ostria Restaurant is a family-owned taverna on the waterfront that specializes in traditional meals like pastitsio (a creamy lasagna). (Open May through early October.)

ANDROS AND NASSAU

A Walk (and Dive) on the Bahamian Wild Side

Andros Island is not the Bahamas you know. This is the Bahamian backcountry, if you will, the largest landmass in a country encompassing 700 limestone islands and 2,400 cays with a total area of 5,358 square miles (13,877 sq km).

NORTH AMERICA

THE BAHAMAS

Andros and Nassau

Andros itself is 2,300 square miles (5,957 sq km). Its interior is primal forests, palm shrublands, and mangrove marshes, home to more than 300 species of birds (including the West Indian flamingo), 25 orchid species, wild boar, and the endangered Andros rock iguana.

Most of its west side is uninhabited national park, one of the largest protected areas in the Caribbean, a mangrove haven for juvenile and breeding marine and terrestrial life.

The east side is more traditional Bahamas: white-sand beaches shaded by palms, but without the high-rises and cruise ships. And this is where you'll find secluded Tiamo Resort, surrounded by a 125-acre (51 ha) nature reserve.

Underwater, the natural wonders continue. Andros is fragmented by three bights (saltwater channels), the southernmost a 93-mile (150 km) fracture connecting one of the world's longest strings of blue holes (also known as cenotes), giving the better-known Yucatán Peninsula (page 280) a run for its money. The world's third largest coral reef runs just offshore, and Andros also abuts a large Mission Blue Hope Spot.

Couple this with a dose of sharks and you'll see why the Bahamas' wild side is worth exploring. ■

An aerial view of the fragments of Andros Island, a wild place cut through by channels, studded by blue holes, and carpeted in forest.

Everything about **Tiamo Resort** reflects its natural surroundings: Cabins are tucked away in the forest, with sand pathways leading to the beach. Juvenile lemon sharks circle the floating docks, overlooked by the main house, with its pool, outdoor deck, and lounge. Stand-up paddleboard excursions became our morning meditations, cruising the flat topaz shallows, watching stingrays float over seagrass beds.

There are plenty of activities to choose from here, including private picnics on secluded white-sand beaches, spa treatments (the seaweed wrap helps repair sun and wind damage), and guided tours.

(Tip: We were weathered out from exploring **West Side National Park,** *but this half-day boat tour to a mangrove habitat that's home to bottlenose dolphins, sawfish, juvenile sharks, loggerhead turtles, and more is supposed to be something truly special.)*

We opted for a fascinating journey into Andros Island's interior, along the **South Andros Blue Hole and Nature Trail.** Our guide, Barbara, led us through a hardwood forest that is a medicine cabinet for those in the know. "This trail has been used for more than 300 years. This is wild cinnamon: We use it for toothaches," Barbara said, fingering the leaves of a plant growing near the trail. "And over here, this bark we use for teas. If you're over 40 on Andros, you still use it, but the younger generation would rather buy Lipton."

Walking on the uneven, twisted gray limestone rocks that make up the trail resembles walking on whale vertebrae, and we all got a start when a land crab darted out of a limestone crevice, brandishing some impressive claws. Barbara, unperturbed, picked it up for us to look at: "These crabs are important to Androsians. They're protected now, but we used to build homes and send kids to college on these crabs. Everywhere, things are changing."

Although much of Andros is protected in national parks, 80 percent of the island is less than five feet (1.5 m) above sea level, which makes it vulnerable to rising sea levels and climate change. Limestone caves abound, above and below water. Above, they're filled with chirruping buffy flower bats, and below they're similar to Mexican cenotes, but less crowded and even more unexplored.

This diving paradise straddles the Atlantic Ocean and Caribbean Sea, and there is much about Andros to recommend it to brand-new or inexperienced divers (especially kids): warm water, good visibility, lots of marine life, small dive groups, and even entry-level cavern dives.

The reef is filled with bommies and cracks, a maze of tunnels favored by schooling fish and critters (such as banded coral shrimp and lobster) that like to hide. The coral is colorful, but pressure is visible: Algae coats some of the shallower coral, and bleaching estimates in the area aren't positive.

Peace and romance abound at Tiamo Resort, an eco-friendly boutique lodge near the northern tip of South Andros island.

Make a Difference

Sharks need more protection, even in progressive areas like the Bahamas. There are many ways you can help: Diving with sharks is one way to learn more and place an economic value on their lives. (Check out **Stuart Cove's Shark Awareness Specialty Course**, a certification focusing on shark education and proper behavior for diving with them.) Supporting the work of nonprofit **Pew Charitable Trusts** (*pewtrusts.org*) is another: The Bahamas' shark sanctuary is a result of their partnership with the Bahamas National Trust. The Bimini-based **Shark Lab** (*biminisharklab.com*) is a conservation heavyweight in the area, undertaking shark and ray research, educating future scientists, and enhancing conservation awareness. (Facility tours, sponsorship opportunities, and internships are available.)

Lisbon Creek is a roller coaster of a cavern dive in the channel in front of Tiamo. It can only be dived on an outgoing tide. You swim into the cavern as hard as you can, then crawl down to a crack. Thick clouds of schooling fish obscure the entrance, which is filled with lobster. When you're ready to wrap up the dive, simply let go, and the current will carry you out in a rush.

(Tip: This is not a dive for beginners: The water is pushed through the cavern at an alarming rate.)

As difficult as it was to say farewell to the wilds of Andros, we headed to **Nassau** for an adventure of another kind: shark diving.

The Bahamas is one of the few places in the world with a relatively healthy shark population. In 1992, the country banned long-lining. In 2011, the Bahamas doubled down even further, creating a 243,244-square-mile (630,000 sq km) shark sanctuary. This not only establishes shark protections throughout the Bahamas' territorial waters, it also bans the sale, trade, and possession of shark parts, as well as commercial shark fishing.

Now people travel to the Bahamas from around the world to dive with sharks. Nearly half the divers who visit the Bahamas come here just to see sharks, with shark tourism generating $113.8 million USD annually for the Bahamian economy.

Shark diving can be a controversial topic, but the benefits vastly outweigh the negatives. First, it helps dispel myths and changes the way people

People travel to the Bahamas to dive with sharks (one of the best operators is Stuart Cove's Dive Bahamas, pictured). The economic value of shark tourism helps protect them.

see these creatures. Second, if done properly, with the sharks' welfare and diver safety paramount, there are minimal adverse effects on the sharks' behavior. (Resident species are receiving the equivalent of an apple during each feed—they don't depend on shark dives for food.)

Most important, shark diving places an economic value on the animals and their natural habitats, as evidenced in the Bahamas: Shark diving led to shark protections.

In Nassau, there's one company to go shark diving with, and that's **Stuart Cove's Dive Bahamas.** Divers

Parents and teachers: Check out Florida-based **Sharks4Kids,** which has a dynamic range of activities and educational materials (including info on Bahamas' sharks) for kids, all designed to inspire the next generation of shark advocates.

descend to the **Shark Arena,** kneeling in a large circle with the shark feeder in the middle, slowly distributing 17 small fillets of fish to the circling Caribbean reef sharks (we counted 21), nurse sharks, and even a goliath grouper. The sharks are definitely excited, swimming in between divers (we received a few bellies and tails to the head), but it never felt frenzied. And as soon as the food ran out, the sharks faded away, leaving divers marveling at the experience. *(Tip: This dive is suitable for beginners.)*

But an even better dive than the Shark Arena was the nearby ***Ray of Hope*** **wreck,** a 200-foot-long (61 m) freighter purpose-sunk in 2003 to be an artificial reef, resting at around 69 feet (21 m).

We descended to the bow segment of the ship, which has separated from the main cargo hold.

Beams of sunlight filtered down through the warm, clear water. Overhead, we counted more than a dozen Caribbean reef sharks and nurse sharks cutting through the light, circling the ship, coming in close out of curiosity, never aggressive, always relaxed. We floated there, suspended, and appreciated the gift of the moment.

It would be great if more dives were like the *Ray of Hope:* Divers experiencing plentiful populations of protected sharks in a natural environment, on the sharks' terms. But we're not there yet—we've decimated more than 70 percent of the world's population of sharks and rays in the past 50 years, with overfishing the primary cause of decline. (It's estimated that 100 million sharks are killed by humans every year.)

Until we restore balance, we need more countries to follow the Bahamas' lead in valuing *live* sharks over dead ones, in keeping the ocean wild, and in providing a ray of hope.

Sharks cruise wrecks near Nassau, sharing the water with divers and snorkelers.

NEED TO KNOW

GETTING HERE: Nassau welcomes multiple international flights per day. From there, it takes 50 minutes (a short interisland flight and boat ride) to get to Tiamo Resort, which can only be accessed by air or sea.

GETTING AROUND: On Andros Island, getting around involves boats, feet, and stand-up paddleboards. On Nassau, the public buses (called "jitneys") are convenient and cheap (exact change is required).

PACKING TIPS: We highly recommend packing tropical-style long pants and long-sleeve shirts for the evenings. Tiamo Resort has come up with clever ways to keep the effervescent population of mosquitoes and sandflies at bay (including repellent stations throughout the resort), but covering up helps. Sturdy shoes are handy for exploring the island's inland terrain.

WEATHER: Summers are warm (80°F/27°C); it's milder autumn through spring. The Bahamas is in the hurricane belt: Storm season usually runs around mid-June to mid-December, peaking in mid-August to mid-September.

IN ADDITION: Although Tiamo definitely has a honeymoon or anniversary vibe, it is a great place for families with children: quiet, safe, and plenty to explore. Tiamo Resort closes in September and October.

Diving

OVERVIEW: The Bahamas has it all: a great diversity of sites (reefs, cenotes, and wrecks), a variety of locations (from quieter Andros to bustling Nassau), good conditions, and a successful shark sanctuary, the direct result of dive tourism.

- **Visibility:** Around 66-plus feet (20+ m)
- **Water Temp:** 80°F (27°C) year-round
- **Depth Range:** 66 to 98 feet (20 to 30 m)

MARINE LIFE: Reef fish (midnight parrotfish, French and queen angelfish), Nassau grouper, cubera snapper, triggerfish, banded coral shrimp, barracuda, sharks (nurse and Caribbean reef), and green turtles

SHOP INFO: Tiamo Resort's dive shop has high-quality rental gear and fast speedboats. Due to resort exclusivity, most dives are valet dives (just you and your buddy). This is a great place to learn to dive or to gain more confidence. On Nassau, we dove with **Stuart Cove's Dive Bahamas,** a large and successful dive operation with a global reputation. Stuart Cove's is a busy marina-based shop (bus pickup around Nassau available) with high standards and a fun team.

Accommodations

HIGH-END: Tiamo Resort doesn't just strive to blend in to Andros' natural environment for aesthetics; it also implements sustainable eco-friendly practices: conserving precious water supplies, minimizing single-use plastic, and employing staff from local communities. The result is a boutique resort that feels very much a part of the island, equally elegant and rustic. Thirteen beachfront rooms and villas dot the nearly four miles (6.4 km) of private beach. The three-bedroom Bird's Nest is the premier accommodation, including living room, kitchen and dining room, a private heated pool, and hot tub. ~$1,400 USD

MID-RANGE: Most of Tiamo's villas are one-bedroom, encased with a private patio; some include a plunge pool. ~$550 USD

BUDGET: The cabin-style bungalows are smaller in size: one-bedroom, with a private patio. ~$450 USD

Food & Drink

Dinner at **Tiamo Resort** is the showcase: haute Bahamian cuisine (like seared fish served with a fresh fruit and vegetable salad), usually served alfresco on the terrace, with striking views of the sun setting over the ocean. Tiamo's head chef is Michelin-trained, and he returns to France regularly to experiment with new flavors.

Lunch is light, tasty, and fresh: Think sliced buffalo mozzarella and tomato salad, island jerk chicken, and strawberry mousse.

Breakfast is a casual affair: a light American-style buffet continental breakfast, with a few hot selections to choose from.

SYDNEY

A Different Side of Sydney

Australia's largest city has the feel of a summer's day: light, bright, and full of possibilities.

It has everything you want from a major metropolis: iconic landmarks (soaring Harbour Bridge and shell-like Opera House); culture (world-class museums and mouth-watering restaurants); and a strong history (Aboriginal Australians are one of the longest continuous cultures on Earth having lived in Australia for more than 60,000 years). On top of all that, Sydney glows with natural beauty, populated by parks and folded around a spectacular harbor.

There are three main reasons we love spending time here. First, Sydney's residents make the most of their city. They are rarely found indoors; any nonworking moment sees them flocking to their city's parks, beaches, and promenades to indulge in their dual passions of salt water and sport. It creates an invigorating atmosphere of cosmopolitan adventure.

Second, diving is right on your doorstep. Sydney Harbour is home to more than 3,000 species, more than any other harbor in Australia. This is due to a combination of tidal flushing and environmental diversity, including rocky reefs, sand flats, and seagrass beds. Shore diving rivals boat diving in popularity, and is oh-so-easy here—right in the shadow of the city.

Third, of all the major cities we've visited, Sydney is the easiest to experience without breaking the bank, offering up a wealth of inexpensive and free activities.

This is a different side of Sydney, and one that surprises us every time we visit. ■

Sydney Harbour is home to more than 3,000 species, including sea stars (starfish).

Sydney's boundless energy doesn't tolerate boredom. Every visit to this remarkable city whisks by in a flash, so let yourself be invigorated and make the most of your stay.

The icons are the places to start. The **Sydney Harbour Bridge** arcs up and over the harbor, with sweeping views of the city skyline and the Opera House. The adventurous **Bridge Climb** is well known, but visitors are often surprised to learn they can walk or cycle across the bridge for free.

The **Sydney Opera House** is also a must-do. This lyrical landmark is as pretty in person as it is on postcards. While seeing a show or taking a guided tour are special experiences, walking around the grounds, or—our pick—having a drink at the harbor's-edge **Opera Bar** is a great way to soak in the atmosphere.

Sydney's parks, however, are what bring this city to life. There are more than 400 of them, ranging from the 74-acre (30 ha) **Royal Botanic Gardens,** the oldest scientific institution in the country (1816) and home to an abundant collection of plants (free guided tours available; book in advance), to heritage-listed **Hyde Park,** Sydney's oldest parkland. This 40-acre (16 ha) park is located in the heart of the city and is a tree-filled oasis bordered

by skyscrapers. Don't miss the **Australian Museum,** the country's first, located on the park's east side. The museum is home to cultural and historical exhibits and delights in sharing behind-the-scenes stories. (Ask about Krefft's Chair.)

(Tip: Love history and have a little spare time? Volunteer to help the museum decipher old handwritten labels and notes. Visit digivol.org *to sign up.)*

We're learning more and more about the importance of green spaces in urban environments. Parks are valuable. They support the community and spending time in nature works wonders on mental and physical health. (If the pandemic helped underscore anything, it's that parks are an essential part of public health infrastructure.)

And then there are the environmental benefits: Mature trees and native bushland offset carbon. Plus, parks provide valuable pockets for wildlife that have otherwise lost their habitats due to urban growth, helping with the much needed preservation of biodiversity, from bats to birds to insects.

Sydney's parks extend beyond the city to its wider suburbs, some of which—like **Manly**—are an easy and fun ferry commute to the city, and a good base for divers.

If you think of Sydney Harbour as a half-open dragon jaw, Manly is the top tooth. This vivacious peninsula boasts a collection of cafés and shops, many of which line the **Corso,** a pedestrian mall connecting the harborside wharf with Manly Beach. Here, you'll find everything from surf shops to high fashion.

North Head Sanctuary overlooks Manly. This is a place of significance to the Gayamagal people, the traditional custodians and owners of the land,

The Sydney Opera House, the city's most iconic landmark, is a vibrant performance space for opera, theater, dance, music, and lectures.

Make a Difference

Seaweed has two things working against it: First, it isn't sexy. Second, it's out of sight, and therefore out of mind. When crayweed, a type of seaweed that formed dense underwater forests off Sydney's coast, disappeared (and we're talking 43+ mi/70+ km of it), it went largely unnoticed, until a group of marine scientists at the Sydney Institute of Marine Science launched **Operation Crayweed** (*operationcrayweed.com*). Seaweeds provide critical habitat and food for hundreds of species. They also capture carbon and produce oxygen, so they support us, too. Operation Crayweed is replanting healthy crayweed onto deforested rocks using biodegradable mesh. What they need most is funding (donations can be made via their website). If you're in the area and interested in lending a hand, get in touch.

and it was also one of Australia's most heavily fortified WWII sites. The dramatic cliffs and peaceful bushland are crisscrossed with walking and cycling tracks. (Guided tours are available through the Harbour Trust.)

Below North Head stretches golden **Manly Beach,** its pine-lined promenade a favorite with locals and visitors alike. Surfing is popular. Check out **Manly Surf School** if you want to give it a try, or sit back and watch locals of all ages take to the sea as if it's their second home.

(Tip: Surf Life Saving is an iconic part of Australian culture, and there's a reason for that: People get into trouble here, in riptides and getting swept off rocks. Exercise caution and ask advice.)

The southern curl of Manly holds **Fairy Bower Beach** (home to the uber-cute **Fairy Bower Pool,** a rock pool built into the coastline by Manly residents in 1929, and a delightful place for a soak), **Shelly Beach,** and the **Cabbage Tree Bay Aquatic Reserve,** a favorite with snorkelers and divers.

This no-take sanctuary zone has been fiercely protected and tended to by the local community since its establishment in 2002. The result is a thriving marine area and nursery, with more than 160 species of fish and 50 species of invertebrates identified, including sharks (spotted wobbegong, juvenile dusky whalers, and the adorable Port Jackson), giant cuttlefish, weedy sea dragons, and blue grouper.

For an urban area, Sydney has diverse diving: coastal and harbor sites, accessible by boat and shore, ranging from beginner to technical.

Both Fairy Bower Beach and Shelly Beach are entry points for snorkelers. We were amazed at how good the snorkeling was so close to such a busy promenade. Sunlight filtered through kelp that is a wobbegong's preferred cover, their long tails waving to and fro in the surge. Large schools of baitfish and squads of squid scooted by, and blue grouper were easy to spot, given their vibrant blue coloration.

(Tip: Cabbage Tree Bay is largely protected from the swell, so conditions are usually calm with good vis. If you have your own gear, this fantastic snorkeling is free. Snorkel gear rental and snorkel tours are offered by Dive Centre Manly and other local shops.)

Two hours from Sydney (by train or car) are the Blue Mountains, a UNESCO World Heritage site with lots to do: hiking, rappelling, visiting caves and waterfalls, a cultural center, and walks with Aboriginal guides.

Shelly Beach is also a favorite with divers. This beach-entry dive is sheltered and shallow (39 ft/ 12 m max), and there are two options: Follow the right-hand reef wall from the beach, or take a left turn, paralleling the promenade back toward Manly Beach. Take your time, and peer into seaweed and under rocks for good macro. This area also has good night diving.

More than 40 dive sites dot Sydney's coastline and harbor, a mix of boat and shore dives, ranging from beginner to technical. **Chowder Bay** is a protected shore dive that is a favorite with underwater photographers. There is always something special to see, from cuttlefish, to decorator crabs, to seahorses (like the pot-bellied or endangered White's, which are endemic to Sydney Harbour).

Long Reef on Sydney's northern beaches is an aggregation area for gray nurse sharks, which swim around this boulder-studded underworld, rife with caves, swim-throughs, and thick schools of fish.

Inner and Outer Colours are slightly more advanced sites along an offshore reef at a depth range of 66 to 98 feet (20 to 30 m). Both offer great topography (boulders, caves, trenches, and overhangs), with soft coral and schooling fish.

In 2019, Sydney's coast was named a Mission Blue Hope Spot due to its diversity and abundance of marine life, which is unique, given its proximity to a major city. At the time of writing, less than one percent of Sydney's waters are protected. Given how overwhelmingly important Sydney's seaside is—to marine life, and to salt-proud Sydney-siders themselves—hopefully underwater park protections will soon reflect what's happening topside as well.

Manly, one of Sydney's golden suburbs, is a favorite with divers, snorkelers, walkers, and—especially—surfers.

NEED TO KNOW

GETTING HERE: Sydney Airport is the country's busiest, with daily flights connecting Sydney to the rest of the world (including direct flights from the United States). The airport is about 5.5 miles (9 km) outside of the city center.

GETTING AROUND: Sydney has an enviable public transportation system, including light rail, trains, buses, and—our favorite—ferries (a sightseeing trip and commute rolled into one). Look into an Opal card if you plan to be mobile: It's a convenient way to pay for public transportation. Rental cars and taxis are available, but traffic can be gnarly.

PACKING TIPS: You'll be outside in a country with high UV levels, so pack chic and sporty layers and sun cover.

WEATHER: Sydney has an abundance of sunshine, with warm Southern Hemisphere summers (December to February) and mild winters (June to August; this is also prime humpback whale migration season). Spring and autumn have pleasant, cool weather and fewer crowds. Diving is year-round; July through September is cold but has some of the best conditions and visibility.

IN ADDITION: Sydney loves its festivals and the annual darling is the New Year's Eve fireworks display at the Harbour Bridge. From free standing-room spots, to the earlier kid-friendly show, to LGBTQ+ parties, there are a thousand ways to take in this spectacular display. Book early!

Diving

OVERVIEW: Rich and diverse shore and boat diving in a vibrant city.

- **Visibility:** Up to 49 feet (15 m)
- **Water Temp:** 61°F (16°C) in winter / 77°F (25°C) in summer
- **Depth Range:** 39 feet (12 m) for shore dives; 88 feet (27 m) for boat dives; 131-plus feet (41+ m) for tech diving

MARINE LIFE: Blue grouper, sharks (Port Jackson, gray nurse, dusky whaler, wobbegongs—tasselled, ornate, and spotted), weedy sea dragons, rays (fiddler and Southern eagle), yellowtail kingfish, squid, giant cuttlefish, shortpouch pygmy pipehorses, goatfish, seahorses, and nudibranchs

SHOP INFO: We dove with **Dive Centre Manly,** one of the area's pioneer dive shops. They conduct guided shore dives around the Sydney area, offering scheduled boat dives and weekend outings for all levels. (Check their website for schedules, trips, and events, like underwater cleanups; book in advance.) Dive Centre Manly offers training (including tech), refresher courses, Nitrox, and snorkel safaris. They're centrally located in Manly, which we found to be a good base for diving.

Accommodations

HIGH-END: Splurge on an Opera View suite at the 155-room **Park Hyatt Sydney,** which has uninterrupted views of the harbor and Sydney Opera House. ~$845 USD

MID-RANGE: Staying at centrally located **QT Sydney** is like living in the theater: It's dramatic, quirky, and entertaining. This 200-room hotel has an Italian trattoria, bar, spa and barbershop, and smart elevators. ~$229 USD

BUDGET: **Manly Beachside Apartments** offers simple, comfortable, affordable accommodations one block from the beach. (Tip: Rooms are located up a couple of flights of stairs, and there is no elevator.) ~$45 to $120 USD

Food & Drink

Alibi Bar & Kitchen is a haute cuisine vegan restaurant (part of Ovolo Hotel in Wooloomooloo) that is both elegant and eclectic, with delectable meals and divine cocktails and mocktails. Try the eight-course tasting menu.

The Pantry is an all-day Manly seaside café. The focus here is local and seasonal fare, served in a relaxed and picturesque atmosphere.

Bodhi is a vegan restaurant tucked under fig trees in the middle of Cook+Phillip Park, serving Yum Cha–style meals. There are plenty of exquisite, tapas-style dishes to choose from, but don't miss the sweet Japanese pumpkin dumplings—we could have eaten our weight in these.

BAY OF ISLANDS

Classic Kiwi Road Trip Around the Bay

New Zealand's Bay of Islands is a region in the northeast of the North Island famed for its beaches, water activities, natural beauty, and rich history.

Charming seaside towns like Paihia and Russell (once known as the "hell hole of the Pacific," now a beauty with flower-lined promenades) rub shoulders with the Waitangi Treaty Grounds, New Zealand's most important historical site. This is where the Treaty of Waitangi, New Zealand's founding document, was signed in 1840. It is a powerful place of museums, culture, and reflection.

Slightly farther south is the incomparable Poor Knights Islands, a marine and nature reserve located 14 miles (23 km) off the Tutukaka Coast. The islands are the remnants of 11-million-year-old volcanoes carved into tunnels, arches, and cliffs. It's also home to a crush of marine life that doesn't give a toss about divers (or snorkelers). This place is so special, it's captured the hearts of ocean legends, including Dr. Sylvia Earle. "Poor Knights is one of the places I really treasure the most," she said. "Here's this tiny little place that has been protected for longer than most places in the ocean and it shows."

After 17 years of living in New Zealand, we maintain that road trips are the best way to experience the country, and this one's a goodie: Starting in Auckland, you can whizz round in a handful of days, or explore as long as you'd like. There's no hurry, and no worries. ∎

Bay of Islands
NEW ZEALAND

Fish shelter inside the bridge of the H.M.N.Z.S. *Canterbury,* a large, purpose-sunk frigate that is one of the Bay of Islands' iconic wrecks.

Northland (which includes the Bay of Islands on its northeastern coast) is a thin strip of land arching gracefully away from Auckland. This cultural stronghold is home to small towns, beaches, a handful of rural roads, and rolling farmlands, with the sea always within reach. It is an ideal spot for a road trip, so rent a car in Auckland, chuck your fins in the back, and head north.

Tutukaka is a small town about 132 miles (212 km) from Auckland Airport (around three hours' travel time). It's dotted with art shops, cafés, and holiday homes. Lush green forest borders white-sand beaches and turquoise bays, with large pōhutukawa trees gifting shade to faded beachside picnic tables. Known as "New Zealand's Christmas tree," these stately evergreens burst with crimson flowers in the summer (November and December). The coastline is ideal for kayaking and walking, and there are plenty of opportunities (guided or independent) for visitors of all ages and abilities.

Tutukaka is also the gateway to the world-renowned **Poor Knights Islands Marine Reserve,** comprising two large offshore islands and numerous smaller islets, covering around 494 acres (200 ha). This is a popular area for diving, snorkel-

_____NEARBY_____

Visit Cape Reinga, the North Island's tip, where the Tasman Sea meets the Pacific Ocean. According to Māori history, this is where spirits begin their final journey to their ancestral homeland. (It's a 3.5-hour drive from Russell by bus or car.)

ing, and boat-based day trips—no one is allowed to venture on the land of this restricted nature reserve and culturally sensitive area.

This thriving ecosystem is located at the intersection of temperate and subtropical currents. Arches, walls, canyons, and caves are coated with kelp forests, swaying in the cold-water surge. The sheer amount of fish is staggering, and they are accustomed to (and therefore oblivious of) divers, secure in their no-take reserve.

At the **Northern Arch,** we followed a kelp-coated wall, past pairs of Lord Howe coralfish, conger eels tucked into rocky crevasses, and large scorpionfish. The wall curves into a deep cutting, filled with thick schools of pink and blue maomao, exiting toward the open ocean. Here, kingfish and snapper burst into action, cutting through a bait ball. Bronze whaler sharks are frequent visitors, and we were advised (pre-dive) not to get so caught up with the life on the walls that we forget what might be in the blue—manta rays, paper nautiluses, mola mola, and orcas have all been sighted at the Poor Knights.

Moorish idols were also spotted for the first time in May 2019, which isn't necessarily a good thing, to see tropical fish in New Zealand's cooler waters. Climate change is both warming and acidifying the ocean at an alarming rate. Recent studies have shown marine life is fleeing the equator, searching for cooler waters, which, in turn, displaces cold-

The Poor Knights' Rikoriko Cave is the largest surveyed sea cave in the world, yawning 262 feet (80 m) wide and 427 feet (130 m) long.

water species. What does that mean for us? We don't know yet, but scientists warn it isn't going to be good. (The only way to tackle this problem is to aggressively reduce our emissions—now.)

Diving is an all-day activity at the Poor Knights, and many dive trips have non-divers along, who enjoy the area via snorkel, kayak, or stand-up paddleboard. On the 35-minute boat trip to and from Tutukaka Marina, boats are often joined by common and bottlenose dolphins, Bryde's and pilot whales, and orcas. On one of our return journeys, we were surrounded by hundreds of dolphins and pilot whales, surfing the bow wave, breaching, and tail slapping. It was one final gift after a perfect day of diving.

· **Russell** is located about two hours (and one short car ferry) north of Tutukaka. We love this charming town, which has the renegade history of a whalers' port.

A jetty reaches out from a golden beach lined with pōhutukawa trees, whose roots have buckled the pavement of the ocean promenade stretching in front of balconied buildings like the

A carved figurehead adorns the bow of a traditional Māori *waka* (canoe), displayed at the Waitangi Treaty Grounds near Paihia.

stately **Duke of Marlborough Hotel.** The Duke is New Zealand's first licensed hotel, bar, and restaurant, "refreshing rascals and reprobates since 1827" (legally since 1840).

Down the other end of the promenade is the **Pompallier Mission and Printery,** home to a gift shop and café in gardens bursting with flowers. (Don't miss a guided tour of the printery, which was fascinating.) **Christ Church,** set a few streets back, is New Zealand's first—Charles Darwin donated to its construction, the grounds contain headstones of some of New Zealand's first settlers, and the walls still have musket holes from an early battle. Stretch your legs up **Flagstaff Hill** (a 1.6-mi/2.5-km loop) for 360-degree views and a lesson in civil disobedience: Hone Heke, an influential Māori leader, felled the British flag here four times in protest of British rule.

Across the bay from Russell, **Paihia** is the base for diving the area's shallow, flat reefs riddled with caves and crevices favored by moray eels, crayfish, and grouper (gold ribbon and toadstool). During the summer months, stingrays aggregate in the caves to mate, attracting orcas. (*Tip: Paihia-based shops can arrange pickups at the Russell jetty; or base yourself in Paihia, a lively town with plenty of shops and eateries.*)

Paihia is also home to a couple of well-known wrecks: the **Rainbow Warrior,** Greenpeace's flagship that was sunk by French saboteurs in the 1980s (now an artificial reef in the Cavalli Islands; this is a full-day outing, including a launch from Matauri Bay), and the **H.M.N.Z.S. Canterbury.** This large frigate was purpose-sunk in Deep Water Cove—a marine reserve with an abundance of life—and sits upright, with the bow at 66 feet (20 m). It has an accessible helicopter hanger, wheelhouse, command bridge, and engine room (this for more experienced divers).

Don't leave the north without spending a day at the **Waitangi Treaty Grounds** near Paihia. The grounds hold two modern museums, an authentic meeting house, traditional *waka* (canoe), visitors center, and café, all set within native forest and gardens. (*Tip: Plan to spend most of the day here; we recommend a one-hour guided tour and cultural performance, followed by time to look around.*)

The treaty was signed on the flat lawn, with its unmissable white flagstaff, overlooking the sea. It set out the terms on which the peoples of two nations agreed to live together—terms that are still being debated and discussed. The treaty is so much more than history: It is a living document, part of New Zealand's present and future.

The Bay of Islands will bring New Zealand to life for any visitor. It is a place to experience the cultural lifeblood pumping through this country's veins, as well as the richness and importance of the natural landscape, both of which help make New Zealand the remarkable country that it is.

"Refreshing rascals and reprobates since 1827": Russell's iconic Duke of Marlborough Hotel is still one of New Zealand's most popular spots.

Make a Difference

Hector's dolphins, found only in New Zealand, are among the smallest dolphins, growing to about five feet (1.5 m) in length, with a distinctive "Mickey Mouse ear" rounded dorsal fin. The two unique subspecies (the South Island Hector's dolphin and the Māui dolphin, found on the North Island's west coast) are near extinction; there are fewer than 55 Māui remaining. Although there have been partial bans on gill nets and trawl nets (their biggest threat), more needs to be done. What can you do? Public outcry in New Zealand and around the world is keeping them alive. Sign petitions. Write letters. This is a great topic for school kids. Visit **New Zealand Whale and Dolphin Trust** (*whaledolphintrust.org.nz*) and **Black Cat Cruises'** Protect Hectors (*blackcat.co.nz/protecthectors*).

NEED TO KNOW

GETTING HERE: Auckland Airport receives daily flights from around the world.

GETTING AROUND: A rental car is best. Take your time navigating Auckland, New Zealand's biggest city.

PACKING TIPS: Layers. New Zealand can have four seasons in one day, and the sun is incredibly strong here, even when cloudy. Kiwis tend to be casual, and jandals (flip-flops) are the north's mandatory wardrobe item.

WEATHER: Southern Hemisphere summer (November to March) averages around 75.2°F/24°C, with a slightly cooler winter (May to September)—60.8°F/16°C. Diving is year-round.

IN ADDITION: Outside major cities, New Zealand roads tend to be windy, two-laned affairs. Endear yourself to Kiwis by pulling over to let faster traffic by (since passing can be difficult), and it will always take longer than you think to get somewhere. Pad in extra time so you can take your time.

Diving

OVERVIEW: New Zealand's most famous dive destination, with temperate reefs and impressive wrecks. The Poor Knights Islands Marine Reserve is spectacular in its diversity and abundance. This is special diving, and suitable for divers of all levels.

- **Visibility:** From 33 to 115 feet (10 to 35 m)
- **Water Temp:** 61°F (16°C) in winter / 72°F (22°C) in summer
- **Depth Range:** Up to 131 feet (40 m)

MARINE LIFE: Pink and blue maomao, bronze whaler sharks, manta rays, bull rays, smooth stingrays, moray eels, trevally, New Zealand demoiselle, koheru, golden snapper, nudibranchs, kingfish, soft coral, sponges, kelp forests, pilot whales, dolphins, and orcas

SHOP INFO: In Poor Knights, we dove with **Yukon Dive.** This knowledgeable team favors small groups and prioritizes conservation. They have comfortable boats, running trips out of Tutukaka or Marsden Cove. In Paihia, we dove with **Paihia Dive.** Like Yukon, Paihia Dive is a small, locally owned shop that is passionate about customer experience and their beautiful backyard. Both shops offer snorkeling trips and dive training.

Accommodations

HIGH-END: The storied **Duke of Marlborough Hotel** is right on the waterfront. The Duke has 38 varied rooms and the hottest restaurant in town. *~$150 USD*

MID-RANGE: **Hananui Lodge & Apartments** is just down the waterfront promenade from the Duke (same amazing waterfront view), but it's quieter, perfect for couples and families, with lovely hosts. There are 16 units: 10 are in the main waterfront lodge and six apartments are on nearby York Street. We've stayed here many times and will return. *~$140 USD*

BUDGET: **Quality Hotel Oceans Tutukaka** overlooks the Tutukaka Marina, ideally situated for Poor Knights excursions. This 28-room hotel has a range of rooms (from marina views to two-bedroom apartments) and a good house restaurant. *~$120 USD*

Food & Drink

The **Duke of Marlborough Hotel** is a dining experience. The indoor area has a timeless elegance (our favorite touch is the stained-glass windows), while the outdoor balcony area is a lively spot with unparalleled waterfront views. The menu focuses on local, seasonal produce, paired with New Zealand wine and beers. Reservations recommended.

We always eat at the **Bay of Islands Swordfish Club** (BOISC) when we're in Russell. Visitors can dine as guests of the oldest game fishing club in New Zealand, which overlooks the waterfront. They have a diverse menu (seafood, burgers, salads, dim sum), and the chef will even cook your own catch.

Hone's Garden is exactly what the name suggests: a garden oasis serving up delectable wood-fired pizzas. This is the best lunch spot in Russell.

TOFO BEACH

Mega-fun and Megafauna

AFRICA

MOZAMBIQUE

Tofo Beach

Tofo Beach is a southern spur on Mozambique's biodiversity-rich coastline. This small town is tucked away in the southeastern province of Inhambane, bordered by empty, sweeping arcs of golden beaches.

Smelling of dust and smoke, Tofo is a small fishing village that's ensnared decades of soul-searching travelers with its azure surf breaks, vibrant reefs, warm people, and laid-back lifestyle. The result is a quirky culture, spiced by African, Arabic, and Indian influences, past Portuguese colonial rule, and an integrated expat community. The food is tasty, the conversation lively (in the national language of Portuguese, the local language of Bitonga, and a smattering of English), and days are filled with the bustle and ebb of living. Tofo is used to visitors and welcomes them.

This culture captured us, although we were drawn here by the megafauna. The warm and plankton-rich Indian Ocean waters attract whale sharks and manta rays year-round, and migrating humpback whales June through October. As a result of these bountiful reefs and waters, the dive (and snorkel) industry is well established here.

Adventurers be warned: Mozambique has a siren-song stretch (roughly 1,500 mi/2,414 km) of marine life–filled coastline stretching all the way to the remote and rugged Quirimbas Islands that is waiting to be explored, studied, and hopefully protected—if it can withstand the constant sieges from oil and mining exploration.

Intrepid travelers should also take heed: Tofo Beach is filled with people who came for a few days and stayed for the rest of their lives. Will you be the next to fall in love with Mozambique? ■

The long, empty arcs of Tofo Beach are favored by surfers, fishermen, and beach wanderers.

Mozambique is a place of morning and night, and days have a natural rhythm. The morning finds fishermen, surfers, and divers heading out to sea, and the market begins to bustle.

Afternoons are languorous, waiting out the heat wearing next to nothing on mosquito-netted beds, reading dog-eared paperbacks like the Alexandria Quartet or *Desolation Angels,* drifting in and out of a sleep interrupted by the sound of squeals coming from the pool.

Mozambeat Motel has partnered with the Marine Megafauna Foundation (MMF) to offer swimming lessons to local kids twice a week, and it is fun to cheer the eager students on. As in the Galápagos (page 124), most locals—despite the fishing culture—have never learned to swim; we were told that nearly every Mozambican has lost a family member to drowning. Along with swimming lessons, the kids learn about marine biology, undertake beach cleanups, and some even go on to become dive guides, which is one of the best paid jobs in the community.

(Tip: To learn more or to get involved, speak to Mozambeat, MMF, or your dive shop; this is a good spot to sponsor a dive guide.)

NEARBY

Mad-keen divers should also check out other hot spots like Quirimbas National Park (remote, rugged, and unexplored); Bazaruto Archipelago (a group of six white-sand islands); or Morrungulo (an unexplored, offshore, and life-filled plateau).

In the evenings, there is always something on in this serendipitous town, but you never know what it might be, or who you might meet. Restaurants and bars buzz with energy and music, which spills out onto the roads and beaches. Venture out and leave space for things to happen. *(Tip: Bring a flashlight: Streetlights aren't a thing here yet.)*

The long, lonely beaches that arc the coastline seem purpose-built for favorite traveler pastimes: surfing, walking, snorkeling/diving, and sailing. Tofo's main beach suits beginner surfers, and the **Surf Shack** rents out boards and offers small-group or private lessons. Surfers with some experience prefer breaks like **Tofinho Point,** a right-hand reef break on a rock ledge wrapping around the headland. *(Tip: This is an all-year surf spot, but peak season is May through August.)*

Beach walkers often end up at Tofinho Point, as well, which is a great spot for watching the surfers and spotting whales. Check out the **Monument of Fallen Heroes** to those lost in the fight for liberation in the 1960s and '70s.

Whether it's the empty beaches or the somber history, Mozambique does have a weighty feel to it. Gold first attracted the Portuguese to Mozambique around 1498. After that, Inhambane became a major port in the ivory and slave trades. And if you think Mozambique has weathered the storm, batten down the hatches: As in so many places (especially countries vulnerable to exploitation),

Happi, Liquid Dive Adventures' on-site vegetarian restaurant, is one of many delectable eateries in Tofo Beach.

too often nature is sold to the highest bidder here, especially oil, gas, and mining interests.

As we were writing this chapter, rights had been granted to extract minerals from Inhambane's exquisite beaches and to drill for oil on the borders of Bazaruto Archipelago National Park, a biodiversity hot spot that's home to endangered marine species like manta rays, whale sharks, and dugongs. The park also supports hundreds of coastal communities and is an epicenter for marine tourism.

But this time there's a happy update: Pressure from community groups and scientists (including MMF) persuaded the oil company to withdraw from Bazaruto, a welcome reminder that we can make our voices heard, and make a difference.

Riches come in many forms, and divers and snorkelers know where Mozambique's real wealth lies. From **ocean snorkel safaris** (with the Tofo Big Five: whale sharks, manta rays, dolphins, turtles, and seasonal humpback whales), to **megafauna-filled dives,** Tofo Beach's turquoise waters are a target-rich environment.

(Tip: There are shallow reefs for beginners, but

Marble Arch is a site with schooling fish and beautiful topography, including archways and a sandy-bottom bowl encircled by reef walls.

---

the exciting diving is out deeper, usually with stronger currents requiring group negative entries.)

There are 25 reefs within a 20- to 40-minute Rigid Inflatable Boat (RIB) ride of Tofo Beach, ranging from 40 to 131 feet (12 to 34 m). Most sites double as manta ray cleaning stations, where mantas queue up to have small reef fish remove parasites. Nearly 1,400 individual manta rays have been identified in the area, and divers can help support manta ray research and protection efforts by sharing ID photos with MMF and other organizations.

The aptly named **Manta Reef** is one of the area's iconic cleaning stations, a place of pinnacles and small caves. If you can tear your eyes away from circling mantas, keep an eye out for exquisite macro—frogfish, weedy scorpionfish, and robust ghost pipefish—blending in with coral in eye-popping colors and variety.

The Office is often paired with **Amazon** on a double-tank dive, since the two reefs are only a couple of miles apart. *(Tip: During humpback whale season, the surface interval in this area is often a breachfest. Keep your camera handy!)* The conditions need to be just right for a day at the Office and in the Amazon, as both sites have tricky currents. If you're lucky enough to take the dive, you'll have your eyes full: honeycomb moray eels, whitetip reef sharks resting under overhangs, turtles, and, of course, mantas.

Look for smalleye stingrays, too. They are the world's rarest and largest stingray (with a 7-ft/2-m wingspan). Almost nothing is known about these mysterious creatures, and this is one of the few areas where they are regularly spotted.

Tofo can be a place where it's all too easy to while away the hours underwater and spend topside time eagerly awaiting the next dive, but take a day to sail back in time on the **Mozambeat Motel's "Carlos's Tour."**

It begins with a sailing trip in a traditional dhow, a wooden concave boat with a lateen sail of patched canvas. There is something deeply stirring about sailing the Mozambique coast in a dhow, that ancient mode of transport, skimming along aquamarine seas, skirting in between long-lapping tongues of white sand, passing men fishing and women in headscarves, skirts, and snorkel masks duck-diving for mussels and crabs.

The tour includes a snorkel stop and a visit to a small island, home to a village of 800 people,

Tofo Beach is a megafauna hot spot, with year-round opportunities to dive and snorkel with whale sharks and manta rays.

before returning to Carlos's home village of Barra to enjoy lunch with Carlos and his family. On the menu is *matapa* (a cassava dish served with peanut, coconut, and rice), homemade coconut beer, and lots of laughter.

This relaxed but full-day outing is about as real as you can get, connecting Mozambique's past with its present, marveling at its jaw-dropping beauty, awakening an ancient wanderlust, and sharing a meal with kind people willing to open their home to strangers.

In Tofo, every day is a good day out. Perhaps that's why so many people choose to return—or stay.

Make a Difference

The **Marine Megafauna Foundation** *(marinemegafaunafoundation.org)* is a research and advocacy organization for threatened marine life (like whale sharks and manta rays). They have been instrumental in getting megafauna on threatened species lists and expanding marine protection strategies, working closely with policymakers and governments. In 2021, after nearly 20 years of research and lobbying, they achieved formal protection for manta rays and whale sharks in Mozambique. Get involved: Donate, adopt a shark or manta ray, or become an MMF member ($25 per month helps teach a child to swim every year, for example). Their website has lesson plans, or you can join an MMF expedition to a global megafauna hot spot. Visiting Tofo Beach? Contact MMF to see if it's a good time to visit their research center.

NEED TO KNOW

GETTING HERE: Flying into Inhambane Airport is easy but expensive, especially with dive gear. Many people fly into Johannesburg or Maputo and undertake the long drives (13 and seven hours, respectively) to get to Tofo via rental car, bus, or shuttle.

GETTING AROUND: Inhambane Airport is about 12.5 miles (20 km) from Tofo Beach. Taxis can be prebooked or arranged upon arrival at the airport; some hotels offer shuttle services (ask in advance). You don't need a car in Tofo—most places are within walking distance.

PACKING TIPS: Sun protection, robust travel insurance (there is a hospital in Inhambane, but most medical emergencies are treated in South Africa), and malaria medication (this is a high-risk area; speak to your doctor) are musts; otherwise, casual is the way to go.

WEATHER: Southern Hemisphere summer (December through April) is hot and rainy; April through early July is favored by divers (uncrowded sites with calm seas and good visibility).

IN ADDITION: Check out our tip about Ethiopian Airlines via Addis Ababa in the Zanzibar chapter on page 201.

Diving

OVERVIEW: Mozambique is all about the megafauna. This Mission Blue Hope Spot is a year-round hot spot for manta rays and whale sharks. Although there are shallow reefs for beginners, the amazing sites (reefs and walls) are deeper with strong currents, so Tofo is better suited to divers with some experience.

- Visibility: Around 49 feet (15 m)
- Water Temp: 72°F (22°C) in winter / 82°F (28°C) in summer
- Depth Range: 62-plus feet (19+ m)

MARINE LIFE: Manta rays, smalleye stingrays, sharks (whale, leopard, whitetip reef, and bull), grouper (giant and marbled), turtles (loggerhead, green, olive ridley, leatherback, and hawksbill), macro (frogfish, pipefish), and—if you're lucky—humpback whales and dugongs

SHOP INFO: We dove with **Peri Peri Divers,** the "hottest" (their joke) shop in town. They have more than 30 years of experience in the area and are close partners with MMF on conservation efforts. They have a good setup, with a 16-foot-deep (5 m) training pool, gear rental and storage, and stay-and-dive and free Nitrox packages. We love that they have a lot of local guides, all of whom love sharing their ocean backyard.

Accommodations

HIGH-END: Liquid Dive Adventures has a resort in downtown Tofo Beach. Their 11 beachfront cabins have all the basic trimmings (AC, Wi-Fi, mosquito nets). Non-divers welcome and on-site restaurant. ~$105 USD

MID-RANGE: Mozambeat Motel is a blast. This vibrant spot features a mix of eclectic cabins, standard rooms, and a dorm room, centered around an outdoor pool, bar, and restaurant. Located about one mile (1.6 km) from town and walking distance to the beach. ~$65 USD for a cabin; ~$10 USD for a dorm

BUDGET: Turtle Cove Lodge has a yogis and surfers vibe. This family-friendly spot has a variety of accommodations (from dorm rooms to family units), offering daily yoga classes and a vegan restaurant. Similar distance from town and the beach as Mozambeat. ~$36 USD for a chalet; ~$24 USD for an economy room

Food & Drink

Sumi Bar & Kitchen serves authentic Japanese cuisine in downtown Tofo Beach. This is a favorite spot with expats and the dive crew.

Happi is Liquid Dive Adventures' on-site vegetarian restaurant, serving fresh seasonal fare (like roasted cauliflower salad with feta) and drinks from a beautiful seaside spot. Bring your reusable bottle—they offer free drinking water.

Mozambeat Motel's restaurant has crowd favorites: homemade breads, burgers, and vegetarian options, utilizing local produce (some from their own garden).

HVAR

The World's Stage

A colorful cast of cultures and characters have all had their moment in the spotlight on the Croatian island of Hvar. Greeks, Romans, Venetians, Austrians, French, Yugoslavians, and more—they've all laid claim to Hvar at one point in time; sometimes more than once.

Despite its revolving ownership, this island in the Adriatic Sea has welcomed visitors for thousands of years. Its strategic location on main trade and pilgrimage routes, coupled with its beauty and climate, made Hvar a popular holiday spot for nobility as far back as the 15th century (a trend that continues today). Organized tourism has flourished here for more than 150 years.

You couldn't ask for a more breathtaking backdrop. This 42-mile-long (68 km) island is outlined with smooth-pebbled and sandy beaches, washed by the glittering emerald-sapphire Adriatic. The coastline and the interior's rolling hills and flat, fertile plains are dotted with hamlets of cream-colored stone houses capped by fading coral-colored roofs, bleached by the almost ever present sun. (With more than 2,700 hours of sunlight a year, Hvar is one of the sunniest spots in Europe.) This includes the Stari Grad Plain, a UNESCO World Heritage site cultivated by ancient Greeks as far back as 384 B.C.

Hvar is still shaking off its unwanted reputation as a party town, but it's quickly becoming a go-to destination for outdoor enthusiasts: hikers, cyclists—and divers. With clear water and intriguing underwater formations, Hvar has something for divers of all levels.

From people-watching in the town square to seahorse-spotting underwater, Hvar puts on a performance that's the hottest ticket in town. ∎

Hvar's romantic harbor has welcomed visitors for thousands of years.

Hvar Town is the island's capital and largest settlement, resplendent with Venetian architecture. The town's horizon is dominated by a striking fortress with two encircling stone arms. In Hvar itself, the captivating feature is **St. Stephen's Square**—a long, rectangular 15th-century piazza that's the largest in Dalmatia.

Although the square is flanked by the **Historical Theatre** (circa 1612, the oldest communal theater in Europe), St. Stephen's holds its own performances in the form of spectacular people-watching. Sit behind a pair of sunglasses sipping an iced coffee at one of the cafés that border the square and you'll see what we mean about Hvar being a stage. Everyone gravitates here, from backpackers to superyachters, and the stones that pave the piazza are worn smooth and polished from centuries of foot traffic.

That proximity to history is part of what makes Hvar so special. We took a half-day driving tour with **Secret Hvar** to see some of the island's most special sites. The tour began at the highest point,

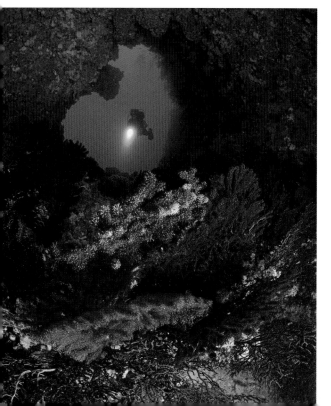

Saint Nicholas Hill (2,060 ft/628 m), and a brief visit of the chapel at its summit (built at the end of the 14th century), but mostly our eyes were drawn to the view. The hill slopes down to the village of **Sveta Nedilja,** surrounded by happy (and steep) vineyards producing the area's plavac mali grapes. "We have had 2,400 years of Greeks, so we've had 2,400 years of winemaking," our guide said. "We're pretty good at it."

From there, we drove down to **Stari Grad Plain** and took a short walking tour of this fertile farmland. It is a patchwork quilt of reds, oranges, and greens that has been carefully tended and valued for more than 24 centuries.

But Hvar's landscape isn't always kind: In 1909, a pest called phylloxera decimated the vineyards, wiping out the wine exportation industry. To combat the damage, locals began planting lavender, eventually producing 10 percent of the world's supply. Forest fires destroyed the lavender fields, leaving behind old stone terraces that still cobweb the hills. People eventually abandoned villages that had been settled since the 15th or 16th centuries and moved to more developed coastal areas that offered water, electricity, and tourism jobs.

It was these nearly deserted interior towns that captivated us the most, like **Velo Grablje,** a picturesque village with pink-stoned and orange-roofed buildings settled among scrubbed hills overlooking the blue Adriatic. Fourteen people still call the village home and attend its 1886 church.

Nearby **Malo Grablje** has seen better days, but it is the place to find the **Stori Komin** ("old fireplace") restaurant, a truly special dining experience. Berti Tudor opened the restaurant in his family's old home in this deserted medieval village,

Experienced divers will love exploring Hvar's deeper sites like Vodnjak (138 ft/42 m), a pinnacle with schooling fish and large gorgonians.

Make a Difference

Hvar's dive community has been encouraging the government to establish a much needed marine park. Visiting divers have helped by placing an economic value on protecting the area and through citizen science efforts. "It takes people as well as presidents to make things happen," said Dr. Sylvia Earle. "Laws are important, but people caring—that's what makes the difference." In the past, public awareness-turned-action has moved mountains, from bringing bald eagles back from the brink of extinction to nearly eradicating the practice of whaling. Never underestimate your ability to effect change. Responsible dive tourism, citizen science efforts, spreading ocean awareness, and active encouragement of marine protections are all ways to get involved and lend a hand.

located about 10 minutes' drive from Hvar Town.

"It was my grandfather's house; my father was born here," Berti said. "They moved to the coast to look for work, just like everybody else, but I decided to come back. It is our home. Maybe it will encourage others to return, as well."

A broken stone path leads to a repaired terrace that holds a handful of outdoor tables. Surrounded by stone ruins, we dined on *peka*, a traditional dish of meat, potatoes, and vegetables. Peka is cooked in a large metal baking dish with a bell-shaped lid, engulfed with hot coals and slow-roasted. It's exceptional, especially in this storybook setting. Moths fluttered around the candlelight and the night kept still as we dined and sipped our wine, listening to quiet laughter coming from the kitchen.

Traditionally, Hvar's surrounding sea has been utilized for fishing and recreational swimming, but the area's scuba diving is turning heads. Hvar is known for its good visibility, which makes it all the easier to admire the area's wrecks (some with artifacts like ancient amphora), coral reefs, seagrass beds, and impressive rock formations. The underwater topography eclipses the topside in drama: walls, caves, mushrooms, and pinnacles, some with cold thermoclines.

Although there are shallower dive sites suitable for beginners, this is a great place to explore deeper diving—most of the sites tend to be around 66-plus feet (20+ m). Most diving is from boats

Native son Andro Tomić has dedicated his life to Hvar's long tradition of winemaking, including the indigenous varietal Plavac Mali.

from Hvar or the neighboring island of Brač, with half- and full-day dives.

Vela Garška is an all-rounder dive from a shallow entry following a wall to an underwater cave around a depth of 16 feet (5 m). This 66-foot-long (20 m) cave has an opening that glitters with light effects and is a favorite haunt for moray eels and octopuses. The wall itself is covered in yellow and orange sponges, populated by a variety of nudibranchs.

Vodnjak is also known as **Campanile,** the "bell tower." This deep, open ocean pinnacle rises to a depth of 42.7 feet (13 m) and is carpeted in sponges and—farther down—large red gorgonians. Look for

The nearby island of Vis is worth a day trip: It has Hvar's historical feel coupled with Brač's tranquility, with a little wildness thrown in. Check out **Alternatura's Three Caves Trip** to the extraordinary Blue Cave, Green Cave, and Stiniva Bay.

scorpionfish and moray eels, and you'll see plenty of schooling fish around the pinnacle. Around the 115-foot (35 m) mark, there's a 17-foot-long (5 m) tunnel.

(Tip: This dive is suited to more experienced divers due to its depth—138 ft/42 m—and potentially strong currents.)

One morning, we took the ferry from Hvar to Brač for a day's diving. We traveled by boat to a site **(Smočiguzica)** that was, ironically, close to Hvar, but more easily accessed from Brač. We followed a rocky, sloping ridge that ended in a spectacular mushroom-shaped pinnacle, shimmering with a cold thermocline and overlooking a deep drop-off. We circled the pinnacle, surrounded by schools of bream and sarpa salpa, returning to a shallow reef carpeted in seagrass beds. This area was great for spotting macro like seahorses and fireworms.

(Tip: Make sure you have your deep-dive certification or have experience at depth to get the most out of diving here. Most shops dive to CMAS standards, so more experienced divers will notice deeper/decompression dives are more common here, although dives can be tailored to suit any level. Remember there is a lot of boat traffic in the area, and not all boats seem to know—or respect—dive flags. Be aware and try to surface near your boat.)

The diving puts on quite a show, but our favorite Hvar performance was our evening walks. We'd stroll along the pine-tree-bordered *riva* (waterfront promenade), cooled by the Adriatic winds, which Hvar's residents can read like tea leaves. We watched wiry, white-haired locals slipping into coastal coves with roped-off lanes for their nightly swim in the sea, making the most of every moment in their extraordinary home.

The aptly named Blue Cave on the nearby island of Vis gets its striking sapphire color from the reflection of filtered sunlight.

NEED TO KNOW

GETTING HERE: It's around a two-hour ferry ride from Split to Hvar. If taking a car (recommended), allow time. There are signs aplenty, but also traffic, and navigating the terminal queues can be confusing.

GETTING AROUND: Rental cars, taxis, or guided tours are best for traveling outside the main township of Hvar, which is very walkable.

PACKING TIPS: This is a no-high-heels location, as the cobblestone streets are begging to twist an ankle. "Ladies in high heels are part of our theater," a local told us. Apart from good walking shoes, Hvar is a fun place to try on a little style.

WEATHER: Hvar is at its warmest—and most popular—in summer, with temperatures above 70°F (21°C). September is an ideal month, especially for divers. Winters are quiet, with most businesses closing in December, but many visitors enjoy this more laid-back time and cooler (but still sunny) weather. In spring, Hvar wakes up (a good time for hikers and cyclists).

IN ADDITION: As with the Split-to-Hvar ferry, inter-island ferries (to Vis, Brač, etc.) can also be a bit chaotic, but it's organized chaos. Arrive early, be prepared to wait, ask questions, and double-check you're boarding the correct boat. It's all part of the fun.

Diving

OVERVIEW: Deep dives, clear water, spectacular underwater formations, and plenty of macro.

- Visibility: 72-plus feet (22+ m)
- Water Temp: 53°F (12°C) in winter / 80°F (27°C) in summer
- Depth Range: 59 to 131-plus feet (18 to 40+ m)

MARINE LIFE: This area has been overfished for centuries, so much of the marine life is smaller fish and macro: two-banded sea bream, lots of fireworms, seahorses, salpa. We also saw octopuses, barracuda, and moray eels.

SHOP INFO: On Hvar, we dove with **Aqualis Dive Center Hvar**, a well-set-up shop staffed by an enthusi-astic team located right on the waterfront. On Brač, we dove with **Big Blue Diving,** which is especially well-suited for families. Both shops offer guided dives and courses.

Accommodations

HIGH-END: As you're likely to be spending a night or two in Split, the **Cornaro Hotel** is an elegant and modern hotel centrally located in Split's stunning historical sector. The staff doesn't miss a beat here, and the Rooftop Bar has cinematic views. ~$183 USD

MID-RANGE: The **Amfora Hvar Grand Beach Resort** is modern with an old-school Mediterranean flair. It has a massive pool complex and is located right across the road from a beautiful ocean cove. (You won't regret splurging on a room with an oceanside balcony here.) It's an easy walk to town. ~$101 USD

BUDGET: Pharos Hvar Bayhill Hotel caters to younger travelers, with minimalist rooms resembling college dorms (although they're private), featuring pop art, plenty of cubbyholes, and colorful, plastic furniture. Everything's on-site (pool, restaurant, and bar), and it's an easy walk to town. ~$95 USD

Food & Drink

While in Split, book a table at **Bokeria Kitchen & Wine Bar,** located in Split's historical sector. Bokeria serves good food (like grilled steak with truffle mashed potatoes) paired with good wine.

Grande Luna is a family-owned restaurant with windows overlooking Hvar's narrow stone streets. The restaurant specializes in traditional Dalmatian dishes (such as *makaruni* with truffles), and the friendly atmosphere elevates dining to an experience.

Stori Komin in Malo Grablje is a rough-and-ready dining experience we absolutely loved. This atmospheric spot serves delicious food. You have to call in advance to book and preorder food so the owner has time to shop and cart the ingredients to the restaurant. Cash only.

BYRON BAY

A Pelagic Party in a Cool Little Town

There's a buzz to laid-back Byron Bay. This coastal town (population around 9,500) is located on Australia's most easterly point, about 110 miles (177 km) south of Brisbane. It's a travel hot spot, known for surf beaches, outdoor markets, yoga retreats, music festivals, and its lush hinterland.

The Arakwal Aboriginal people, the traditional custodians and owners of the Byron Shire area, called it *Cavvanbah* ("meeting place"). When Captain Cook sailed past in 1770, he named it after Vice Admiral John Byron, a legendary navigator and grandfather of the notorious romantic poet Lord Byron. It is somehow apt that Byron Bay's origins are loosely connected to gathering together, exploration, and hedonism.

Twenty million years before our history with Byron Bay began, however, something remarkable happened: A volcano blew its top and hurled a chunk of granite into the sea. And so Julian Rocks was born.

"The Rock," as it's known, is located 1.6 miles (2.5 km) offshore. It is a pelagic party in the middle of the East Australian Current, where any migrating creature (more than 1,000 marine species, including 500 species of both tropical and cold-water fish) stops by for a visit—humpback whales, manta rays, leopard sharks, and more. They join the resident population of wobbegong sharks, turtles (green, hawksbill, loggerhead), mulloway, and eagle rays.

Chris's first Open Water dive was at the Rock, and the very first animal he saw on his first dive was a gray nurse shark. From that moment, Julian Rocks had his heart. It remains his favorite place to dive. (And yes, he wants us to move here.)

Such is the power of this place. ■

A pair of wobbegong sharks snuggle up at Julian Rocks. It's not unheard of to see more than 50 of these Rock residents on a single dive.

It's easy to understand why everyone loves Byron. The weather is warm, there's always something happening in town, and the area is a natural beauty, with a mix of rich forest and long stretches of golden beaches.

Byron's town center is laid out in a walkable grid: three roads down, five roads across, with one main road leading in and out. Traffic can get snarled, especially during peak times/seasons, so save yourself the hassle: Park near North Beach station and hop on the **world's first solar-powered train.** This restored 1949-era, two-carriage train takes you into town in eight minutes for less than it costs to park, plus it's a joy to ride.

The **Byron Bay Hat Company** should be your first stop to pick up the staple Byron Bay wardrobe item, followed by a leisurely browse at the **Book Room Collective.** This bookstore stocks everything from best sellers, to the classics, to obscure titles.

Keep an eye on what's happening in town. Byron is fond of festivals and concerts, which attract everyone from Iggy Pop to Mary J. Blige to Australian bands like the John Butler Trio. Why are they playing a town of 9,500 people? They come here for the atmosphere, just like you.

A short drive, however, transports you from the coastal scene into another world entirely. Byron's

Surfers make the most of every drop of sunlight at Byron Bay's Wategos Beach.

NEARBY

South West Rocks is another one of Australia's great dive spots. It is its own unique ecosystem, with a large, shark-filled ocean cave (410 ft/125 m). It's about a 3.5-hour drive south from Byron Bay, just past Coffs Harbour.

surrounding area is rolling green hills and rich farmlands interspersed with quaint, picturesque towns like **Bangalow** and **Mullumbimby.** There are also tracts of rainforest, ripe with walking tracks and waterfalls, like the 328-foot (100 m) **Minyon Falls,** which cascades over a rhyolite cliff. Minyon Falls is located in **Nightcap National Park,** which is part of the Gondwana Rainforests of Australia World Heritage Area, the largest area of subtropical rainforest in the world. This is also a place of cultural significance. It contains ceremonial and sacred sites that have been used for thousands of years, and are still being used by Aboriginal people today.

Indigenous Australians are the world's oldest remaining civilization and one of the most diverse. One of the must-dos in Byron is to experience this place, hear its stories, and learn about its significance from its traditional custodians and owners. Aunty Lois, a Nyangbul Bundjalung Elder, runs half- to full-day guided tours to sacred sites, sharing history, stories, and teachings through **Aboriginal Cultural Concepts.** Arakwal Bundjalung Elder Delta Kay shares the knowledge passed down to her in **Explore Byron Bay's guided Aboriginal tours.** (For example, learn about bush tucker—traditional food sourced from the wild—in a walk along the banks of Byron Creek.)

Cape Byron Lighthouse is also a must-visit. This spectacular lookout is located on the Australian mainland's most easterly point on a hill that's visible

The 328-foot (100 m) Minyon Falls spills over a rhyolite cliff in the ancient forested area of Nightcap National Park.

throughout town. It features a 1901-era working lighthouse, café, and museum, and is the prime spot for whale-watching (June through October). There is a popular 2.3-mile (3.7 km) walking loop that winds along clifftops, grasslands, and beaches. It also passes **Wategos Beach,** which is emblematic of Byron's current crossroad.

Byron's relaxed beach town ethos attracted the rich and famous, and now it is the most expensive place to live in Australia; it also has the country's second highest rate of homelessness. A few decades ago, no one wanted to live in Wategos Beach because it was considered too far from town; now homes sell for around $17 million USD.

This battle for Byron's soul is consuming the community, but it's nothing that Byron hasn't weathered before. Byron evolved from whaling port to hippie haven to lifestyle hot spot and along the way there was a clash over a marine protected area.

Julian Rocks Nguthungulli Nature Reserve was established in 1982, a 10,000-acre (4,047 ha) protected area banning all fishing within a 1,600-foot (500 m) range around Julian Rocks. Community pressure sparked the marine reserve, but its creation wasn't welcomed by local fishermen. In time, however, the marine reserve did its work and fish populations rebounded, spilling over into fishing grounds. Now local fishermen are some of the reserve's biggest supporters and defenders. Surrounding the reserve is Cape Byron Marine Park, established in 2002, which extends roughly 23 miles (37 km) along the coastline, providing an extra layer of protection for the area's rich biodiversity.

And this is where we dive into the extraordinary diving on offer here at Byron Bay. There are basically two directions you can travel around **the Rock** (as drift or return dives, depending on currents and vis). Despite limited dive sites, Julian Rocks is worth multiple days of diving, due to ridiculous amounts of wildlife. You will never have a boring dive here.

It's a five-minute boat ride to the Rock. Conditions are very weather-dependent: You can have strong current, low vis, or flat calm days with great vis. Underwater, the terrain is a shallow (max 70 ft/ 24 m) mix of rocky outcrops, trenches, caves, and pinnacles, with sandy stretches in between.

(Tip: Diving isn't always easy, but this is a good place to push your skills a little, given the quality shops and focused dive area.)

The Nursery is where most dives begin, a protected aquarium filled with tropical fish and favored by wobbegong sharks that often stack themselves like Jenga blocks. From there, dives might continue to the **Cod Hole,** a wide swim-through which begins around 46 feet (14 m) and descends to around 66 feet (20 m). Here you'll find large schools of good-size cod, kingfish, and mulloway, as well as gray nurse sharks, Queensland grouper, manta rays, bull rays, cuttlefish, crayfish, and cleaner shrimp.

Or you might travel the other direction around the Rock, beginning at the Nursery and continuing to **the Needles,** a maze of sandy channels through towering rock formations. This spot is another magnet for big schools and big critters, including manta rays, turtles, and leopard sharks. Weather and air permitting, **Hugo's Trench** is a long gully filled with all manner of marine life seeking a break from the current. It holds everything from nudibranchs to gray nurse sharks,

A pair of old wife fish. Julian Rocks is our favorite place to explore, thanks to the sheer variety of marine life seen on every dive.

which pack into Hugo's during the winter months.

(Tip: Julian Rocks is also a great snorkel spot. Tours are offered daily to shallow, sheltered areas around the Rock.)

Byron is a place of abundance. It's easy to understand why it's been a gathering place for thousands of years.

Make a Difference

Byron Bay Wildlife Hospital *(byronbaywildlifehospital.org)* is a mobile hospital in a 52-foot (16 m) semi-trailer truck designed to treat injured wildlife at any crisis hot spot. The project sprang from Australia's catastrophic bushfires in 2019 and 2020, which, according to WWF Australia, killed or displaced more than three billion native animals (such as koalas and kangaroos), often because expert wildlife medical care wasn't available. The hospital is equipped with operating and recovery areas and staffed by a small team of veterinary specialists. It is a clever solution to what, unfortunately, will be an ongoing problem. Keen to help? Donate online, follow on social media, and volunteer (fund-raising, administrative support, and other professional services can be done from your home).

NEED TO KNOW

GETTING HERE: There are three airports near Byron Bay: Brisbane (the largest, international and national arrivals, a two-hour drive from Byron), Gold Coast (mid-size, international and national, 45 minutes from Byron), and Ballina Byron Gateway (small and regional, 30 minutes from Byron); shuttle services and car rentals are available from all airports.

GETTING AROUND: It is handy to have a car in Byron, but traffic can get congested, especially during summer or holidays. It's best to park on the outskirts, and walk or cycle through the compact town.

PACKING TIPS: Outdoor clothes and hippie chic; a sun hat is a must. Pack light: Shopping is so good here, you can buy what you need and fit right in.

WEATHER: Byron Bay enjoys warm Southern Hemisphere summers (79°F/26°C) and mild winters (64°F/18°C).

IN ADDITION: If flying in/out of Brisbane, note Brisbane is in a different state (Queensland) than Byron (New South Wales), and Queensland doesn't observe Daylight Savings. That means in summer there is a one-hour time difference between Byron and Brisbane.

Diving

OVERVIEW: One of the world's best dive destinations just offshore from a cool little town, suitable for divers and snorkelers of all levels. Julian Rocks has a huge amount of varied marine life that changes with the seasons, which keeps us all coming back.

- Visibility: From 16 to 82 feet (5 to 25 m)
- Water Temp: 61°F (16°C) in winter / 79°F (26°C) in summer
- Depth Range: Max 79 feet (24 m)

MARINE LIFE: Winter (May to November): gray nurse sharks and humpback whales. Summer (December to June): leopard sharks and manta rays. Year-round: wobbegong sharks, mulloway, kingfish, turtles (green, hawksbill, loggerhead), squid, cuttlefish, octopuses, crayfish, black cod, nudibranchs, guitarfish, and dolphins (bottlenose and common).

SHOP INFO: All of Byron's operators (Byron Bay Dive Centre, Blue Bay Divers, and Sundive) are quality, but we have an experience bias for **Sundive,** where Chris did his first dive and later worked. This is the original shop in the area, and it has a stellar reputation, with a host of knowledgeable guides and skippers—a fun, experienced team. Courses and snorkel trips offered.

Accommodations

HIGH-END: Stay in one of two **Assistant Lighthouse Keepers' Cottages** in Cape Byron Conservation Area. These heritage-listed, three-bedroom cottages have stunning coastal views and are a half-hour walk or short drive to town. ~$336 USD

MID-RANGE: **Elements of Byron** holds a variety of freestanding villas set within 20 acres (8 ha) of native forest. They are furnished with elegant interiors complete with kitchen, private bathhouse, and screened porch. There is an on-site restaurant, spa, multiple pools, and a private beach. Elements is also a short walk from the solar train. ~$303 USD

BUDGET: **Byron Bay YHA** is a centrally located hostel offering a mix of tidy private and shared rooms, with access to a huge communal kitchen and pool. While fun, the YHA tends to be quieter than most backpacker-style accommodations and is a good option for divers on a budget. ~$25 USD shared/$73 USD private

Food & Drink

Balcony Bar & Oyster Co. is a relaxed and elegant joint overlooking Byron's main streets, serving shared plates, seasonal food, and signature cocktails.

The **Rails Hotel** is Byron's best-loved live music venue. (It's a favorite with dive guides.) This relaxed pub has an outdoor beer garden, features live music nightly, a menu of casual food, and a raft of beers on tap.

Bella Rosa Gelateria & Espresso Bar can quickly become a habit. This family-owned business makes delish small-batch gelato from scratch using natural, seasonal ingredients.

MALAPASCUA ISLAND

Thresher Sharks and Karaoke

Malapascua is a small island (roughly 0.6 mi/1 km wide and 1.6 mi/2.5 km long) in the Visayan Sea, off the northern tip of Cebu Island.

It's shaped a little like a beaker, with the majority of its population bottled at the base. White-sand beaches rim the island. White-sand paths wind throughout the town, a few of which lead north to empty stretches of coastline. Palm trees provide shade, hammocks are strung everywhere, and the water is crystal and topaz.

Malapascua's three main pastimes are karaoke, basketball, and cock-fighting. You'll pass loads of glossy roosters on perches when passing through the village. "If you're rich, you have a cock," we were told.

Malapascua is also a mecca for divers, with vibrant reefs and one of the world's premier tech diving shops, Evolution Diving Resort, situated on the southeast coast. Most important, Malapascua is the only place in the world where you can consistently dive with thresher sharks, which frequent a nearby shoal every morning for a clean. Threshers are so important to this island (which lives primarily off tourism, fishing, and boatbuilding) that Malapascua has adopted the shark as its town sigil.

Sure, there are coral reefs, wrecks, and underwater tunnels, seamoths, devil stingers, and blue-ringed octopuses—but the threshers? They are the stars of this intriguing island's show. ■

A traditional *bangca* (outrigger canoe) positions itself near Gato Island. Most of the diving in Malapascua is done from bangca-style boats.

Malapascua is an island that enjoys tourism—needs it—but it is not a "touristy" island. It is home to a vibrant community of around 5,000 people, with a daily routine that follows many generational traditions.

This is not a wealthy island: It has little infrastructure, a plethora of plastic is employed in solutions for day-to-day chores, and many residents still fish for sustenance, their small outriggers lining the beach.

Historically, fishing was the island's primary source of income. Then, around 1999, the shark was out of the bag: Word had gotten round that the tiny island of Malapascua had regular sightings of thresher sharks and divers started flocking.

Thresher sharks are named for their unusually long, scythe-like tails, which they wield with amazing dexterity, stunning fish. They are a shy shark and deepwater species, usually staying well below recreational and even technical dive limits. This might explain their permanent expression of surprise—big-eyed and slightly open-mouthed—when they find themselves sharing their morning bath with a crowd of eager divers.

Monad Shoal is their spa, their morning ritual. This underwater seamount rises 820 feet (250 m) from the seafloor, around five miles (8 km) east of Malapascua. The top of the seamount is around 66 feet (20 m) deep, and divers descend mooring lines to a sloping sand and coral wall around 98 feet (30 m) to wait quietly, hoping to catch a glimpse of this rarely observed shark. (There are three species of threshers; pelagic thresher sharks are the ones that visit Malapascua.)

One after another, the threshers circle, enjoying the attention of cleaner fish. They aren't the only visitors: Manta rays often make appearances, as well as gray reef sharks and whitetip reef sharks, all sharing the same cleaning station.

Diving with the threshers (and their spa friends) isn't difficult, but it does require some attention to detail and a predawn start. Divers gather at 5 a.m. for an extensive briefing (there are strict thresher dos and don'ts), followed by departure, converging upon Monad Shoal at sunrise with every other dive boat in the area.

(Tip: Divers need proof of 30-plus dives beyond 59 ft/18 m or Advanced Open Water certification. The dive can be done as part of your AOW course. There can be current and low vis.)

The reason for the crowds? Early morning provides the best opportunity of seeing sharks (which don't always turn up). Also, due to diver traffic and a desire to protect the area, the friendly agreement among dive shops is to congregate all the

Long days are over too soon in Malapascua: This small island doesn't have a lot of tourist infrastructure, but there's always plenty to do.

Make a Difference

divers in one area at one time in order to contain pressure on the shoal.

As we hovered in place (one of the rules—no lying, sitting, or standing allowed), the threshers weaved in and out of the gloom, spotted by our experienced guides as they cruised the edge of visibility. It was a joy to simply float and watch them, these perfectly sculpted fish with their perpetually surprised expressions.

Thresher sharks turned Malapascua upside down: Shark diving tourism is responsible for around 80 percent of the regional economy. Many fishermen swapped jobs to tourism.

In 2013, when Typhoon Haiyan (Yolanda) leveled much of the Philippines, including Malapascua, the island was the first to be up and running again. Divers who knew and loved Malapascua pooled resources to help. Within two weeks, shark tourism was back in business, with divers returning to a down-but-not-out island, their tourism dollars not only helping Malapascua, but other nearby communities.

In return, when it came time to protect thresher sharks (classified as "globally vulnerable" due to being overfished for their highly prized meat and fins), there was a huge push throughout the Philippines to back greater conservation efforts at the 2016 Convention on International Trade in Endangered Species of Wild Fauna and Flora (CITES), a substantial victory for the sharks.

Malapascua is the only place where divers can reliably see thresher sharks, which visit a nearby shoal every morning for a clean.

It's not all happy families, however. Although Monad Shoal and nearby Gato Island became the Philippines' first shark and ray sanctuary in 2015, illegal fishing (including dynamite fishing) is still rife.

We saw evidence at a few sites, because—although thresher sharks are the stars of the show—diving around Malapascua is varied and fantastic. There are around 22 dive sites, many of which are suitable for families, partners, and snorkelers.

Lapus Lapus is a gentle drift dive over bommies and rocks, home to crazy macro critters like frogfish, demon stingers, seamoths, and more than 100 species of nudibranchs. (Chris firmly believes there's only one species of nudibranch, and the rest is "just a fashion choice.")

NEARBY

Pair a visit to Malapascua with another diving mecca in the Philippines—Palawan's coral gardens. Or book a liveaboard to Tubbataha Reefs Natural Park, a UNESCO World Heritage site and current-filled home to a rich diversity of marine life.

Gato Island, a little triangular rock about an hour's boat ride from Malapascua, is unique because there is a 98-foot (30 m) underwater tunnel bisecting the island. In small groups, divers make their way through the tunnel, sharing it with whitetip reef sharks. (There is also the opportunity to swim around the island, if overhead environments aren't your cup of tea.) Surrounding Gato Island, soft coral radiate in pinks and purples, well matched to the large number of colorful giant clams and color-changing cuttlefish. We even spotted a couple of blue-ringed octopuses.

Chris also seized his chance to take a **rebreather course** at Evolution (called a "DiscoTech"). The course consisted of on-site classroom work to understand the principles involved, followed by a shallow dive on the house reef. He described the experience as an awakening, with marine life approaching extremely close due to the lack of bubbles. (Technical training is suitable—and beneficial—to divers of all levels because it increases awareness and problem-solving skills; you won't simply be thrown into deep dives.)

What else is there to do in paradise? Hopping on the back of a motorbike taxi to camp out at remote beaches, where you'll spot a few entrepreneurial women selling drinks from the only patch of shade and a few stray dogs napping in the sugary sand, is a good way to while away a day.

And then there's the karaoke, a favorite part of Filipino culture, which takes place at multiple venues in town, several nights a week. Just turn up and enjoy the show—bonus points if you get on the mic!

Keep an eye out for weekend community discos, as well, beloved by Malapascuans of all ages and usually held on one of the basketball courts. This is a special way to socialize with the people who call this unique little island home.

Tech divers descend on the *Mogami Maru*, a WWII Japanese wreck that rests at a depth beyond recreational dive limits (170.6 ft/52 m).

NEED TO KNOW

GETTING HERE: Mactan-Cebu Airport is the closest. From there, it's around a three-hour drive to Maya, the port where ferries depart for Malapascua. (Buses available, but private transfers/taxis recommended; often dive shops and hotels can help with travel plans.) Having a full day for this journey is advisable. If arriving in Cebu after noon, overnight in a hotel (like the Appleton Boutique Hotel) and travel north the following day.

GETTING AROUND: There are no cars on the island—walking, bikes, and scooters are the ways to get around. (Taxi scooters available.)

PACKING TIPS: Board shorts/sarongs, reef shoes, reef-friendly sunscreen, wind jacket for spray, and a knit hat for early mornings, and buy a T-shirt at Evolution (they have some good ones).

WEATHER: February to May is the dry season and busier. July to December is the wet season. November and December can have rougher weather and reduced vis. September to October is the "insider" time to visit (after everyone heads home from summer holidays).

IN ADDITION: There are no ATMs on the island, and only a few hotels accept credit cards. Cash is king. If you have space, speak to Evolution about bringing children's books (sorely needed in the community) to donate to their Kids' Book Club.

Diving

OVERVIEW: The small island of Malapascua is a big, big diving destination, with macro-filled reefs and the only place in the world to consistently dive with thresher sharks year-round.

- **Visibility:** From 33 to 66 feet (10 to 20 m)
- **Water Temp:** 75°F (24°C) in winter / 86°F (30°C) in summer
- **Depth Range:** 66 to 394 feet (20 to 120 m)

MARINE LIFE: Thresher sharks, whitetip reef sharks, blue-ringed octopuses, frogfish, scorpionfish, pygmy seahorses, harlequin ghost pipefish, nudibranchs, seamoths, demon stingers, and manta rays

SHOP INFO: We dove with **Evolution,** a dynamic waterfront shop with on-site accommodations and restaurant. They have multiple classic-style boats and focus on small dive groups. Along with recreational dives (thresher, reef, and more), Evolution is a great place to extend your dive skills (Open Water to tech—they have a global reputation as tech specialists). Two things we love about this shop: They try to give all of their staff the opportunity to dive (and develop careers in diving if they want). They also walk the sustainability talk. We can't recommend this place highly enough and will definitely be back.

Accommodations

HIGH-END: Ocean Vida Beach and Dive Resort is a sumptuous resort right on Bounty Beach with 20 rooms (sea or garden views) and an on-site restaurant. ~$100 USD

MID-RANGE: Evolution Diving Resort is located on a quiet beach. It has 16 comfortable rooms, an on-site restaurant and bar, open-air instruction area, and well-appointed dive shop. This is a welcoming spot with a relaxed vibe, ideal for families, solo travelers, and couples. ~$92 USD per room (one or two people)

BUDGET: The **Malapascua Budget Inn** is located in the center of town, offering a variety of accommodations (mixed dorm to private room), and an on-site bar and restaurant. ~$27 USD

Food & Drink

Amihan Restaurant is a hillside establishment located next to Tepanee Beach Resort, serving up a mix of Italian, Mediterranean, Filipino, and Asian dishes.

Ocean Vida's in-house restaurant has a range of choices (from Filipino to European) and serves up one of the best breakfast buffets on the island, with fresh fruit juices made daily. (Breakfast is for guests only.)

The **Craic House,** Evolution's in-house restaurant, is the place everyone gravitates to after a day's diving to swap stories. It's the only authentic Irish bar in the region, with ever changing specials and a great soundtrack.

BRITISH VIRGIN ISLANDS

Indulge Your Inner Pirate

The British Virgin Islands are known as BVI, which locals joke stands for the "better Virgin Islands," a not-so-veiled rub at the U.S. Virgin Islands: BVI is smaller, more personable, more piratical.

And these islands are very much the place of pirates: not only the historical variety, who plied these waters and contributed to the wrecks that litter the reefs, but the modern-day type. Offshore banking is BVI's number one income generator, followed by tourism. More sailboats are rented here than anywhere else in the world—people seeking to trade their everyday lives for the high seas, if only for a week or two. And modern-day pirating is a family tradition. BVI sees a lot of repeat visitors: Parents bring their children, who, in turn, bring theirs.

When Hurricanes Irma and Maria swept through in September 2017, wielding 178-mile-an-hour (286 kph) winds and destroying 90 percent of homes and businesses in the area, BVI's pain was felt not just by the badly affected local population, but by visitors who leave their hearts here. The one silver lining wrought by the destruction was a golden opportunity: The hurricanes carried the islands 20 years back in time. BVI could be rebuilt more sustainably, regulating the tourism that had swelled out of hand.

Ironically, that tourism is what's needed right now: BVI is still struggling to recover, and your visit can help. Go now, and sail back in time. ∎

Paradisiacal coves like Virgin Gorda's Spring Bay have long called out to sailors.

NORTH AMERICA

British Virgin Islands

The British Virgin Islands are made to be explored by boat. It's a collection of four main islands—Tortola, Jost van Dyke, Anegada, and Virgin Gorda—in the Caribbean Sea, part of the Lesser Antilles. There are plenty of uninhabited coves to pull into, towns to plunder, and floating bars to revive at, like the famous **Willy T.**

These forays can be done in one of two ways: from a liveaboard or an island base. We tried both.

The worthy vessel we selected was the **Cuan Law,** the world's largest sailing trimaran, purpose-built in Lake Erie where she was put through her paces (think five tons of ice on the decks) before settling into a more relaxed life in BVI.

She's a floating luxury hotel with comfortable rooms, an air-conditioned shared lounge, teak decking, and plenty of toys: Hobie Cats, stand-up paddleboards, kayaks, and more. A professional, friendly crew of seven look after the maximum 20 guests, sailing where wind, weather, and inspiration takes them. "We never set an itinerary or routine," one crew member told us. "We want to make sure we never fall into a bus route."

The *Cuan Law* is first and foremost a diving boat, but unlike other liveaboards, non-divers aren't treated as afterthoughts.

(Tip: BVI is a great place to learn to dive, and the Cuan Law—with its boutique size and personable service—is ideal for new or inexperienced divers.)

Days begin with the quiet hum of the ship's generator, the lapping of waves, and bird cries guiding you to breakfast on the back deck, after which the day's dive plan unfolds. BVI has more than 100 sites to choose from, and with an onboard tender boat, Chris and I would often dive separately: I explored the shallow, plentiful reefs, which are nurseries for juvenile fish. Chris preferred exploring the numerous caverns, like **Grand Central Cave** (a small entrance opening into a large cavern filled with shrimp and lobster, before exiting through a narrow tunnel), and wrecks like the **Chikuzen,** a Korean refrigerator vessel resting in 79 feet (24 m) of water. Because of its offshore, open-ocean location, the *Chikuzen* is visited by few dive operators, and can only be dived in calm conditions. Its exposed location also makes it a fish oasis in a desert of sand, attracting barracuda, grouper, cobia, stingrays, jacks, and more.

If we weren't diving in the afternoons, we would moor up for a paddleboard, or to simply relax on the back deck, cocktail in hand, watching splashes of sunset give way to lights on sailboats bobbing in the evening dark. Occasionally the sound of laughter would carry from one boat to the next. There's a strange sense of camaraderie with other ships, as if you've discovered a shared secret.

If you base yourself on an island, like at the **Cooper Island Beach Club** (a 10-room, family-owned eco-resort on the shores of Manchioneel Bay), the

Sunset chasing aboard the *Cuan Law*, the world's largest sailing trimaran and a luxury liveaboard that sails the British Virgin Islands

Make a Difference

Tourists understandably avoid places struck by natural disasters, but that leaves communities struggling with a loss of income, as well as recovery. In the Caribbean, where tourism accounts for 35 percent of the economy (one in three jobs), that loss can be catastrophic. Visiting helps destinations recover, but you have to walk a fine line: "Disaster tourism" (i.e., rubbernecking at an accident), or visiting while relief efforts are still underway and essentials such as water and food are in short supply, isn't helpful. But once the community says it's open for business, visitors bring a welcome infusion of money, as well as much needed outside perspectives. What else can you do besides visit? Support places that are investing in sustainable, resilient solutions—i.e., rebuilding in the right way.

pirates come to you: Every afternoon and evening, Cooper Island buzzes with a lively population of visiting sailors. Those staying on the island, however, have the benefit of a large and comfortable room with ocean views, permanent dinner reservations (which can be a battle with pirates), and a central base from which to explore, including an on-site dive shop.

BVI's land-based activities revolve around day trips (half or full day), offered by resorts or independent operators, many of which will arrange to pick you up or drop you off. There are island tours and snorkel excursions, day sails and day hikes. **Road Town,** BVI's capital on Tortola, is worth a wander. Seek shade in the **J. R. O'Neal Botanic Gardens,** a four-acre (1.6 ha) garden lush with tropical plants, or during a tour of the **Old Government House Museum,** the former residence for BVI's governors now filled with historical artifacts.

Don't miss a tour of the **Baths on Virgin Gorda,** a spectacular maze of natural rock formations enclosing secret turquoise sea pools and pockets of sandy beaches. This is a place where words and images fall short—you have to see it for yourself, and it is jaw-dropping.

BVI diving is mostly protected bays filled with reefs or wrecks, and there are some famous wrecks here, including the *Kodiak Queen* (purpose-sunk for divers) and the **R.M.S. *Rhone,*** a 310-foot (94 m) iron-hulled ship that sailed through a hurricane in

The Baths on Virgin Gorda is a spectacular maze of granite boulders that conceals secret pools and slivers of sandy beaches.

1867, resulting in a tragedy that killed most of the people on board.

The *Rhone* lies in two parts on a site that became BVI's first national marine park in 1980. It can be snorkeled or dived, and two dives are recommended: one for the bow, lying in 80 feet (24 m) of water, and one for the shallow stern, which has one of the oldest brass propellers in the world. Penetration isn't possible due to structural degradation, but that's not really the point of the *Rhone*. Its story is incredible, and to be there, and see just how close to shore this ship actually sank, really brings the disaster home, especially in an area prone to hurricanes.

The hurricane damage from Irma (the most powerful Atlantic hurricane ever recorded at the time of writing) and Maria needed to be seen to be believed. More than 300 boats were strewn on BVI's shores, abandoned. Debris and the occasional wind-lifted roof were caught in tree branches stripped of every leaf, a bundle of sticks poking the air. ("If there was a goat in the hills, you could see it from miles away," one local said.) The main island of Tortola looked like a war zone, with boarded-up buildings, few of which had a second story.

Nobody was spared. The *Cuan Law*'s mast tore through one of the cabins. The Cooper Island Beach Club had waves breaking through the kitchen and restaurant. It was one of the first resorts to reopen, saved by a "good hurricane plan," said Meron Napier, the operations manager and an aerospace engineer (and brewer) by trade. "We knew what was coming and we had a plan,

FOR FAMILIES

Sail Caribbean (*sailcaribbean.com*) offers a variety of camps and programs for kids and young adults, including introductions to diving, live-aboard sailing adventures, and marine biology camps, focusing on hands-on field experience.

backed by the owners. We're trying to see this as an opportunity to upgrade some stuff we've been planning to do for years."

It's also an opportunity to band together in a shared camaraderie. When we visited, the Cooper Island Beach Club had just reopened, and everyone in the area turned out to celebrate. Just after we left, Willie T was due to reopen, and the islands were filled with plans to mark that occasion.

Whatever the world throws at us in the years to come, we could all use a little more of that spirit: banding together instead of drifting apart. It's no wonder people love the British Virgin Islands: We left a little piece of our hearts behind, too.

A diver explores the R.M.S. *Rhone,* sunk during a hurricane in 1867, and one of many wrecks in British Virgin Islands' waters.

NEED TO KNOW

GETTING HERE: Most flights connect through another Caribbean airport (Puerto Rico or St. Thomas, for example) before arriving in BVI.

GETTING AROUND: Keen sailors can charter their own vessel and explore at will. Landlubbers can either hop on a crewed ship (like the *Cuan Law*) or base themselves on an island, setting off on interisland day trips.

PACKING TIPS: Lightweight, sporty layers: To pack, just picture yourself on a yacht (T-shirt, shorts, hat, sunglasses, windbreaker, sweater, sneakers or reef shoes).

WEATHER: December to April is the best time to visit. June through November is the Named Storm (i.e., hurricane) season, with the greatest possibility of storms August through October.

IN ADDITION: Many places close mid-August through late October. BVI isn't the place to skimp on travel insurance, as hurricanes have a habit of changing plans. Make sure you're covered.

Diving

OVERVIEW: BVI has long been beloved by divers for wrecks and reefs, and the option of sailing from dive site to dive site (a different feel from a liveaboard) or diving from an island base.

- Visibility: Around 65 feet (20 m)
- Water Temp: 79°F (26°C) in winter / 84.2°F (29°C) in summer
- Depth Range: 36 to 79 feet (11 to 24 m)

MARINE LIFE: French and gray angelfish, arrow crabs, spiny lobster, slender filefish, reticulated brittle stars, schools of blue tang and barracuda, and stingrays

SHOP INFO: We dove on the *Cuan Law,* which was fantastic. It's crewed by experienced dive instructors who put safety first and foremost. Let them know what gear you'll need in advance. From Cooper Island, we dove with **Sail Caribbean Divers,** which has a shop down the beach from the Cooper Island Beach Club (it also has shops on Tortola) and a nicely set-up dive boat.

Accommodations

HIGH-END: The *Cuan Law* has 10 comfortable staterooms, each with a private bathroom. It can hold up to 20 guests, making it ideal for groups of friends or families. This is a special, elegant ship, great for making holiday memories. *~$3,050 USD per person for six nights/ seven days; whole boat rental available*

MID-RANGE: The **Cooper Island Beach Club** features 10 guest rooms decorated with driftwood tones, each with a private balcony. It's convenient (coffee shop, brewery, restaurant, nearby dive shop, and more), and it's doing great things. Eighty-five percent of the resort's power is solar. They don't sell bottled water. They don't use straws. Cups are either washable or disposable ones made from corn or paper. A sand-glass crusher reduces empty bottles to fine sand, to be used in building or landscaping. This peaceful place livens up every evening with visitors. *~$250 USD*

BUDGET: **Guavaberry Spring Bay** on Virgin Gorda, near the iconic Baths. They offer a range of one- to three-bedroom home rentals, all of which have large private porches with ocean views. *~$185 USD*

Food & Drink

Cuan Law's fresh and varied menu is adapted to guests' wants and needs (let them know about food allergies in advance). Food is delicious and there's plenty of it. Dinner is an occasion—dress smart and enjoy the ambiance.

Cooper Island Beach Club's beachfront restaurant and bar serves lunch and dinner, utilizing locally sourced fruits and vegetables, including produce from their own garden; they've also partnered with local farms and fishermen.

Don't miss Cooper Island Beach Club's custom-built **brewery** and **Rum Bar,** which boasts the largest selection of rum in BVI. If you have an extra $100, try a shot of the Black Tot, which used to be served to British sailors and is no longer being made.

BELIZE

A Green-Blue Beauty

Belize is one of the most biodiverse places on the planet: an 8,867-square-mile (22,965 sq km) mix of rainforest rubbing elbows with reef.

NORTH
AMERICA

Belize

Despite its small size, Belize punches above its weight in its commitment to protect its rich and unique environment. There are still issues—illegal logging, deforestation, and shark fishing, to name a few—but there is much to celebrate. The Belizean government announced plans to ban single-use plastics, and Belize was also the first country to ban fishing for parrotfish, a recommendation put forward by local fisher-men after they learned about the critical role parrotfish play in reef health by eating algae.

The Belize Barrier Reef is a UNESCO World Heritage site and part of the 700-mile (1,127 km) Mesoamerican Reef system, the second largest barrier reef on Earth and a Mission Blue Hope Spot. In 2018, the Belize Barrier Reef was removed from UNESCO's List of World Heritage in Danger, thanks in part to a landmark moratorium on oil exploration in local waters. At the time of writing, Belize is one of only a handful of countries in the world to adopt this legislation.

The result of the moratorium has been a slow but steady increase in overall reef health, which is both amazing and encouraging, given the pressures Caribbean reefs are facing.

And on land, Belize had the foresight to create places like the Cockscomb Basin Wildlife Sanctuary, the world's first jaguar preserve and a reservoir for biodiversity.

This laid-back little country is taking giant strides as a world leader in conservation. Supporting it—as well as enjoying the very environ-ment it's protecting—is why now is the time to go. ∎

Belize is beloved by divers and is wonderfully diverse, from the Great Blue Hole to fringing reefs to migrating whale sharks and pelagics.

We took a road trip, beginning in Belize City and driving 115 miles (185 km) south to Placencia, branching off into Belize's lush jungles and white-sand cays along the way.

(Tip: Don't drive at night. This has to do with road safety [i.e., a lack of streetlights], not crime. Also, Belize wields speed bumps instead of stoplights, so slow down or lose your suspension.)

Belize City is the embarkation point to access Belize's most famous dive destination, the **Great Blue Hole,** a sapphire blue, underwater sinkhole more than 984 feet (300 m) across and 410 feet (125 m) deep. It's also an ideal home base for exploring the ancient Maya city of **Altun Ha,** located an hour's drive north. Altun Ha is famous as the discovery site of one of the largest carved jade objects found in Mesoamerica, a 9.75-pound (4.4 kg), six-inch (15.2 cm) head shaped in the likeness of Kinich Ahau, the Maya sun god.

Our guide led us around this ancient complex (settlement dates back to 200 B.C.), with its four ceremonial structures and sealed ponds that used to act as a reservoir and still hold rainwater today. Our visit ended by climbing stairs specially constructed to allow visitors the rare treat of roof access to the 54-foot-tall (17 m) Temple of the Sun God, with its commanding view of the complex.

The ancient Maya city of Altun Ha is famous as the discovery site of one of the largest carved jade objects found in Mesoamerica.

From Belize City, it's a two-hour drive south to **Bocawina Rainforest Resort & Adventures,** located in the lush Maya Mountains within Mayflower Bocawina National Park. The resort sits on 50 acres (20.2 ha) of the national park's 7,000 acres (2,833 ha) of protected rivers, rainforest, and waterfalls, studded by Maya ruins. Bocawina offers a 2.5-mile (4 km) rainforest canopy zip line and more than 10 miles (16 km) of jungle hiking trails. It's an ideal place for families with active, outdoorsy kids.

Guinea fowl wander the property, one of the more than 237 species of birds identified in the area, and jaguars patrol the perimeter. The area has been a jaguar reserve since 1984, and it's believed there's a healthy population of the elusive cats (an estimated 800) around Bocawina, thanks to connected tracts of protected area that create a wildlife corridor.

*(Tip: Request to see a presentation on the **Panthera Project,** an NGO working in Belize dedicated to the conservation of wild cats, supported by the resort.)*

We never missed the opportunity to go on a guided nature hike at dawn or twilight. You never knew what you would see, from busy leafcutter ants (their behavior can predict rain), to keel-billed toucans, to helmeted basilisk lizards.

On one dawn hike, we heard a tremendous commotion in the forest coming toward us at speed. A ball of fur exploded through the brush, landing six

feet (2 m) from where we were standing. Two collared anteaters broke apart, and—seeing us—darted in opposite directions. It was a once-in-a-lifetime wildlife encounter.

Or so we thought.

Later that day, we drove the 15.5 miles (25 km) to the coastal town of Dangriga to catch a water taxi to **South Water Caye,** a semi-private island that is 480 feet (146 m) at its widest point, punctuated with Blue Marlin Beach Resort's brightly painted cottages. The Blue Marlin is a Belizean family-owned resort and has been run by the same family for three generations. "This was my mother-in-law's island; she used to bring the kids here in the 1960s," matriarch Rosalia Zabaneh told us. "It used to be 28 acres (11 ha), but now it's 18 (7 ha). Erosion."

We immediately embarked on a dive to explore this hidden jewel of the **Belize Barrier Reef Reserve** system. The large, fringing reefs have a mid-water ridge around 82 feet (25 m), with a flat, sandy bottom on one side of the ridge (teeming with reef fish), and a steep wall on the other (a great place

An aerial view of Blue Marlin Beach Resort on South Water Caye, which is 480 feet (146 m) at its widest point

to see larger pelagics, as well as eagle rays and barracuda).

In an effort to keep the Caribbean lionfish population in check, Blue Marlin's dive shop has taught resident nurse sharks to eat the invasive species. The result is like taking a bunch of puppies for a walk. We had two nurse sharks following us throughout our first dive at a site called **Paradise,** weaving in and out of our fins, poking into whatever hole we paused to look into.

Chris pointed his flashlight under one coral overhang, encountering an enormous moray eel. As he slowly backed away, one of the sharks charged in, knocking him sideways. The nurse shark shot out with that massive moray attached to its head. Both animals came out of the encounter unscathed, but—along with the aardvarks—it made for a wild day.

Diving is the primary activity on South Water Caye, and it's a great place for divers of all levels (including beginners), guided by a local family who know this area and consider themselves its care-takers. Don't miss the opportunity to take a boat trip to **Twin Caye, Bird Caye,** and **Tobacco Caye,** drifting gently along mangrove-lined corridors while manatee-spotting and bird-watching.

We left South Water Caye before we were ready, returned to Dangriga, and headed south to Placencia.

*(Tip: Before heading south, visit the **Gulisi Garifuna Museum** in Dangriga and have a cultural day at **Palmento Grove,** owned and operated by a Garifuna family, in Hopkins to learn more about the Garifuna culture.)*

It took about 1.5 hours to drive to **Placencia,** a long, low peninsula. We came here to dive with **Splash Dive Center.** "Here, diving is like fashion," our guide told us. "It's the thing to be a dive master or dive instructor. I fished with my father as a kid and learned to dive 17 years ago. My son never fished; he became a dive instructor at 20. The sea knowledge gets passed on; it's just different."

Our first dive was simply dropping into blue water looking for whale sharks, which follow spawning snapper at depth. (We didn't see any, but spotted a few silky sharks.) Our second dive was at **North Wall,** a steep drop-off teeming with life, including Nassau grouper, large moray eels, sponges, crayfish, a loggerhead turtle, and nurse sharks. On the boat ride in between, we snorkeled with spotted dolphins.

Nurse sharks often provide pleasant companionship for divers and snorkelers as they explore Belize's waters.

For us, Belize is a collection of vivid memories and wonderful wildlife encounters. The local awareness and engagement are what impressed us the most. Belize is trying hard with limited resources and innovative practices to protect large areas of the country's ocean and land. The result is some of the Caribbean's healthiest reefs, and a feeling of possibility.

Make a Difference

From South Water Caye, call ahead to arrange a free tour of **Carrie Bow Cay Field Station,** the Smithsonian National Museum of Natural History's long-term field site *(ccre.si.edu)*. Meet scientists and learn more about their coral reef field studies. **Splash Dive Center's Junior Dive Club** *(splashbelize.com)* teaches local Belizean kids to dive free of cost, so they can experience the Belize Barrier Reef for themselves. Club members have gone on to careers in diving, which gives them a profession and strengthens the community's commitment to the reef. Diving with Splash supports this initiative; you can also provide sponsorship. Placencia-based **Fragments of Hope** *(fragmentsofhope.org)* focuses on coral and mangrove restoration and sustainable management. Donations accepted; they also offer kayaking tours.

NEED TO KNOW

GETTING HERE: There are daily direct flights from many major cities to Belize's international airport (located on the outskirts of Belize City).

GETTING AROUND: Driving is a great way to explore this compact country. Cars can be rented at Belize's international airport.

PACKING TIPS: Sporty casual: Belize is the place for quick-drying adventure gear, including hiking boots, lightweight long pants, long-sleeved shirts, and reef shoes. Don't forget a pair of binoculars.

WEATHER: The average annual temperature is a pleasant but humid 84°F (29°C). February to May is the dry season, and the best time to visit. June through December is the wet season, and the Caribbean hurricane season can send wild weather Belize's way.

IN ADDITION: Belize charges 12.5 percent tax on all goods and services—factor that into your budget, or you'll be in for a shock! Drone enthusiasts: You'll need to acquire a permit before you arrive in Belize.

Diving

OVERVIEW: The Belize Barrier Reef Reserve System is one of the most biodiverse places on the planet, with healthy reefs thanks to a monumental and ongoing effort by the country. This is a great place to dive with lots to see, and most of the reef is yet to be explored.

- **Visibility:** 100-plus feet (30 m)
- **Water Temp:** 80°F (26.6°C) in winter / 85°F (29.4°C) in summer
- **Depth Range:** Average 82 feet (25 m)

MARINE LIFE: Sharks (Caribbean reef, nurse, silky, lemon), coral (brain, staghorn), barrel and other sponges, barracuda, moray eels, turtles (hawksbill and green), and snapper. Whale sharks migrate through March to June, and keep your eyes peeled for manatees.

SHOP INFO: We dove with **Splash Dive Center** in Placencia, a professional outfit with multiple boats and good safety standards. They also support a number of community and environmental projects. On South Water Caye, we dove with **Blue Marlin Beach Resort,** a well-run, locally owned and operated shop with great intel.

Accommodations

HIGH-END: The **Blue Marlin Beach Resort's** high number of return guests, some of whom have been coming here for more than 17 years, should tell you all you need to know about this Belizean family-owned property. The 15 units are furnished comfortably in decor your grandmother would choose, with captivating outside views, the sound of the wind and waves ever present. ~$425 USD

MID-RANGE: **Belizean Nirvana** can be tricky to find (down a side street, no car access), but its beachfront location, well-equipped suites, and proximity to John the Bakerman (pick up some freshly baked bread before your dive) make this a great place to stay. ~$216 USD

BUDGET: **Bocawina Rainforest Resort** is a place you'll want to spend more time. Located in the foothills of the Maya Mountains, this small eco-lodge offers a comfortable range of accommodations (12 rooms and suites) and is completely off-grid, utilizing hydro and solar power. Day visitors and diners welcome. ~$165 USD

Food & Drink

Blue Marlin Beach Resort is too small and remote to offer a menu, so they serve up one main meal with variations: Think pan-fried snapper with coconut rice, fried plantains, and limes. (Advise any food issues prior to arrival.)

Bocawina's **Wild Fig Restaurant** is comfortable dining with a farm-to-table focus: Most produce is sourced from local farmers or grown on the property. Non–hotel guests welcome.

The **Roadhouse Restaurant** in Sand Hill is an easy stop (15 mi/24 km) from Altun Ha. This is basic Belizean cuisine, and it's oh-so-tasty: rice and beans with homemade sauce that straightens the curls, accompanied by a tall glass of grapefruit juice.

EASTER ISLAND

Past. Present. Future.

If rugged New Zealand conceived a love child with warm Hawai'i, it would be Easter Island: a wild and windswept peak of a submerged mountain range, 64 square miles (166 sq km) in size, 42 percent of which is national park (and a UNESCO World Heritage site).

This island has seen it all, including the rise and catastrophic demise of a civilization. And that experience is palpable, as if the soil and sea were trying to tell the story.

It's believed Easter Island (also known as Isla de Pascua or Rapa Nui, after the Indigenous culture) was first settled between A.D. 800 and 1200. We don't know much for certain. We can speculate, we can carbon-date, but what was known is lost.

For more than 500 years, the population of Easter Island flourished, coexisting in peace and arcing toward a cultural zenith. Parallel to progress, however, was the destruction and overexploitation of the island's natural resources. There is archaeological evidence that Easter Islanders had to adapt to increasingly challenging conditions, leading—inevitably—to civil war, cannibalism, the abandonment of great works, and the rising of a new cult.

When European visitors and Peruvian slave raiders found the island, that was the nail in a self-built coffin.

Today, this extraordinary island has been reborn. We desperately wanted a time machine while we were there. More than that, we want to return. ∎

Easter Island is a living museum, populated with sites like Rano Raraku, the quarry where the island's legendary *moai* statues were carved.

Easter Island is one big open-air museum, with an estimated 20,000 archaeological sites (some of which are 200 years older than Machu Picchu) scattered around the island, and a variety of different ways to experience them.

A guided tour is the best way to start. While most archaeological sites have some signage, they only cover a small percentage of the stories, detail, and history a guide can share.

Here are four of our favorite sites:

Rano Raraku: Welcome to the *moai* factory, the birthplace of Easter Island's legendary and enormous monolithic statues, built by the Rapa Nui people. It takes about an hour to walk the undulating loop trail through the quarry, past 387 moai that rest in various stages of completion. It's a fascinating insight into how the statues were created.

Ahu Tongariki: The island's largest ceremonial structure (328 ft/100 m long) is set in a rolling, open field, a pleasant place to sit and contemplate, or to circumnavigate the massive *ahu* (platform) with its line of 15 standing moai, their backs to the nearby ocean.

Rano Kau: En route to Orongo village is the impressive 3,000-foot-wide (915 m) crater of Rano Kau, an extinct volcano filled with freshwater that

——— SOMETHING SPECIAL ———

Get ink. **Mokomae Araki,** one of the island's premier artists, tattooed a traditional design on Carrie's wrist. He can also arrange to body paint you for a fierce natural photo shoot, a souvenir like no other.

was once the island's primary water supply, as well as an ancient *manavai* (wild garden). A viewing platform provides information and uninterrupted views of this special microclimate, a haven for biodiversity, separated from the ocean by a razor-thin rock wall, and still home to the totara reeds, bananas, taros, and avocados that were planted during the island's cultural heyday. "Rano Kau is the closest to the island the way it was," our guide told us.

Orongo: The ceremonial village of Orongo is a spellbinding cliffside collection of history and legend. On the heels of 200 years of brutal civil war (14th to 16th centuries) came the Birdman cult, a bloody tournament held every spring to determine which clan chief would rule the island for the coming year. Visitors can follow a hillside path next to 54 elliptical stone houses once used by visiting dignitaries during the ceremony. This windswept vantage point provided them with unobstructed views as the chiefs' selected champions scaled a 984-foot (300 m) cliff, swam nearly a mile (1.6 km) to the Motu Nui islet, collected the egg of a migratory sooty tern, and returned with it. The first chief to receive an egg from his designated warrior was crowned king for a year, and the warrior was commemorated in a stone carving with the body of a man in a fetal position, and the neck and head of a frigate bird. This political system, the antidote to civil war, continued for more than 200 years, the last competition being held around 1867.

A guineafowl puffer fish swims above a bed of coral. Easter Island offers unique, exploratory diving in remarkable visibility.

Idyllic Anakena Beach. Oral tradition holds this was the landing place of Easter Island's first king, Hotu Matu'a.

It takes around 30 to 60 minutes to navigate the half mile (0.8 km) of trails that wind past nine interpretive points, and there is also an indoor information center with a plethora of signage.

There are other ways to experience Easter Island's unique history and culture, beyond walking tours of archaeological sites. Spend five hours on horseback with **Kotelo Horse Riding** traversing the northern tip of the island, from Ana Te Pahu to Anakena, the landing place of Rapa Nui's first king. Together with our Spanish-speaking guide and English-saddled horses, we picked our way through sloping, lava-rock-strewn terrain: no roads, no trails, no crowds, just the hint of a path that took us up and down crevasses and past fallen moai, ancient petroglyphs of tuna (a species rarely seen in the surrounding ocean these days), and the outlines of old boat-shape homesteads, with million-dollar views of the sapphire sea.

(Tip: Beginner riders might find this ride challenging; it's a big day in the saddle.)

Ah, that sapphire sea. It's still rare for people to come to Easter Island to dive: They come here for the culture, not knowing how much it extends beneath the surface as well.

Easter Island's underwater realm is strange: The landscape is a network of twisted, contorted features. The **Coral Gardens** is a flat coral reef full of cracks and channels emerging onto a large, sandy plain, while the **Wall** is a steep drop to around 105 feet (32 m), with caves and swim-throughs. The **Pyramid** is a deepwater site, an offshore pinnacle under Easter Island's imposing cliffs, with breathtaking scenery topside and underwater. Divers follow the pinnacle down to the 131-foot (40 m) mark, slowly circling while ascending until reaching a giant archway to swim through. There's even an **underwater moai,** though not the real thing. It's a movie prop from the 1994 film *Rapa Nui,* purposefully sunk at 72 feet (22 m) and a fun underwater photo opportunity.

Along with a large number of native and endemic species (keep your eyes peeled for the Easter

Island butterflyfish, which is black with a striking white outline), Easter Island has the second best visibility in the world after Antarctica, a staggering 230 feet (70 m), thanks to volcanic-soil-filtered rainwater and a lack of ports and rivers. (We dove in 115-ft/35-m visibility and the dive shop apologized for the "murkiness" of the water.)

(Tip: The diving isn't hard, but it's a bit rough-and-ready, which some beginners might find daunting. You need to be comfortable taking your gear on and off in the water, and a lot of it is on the deeper side, so having your deep-dive certification and knowing how to be conservative with your profiles is advantageous, especially given that this is one of the most remote places on Earth.)

Larger marine life is notably absent, possibly due to pressure from the fishing fleets that sit on the edges of the marine parks, but there is a multitude of turtles, moray eels, small fish, and macro life on display. Remember that fish hide in good visibility: Patience pays off here.

This is one of the best and most special dive locations in the world, in waters surrounding one of the best and most special places in the world. But marine life needs the chance—and time—to bounce back. If given the opportunity, diving could be as good as the Galápagos (page 124), but with better visibility.

Easter Island is one of the bright sparks in the natural universe, but there's an unmissable lesson

This underwater *moai* (which is actually a purpose-sunk movie prop and not the real deal) is a favorite photo op with divers.

here: It is rare to visit the bones of a civilization that wrought its own demise in almost absolute silence. It seems analogous with the direction our world may be heading. This place is an alluring reminder of what can happen if we're not careful, and what we have that is worth protecting.

Make a Difference

Te Mau o Te Vaikava o Rapa Nui—Mesa del Mar is helping to raise community awareness around ocean protection. One of their biggest victories was convincing the Rapa Nui people to overwhelmingly support the Rapa Nui Marine Protected Area (established in 2018 and one of the world's largest), overcoming initial opposition through education and community engagement. "I was a spear fisherman until a few years ago. I went scuba diving and was amazed by what I saw," said Ludovic Tuki, the organization's executive director. "Environmental education is the key: I say to my people: What do we want Easter Island's future to be? It is in our hands." Follow their work on Facebook. Sometimes they hold ocean and coastal cleanups and events that visitors can join in.

NEED TO KNOW

GETTING HERE: Easter Island is roughly 2,300 miles (3,700 km) west of South America, a five-hour flight from Tahiti or Santiago, Chile.

GETTING AROUND: Hanga Roa is the waterfront township home to most of the population; the rest of the island runs largely wild. It's beneficial to hire a guide for the first few days (for bearings and background information). After that, renting a car and self-exploring is a good way to go.

PACKING TIPS: A sturdy, rugged wardrobe comes in handy here, especially shoes: The only even terrain is the airport runway. Red volcanic dust settles on everything.

WEATHER: Pleasant, warm, and moderately humid year-round, with sporadic showers. Easter Island's Southern Hemisphere summer is busier for visitors; winter has the best diving conditions. The wind is always a factor here and can cancel some dive days—pad in flexibility.

IN ADDITION: It should go without saying, but don't touch, climb, or lean on the *moai* or archaeological sites. Don't walk off paths and damage fragile vegetation. Hire certified guides that enforce rules. All visitors must purchase a national park ticket, valid for 10 days. No one can enter park sites without this ticket, so carry it on you.

Diving

OVERVIEW: Easter Island's isolated, unique underwater ecosystem has at least 140 species endemic to the area, including Easter Island butterflyfish, Michel's chromis, Rapanui filefish, and more. This is deeper, exploratory diving in remarkable visibility.

- **Visibility:** From 100 to 230 feet (30 to 70 m) and beyond
- **Water Temp:** 66°F (19°C) in winter / 81°F (27°C) in summer
- **Depth Range:** 59 to 130 feet (18 to 40 m)

MARINE LIFE: Strange. Along with the large population of endemic species, there is an abundance of turtles, coral (which appears electric blue), and twisted volcanic rock formations (arches, tunnels, cliffs, and chasms).

SHOP INFO: There are several dive shops on Easter Island based in Hanga Roa. Most of the diving is on the west side of the island close to the harbor. All shops use local fishing boats for dive excursions, which adds a splash of adventure. We dove with **Mike Rapu Diving Center,** one of the oldest shops on the island: experienced, friendly, with great local knowledge.

Accommodations

HIGH-END: Explora Rapa Nui is an all-inclusive 30-room hotel located in a secluded spot on the southern coast, surrounded by Easter Island's natural beauty. Its stunning architectural design is LEED-certified (Leadership in Energy and Environmental Design). ~$816 USD

MID-RANGE: The hacienda-style **Iorana Isla de Pascua Hotel** has been owned and operated by the same family for more than 30 years: friendly people who know and love their island, and are happy to share their experience with visitors. Located a 15-minute walk from town, this 52-room hotel overlooks the ocean and has an on-site restaurant and comfy, simple, spacious rooms. ~$194 USD

BUDGET: The **Kaimana Inn Hotel & Restaurant** has an unbeatable central location in Hanga Roa. It's small, family-owned, and friendly, with simple facilities. This is a great base if you're looking to save money for diving and adventures. ~$56 USD

Food & Drink

You can't beat the views from the two-story **Te Moai Sunset.** Enjoy dinner while watching the sun set over the Pacific Ocean, silhouetting the Ahu Tahai moai that lend the restaurant its name.

Te Moana is hip and Polynesian proud, with a wooden deck overlooking the ocean. Ceviche (more than four varieties) is the specialty of the house.

Tataku Vave is a great oceanside lunch spot, filled with rustic charm and a steady sea breeze, serving up dishes like *pescado encostrado en sesame y pimiento*—fish seared in a sesame seed and pepper crust.

EXMOUTH

Diving in the Desert

Exmouth is a place of crazy colors and wild contrasts. The landscape is ablaze with pinks, turquoises, crystal whites, scrub greens, and rust reds, all under a robin's egg blue sky. It's one of Australia's driest landscapes, and one of its best dive destinations.

AUSTRALIA
Exmouth

Located a two-hour flight or two-day drive north of Perth, Exmouth is perched on the northeastern side of a spur, facing the mainland. Rugged Cape Range National Park faces the open Indian Ocean on the spur's western side.

The Ningaloo coastline (the southwestern side of the spur) is a Mission Blue Hope Spot and UNESCO World Heritage site encompassing nearly 1.5 million acres (604,500 ha) of marine and terrestrial areas. This is a place revered for its Indigenous history: Evidence shows it has been continuously occupied for more than 40,000 years. Topside, the arid and rugged landscape is home to an extensive network of canyons, caves, and underground watercourses. Underwater, it holds remarkable biodiversity. The Ningaloo Coast, one of the longest near-shore reefs in the world, is a whale highway (scientists have counted up to 30,000 humpback whales traveling the Western Australia coastline) and an annual aggregation area for whale sharks and manta rays.

This is a true reef-to-range destination where adventurers of all ages can revel in the wonders of both the sea and the desert. ∎

Sunset illuminates a sand dune in Cape Range National Park. Exmouth is one of Australia's driest landscapes, and best dive destinations.

Exmouth is archetypal Australia: a raw red landscape soothed and surrounded by impossibly turquoise seas—lonely and beautiful, wild and harsh.

This town of around 2,500 people is a choose-your-own-adventure kind of place, from driving and hiking outings to renting a "tinny" (a small aluminum boat) for your own coastal snorkel excursions. Whatever you choose, wrap up adventures with good food and music at one of Exmouth's lively bars and eateries.

(Tip: Take the sun seriously and let someone know your plans. Bring more water than you think you'll need, and enjoy the wonderful wildlife—kangaroos, dingoes, emus, and snakes—from a respectful distance. Keep a watchful eye for animals while driving, too.)

Visiting **Cape Range National Park** is one of Exmouth's must-dos. This ancient rugged limestone range is cut through with deep canyons and pockmarked with caves, rising to weathered plateaus. It is home to a staggering amount of life: animals (like black-footed rock wallabies, echidnas,

and lizards), birds (corellas, ospreys, and sea eagles), and more than 600 species of plants.

One of the most popular ways to experience the park is to drive it, stopping at your leisure for short walks. There are also several fantastic hikes for people with a moderate level of fitness who don't mind a little rough terrain. These include the **Mandu Mandu Gorge** (reef views), the **Badjirrajirra Loop Trail** (gullies and gorges), and the **Yardie Nature Trail/Yardie Creek Gorge Trail** (gorge and reef). *(Tip: Park entry fees apply; day passes available.)*

Another way to experience Yardie Creek is an outing with **Yardie Creek Boat Tours** to soak in the beauty of the gorge while slowly cruising the waterway, learning from expert guides about the area's flora, fauna, and history along the way.

That turquoise ocean, however, is far too inviting to stay put on land. Visibility can vary for snorkeling and diving, but given the large number of sites around the peninsula, operators usually have weather work-arounds.

The **Murion Islands** are located about nine nautical miles (17 km) north of Exmouth, and they are a popular spot for snorkelers, divers, and fishermen. (Divers will immediately notice a skittishness to the marine life and a lack of medium-size fish that are telltale signs of favored fishing areas.)

Bommies stud the sandy bottoms, forming living sculptures for divers to swim around, through, and over. There is an abundance of healthy soft coral in bright colors here, and we spotted nudibranchs, turtles, sweetlips, cod, and schools of juvenile barracuda.

Don't pass up the opportunity to dive **Exmouth Navy Pier.** This active Australian military base is home to a heavily restricted T-shaped pier that divers can share with a crush of marine life.

Vlamingh Head Lighthouse keeps watch over Ningaloo Reef. It's a great spot to watch the sunrise or sunset over the sea.

Make a Difference

Ningaloo's beaches are important nesting grounds for turtles, with hawksbill, green, and loggerhead the most frequent visitors. Most laying occurs November through February, with hatchlings emerging January to March to run the gauntlet of birds, lizards, crabs, and fish. Few live to see adulthood. The **Jurabi Turtle Centre** (parks.dpaw.wa.gov.au/site/jurabi-turtle-centre), about 12 miles (20 km) from Exmouth township, is an open-air, interpretive educational facility placed near known nesting beaches. Visitors can learn more about turtle biology and the threats they face. Guided Turtle Eco-Education Tours are offered December through early March, increasing the chances of witnessing nesting or hatching turtles while learning how to do so as unobtrusively as possible. (Book at the Ningaloo Visitor Centre.)

After a robust briefing, it's a giant-stride entry off one of the pier's platforms (around a 7-ft/2-m drop), down the mooring line to a mysterious maze of beams, shot through with filtered sunlight and shadows. From there, you have the option of participating in a small-group guided dive, or self-guiding with your buddy, which is what we did.

The restrictions (no fishing allowed) work in divers' favor, resulting in accumulation of species rarely seen in such a concentrated area. (For example, we spotted a dugong.) As we slowly finned over and under the supporting beams of the pier, we admired pylons carpeted in macro life. Thick schools of trevally and snapper refused to give way: We had to gently bump into them before they'd begrudgingly part to let us through. Pregnant whitetip reef sharks lay alongside beams resting on the sand, and we had the pleasure of meeting the resident BFG (big friendly grouper), a massive Queensland grouper with no qualms about getting up close and personal with divers.

(Tip: Dive operators have to follow strict protocols on this active naval base. Roll with the red tape. For example: A valid photo ID is required. Carrying a snorkel and PLB is advised due to currents in the area.)

Another special experience is the opportunity to **snorkel with whale sharks.** Ningaloo is one of few places in the world where whale sharks appear regularly in large numbers (about 200 to 400 per year) near the shore. Two currents form an eddy trapping

Whale sharks appear every year in Ningaloo to feast on plankton, and visitors have the opportunity to snorkel with these gentle giants.

plankton on the edge of a deep, offshore shelf, and that's what attracts these giant filter feeders.

We went out on a full-day tour with Live Ningaloo, a small company specializing in bespoke experiences (high-quality, small-group). Whale and whale-shark tourism is managed and monitored here, and one of the protections in place is limiting the number of people in the water with the animals. Tours accommodating larger groups have to rotate swimmers; Live Ningaloo does not.

When a whale shark is spotted, the boat approaches cautiously, and snorkelers slide into the water on either side of the whale shark, finning

NEARBY

Coral Bay is a 1.5-hour drive south of Exmouth, a tiny resort town right on the shores of Ningaloo Reef. This is a great area for snorkeling among crystal waters and coral gardens with turtles, manta rays, tiger sharks, whale sharks, and more.

alongside and keeping a mandatory distance so it can go about its business. In between swims, an onboard marine scientist shares information about whale sharks, which enhances the experience.

We enjoyed six swims with five beautifully patterned individuals. On our final swim, we kept pace with one steadily swimming behemoth for 27 minutes. (It's what I hope the afterlife is like: gliding peacefully through a blue abyss with a whale shark below and loved ones at my side.)

(Tip: Live Ningaloo offers complimentary transfers from Exmouth, and all gear is included; children and non-swimmers welcome.)

It's estimated that whale shark ecotourism contributes at least $15 million USD to the local econ-

omy every year. This remarkable area also supports thousands of species on reefs, seagrass beds, estuaries, and mangroves. That, however, is not enough to keep it protected and out of harm's way. Large-scale industrial developments, like deepwater ports and pipelines for the fossil fuel industry, keep getting proposed, approved, and fought against.

Like many countries, Australia is at a turning point regarding its future. It has long relied heavily on mining and coal exportation as the cornerstones of its economy. However, given its unique landscape and industrial acumen, Australia has enormous capacity to make cheaper electricity from solar and wind, and to be a global player in the clean energy industry. It's an immense opportunity, and one that would help protect its other natural resources, like whale highways, whale sharks, and the wonders of Ningaloo.

Go west, friends. Exmouth is extraordinary.

Reef fish dart around a coral garden. Exmouth is ideal for divers of all levels, with reefs and one of the best pier dives in the world.

NEED TO KNOW

GETTING HERE: Perth is the gateway to Exmouth. QantasLink has daily flights from Perth to Learmonth Airport, which is a 30-minute drive south of town.

GETTING AROUND: Rental cars are definitely handy here. Driving is easy.

PACKING TIPS: Pack casual clothes for outdoor activities (sun cover, reef-friendly sunscreen, sunglasses, good walking shoes, insect repellent, and head nets). Evenings smarten up a little. Warm layers are useful.

WEATHER: Exmouth has 320 days of sun and a desert climate: Days can be hot (104°F/40°C) and nights cool down. Southern Hemisphere summer (December to February) and Australian public holidays can be busy. Mid-March, May, June, September, and October are the insider months, with good weather and fewer crowds.

IN ADDITION: Prepare to be assailed by flies in certain parts of Exmouth. We didn't get bitten, but they seem to aim for eyes, ears, and nostrils, a pesky annoyance that sheds light on why some people wear head nets.

Diving

OVERVIEW: The world's largest fringe reef and a marine park, part of the Ningaloo Coast World Heritage Area. This area is home to whale sharks, manta rays, and humpback whales, as well as one of the best pier dives in the world. Divers of all levels will love it (snorkelers, too).

- **Visibility:** Navy Pier: 13 feet (4 m); reef: 66-plus feet (20+ m)
- **Water Temp:** 70°F (21°C) in winter / 86°F (30°C) in summer
- **Depth Range:** 66 feet (20 m)

MARINE LIFE: Whale sharks, manta rays, dugongs, turtles, humpback whales, nudibranchs, snapper, grouper (goliath and marbled), sharks (whitetip reef, tiger, blacktip reef, gray reef), batfish, octopuses, and soft coral. Whale sharks (April to August), manta rays (May to November), and humpback whales (June to November). December to February is turtle breeding season.

SHOP INFO: We dove with **Dive Ningaloo,** a locally owned and operated business that (at the time of writing) owns the exclusive license for Exmouth Navy Pier. Courses, reef diving, snorkel trips, and whale shark swims also offered. We dove with **Exmouth Dive & Whalesharks Ningaloo** in the Muiron Islands, another good shop that focuses on quality experiences. They, too, offer courses, diving excursions, snorkel trips, and whale shark swims. For our whale shark swim, we went with **Live Ningaloo,** which specializes in small-group, bespoke experiences.

Accommodations

HIGH-END: Mantarays Ningaloo Beach Resort feels like a cool breeze encapsulated in a hotel. This elegant and casual resort is set three miles (5 km) outside of town. It has 68 rooms, most with marina or ocean views, a pool, beach access, and a restaurant and bar. ~*$220 USD*

MID-RANGE: Exmouth Escape Resort is a village of self-contained villas and apartments set around a swimming pool within walking distance from town. The on-site car rental is a useful amenity, and their restaurant, Whalers, is one of the best in Exmouth. ~*$185 USD*

BUDGET: Potshot Hotel features a range of accommodation options, from backpacker-style to luxury apartments, in a complex that has a restaurant and pool, and is within walking distance of town. ~*$26 USD*

Food & Drink

Whalers Restaurant is a family-run spot serving steak and seafood meals in an elegant indoor-outdoor setting.

Adrift Café in Exmouth township is a relaxed, rustic eatery serving up fresh classics like an eggs Benny breakfast, or roast pumpkin and spinach salad with Persian feta for lunch.

Locally owned **Whalebone Brewing Company** is an outdoor venue perfect for after-work/dive meetings with friends over pizza and craft beer. They have excellent live music and an ingenious playground for kids.

SEYCHELLES

FRÉGATE

Returning to Nature

Frégate hums with life. There are more than 3,500 Aldabra giant tortoises on this 0.8-square-mile (2.2 sq km) Indian Ocean island, one of 115 that make up the Seychelles. These lush granite-and-coral islands—fringed by lacy white surf and sugary beaches, and studded with boulders shaped in a strange dream—were left behind when India broke away from Gondwanaland 100 million years ago. Scattered nearly 1,000 miles (1,600 km) from the east coast of Africa, the Seychelles evolved in Edenesque isolation until settlers arrived in the 18th century, upsetting the ecological apple-cart. Plantation-era farming for crops stripped the Seychelles of its native flora, and the effects rippled throughout the wealth of wild-life that can be found here: exotic birds and bizarre insects, endangered sea turtles and coral reefs.

When private owners purchased Frégate with the intention of turning it into a conservation sanctuary, restoring and protecting the island's land and marine environments, there were fewer than 100 tortoises left. Their rebounding numbers are one of Frégate's many success stories, none of which would be possible without visiting guests.

Fair warning: Frégate isn't cheap, but the wildlife is worth every penny. On our first day, from the vantage point of our infinity pool, we saw hunting tuna, cruising manta rays, and a squadron of cow-nosed rays in the turquoise sea. And that was all topside. Underwater, Frégate reveals coral gardens, clouds of batfish, giant clams, and submerged pinnacles, ideal for shark-spotting.

Every day brought extraordinary new encounters. Keen to return to nature? Frégate is as good as it gets. ∎

Dreamlike and paradisiacal, Frégate is a small island sanctuary teeming with life and supported (in part) by an elegant luxury lodge.

Frégate is a lush, living laboratory, scented with frangipani and ylang-ylang. Decades of research and restoration work has yielded a paradise the likes of which we've never seen. At dawn and dusk, the sky is filled with the angled shapes of thousands of rare and endemic bird species, including fairy terns, noddies, and the Seychelles magpie-robin, one of the rarest birds in the world, brought back from the brink of extinction by the Frégate team. (At one point, only 14 of these birds remained.)

Their sanctuary is the tens of thousands of replanted indigenous trees—including banyan trees and the rare coco de mer (producing the largest seed in the world)—that also provide shade for the giant tortoises that flourish under Frégate's protection. Frégate is home to the second largest wild-roaming population of Aldabra giant tortoises (after the Galápagos, page 124), a species that is still endangered due to poaching. We saw them everywhere: sneaking into the garden; wal-

lowing in muddy pools; stretching their necks to pull low-hanging star fruit from the trees; grazing and snoozing on the island's airstrip, one of their favorite haunts. (Tortoise wranglers are employed to gently shoo the 551-lb/250-kg giants out of the path of incoming helicopters carrying arriving guests.) The majority of Frégate's tortoises are wary of humans, pulling in their necks with a disconcerting hiss (an exhalation of air to make room in their shells for their heads and necks) as we strolled past.

A network of nearly seven miles (11 km) of inland nature trails and concrete paths link the **museum** (the former plantation owner's house; well worth a visit), the **marina** (stocked with water toys like kayaks and Hobie Cats), and the **Rock Spa,** a teak house that holds a gym, spa, and yoga studio. *(Tip: You haven't known peace until you've taken a yoga class in the presence of wandering baby tortoises.)*

Don't miss a **tour of the garden,** which provides more than 80 percent of the island's food. "For some guests, the garden is their favorite place on the island. They'll come down here with a basket, collect what they want to eat, and bring it back to the chef," said Simon Love, Frégate's agricultural manager. "The tortoises," he added, "are less-welcome guests. I catch them in the garden, and they always look at me sheepishly. They know they aren't supposed to be here."

Guests are encouraged to get involved with daily conservation activities, from lending a hand with Frégate's coral restoration project to safeguarding sea turtle nests. (Frégate is one of the few places in the world where hawksbill turtles nest during daylight.)

Morning and nighttime nature hikes (when the island is at its most active) with one of the resident

Frégate's warm, clear water and varied diving (sheltered reefs, spicy currents, and sharky pinnacles) make it a dream destination for divers.

Make a Difference

Frégate *(fregate.com)* is justifiably proud of its ongoing protection and preservation, and guests can be as hands-on as they want to be. Divers and snorkelers can get involved with the coral nursery; tortoise enthusiasts can sponsor a baby tortoise and/or help out in the nursery; tree lovers can plant endemic saplings; and sea turtle fans can join ecologists on the beach during nesting season (October to January) to ensure successful hatchings. Every now and again, Frégate recruits long-term (six months-plus) conservation volunteers; contact the team if you'd like to learn more or if you'd like to get involved in other ways (donations, etc.). And remember: Simply by staying on the island, you're contributing to the work being done here.

biologists are definite must-dos. The night hike was a revelation in the wonderfully weird. The experience was an hour-long search in the dark for the "Five Freaks of Frégate," the often overlooked nocturnal species that are as mesmerizing as the diurnal ones. We spotted them all: the Seychelles giant millipede, the Seychelles giant scorpion, the tailless whip scorpion (which is actually a spider), the tenebrionid beetle (a critically endangered beetle endemic to Frégate), and the Seychelles house snake, which we watched scavenge a small fish that had been dropped by a seabird.

The Seychelles is one of the wealthiest countries in Africa, and an island nation heavily reliant on the ocean for its livelihood. In 2020, the Seychelles announced 13 new marine protected areas. The declaration means 30 percent of its territorial waters (an area larger than Germany) are protected, 10 years ahead of international targets.

This good news is especially sweet for divers, who will find an underwater Eden at Frégate that's as rich as the terrestrial paradise. An upwelling of cold, nutrient-rich waters surrounds the island, attracting and sustaining life. There are about eight established dive sites within a 15-minute boat ride, and several more at longer range.

This is an area to be dived over and over again as there's always something new turning up. With warm, clear water and a plethora of wildlife, Frégate is ideal for divers of all levels, and there are plenty of sheltered spots to explore, like **Grand Anse,** a flat

Frégate is a conservation success story: The number of Aldabra giant tortoises on the island has grown from 100 to more than 3,500.

reef covered in coral, including fragile staghorn. This reef is filled with thick schools of juvenile fish, giant clams, anemones with resident clownfish, leaf fish, and those powerful punchers, mantis shrimp.

Chill Out can get frisky with current, but the wildlife is off the hook: clouds of big, inquisitive batfish, massive stingrays and tawny nurse sharks, and we even watched an epic battle of an octopus trying to drag a fully inflated (and very much alive) puffer fish into its den.

Lion Rock is another special dive site, superb for shark-spotting and suitable for divers with some

If Frégate is out of reach, look into other Seychelles islands like Alphonse Island. A one-hour flight from Mahé, Alphonse is also populated by tortoises and has great diving. Accommodations run around a third of Frégate's cost.

experience. This large granite pinnacle is located offshore, dropping down to 98 feet (30 m), and seems to be a magnet for manta rays and especially sharks.

Frégate is bespoke diving at its best: beautiful conditions, flourishing wildlife, very small groups, immaculate boats, and hands-on, conservation-minded guides. They treat their island home with respect and insist on the same from their guests.

We were staggered to learn that only 25 percent of Frégate's guests take part in the nature hikes. The island attracts two types of visitors: those interested in the ecology of the island, and those attracted to the beauty, luxury, and exclusivity of Frégate. Both are crucial to the success of the island.

Conservation right now is considered a luxury; many people can't afford it, and others choose to ignore or politicize it. But here's what it boils down to: Our collective survival depends on the protection and restoration of our environment, and places like Frégate have turned conservation into a priority. Visitors can be as involved as they want to be, and if they prefer to relax on a beach, they're still funding the work being done here. It's a good model, and one the Seychelles seems to be embracing.

This island filled us with hope. On our journey, we witnessed so many examples of people—from all backgrounds—making a difference in their corner of the world, and Frégate is a shining example of that, returning the island to nature, and restoring its balance.

Tranquil views from infinity pools. The island holds 16 secluded luxury villas and one grand estate, each with breathtaking vistas.

NEED TO KNOW

GETTING HERE: Mahé is the largest island in the Seychelles and its entry point. From there, it's a 15-minute helicopter flight or 1.5-hour boat trip to Frégate, arranged by the resort.

GETTING AROUND: Guests are assigned their own buggy to navigate the island (or you can walk). Mind the natural hazards: tortoises by day (if they're camped out on the path, walk up and gently pat their shells to encourage them to shift) and the cigar-size Seychelles giant millipede at night. Harmless, endangered, and going extinct, these important caretakers of the forest can be difficult to dodge, but please try.

PACKING TIPS: Relaxed resort wear. Sun cover is important. The lodge provides special insect repellent that's safe for wildlife.

WEATHER: This Southern Hemisphere destination is warm year-round. October through May is best for diving: calm seas, good visibility, short bursts of rain. May through October is drier with steady winds. Avoid the busy European holidays.

IN ADDITION: Families are most welcome here and kids will fall in love with the wildlife. Frégate is undergoing ambitious restoration efforts and will be closed to tourists until 2024.

Diving

OVERVIEW: Heavenly, bespoke diving from a private island base with options for all levels of divers. The Seychelles has protected 30 percent of its territorial waters, and therefore the area is teeming with marine life.

- Visibility: 98-plus feet (30+ m)
- Water Temp: 77°F (25°C) in winter / 88°F (31°C) in summer
- Depth Range: 53 to 98 feet (16 to 30 m)

MARINE LIFE: Manta rays, sharks (gray reef, tawny nurse, and whitetip reef), turtles (hawksbill and green), trevally (giant and bluefin), octopuses, batfish, bumphead parrotfish, Napoleon wrasse, barracuda, tuna, staghorn coral, leaf fish, mantis shrimp, and so much more

SHOP INFO: Frégate has a private harbor and top-notch team; guides and boats are exclusive to your dive party. If you want to focus on diving, learn to dive, or use Nitrox, prebook in advance; otherwise, adding a few dives to your stay is easily organized on-site. All gear included.

Accommodations

HIGH-END: Frégate Island Private has 16 secluded luxury villas and one grand estate scattered throughout the island. Villas are divine, with elegant furnishings, verandas with a view, infinity pools, and hot tubs. It's easy to feel instantly, happily at home here. A private butler, meals, and most nonmotorized activities are included. The **Banyan Hill Estate** is three villas in one, perfect for families or groups of friends. ~$16,230 USD

MID-RANGE: There are three family-style **Private Pool Twin Villas** on the island, with two bedrooms, living room, and dining room. ~$8,520 USD

BUDGET: The remaining 13 rooms are **Private Pool Villas,** ideal for couples. ~$4,600 USD

Food & Drink

Frégate Island Private's meals are sourced from their organic garden complex and the sea. The lodge offers a range of dining venues, including two restaurants and a beach bar. Occasionally, the culinary team puts on something special, like a **Creole-inspired dinner at the Plantation House,** serving Seychellois fish curry, pumpkin soup with lemongrass, Frégate palm heart salad, and creole meatballs in tomato sauce.

Don't miss having breakfast in the **Banyan Treehouse,** an ancient tree with a platform located 49 feet (15 m) up. Enjoy coffee and a delicious cold breakfast to the accompaniment of birdsong, an amazing way to begin the day.

A **picnic lunch on a private beach** (one of seven around the island) is also a must-do experience. A packed Mediterranean-style lunch is laid out with a cooler of iced drinks on a beach of white sand. Nothing to do but relax and enjoy the wild beauty.

GRAND CAYMAN

Reputations Can Be Misleading

The Cayman Islands conjure up images of seduction, sea, and sundowners laced with larceny, but there's so much more to this white-sand playground than cruise ships and the euphemistic tax haven.

Geographically speaking, the Cayman Islands are three islands: Grand Cayman, Little Cayman, and Cayman Brac. They are umbrellaed by Cuba, Jamaica, and the Yucatán Peninsula (page 280), and border the deepest spot in the Caribbean: the 26,247-foot (8,000 m) Cayman Trench.

Grand Cayman is 22 miles (35 km) long, with a high-rise reputation that primarily applies to the west coast's famous Seven Mile Beach. The other 15 miles (24 km) are a stark surprise, a low-lying landscape filled with trees and a central mangrove wetland covering more than 8,655 acres (3,500 ha). All of that is encircled by a dramatic ocean covering reefs to plunging walls.

"True Caymanians measure our lives by storms," one local told us. "The sea is everything to us: our misery and salvation."

We've wrought a lot of damage in the Cayman Islands, from slavery to habitat destruction, but the past few years have been a wake-up call in preserving what makes this place unique.

This is the only place in the world with blue dragons, one of six places with permanent bioluminescence, and an oasis for endemic bird and orchid species (one of which is no bigger than a thumbnail). Throw in a mermaid, and have we got your attention? The Cayman Islands got ours. ∎

There's more to Grand Cayman than the sugary white sand and turquoise water of popular Seven Mile Beach: The island is remarkably diverse.

Understanding the strong connection Caymanians have with their islands—measuring their lives by sea, sun, and storms—is understanding the heart and soul of this place. Two spots in particular (worth visiting early in your stay) will provide a good introduction and probably a few surprises.

The **Cayman Islands National Museum,** located in George Town and housed in a 200-year-old building, is home to a series of exhibits on the islands' natural and cultural heritage. We found the informative display on conservation—including status updates on species and natural environments—particularly captivating.

Pedro St. James (just outside Bodden Town) is the oldest surviving structure in the Cayman Islands, and it has more than a few stories to tell. This 7.5-acre (3 ha) National Historic Site was built in 1780. It's seen the beginning of democracy, the end of slavery, and weathered more than a few storms. Visitors can experience a multisensory 3D presentation, explore the three-story restored Great House, and wander the seaside grounds. *(Tip: Take a guided tour—some of the guides are descendants of the original owners.)*

At the **Queen Elizabeth II Botanic Park,** the

Cayman Brac and Little Cayman (an easy interisland flight from Grand Cayman) each have distinct personalities: Cayman Brac is wilder and quirkier; Little Cayman is more natural and serene. Both are superb diving destinations worth visiting.

surprises keep coming. One of the biggest revelations to us was the discovery of blue dragons.

Sir Francis Drake first wrote of these "great serpents" in 1586, bright blue beauties with disconcertingly blood-red eyes that can surpass five feet (1.5 m) in length.

"The whole point of the blue is to show off: Once these iguanas reach a mature size, they have no natural predators—except us," said the operations manager of the park's Blue Iguana Conservation (BIC), which breeds and releases blue iguanas back into the wild.

These blue dragons are found only on Grand Cayman. In 2001, fewer than 30 individuals remained. By 2018, BIC had released 1,000 blue iguanas and changed their focus from restoring the wild population to conserving the species.

Visitors to the botanic park might come across a blue iguana while exploring the park's 65 acres (26 ha) of themed gardens and woodland trails. Those who want to make sure they see one of these rare and beautiful creatures can book a tour of the BIC facility (self-guided or a half-day behind-the-scenes experience with BIC iguana wardens; Zoom tours are also available).

(Tip: BIC welcomes volunteers—for the day, two-week stints, or ongoing. Contact BIC in advance.)

Although not as rare as a blue iguana, an after-dark tour with **Cayman Kayaks** to **Bioluminescence Bay** ("Bio Bay," near Rum Point) is another

Mermaid meeting: Author Carrie Miller visits "Amphitrite," a nine-foot-tall (2.7 m) bronze statue located at Sunset House resort's house reef.

special and unexpected Cayman twist. Thanks to a cocktail of sunlight, nutrients, and shelter, Bio Bay is one of six places in the world with year-round bioluminescence. This 1.5-hour tandem kayak tour begins at twilight. At first, the water seems effervescent, filled with gleaming white bubbles. Soon the bubbles begin to flush greenish-blue, then light blue. Paddle strokes create a wave of color that surges and dissipates, and scooping a handful of seawater gives you a fistful of stars.

(Tip: This delightfully informative tour is a great evening out for all ages. They also run an electric boat as an option for elderly or disabled guests. Do not wear any lotion or repellent, as this harms the bioluminescence.)

Another fun and educational activity for families is **Jean-Michel Cousteau's Ambassadors of the Environment program,** based at the Ritz-Carlton Grand Cayman (but open to the public). This summer camp for everyone started as kids-only, but the kids were having so much fun the parents wanted to participate, too. Their selection of ecotours

Blue iguanas are Grand Cayman's most endangered species. You can see them (and help conservation efforts) at Queen Elizabeth II Botanic Park.

transforms the island into an outdoor classroom, led by knowledgeable and enthusiastic guides.

We chose the Mangrove Kayak Adventure, a three-hour, glass-bottomed kayak tour through Grand Caymans' red mangrove forests. On the tour, we slowly paddled through a trail surrounded by tangled roots, stopping frequently to talk, look, and learn.

Mangroves are a marvel, and our guide Cara Heller, an engineer by training, is equally impressed by this force of nature. "If a company came to me and said: 'We need you to design something that is incredibly strong, flexible, self-regenerating, and eco-friendly, something that can act as coastline protection, a filtration system, a nursery for marine life, and a sanctuary for birds,' it would cost billions of dollars to design, if it was possible at all," Cara said. "Yet here it is, growing for free, and it's being torn up to make room for development."

Mangroves are the magic behind the Cayman Islands' legendary reefs, which have lured recreational divers since 1957. Grand Cayman is a year-round destination for divers of all levels (snorkelers, too). There are more than 240 dive sites accessible by boat or shore, and most of the dive sites are named after the bars they are offshore of.

Each side of the island has a personality. The north side has a wall running parallel to shore that plunges beyond 6,000 feet (1,829 m). (Look for turtles, spotted eagle rays, and sharks.) The south side is a sheltered spot favored in winter, with canyons, arches, and swim-throughs. The west side is the most dived coast, with reefs and walls and favorable conditions. (This is where you'll find the wrecks.) The east coast is uncrowded, unspoiled, and more remote, with reefs, pinnacles, and walls.

The house reef in front of **Sunset House** (located in the southwest corner of the island) is a gem for beginner divers. This shore dive begins in a shallow, squid-filled ocean pool, before exiting along a channel. The sloping reef is filled with nooks and crannies, extending onto a sandy bed that's home to a community of garden eels. The dive takes you past a nine-foot-tall (2.7 m) bronze statue of a serene mermaid, and the fish-filled, shallow (60 ft/18 m) wreck of the **LCM _Nicholson._**

Divers with some experience shouldn't miss the **U.S.S. _Kittiwake,_** a spectacular, 251-foot-long (77 m) wreck that can get crowded. The _Kittiwake_ rests at

There is something for every diver in Grand Cayman, from house reefs to wrecks like the U.S.S. _Kittiwake._

a depth of 72 feet (22 m) and used to sit upright on the sand until it was knocked on its side by a hurricane in 2016. There are still a lot of penetration opportunities, and it's a favorite with turtles, barracuda, tarpon, macro life, and schooling silversides.

Grand Cayman is filled with marvelous treasures. Few places offer a gentle lesson in the interconnectivity quite the way this place does. It defies its reputation—and expectations.

Make a Difference

It's worth learning more about two current issues in Grand Cayman. First, the western side of the island has already lost more than 70 percent of its mangroves, largely due to development. Second, the cruise ship industry and government are fighting to open George Town Harbour for dredging to accommodate bigger ships. Dredging would destroy acres of precious coral reefs, at a time when the world is losing reefs at an unprecedented rate. The reefs are also critical to attracting and maintaining overnight visitors, which bring in 78 percent of tourism revenue. Both mangroves and reefs are important, fragile ecosystems that are notoriously difficult to relocate and regenerate. Check out the **National Trust** (nationaltrust.org.ky) for tours, to learn more, or to donate.

NEED TO KNOW

GETTING HERE: Canada and the United States have direct flights to the Cayman Islands, with Miami being the main gateway.

GETTING AROUND: Renting a car is a great way to explore. Driving is on the left side, but many cars also have the steering wheel on the left side (specify with the rental car agency if you want one on the right side). Watch out for endangered blue iguanas!

PACKING TIPS: Mix and match: You'll want a few outfits that blend in with the glitterati, but the rest can be active and functional. Sun hats and reef shoes are a must.

WEATHER: Pleasant temperatures year-round, ranging from 80°F (26.6°C) in winter to 90°F (32°C) in summer. November through March is clear and calm, while May through October can be humid and rainy. Hurricane season is June through November.

IN ADDITION: Grand Cayman is a place where best practice and bad practice rub shoulders. (For example, some of the island's largest and most popular land-based attractions are places where you can touch and handle wildlife for photographs.) It's a good reminder that everything we spend money on—from accommodations to activities—is a direct message that we want more of the same. Spend sustainably!

Diving

OVERVIEW: Grand Cayman has walls, reefs, and wrecks in warm, clear water. This is varied diving in great conditions, with something for divers of all levels (and snorkelers).

- Visibility: 65-plus feet (20+ m)
- Water Temp: 78°F (25.5°C) in winter / 86°F (30°C) in summer
- Depth Range: 40 to 99 feet (12 to 30 m)

MARINE LIFE: Good macro (lettuce leaf slugs, Pederson cleaner shrimp, pistol shrimp), fish (tarpon, Nassau grouper, bluestriped grunt, stoplight parrotfish), turtles (loggerhead, green, hawksbill, and leatherback), garden eels, sharks (nurse and Caribbean reef), spotted eagle rays, and coral (elkhorn, staghorn, brain, sea fans)

SHOP INFO: We dove with **Sunset House's Sunset Divers** on Grand Cayman. The shop is integrated into the dive resort, and both are fun, energetic, and welcoming. Boat dives are offered, and there is also a nice house reef.

Accommodations

HIGH-END: The **Ritz-Carlton Grand Cayman** is a 144-acre (58 ha) resort on Seven Mile Beach, offering elegant comfort, as well as a few surprises, including a local art gallery and a kid-friendly vibe. ~$803 USD

MID-RANGE: **Shangri-La** is a family-owned and operated B&B located in the quieter West Bay area of Grand Cayman, a convenient 3.5 miles (6 km) from Seven Mile Beach. It offers 11 individual rooms and suites, shared complimentary bikes, and a specially designed diver's locker for rinsing and drying dive gear. ~$282 USD

BUDGET: **Sunset House** is a great base for divers, with an on-site dive shop, unlimited shore diving, and room-and-dive packages. Non-divers and snorkelers will also love it here. There are 36 rooms, a friendly atmosphere, two pools (standard and ocean), a cruise-ship-free house reef, and proximity to George Town (a 15-minute walk). The restaurant/bar is a great spot to watch the sunset, cold drink in hand. (Visitors welcome.) ~$260 USD

Food & Drink

Since 1988, the **Wharf** has offered seaside dining tailor-made for groups of friends, families, or couples.

Guy Harvey's Restaurant was a wonderful find. Located on the George Town waterfront with harbor views, the menu was exceptional (we loved our Parmesan-encrusted fish with lemon caper butter sauce and crab cakes) and the atmosphere casually elegant, filled with Guy's ocean-themed artwork.

Kaibo is a quintessential beach shack at Rum Point (great for a pre–Bio Bay meal). This restaurant does Caribbean beachside cuisine very well: burgers, pizzas, and salads.

GOZO

Ready, Set, Go(zo)

Gozo is like no place you've seen before.

Flat-topped hills crowned with medieval architecture (fortresses and domed basilicas) terminate into sheer limestone cliffs, arching over and hollowed out under the aquamarine Mediterranean. This 26-square-mile (67 sq km) island is the second largest in the Maltese archipelago. The exposed, harsh, and surprisingly natural landscape (given its close proximity to wall-to-wall Malta) feels more Middle Eastern than European.

Gozo is part of the Republic of Malta. Its inheritance is culture, and its location is the crossroads of history, encircled by Italy, Greece, Tunisia, and Libya.

Everything is in close proximity on this fiercely independent island, where history and legend rub shoulders. You can tour Xewkija—Gozo's biggest church with the third largest unsupported dome in the world—in the morning. In the afternoon, sunbathe on red-sanded Ramla

Beach, which is overlooked by the "love cave" where the sea-nymph Calypso imprisoned Odysseus in Homer's *Odyssey*.

Gozo is also a place of adventure. Travelers can kayak the coves that cut into Gozo's dramatic coastline, or try their hands at climbing spectacular rock faces. They can snorkel or dive the legendary Blue Hole.

The unholy surprise of Gozo is that the island keeps on giving, and just when you think you have a handle on it, you uncover something new. Are you ready? Then Go(zo). ■

Aptly named fried egg jellyfish (also known as egg-yolk jellyfish) are often spotted in the waters surrounding Gozo.

The ancient and formidable **Cittadella** is the perfect place to begin your exploration of Gozo. The Cittadella looms over the capital city of Rabat, also known as Victoria, its hilltop battlements providing sweeping views.

This winding maze of narrow alleys flanked by high walls empties onto open courtyards baking in the hot sun. There is something to discover around every corner, from museums to craft shops and restaurants. (Self-explore, or guided tours available.)

Gozo has been a prize to be won since war was invented, and the Cittadella grew defensively during centuries of raids by pirates and slavers. It all culminated in a devastating siege by the Turks in 1551, who enslaved or killed nearly all of Gozo's population (around 5,000), leaving fewer than 100 people behind. Rebuilding took generations. Until 1637, all Gozitans were required by law to shelter at night within the Cittadella. It took a lot longer than that for Gozo's distrust of foreigners to ease into detached interest.

Gozo's **13 villages** (depending on how you count) radiate outward from Rabat. All are worth exploring on driving day trips, and if you're visiting during the summer months, you are in for a treat. Every weekend from the end of May until mid-

September, each village organizes a *festa* **(festival) in honor of its patron saint** (complete with bands, fireworks, processionals, and horse racing), and there are fierce rivalries to outshine the neighbors. (Visitors welcome.)

Gozo's landscape makes you want to be a kid again, with rocks to scramble over and coves to swim in. With more than 26 miles (43 km) of coastline, it's easy to understand why **kayaking** is such a popular sport here, but—in the Gozitan spirit—Chris and I decided to split up for a day and each of us try something new.

I opted for a half day of **climbing with Gozo Adventures.** I haven't done much climbing before, and I struck gold with my instructor, the legendary Stevie Haston, one of the United Kingdom's most accomplished climbers and alpinists. (I didn't know this until I Googled him later; Stevie doesn't boast about his achievements.)

We based ourselves in an ancient, curving riverbed, beginning with a 40-foot (12 m) face and working up from there. I was roped in for safety but climbing on my own. Under Stevie's watchful eye, I completed four exhilarating routes I never would have imagined trying at the beginning of the day.

(Tip: Gozo is an ideal place for beginners to give climbing a try. For experienced climbers, Gozo is a playground! More than half its coastline is cliff faces, offering natural holds and uncounted adventures.)

The exquisite Xewkija Church commands the skyline. Xewkija is Gozo's biggest church and holds the world's third largest unsupported dome.

While I was climbing with Stevie, Chris was taking a **free-diving clinic** with another legend, world champion free diver Jesper Stechmann.

The course begins with breathing exercises, the core to free diving, as well as yoga (stretching and relaxation helps you fill your lungs to capacity). Following the classroom instruction, Jesper takes students down to a sheltered lagoon to put it into practice. One of the most peculiar aspects was understanding and experiencing diaphragm fluttering, a precursor to wanting to draw a breath. A trick to free diving is both recognizing and shelving that feeling so you can relax and safely push past it.

Chris was, unfortunately, battling a cold, and his sinuses kept him restricted to 33 feet (10 m), a hair shy of Jesper's personal best of 334.6 feet (102 m). Still, Chris was hooked: He thrived on the instruction (physiology, philosophy, and techniques) and is keen to return when he's cold-free.

Climbing and diving are both activities that give you a different perspective on the world—you see

With striking rock formations and plenty of wrecks, Gozo puts on a show for divers.

in vertical, beyond the horizontal. They also require being present and mindful, to be a part of your environment rather than working against it.

Gozo has surprisingly diverse diving for such a small island. Even though there's diving for all levels here, technical diving is popular—even the local tourism advertisements feature a tech diver, which is unusual. The underwater topography mirrors the terrestrial, with flared arches, yawning caverns, V-shaped trenches, and underwater caves. It's a work of art, surrounded by jewel-colored seas.

There are wrecks like the **M.V. *Karwela,*** a 164-foot (50 m) former tourist ferry with perhaps one of the most photogenic and famous underwater staircases in the world. It stands upright around 131 feet (40 m) on a sandy bottom, easily penetrable and an easy dive, but deco due to the depth.

The **Blue Hole** in Dwejra is legendary. This natural rock formation resembles an upright tube, carved by wind and rock. Divers descend through a cloud of snorkelers and swimmers, and soon have the sapphire world to themselves, exiting through an underwater archway that leads into the open sea, sharing it with larger fish like grouper, dentex, or tuna.

However, it was the **Inland Sea** (adjacent to the Blue Hole) that took our breath away with its spectacular topography. The ocean spills through a channel, connecting a semicircle inland lagoon with the open ocean via a 263-foot (80 m) tunnel with deep, vertical, overhanging walls. The dive begins on the shore of a small fishing village, following the tunnel around 33-foot (10 m) depth before exiting onto a steep wall. From there, you can travel left or right before returning through the tunnel. (*Tip: Be wary of boat traffic, especially in the tunnel.*) There's good marine life here, including parrotfish, bream, octopuses, and mesmerizing fried egg jellyfish, which look exactly like their name suggests.

As with most places in the Mediterranean, fishing is a centuries-old culture here, and the surrounding waters show it. There is also a disappointing amount of rubbish, which is carried by ever present winds and snagged in sea caves and crevices. However, there is a growing environmental awareness, particularly around the country's terrestrial habitats

The Gleneagles Bar (an authentic Gozitan watering hole) keeps watch over Mgarr Harbour.

(home to a large number of native and endemic species). In 2016, the Republic of Malta extended its marine protected areas to cover about 30 percent of their waters, roughly 11 times the size of the Maltese Islands. It's a step in the right direction.

Things here take time. Give it time, and Gozo will gift you back something you never expected. Ready, steady . . .

Make a Difference

Even if Malta wanted to take a strong environmental stand (and it could do better), the country sits astride the Mediterranean's principal shipping routes and commercial fishing areas, a prime example of the need for global (as well as local) change. Land conservation must double by 2030 to prevent an unraveling of the ecosystems our lives depend on. Studies estimate protecting half the Earth would cost around $140 billion per year, considerably less than the trillions the 2009 U.S. bank bailout cost. We can find the money if we need to—and we need to. What can you do? Vote and support global conservation efforts. Check out the **Wyss Campaign for Nature** (*wysscampaign.org*) and the **Global Deal for Nature** (*globaldealfornature.org*) to learn more and get involved.

GETTING HERE: It's an hour's drive from Malta International Airport to the ferry terminal at Cirkewwa Harbour, and then a 25-minute crossing to Mgarr Harbour in Gozo. Gozo is only accessible by ferry: They operate regularly, and you pay for your round-trip ticket on your *return* journey from Gozo to Malta.

GETTING AROUND: Renting a car is a good way to get around, but bear in mind Gozo's unwritten rule: The bigger vehicle has right of way. Take your time and take it slow. Mayjo Car Rentals is a good establishment offering everything from car rentals to tours to transfers.

PACKING TIPS: The sun is intense, the wind can be cool (especially on boats), walking surfaces are uneven, and the locals dress with style. Pack accordingly.

WEATHER: Summer is hot (over 100°F/38°C) and crowded. Temperatures cool and crowds thin in October, and November/December bring rain. January through March is mild (63°F/17°C) and uncrowded, and April and May are ideal for outdoor activities: warm (72°F/22°C), with long hours of sunshine.

IN ADDITION: Many places are closed on Sundays.

Diving

OVERVIEW: A mecca for tech divers and free divers, this year-round Mediterranean dive destination has reefs, walls, caves, and wrecks, and is suitable for divers of all levels.

- Visibility: 65-plus feet (20+ m)
- Water Temp: 57°F (14°C) in winter / 81°F (27°C) in summer
- Depth Range: 17 to 131-plus feet (5 to 40+ m)

MARINE LIFE: Fried egg jellyfish, conger and moray eels, yellowfin tuna, blue runners, grouper, dentexes, umbrella snails, parrotfish, and crayfish

SHOP INFO: We dove with **Atlantis Diving Centre,** a family-run shop offering guided dives and courses; they see a lot of return visitors. One of the owners is a very experienced tech instructor (Atlantis's basement is a massive tech diving shop). Chris did his free-diving course with **InnerDive.** Founder and world champion free diver Jesper Stechmann is one of an elite team of instructors teaching absolute beginners through pros at their purpose-built free-diving center. Safaris (guided free diving around Gozo) are also offered.

Accommodations

HIGH-END: Hotel Ta' Cenc and Spa, located near Sannat on the southern coast of Gozo, is large (84 ground-floor rooms, three restaurants, a pool, and spa), but surrounded by nature. Stay in a *trullo,* unique bungalows with beehive-style ceilings. ~*$236 USD*

MID-RANGE: Dar tal-Kaptan is a hospitable bed and breakfast in the quiet village of Ghasri (2.5 mi/4 km from Rabat). This 400-year-old farmhouse has five individual rooms, eclectic and somewhat sensual decor, and an outdoor pool. (Adults only.) ~*$105 USD*

BUDGET: The 40-room **Downtown Hotel** in Rabat attracts visitors from around the world (making for a fun atmosphere) with its central location, welcoming staff, and reasonable rates. Rooms are simple, and amenities include on-site dining, a rooftop pool deck, bowling alley, and play area for kids. ~*$60 USD*

Food & Drink

Family-run **Tmun Mgarr** specializes in seasonal dishes showcasing Gozo's natural flavors, like prawn tartare with strawberries, lemon pearls, and micro herbs. This is the spot to dine with friends.

Ta' Rikardu is located down a winding alley in the Cittadella, serving a delicious menu of traditional food centered around the owner's homemade wine and cheese, and homegrown produce.

The **Gleaneagles Bar,** overlooking Mgarr Harbour, is as authentic as they get. This watering hole (decor: unvarnished maritime) welcomes locals meeting at the end of the day, people studiously drinking alone, and wide-eyed travelers keen on visiting a Gozitan institution.

MUNDA AND GIZO

History, Mystery, and Adventure at Its Best

We've seen some beautiful islands on this journey, but the Solomon Islands? Wow.

Hard and soft coral in jewel tones shimmer under an ocean that has crystal channels and turquoise bays. Richly forested islands are framed by a deep sapphire sea. Divers will have to fight the urge to take a giant stride out of the airplane flying over the Solomons—the underwater opportunities appear endless, unexplored, and tantalizing.

The Solomon Islands are located in the middle of the Coral Triangle, forming a geographical crown for northern Australia along with Papua New Guinea and Indonesia, which lie to the west.

There are 992 islands in the Solomons (147 inhabited), covering a vast swath of ocean. Rain always seems to be on the horizon, but rarely where you are. If it does arrive, it's over in a burst, and the sun appears again, preparing to cast a sunset the likes of which you've never seen.

It is said that a Spanish explorer named the islands after the riches of King Solomon, but once you slip beneath the surface, you'll see where the true riches lie: Reefs here hold more than 500 species of coral, 1,000 species of reef fish, and healthy populations of sharks.

The Solomons are a great destination for travelers seeking something off the beaten track, who are willing to trade a few comforts and conveniences for adventure. Come visit this naturally beautiful country, which is populated by shy but welcoming people. You'll find history and a little mystery tucked around every bay and inlet. ∎

There are 992 islands in the Solomons, 147 of which are inhabited. Cultural traditions are strong, rich, and varied throughout the islands.

Honiara is the Solomon Islands' capital and largest city, situated on the northwestern coast of Guadalcanal, a name that lives in wartime infamy. When the Japanese invaded the Solomon Islands in 1942, the islands were swept into the Pacific Theater. The strait off Honiara became known as the Iron Bottom Sound, a sunken graveyard of shipwrecks and aircraft.

Now, this proudly independent country welcomes close to 30,000 visitors every year, many of whom are war buffs, scuba divers, or both. This is a great spot for divers and snorkelers of all levels, with warm, clear waters filled with wrecks and reefs aplenty.

We split our time between Munda (a village on New Georgia Island) and Gizo (a small island northwest of Munda).

Munda is making efforts to woo visitors. It has just enough infrastructure (a few hotels, small airport, great guides, and an excellent dive shop) but hasn't sacrificed its personality. Munda is also making concerted strides in ocean conservation by developing no-take areas, educating locals around fishing for sharks and turtles, and making reef conservation efforts. Diving and snorkeling are the main activities here, with more than 40 sites within a 40-minute boat ride.

(Tip: There is a lot of exploratory diving here, too, with more wrecks being discovered every year.)

Mbigo Mbigo (Rainbow Reef) lives up to its name, a wall dive around 98 feet (30 m) with hard coral bommies in blues, yellows, pinks, and greens, and a top reef around 26 feet (8 m) that is ideal for safety stops and snorkelers. **Marlon's Crack** is another shared snorkel/dive spot and similar wall dive, with unique crevices and cuttings in the reef. We spotted a small scalloped hammerhead in the blue off the wall, and endemic white bonnet anemone fish in the shallows.

Shark Point is a fun and fishy spot at the end of a protruding reef. Divers can go deep here (98+ ft/ 30+ m), following the sloping reef on a drift dive, keeping an eye out for sharks (we spotted more than 20 gray reef sharks), as well as large fish, rays, and turtles. This spot is also a favorite with snorkelers: With a guide, snorkelers hold on to a rope attached to the boat, which drifts with the current. The coral isn't as good in the shallows as it is down deep, but the fish! There are hundreds of butterflyfish, good-size snapper, parrotfish, and sharks. After a bit, you get back into the boat, drive back, and do it again, like a sharky amusement park ride.

We did two WWII wreck dives on a single tank here. Since they are small wrecks, we did a 10-minute dive on each using the same tank of air, which is unusual, but worked well. The ***Airacobra*** is an American P-39 fighter aircraft sitting upright on a sandy bed in 89 feet (27 m), and the ***Dauntless*** is a Douglas SBD-4 dive bomber that was hit and put down in Rendova Harbour by pilot Jim Dougherty, who not only survived, but returned to dive the wreck of his own plane 50 years later.

There are plenty of non-diving activities to do in the area, too, including forest walks, river cruises,

Uninhabited Kennedy Island is where former U.S. president John F. Kennedy and the surviving crew of his rammed boat swam to in WWII.

Make a Difference

When COVID closed borders, **Dive Munda** looked to its own backyard, launching a youth campaign that trained young Solomon Islanders to dive, with a focus on underwater cleanups, stopping plastic pollution, coral protection and restoration, and diving as a career. They created a network of partners and former guests to sponsor local young men and women (who couldn't afford the $185 training otherwise). These young people will play an integral part in helping to preserve, protect, and promote the Solomon Islands in the future. In six months, Dive Munda trained more than 100 young people from the Solomon Islands (60 percent female, 40 percent male), and their goal is to continue this program. Want to help? Contact Dive Munda (*divemunda.com*) to donate funds, services, or expertise.

and village tours. Dive Munda guides Sunga Boso and Brian Daga took us to **Skull Island,** a tiny islet with myriad skulls nestled under flat rocks or housed within triangular shrines. This is the resting place of prominent chiefs and warriors vanquished during the head-hunting days. (Head-hunting is complex, but preserving the decapitated head of an enemy was basically a status symbol.) It's peaceful here, but there is a mood.

(Tip: Visitors should only come here with a proper escort, as per cultural protocols.)

Gizo is around 90 minutes by boat from Munda. *(Tip: You can fly, but boat travel is handy for divers, and it's a beautiful trip, weaving through islands, volcanoes looming on the horizon.)* Gizo is the third largest town in the Solomons. Small stores line the main street, and there are markets to explore, selling carvings, fish, fruits, and vegetables.

Gizo is known for its WWII wrecks and vibrant reefs, and it has diving (and snorkel trips) down to a science. Divers meet at the dive shop in the morning and set off by boat for an unhurried morning dive in small groups with experienced local guides. Lunch breaks are spent on serene, lonely islands powdered with white sand and shaded by palm trees. Picnics include grilled fish, pumpkin, pineapple, and rice, eaten with your fingers off of a large leaf, followed by a post-lunch snorkel and a second dive.

The ***Toa Maru*** is one of the most popular shipwrecks. This large (459 ft/140 m) Japanese trans-

The Solomons have exploratory diving and snorkeling for all levels in wreck-filled waters lit up with jewel-colored coral and creatures.

port ship is lying on its starboard side, mortally wounded and sunk a stone's throw from shore. The dive begins around 23 feet (7 m), descending to 121 feet (37 m). Thickets of staghorn coral encrust the wreck, attracting fish, turtles, rays, and octopuses. The boat itself is filled with sake bottles, ammunition, typewriters, and bombs. (Some penetration is possible for more experienced divers; this eerie wreck can also be snorkeled.)

Another favorite is a dive/snorkel on an **American Hellcat fighter plane,** lying intact in a sunlit lagoon at 33 feet (10 m).

Solomon Islands Discovery Cruises (Dive Munda partners) runs a handful of small, seven-night adventure cruises throughout the year, with a focus on hands-on, travel-immersive activities: village visits, bonfires on the beach, learning to dive.

Don't miss the opportunity to visit **Kennedy Island** (either take a guided tour, or pilot your own small boat from Fatboys Resort). This lovely little uninhabited island is where John F. Kennedy and the surviving crew of his PT109 boat swam after being rammed by a Japanese destroyer.

Kennedy Island looks like paradise, with a forested interior, a local parrot named Kennedy that whistles at visitors, and beautiful beaches to snorkel. *(Tip: Bring water, snacks, snorkel gear, a towel, and cash for the caretaker.)*

To PT109's survivors, however, it was a brief respite in a night of terror. Informational placards describe the crew's incredible survival story, and the role played by two Coastwatchers, Eroni Kumana and Biuku Gasa, who paddled 37 miles (60 km) overnight through enemy waters bearing a coconut with a carved message from Kennedy back to Allied troops. He and his men were rescued shortly after.

This story and more are why it's worth visiting the **Solomon Islands National Museum** in Honiara (a short walk from the Heritage Park Hotel). This modest museum features interesting cultural displays (shell money, skull shrines, etc.), as well as extensive information on the Coastwatchers, a network of Solomon Islanders who are credited with saving the lives of more than 600 military men, 190 civilians, and the 35th president of the United States during WWII.

The waters surrounding the Solomon Islands are a sunken graveyard of WWII shipwrecks and aircraft. More wrecks are discovered every year.

NEED TO KNOW

GETTING HERE: The Solomon Islands are a three-hour flight from Brisbane, Australia. Honiara International Airport on Guadalcanal is the main arrival port, but there are also direct flights from Brisbane to Munda with Solomon Airlines, which we loved.

GETTING AROUND: Interisland boats or flights are the way to get around. Solomon Airlines flies to more than 20 domestic ports.

PACKING TIPS: Light, casual, and quick-drying clothing for a humid environment. (Respectful dress appreciated.) Reef shoes, reef-friendly sunscreen, mosquito spray, and basic first-aid supplies are useful.

WEATHER: Average daytime temps of 84°F (29°C), with evenings dipping to 66°F (19°C). April to November is drier and mid-March is the insider time to visit this Southern Hemisphere destination.

IN ADDITION: Malaria is present. Honiara has plenty of ATMs, but cash is preferred on the islands; make sure you have multiple ways to access money.

Diving

OVERVIEW: Exploratory, year-round diving and snorkeling for all levels in wreck-filled waters lit up with jewel-colored coral.

- **Visibility:** From 33 to 98 feet (10 to 30 m)
- **Water Temp:** 82°F (28°C) in winter / 86°F (30°C) in summer
- **Depth Range:** 33 to 131 feet (10 to 40 m)

MARINE LIFE: Sharks (gray reef, whitetip reef, blacktip reef), endemic white bonnet anemone fish, hard and soft coral, octopuses, eagle rays, green and hawksbill turtles, nudibranchs, jacks, and barracuda

SHOP INFO: Dive Munda is based next to the Agnes Gateway Hotel, catering to divers and snorkelers of all levels. There are a variety of sites within easy travel of the shop via two 23-foot (7 m) boats. This shop is staffed by an amazing crew of mostly local guides who know these islands. Facilities are basic, but good quality and well maintained. **Dive Gizo** is the original shop in the region; it is professional, experienced, and also has a great crew of local guides. Like Munda, there is an exciting mix of wrecks and reefs within easy distance of the shop. They cater to divers of all levels (courses offered) and have tours for non-divers, families, and snorkelers.

Accommodations

HIGH-END: Fatboys Resort is a handful of bungalows on Mbambanga Island, about a 10-minute boat ride from Gizo. There is an open-air restaurant located over the water at the end of a 328-foot (100 m) jetty circled by blacktip reef sharks and sparkling with giant clams. This place has reggae on the speakers, Wi-Fi that works (until someone else tries to use it), fun staff, and everything going a little different from plan. *~$258 USD*

MID-RANGE: The modern, seafront **Heritage Park Hotel** in Honiara is one of the country's premier hotels, with multiple accommodation options, helpful staff, on-site restaurant, and swimming pool. *~$163 USD*

BUDGET: The **Agnes Gateway Hotel** is a 28-room seafront establishment close to Munda airport that is basic, welcoming, and comfortable, with a range of rooms (splurge on something with a ceiling fan). *~$150 USD*

Food & Drink

GG's at Heritage Park Hotel has an à la carte menu serving a variety of dishes, from European to Pan-Asian. Try the fish with pepper plum sauce.

Fatboys' overwater restaurant and bar serves up delicious meals concocted from what's available (think local catches like crayfish, pan fried in lime juice and butter). Open for lunch and dinner.

Roviana Restaurant at the Agnes Gateway Hotel has simple, tasty meals (also local and fresh-caught) on a seaside deck with stunning views that will take your breath away: calm seas in the morning and spectacular sunsets at night. Guests order dinner at 5 p.m. and choose what time they'd like to eat.

KENTING NATIONAL PARK

A Coral Kingdom Adept at Weathering Storms

Taiwan is an enigmatic, oblong island in a typhoon-swept sea. Underwater, it is home to a rare and diverse coral ecology. Topside, it is reef pushed skyward, creating a landscape of limestone caves and cliffs, with more than 200 mountain peaks towering above 9,000 feet (2,743 m).

Plenty of rain and a warm climate has carpeted around 60 percent of the island in forest, around 20 percent of which is protected in parks and reserves. This is an endemic wonderland of plants and animals, a bird- and butterfly-watcher's paradise.

Located about 100 miles (161 km) across the Taiwan Strait from China, and bordered by the East China, South China, and Philippine Seas, Taiwan is an independent and democratic society. It has its own elected government and constitution, and is intent on determining its own future. Although Taiwan is perhaps best known for its tech savviness, there is so much more here. Travelers can explore walking tracks that cut through ancient and uplifted coral beds, leading to picture-perfect spots to watch the sun rise—or set. Dive sites surround the island, ranging from turtle-populated coral gardens to wrecks to current-swept walls.

This engaging and energetic island is easy to travel around and flat-out fascinating. So far, word hasn't spread too far west about the diving, hiking, and natural wonders. Now's the time to go. ∎

A close-up of gorgonian coral polyps. There is a mix of shore and boat diving in Taiwan, from coral gardens to deeper drift dives.

For a small country, Taiwan has a lot going on. From north to south, the west coast of Taiwan is a spiderweb of roads and cities. A vast swath of Taiwan's center is rumpled with mountains, and the southern tip is downright tropical. We disembarked in vibrant Kaohsiung City, Taiwan's third largest city, before traveling south to that tropical tip, the Hengchun Peninsula, gateway to Kenting National Park.

Kenting National Park, established in 1982, was the first park in Taiwan to encompass both land and ocean environments. It is a surprising collection of deep gorges, windy tablelands, butterfly-laden lowland forest areas, and beaches.

Inside the national park is **Sheding Nature Park,** a 319-acre (129 ha) encapsulation of everything that makes Kenting special. There is an easy two-hour walking loop to follow that starts with a passage through "butterfly alley," where you're likely to spot shy Formosan rock macaques and some of the

area's more than 216 species of butterflies. You'll walk through sharp cuttings with towering coral walls and emerge onto grasslands bordering a bonsai-like forest, hammered by the strong eastern winds. Here, there are raised platforms for watching the raptor migration that takes place every September and October (tens of thousands of condors, eagles, goshawks, and falcons).

(Tip: Kenting National Park Visitor Center has great displays and information. Although it's easy to self-explore Sheding, guided tours are available and worth it for the flora and fauna intel. Book guides well in advance. Winter weekdays are uncrowded and quiet.)

Bookmark a couple of days to drive around Hengchun Peninsula and self-explore. **Shadao Beach** is breathtakingly beautiful with pinky-white sand lapped by turquoise water. This is an eyes-only ecological reserve, protecting a turtle nesting area, as well as the beach's purity. (Shadao is 98 percent calcium carbonate.) Visit the nearby visitors center to learn more about the beach's significance and to hold sand from the beach in a way that doesn't negatively affect it. (Zoom in with your phone to see tiny, perfectly formed shells in your palm.)

Farther down the road is the still functioning **Eluanbi Lighthouse,** built in the 1880s, near the southernmost point of Taiwan. Purchase a ticket to Eluanbi Park and spend time exploring the network of walking trails, winding through trees (banyan, fig, and ebony) stubbornly anchored in uplifted coral and pausing to soak in the coastal atmosphere on shaded picnic benches.

Continue round to **Longpan Park,** a wild and windy grassland tabletop of uplifted coral reef overlooking the Pacific Ocean. This fragile limestone landscape is well cared for, with winding

Diving in Taiwan is becoming more popular, with healthy species, like the freckled hawkfish, to see.

Make a Difference

This is a good chapter to talk about the high seas. The high seas are huge open ocean areas located beyond any country's national jurisdiction, covering around half the Earth's surface. Why are they important? The high seas are unexplored biodiversity vaults (critical to the ocean's health and therefore our own) and wildlife corridors to migratory and often endangered species, like whales and sharks. What's the issue? No one is really in charge, especially in regard to protection and conservation, and the high seas face threats like unregulated overfishing and deep-sea mining. What can be done? Learn more about the high seas and their importance, spread the word, and urge your political leaders to prioritize a High Seas Treaty that will provide meaningful, regulated protections.

wooden paths, trash cans disguised as tree stumps, and pleasant, shaded pavilions. It is also an ace spot for watching the sunrise.

(Tip: To catch the sunset, hit the opposite coast— **Guanshan,** a temple complex with terraces overlooking the ocean. Leave time to find a prime spot; this place can get crowded.)

Taiwan's underwater landscapes are growing in popularity, too, as more Taiwanese are becoming keen divers. Full disclosure: This was the second place on our journey where we were unable to dive (along with the Outer Banks, page 232; this time it wasn't storms that slowed us down, but bad colds). However, as with the Outer Banks, we did on-the-ground legwork to gather information.

Kenting is home to more than 1,100 species of reef fish and more than 80 species of coral. Along with coral gardens, Kenting also has wrecks, walls, striking topography, and some current-swept deep dives. There is a mix of shore and boat diving here, and a little something for everyone.

This is a popular area for learning to dive, with many novice sites located along the west coast or inside the bay. **Shan Han** is a shore dive with shallow crevices and mini-canyons to explore, frequented by turtles, scorpionfish, and reef fish. **Chu Shui Kou** is also known as "Barracuda Point," thanks to the resident squad that hang out here. There are also cuttlefish, black sailfin blennies, flame scallops, and convict snake eels. Night diving is

Taiwan is known as the "coral kingdom," home to more than 80 species of coral.

popular—keep an eye out for crocodilefish. The **Soft Coral Garden** is a boat dive, and sometimes a gentle drift, known for its namesake soft coral, as well as a large number of nudibranchs.

Farther out, on the outskirts of the bay and near the points of the two peninsulas, are more advanced dives—deeper, and strong currents are possible. **Sha Dao,** near Eluanbi, is a deteriorated wreck favored by lionfish, stonefish, and angelfish, while **Shuang Feng Lan Dong** is a deep (115 ft/ 35 m) boat dive along a soft-coral-encrusted wall. Look for pygmy seahorses, as well as fish like barracuda, jacks, and sweetlips.

__ WISH WE KNEW __

Winter (December to June) is colder, but still has great weather. The area's different dive sites allow for weather workarounds. There are far fewer crowds and prices are about half of what they are during the high summer season.

Experienced divers told us the best thing about Taiwan is its accessibility: No matter where you are on the island, you are close to a dive site. It is possible to visit a large number of sites—from Green Island on the southeastern coast, to the northeastern coast near Taipei—during one visit. They also told us the biggest challenges facing Taiwan are pollution, education around best practice (not walking on coral or handling marine life), and overfishing. Taiwan operates one of the largest longline fishing fleets in the world, a multibillion-dollar industry that is rife with human rights issues and law-skirting practices like shark finning.

According to Dr. Enric Sala, National Geographic explorer in residence and founder of the Pristine Seas project, fishing is the largest hunting operation left on the planet, targeting more than half of the ocean surface, regardless of restrictions. It's a main driver of biodiversity loss. However, commercial fishing isn't just harmful to the planet—it cannibalizes itself. "Some argue that closing areas to fishing hurts fishing interests," Sala said. "But the worst enemy of successful fisheries is overfishing—not protected areas."

Scientists have determined that protecting the right places (a minimum of 30 percent of the ocean) could increase seafood catch by more than 8.8 million tons (8 million metric tons) relative to business as usual now.

Given Taiwan's progressive mindset and technical capabilities, this is an area where a geographically small nation could make an overwhelming positive impact on the world.

Kenting National Park is a surprise collection of windy tablelands, beautiful beaches, and butterfly-laden lowland forest areas.

NEED TO KNOW

GETTING HERE: Kaohsiung City (KC) is the best arrival port for Kenting. Kaohsiung International Airport receives several international flights a day.

GETTING AROUND: Taiwan is well equipped for getting around with a high-speed rail system and buses. From KC, it's easy to take a bus (the Kenting Express) to Kenting (around two hours). There are plenty of car rental companies, some with driver-guide options. Speak to the dive shop or hotel—they can often provide advice and/or help make arrangements.

PACKING TIPS: Casual outdoor clothes with a few nicer options for KC and dinners out. Layers, walking shoes, and a windbreaker come in handy.

WEATHER: Southern Taiwan is diveable year-round. June through September is typhoon season and busy. December to June is colder with some shutout weather days.

IN ADDITION: Travel insurance is recommended during typhoon season (June through September).

Diving

OVERVIEW: A dive destination that is making waves, for all the right reasons. This up-and-coming location has coral gardens for beginner divers, with depths and currents for more experienced divers.

- Visibility: From 16 to 82 feet (5 to 25 m)
- Water Temp: 73°F (23°C) in winter / 84°F (29°C) in summer
- Depth Range: 39 to 131 feet (12 to 40 m)

MARINE LIFE: Lots of macro (pygmy seahorses, short-pouch pygmy pipehorses, ghost pipefish, seasonal nudibranchs), plenty of hard and soft coral, cuttlefish, turtles (hawksbill and green), barracuda, and bluespotted ribbontail rays. Coral spawning occurs around the full moon in April and May, making for great night diving and also attracting whale sharks and manta rays.

SHOP INFO: Many shops in Taiwan don't have English-speaking staff, so you may need to do a little extra research to find one that does, like **CTdiver.** This locally owned shop in Kenting offers small-group courses and guided shore and boat dives. CTdiver knows the area, has a strong focus on safety, and is a leader in marine protection and best practice.

Accommodations

HIGH-END: Howard Beach Resort is a traditional Taiwanese beach resort in Kenting that manages to be fun, elegant, and quirky all at the same time. This seaside resort has 405 spacious rooms, a massive pool complex, and a buffet-style restaurant serving a range of international foods. The staff is incredibly friendly. *~$119 USD*

MID-RANGE: Hotel Indigo is located in the heart of KC. It's on Central Park, surrounded by shopping and just five miles (8 km) from the airport. This vibrant place has great staff and snug, eclectic rooms. *~$113 USD*

BUDGET: Taiwan Dive Center (TDC) in Kenting is a cutting-edge spot for divers. This purpose-built house has bunk and en suite rooms, a shared dining area, an on-site dive shop and classroom, and English-speaking staff. *~$28 USD for a dorm room; $64 USD for an en suite*

Food & Drink

Eatogether Kaohsiung Sando is a buzzy, super-fun buffet in the Sanduo Shopping District Station. It offers a wide variety of food, from Taiwanese to Western to Japanese to Chinese. Reservations recommended.

Piccolo Polpo Bistro is a Mediterranean restaurant with dishes like wild mushroom and truffle risotto, fresh mussels with lime sauce, and Basque burnt cheesecake. Try the zingy mint-and-lime smoothie.

We were told a different name every time we asked, but believe this special place is called **Hengchun Old Shop Spicy Hot Pot Restaurant,** located in Hengchun township. (Look for an inconspicuous, busy spot with colorful walls.) They serve hot pots—boiling bowls of broth and spices where you can cook meat, veggies, and noodles at your table.

BORMES-LES-MIMOSAS

The Garden Does Not Stop at the Water's Edge

The 12th-century village of Bormes-les-Mimosas is part of the Var department in the central-southern region of Provence, sharing the fabled French Riviera coastline with glittering towns like Saint-Tropez, Cannes, Nice, and Monaco. You'll be forgiven if, like us, you've been blinded by the Côte d'Azur's sparkle and overlooked what has to be one of the world's best dive travel destinations: a warm and natural hamlet where the ocean is considered part of the greater garden.

Named after the bright yellow Australian mimosa flowers that herald the beginning of spring, the medieval township of Bormes keeps time under a blue sky crowned with more than 300 days of sun per year. Bormes is home to more than 700 different species of plants, 12 vineyards, and a natural coastline of more than 10.5 miles (17 km) of secluded, sandy beaches and coves, shaded by wild pinewoods.

The garden stretches into the Mediterranean park of Port-Cros, the first marine park in Europe, established in 1963. Although Port-Cros's protection also encompasses terrestrial landscapes, its heart beats underwater. Here you will find a flourishing marine-scape of seagrass beds and rocky landscapes, circled by schools of barracuda and bream, and patrolled by respectably sized grouper. Port-Cros is a vision of what the Mediterranean could be, given time and protection.

Flanked by the historical birthplace of scuba diving (Sanary-sur-Mer, just beyond Toulon) and the Musée Océanographique de Monaco, Bormes's lifeblood runs blue-green. Any lover of living things will feel at home here. ■

The 12th-century hamlet of Bormes-les-Mimosas is perched on a hillside overlooking the Mediterranean.

Bormes-les-Mimosas is plucked from a Provençal fairy tale, a picturesque hamlet of delightfully pink houses with wooden shutters overlooking cobblestone streets. The scents of mimosa and jasmine mingle with those of brewing coffee and baking bread. This is a living, breathing town—not a preserved historical spot—with cafés and shops springing to life as the morning wears on.

At **Les Bibis du Midi,** milliner and force-of-nature Nathalie Papet crafts exquisite, phantasmagorical designs out of hemp, feathers, and silk, her creations perched for sale on shelves and vines outside of her workshop. She also offers introductory hatmaking courses and—for something special—a private interview, to create something uniquely you. *(Tip: Contact in advance to make appointments.)*

Perched on a hillside overlooking the sparkling sea, Bormes is about four miles (6 km) from the (slightly) more urban towns of La Favière (where the harbor and dive center are) and Le Lavandou. Beneath Bormes, the coastal region stretches out like a sunny Sunday afternoon. The area is a **hiking paradise,** with more than 100 miles (161 km) of paths. **Rent an electric bike from Château Malherbe** for a lazy cycle around their vineyard. Sea breezes caress the vines in this area, cultivating rosés and whites with an almost whiskey-like depth.

_____WISH WE KNEW_____

In France, divers need to have a medical certificate of fitness to dive that is less than one year old. You'll be asked to present this at the dive shop before you dive. Get this sorted *before* you travel.

The **gardens of Domaine du Rayol,** a 49-acre (20 ha) protected natural area about 10.5 miles (17 km) east of Bormes, contain the Jardin des Méditerranées—more than 12 Mediterranean landscapes from around the world, including a high-altitude Chilean garden, familiar flora from our New Zealand home (manuka, flax, and Nikau palm trees), and a **Marine Garden.** A guided garden tour of this underwater Mediterranean landscape, examining the life that lives there, was a unique experience.

Equipped with swim fins, masks, and snorkels, we slowly explored Posidonia seagrass beds and life-filled sandy areas, glittering gold with pyrite. We saw schools of fish, anemones, and an octopus (which pulled in rocks around itself when we got close, as if closing the front door). Our guide, Nico, pulled a flotation device behind him, which we gathered around when we paused to talk. "We are all gardeners of the planet, for better or for worse," Nico told us, "and the garden does not stop at the water's edge."

In fact, the garden stretches into Port-Cros National Park, one of the first to protect an area of land and ocean together. The park covers around 4,200 acres (1,700 ha) of land and 7,166 acres (2,900 ha) of sea, including several islands and islets. Port-Cros teems with life in a way that divers never knew the Mediterranean could be. (Only 1.27 percent of the Mediterranean Sea is protected by marine parks that effectively implement management plans.)

The *Spahis,* which sank in 1887, is one of many diveable wrecks in the area.

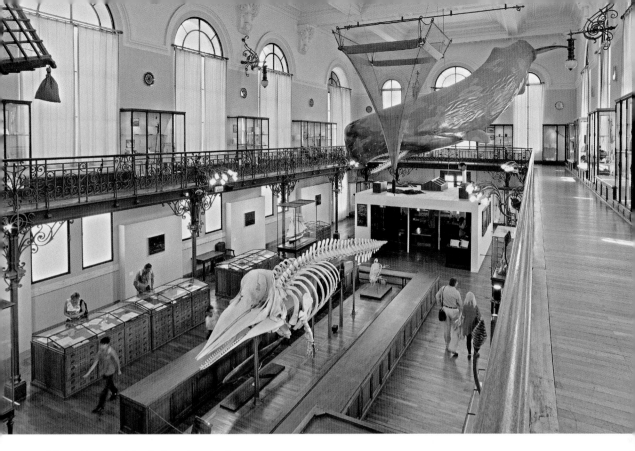

There is a wealth of dive sites in the area, most within a 30- to 45-minute boat ride. There is diving for all levels, although divers with some experience will probably enjoy it more, due to currents and depth.

Gabinière is a tiny island that drops into the sea, with drift dives curving around either side. From the drop point, strong currents push divers over spurs of rock, past schools of barracuda 100 strong, large grouper, and gorgonian fans. Eventually, the current eases and the area shallows into seagrass beds; keep your eyes peeled for small critters tucked away in the rock crevices.

There are also a number of diveable wrecks in the area, like the popular **Le Grec** (*The Greek*), built in 1912. A floating mine tore the bow off this 177-foot-long (54 m) ship in 1945. *Le Grec* lies in 115 to 154 feet (35 to 47 m) of water, is penetrable, and is a deco dive. It is covered in growth, including gorgonians, and

surrounded by life: lots of macro, grouper, moray eels, and scorpionfish, including large schools of fish.

The past 10 years have seen the return of bigger fish to the area (like swordfish) and even a few whales. The marine park is patrolled, but it's also respected by local fishermen who reap the bounty in large, healthy populations of fish close to shore and just outside the marine park's borders. Port-Cros is a special place, one befitting of an area that is home to the beginning of recreational scuba diving.

No visit to Bormes is complete without day trips to two meccas for ocean lovers. To the west is **Sanary-sur-Mer,** just beyond Toulon, about one hour's drive from Bormes. Sanary-sur-Mer is where a group of friends—including Jacques-Yves

Cousteau, Frédéric Dumas, and Philippe Tailliez—pioneered scuba diving techniques and equipment, often at great risk to themselves. Not just in testing unknown equipment underwater—Germans patrolling during WWII made the divers' excursions deadly difficult: Had they been caught with strange equipment, they risked execution.

The **Musée Frédéric-Dumas** is a divers' treasure trove, containing information (much of which is in French, but English translations are coming) and early equipment, including the Aqua-Lung designed by Cousteau and Émile Gagnan, and the first molded weight belt, with weights designed in circular shoeshine tins for size consistency. (Even the first belt was designed to be a quick release with one hand.) This place provides fascinating insight into the beginnings of scuba diving, as well as the love these pioneers held for the ocean.

About two hours' drive to the east of Bormes is Monaco, home to the extraordinary **Musée Océanographique de Monaco,** an elegant institution built into the very rock of the coastline. It has kept a watchful eye on the oceans for more than 110 years.

This dazzling museum holds exhibits, historical collections, and aquariums intermingled with floor-to-ceiling windows overlooking the sea, marble staircases, and mosaic floors. Most aquarium species on display (including all coral) are grown, rather than collected, although the museum is still home to a female brown moray eel brought here

Sun-kissed Château Malherbe is one of a dozen or so vineyards in the area, its vines caressed by sea air.

by Jacques Cousteau. (She's more than 70 years old now.) Displays are informative, interactive, and insightful.

(Tip: Self-guide or book a guided tour in advance; visiting during the uncrowded off-season is something special.)

Spending time here—from the cafés of Bormes, to the magic of Port-Cros, to the history brought to life by the museums—is a wonderful reminder of the role we play in the ocean's life, the role it plays in ours, and the greater garden we share.

Make a Difference

In 1902, Albert I of Monaco said: "The duty of Oceanography is to detect the hazards caused in all countries by the overexploitation, whether poorly regulated or improperly monitored, of the resources of the sea." Since its inception, the **Musée Océanographique de Monaco** *(musee.oceano.org/en)* has dedicated itself to science, research, education, and the sharing of ideas. Today, its main focus is advocacy and outreach, connecting science to the general public and decision-makers. (Find donation and sponsorship opportunities at the museum or via their website.) The **Prince Albert II of Monaco Foundation** *(fpa2.org)* is dedicated to environmental protection and sustainable development on a global scale, with a special eye on the Mediterranean. (Donations can be made via their website.)

NEED TO KNOW

GETTING HERE: It's about a two-hour drive from Marseille Provence Airport to Bormes.

GETTING AROUND: Rent a car. Driving is easy, especially outside main city centers. There are multiple toll roads, which add up, but are easy to pay by credit card (keep a little cash handy, just in case).

PACKING TIPS: This is the French Riviera: Pack a little color and glamor. Good walking shoes and sunglasses come in handy, as do reusable bags. (France has banned plastic bags, as well as many single-use plastics—bravo!)

WEATHER: Summer is hot and busy. September and October are cooler and quieter (the ideal time for divers to visit). The winter off-season is sunny and perfect for outdoor activities like hiking and cycling. Many places are closed, but those that are open are uncrowded.

IN ADDITION: All beaches in France are public.

Diving

OVERVIEW: Port-Cros is Europe's first marine park, uniting terrestrial and maritime protection zones, and the result is spectacular year-round diving in the Mediterranean, with large and healthy schools of fish, wrecks, and rocky landscapes.

- **Visibility:** From 49 to 66 feet (15 to 20 m)
- **Water Temp:** 54°F (12°C) in winter / 72°F (22°C) in summer
- **Depth Range:** 66 feet (20 m) for reef dives; 138 feet (42 m) for wrecks

MARINE LIFE: Far and away the most marine life we saw in the Mediterranean—Port-Cros reminded us of diving in the Caribbean. Large grouper, barracuda, forkbeards, gilthead bream, scorpionfish, brown meagre, two-banded sea bream, moray eels, some pelagics.

SHOP INFO: We dove with **Bormes Plongée,** a professional outfit based in La Favière (a few miles from Bormes), offering everything from guided dives to training from April through November; diving is by request from December to March. Most European diving centers expect divers to be fairly self-sufficient. If you need a little more attention, request a private guide. Also, the meeting point for the shop is in the harbor, via a rabbit warren of alleyways. It's not a bad idea to scope the location prior to dive day.

Accommodations

HIGH-END: Oceanside **Hôtel Le Bailli de Suffren** is tucked away on a secluded cove about 11 miles (17 km) from Bormes. This elegant, 55-room hotel has beach access, a pool, spa, and three restaurants. Closed October through April. ~$250 USD

MID-RANGE: We loved our stay at **Hôtel de la Plage.** It has a traditional feel to it, with owners who really make an effort to get to know their guests. Centrally located and an easy 10-minute walk to the harbor, we met a lot of fellow divers here. The hotel has 43 comfortable rooms, with an on-site restaurant and half-board options (room with breakfast and lunch or dinner included). Closed October through April. ~$130 USD

BUDGET: The **Hostellerie du Cigalou** is located in the heart of the village of Bormes-les-Mimosas. Its 20 rooms are decorated with different themes and lavished with fabrics and colors. Open year-round. ~$100 USD

Food & Drink

Le Loup de Mer, Hotel Le Bailli de Suffren's elegant restaurant, overlooks the Mediterranean and serves up a variety of *terre* (land) and *mer* (sea) dishes, including homemade ravioli and bouillabaisse.

Restaurant de L'Hôtel de La Plage feels like dining with friends. Set on an indoor-outdoor terrace, and sometimes in the garden, the dinner menu (tasty and traditional) changes nightly, as do the bottles of wine they choose to open.

Le Café du Progrès, in the village of Bormes, takes traditional family recipes and turns them into something magic. This is an excellent lunch spot, serving dishes like crepes and salads.

GALÁPAGOS ISLANDS

We Come Here for the Wildlife

The Galápagos Islands are a place where time is standing still and accelerating simultaneously. Nearly 95 percent of the islands' prehuman diversity remains recoverable, yet new discoveries are the norm here. Even Charles Darwin's celebrated finches, an example of his theory of evolution, are still evolving.

This is the magnetism of the Galápagos: *todo cambia*—everything changes.

The Galápagos Islands cover an enormous area: a 53,300-square-mile (138,000 sq km) archipelago of red and dun volcanic islands baking under the equatorial sun, 620 miles (1,000 km) from the Ecuadorian coast.

The islands offer the wildlife-watching of dreams: giant tortoises, Galápagos sea lions, Galápagos sharks, blue-footed boobies, the most northerly species of penguin in the world, and marine iguanas, which Darwin dubbed "imps of darkness."

This is a place walking a razor's edge. The Galápagos Islands are facing climate change, illegal (and legal) fishing pressures, a population boom, a tourism boom, and an onslaught of invasive species, any of which could tip the precarious balance.

ECUADOR
Galápagos Islands
SOUTH AMERICA

And this is where we—visitors—come in: Our hefty national park fees help protect this special place. Staying in hotels (instead of often cheaper home rentals) allows the government to accurately monitor tourism numbers. Strict guide regulations aren't there to curb freedom, but to protect fragile ecosystems. Conducted properly, tourism can help safeguard the Galápagos's future.

"We need to be responsible tourists and adapt to our environment, rather than adapting our environment to us," said Dr. María José Barragán Paladines, science director of the Charles Darwin Foundation. ■

The Galápagos Islands are home to many weird and wonderful things, like marine iguanas, the world's only aquatic lizard.

We based ourselves on Isla Santa Cruz, the most populated island. Although many divers opt for liveaboards in the Galápagos, the local diving is spectacular and the land-based adventures equally so. Here is the best of both worlds, a feast for the eyes and the imagination.

Lunching with giant Galápagos tortoises at **Rancho El Manzanillo** should be a priority. Located inland from Puerto Ayora and surrounded by lush vegetation, we snacked on local specialties (like lemongrass iced tea and green banana chips with tamarind sauce) while watching some of the island's 3,000 wild tortoises roam in their natural habitat. These are the world's largest terrestrial reptiles (up to 550 lb/250 kg) and the longest living of all vertebrates, averaging more than 100 years in age.

For another memorable experience, take a day trip by boat to **Santa Fe Island** to see endemic Santa Fe land iguanas. Santa Fe was the first of the Galápagos Islands to be visited by Europeans, who described it as hell on Earth (no water, no shade). For

us, it was an Eden: On an easy-paced guided tour, we saw jumping mobula rays, frigate birds, Galápagos sea lions, and a half-dozen Santa Fe land iguanas. There's about 1,000 of them on this 9.3-square-mile (24 sq km) island, staking out territories around the prickly pear cactus (also their food source).

Our favorite Galápagos experience, however, was visiting **Tortuga Bay** to see marine iguanas. The world's only aquatic lizard, they are able to hold their breath for more than an hour, swimming out to sea and diving to depths of 30 feet (9 m) to graze on seaweed and algae.

It's a 45-minute walk from Puerto Ayora to Tortuga Bay's Playa Brava. The marine iguanas can be found on the western side of the beach, where there's a mangrove-fringed lagoon they return to after their sea forays.

As we stood quietly, waist-deep in the lagoon, the iguanas swam right past us, propelling themselves with their long tails. They're a velvety red-black in color, wearing contented expressions, collapsing in a reptile heap once they've reached the beach to warm up. Occasionally, they make tiny "pffft" sounds as they expel excess salt from their bodies.

(Tip: Rangers ensure people keep a 6.5-ft/2-m distance, but the iguanas do a pretty good job of avoiding people who approach them. If you stand still in the water or lie flat on the sand, the iguanas will walk or swim right past you.)

To learn more about the extraordinary wildlife we'd been seeing, we visited the **Charles Darwin Research Station**—three times. Along with an exhibition hall that contains nearly 60 years of Galápagos research, there is also an informative walkway past land iguana and tortoise enclosures. The baby tortoise paddock allows the adorable coin- and plate-size youngsters to grow up in relative safety

A diver checks out a school of yellowtail surgeonfish. The Galápagos Islands are one of the most biologically diverse areas in the world.

Make a Difference

The **Charles Darwin Foundation's** *(darwinfoundation.org)* mission is to conserve the environment and biodiversity of the fragile Galápagos Islands. They do this through scientific research, action, advising the government of Ecuador, and community engagement and education. (We were told that six in 10 children in the Galápagos don't know how to swim, a hindrance to understanding the wealth of their natural resources.) Visiting the Charles Darwin Research Station, the operative branch of the Charles Darwin Foundation, is one way to support the work they do. Volunteering is another (vacancies are listed on the website). The foundation is completely dependent on donors, but what's really needed is consistent, ongoing funding, to allow for future planning.

before being repatriated to other islands. (It's estimated more than 200,000 tortoises were removed from the archipelago; perhaps less than 10 percent of the population remains today, hence the need to repopulate.)

(Tip: Factor in at least a half day for this, and bring your passport for a unique stamp.)

We were blown away by the topside action, but the **Galápagos Marine Reserve** sent us spinning. This is one of the most biologically diverse marine protected areas in the world, home to nearly 3,000 marine species and incredible diving. On every dive, we found ourselves twisting round in midwater because there was always something to look at. For example: A mola mola swam past on our right as a school of scalloped hammerheads traveled by in the distance. While we were watching the hammerheads, a sea lion popped up in front of us, as schools of tuna and barracuda circled overhead under a squadron of mobula rays—and that was just on one dive.

The Galápagos Islands sit at the intersection of three ocean currents converging over more than 300 seamounts. Most of the dives are cool-water drifts in low, greenish visibility due to the nutrient-rich waters. (The marine life is here to feed, so creatures don't linger.)

What impressed us most about the diving, apart from the abundant marine life, was the management of dive locations. There are several dive

The Charles Darwin Research Station is essential to tortoise conservation, raising pint-size youngsters in safety before releasing them.

shops in Puerto Ayora, and they've established a unique system of alternating dive sites. For example, on a Tuesday, one shop dives the **Seymour Channel.** This is a murky wall dive in the channel between North Seymour Island and Baltra Island, which can be dived in both directions; it has big stuff like hammerhead and Galápagos sharks, manta rays, and eagle rays. Meanwhile, another shop goes to **Cousins Rock,** another deep wall with Galápagos sea lions, mola molas, large schools of barracuda, and cold thermoclines at depth where Galápagos sharks like to hang out.

Divers can dive with one shop and rotate through different sites, or they can revisit a favorite site by going with the shop that's diving that location on

Divers should add on a liveaboard trip to Wolf and Darwin Islands. These legends surpass their reputations, with schooling hammerheads, whale sharks, Galápagos sharks, silky sharks, turtles, and more. (Negative entry skills required.)

a particular day. This system gives divers a better experience, as you're the only dive boat at the site, and it minimizes impact.

Although 97 percent of the Galápagos Islands' landmass has been protected in a national park since 1959, as usual, the marine area lagged behind: Less than one percent was protected until 2016, when a new sanctuary was established to protect around one-third of the water surrounding the islands.

But even protected areas aren't safe: In 2017, a Chinese fishing ship was captured in protected Galápagos waters carrying more than 300 tons of endangered marine species, including 6,000 sharks, slain for their fins. In 2020, news reports covered more than 200 international fishing vessels anchored at the edge of the Galápagos's exclusive economic zone eyeing any fish that crossed out of the zone.

The Galápagos is one of the most populated shark zones in the world. A shark is worth $200 for its fins, but a living shark generates around two million dollars in its life through ecotourism. When you think of it that way, it's unfathomable sharks aren't being guarded like a bank vault. The economics don't stack up. More than a third of all jobs in the Galápagos are in marine tourism: If the sharks go, the ecosystem collapses, and the economic system fails.

Ecuador is paying attention. In 2022, a presidential decree expanded the Galápagos's marine protected area by 23,166 square miles (60,000 sq km), half of which will be fully protected. This also presents the brilliant opportunity to link with Panama, Costa Rica, and Colombia to protect the biodiversity gold mine that is the Eastern Tropical Pacific seascape.

Hammerhead sharks patrol Darwin Island. The Galápagos's underwater seamounts and converging currents attract around 3,000 marine species.

NEED TO KNOW

GETTING HERE: There are daily flights from Quito and Guayaquil on mainland Ecuador. Arriving 24 hours before your Galápagos-bound flight is prudent. There are strict biosecurity screenings, and carry-on size is monitored. Make sure you understand and are prepared for the national park fee system prior to traveling.

GETTING AROUND: Getting here is chaotic fun—bus to canal barge and back on the bus to the main town of Puerto Ayora. Once here, walking, bike rentals, water taxis, buses, and taxis are the way to get around. Although we based ourselves on land, many people choose to explore the Galápagos by ship. (National Geographic Expeditions offers sensational voyages.)

PACKING TIPS: Bring bags that have carry straps. With all the travel transfers, you will be handling your luggage a lot. Leave the massive wheeled suitcases at home.

WEATHER: The Galápagos Islands straddle the equator, although most islands fall in the Southern Hemisphere. Prepare (and pack for) withering heat, especially December through May, which is also the time for calmer seas and daily rains giving way to sun. June through September are the busiest months for tourism, due in part to the increased animal activity underwater (like big hammerhead schools); prepare for rougher seas.

IN ADDITION: Tap water is undrinkable, but Santa Cruz has free, safe drinking/refilling stations, so bring a reusable water bottle; the islands are desperately trying to cut down on plastic bottles. Toilet paper goes in the trash can due to a delicate septic system.

Diving

OVERVIEW: The Galápagos Islands are the underwater Serengeti. The sheer amount and diversity of wildlife in this Mission Blue Hope Spot is incredible: Fish biomass is approximately twice the amount found in the second highest area known to science.

- Visibility: From 25 to 49 feet (8 to 15 m)
- Water Temp: 70°F (21°C) in winter / 77°F (25°C) in summer
- Depth Range: Average around 75 feet (23 m)

MARINE LIFE: Schools of tuna and barracuda, mobula rays, eagle rays, *Mola ramsayi* (southern sunfish), Galápagos sea lions, and more than 30 species of sharks

SHOP INFO: Galápagos dive guides go through a strict certification process with the National Parks Authority: They're highly skilled and knowledgeable. We dove with **Scuba Iguana,** an excellent shop. Dive trips tend to last most of the day, due to travel to the harbor (via shuttle), plus the boat trip to the site (distances vary).

Accommodations

HIGH-END: We loved our stay at the **Finch Bay Galápagos Hotel.** They keep the environment very much in mind, from the design of their 27 rooms to the programs they support (like coastal cleanups). Located a five-minute water taxi ride from Puerto Ayora, this is a quiet, friendly (and family-friendly) hotel. ~$524 USD

MID-RANGE: La Isla Hotel is centrally located with five cozy rooms and a buffet breakfast. ~$254 USD

BUDGET: **Ikala Hotel** is another centrally located spot (one block to the main pier), featuring 22 rooms, swimming pool, restaurant and bar, and garden surrounds. It utilizes solar panels to heat water. ~$208 USD

Food & Drink

The **Finch Bay Galápagos Hotel Restaurant** serves fresh, sustainably sourced, traditional dishes in an indoor-outdoor flowing restaurant that mirrors the surrounding environment. (Cocktail hour is magical.)

Dine deck-side at **Almar** (located at the Galápagos Habitat Eco Luxury Hotel) as marine iguanas boldly stroll under your table. Don't miss the fenced-off area for resting sea lions, complete with their own private couches.

1835 Coffee Lab is a cool specialty café serving up local coffee in a sustainable way (think glass jars with aluminum straws).

FLORIDA KEYS

A Road Trip of Wrecks, Reefs, and Renegades

A Florida Keys road trip is a rite of passage. Sooner or later, we all seem to migrate to this 125-mile-long (201 km) ribbon of islands, stretching from the southern tip of Florida to within shouting distance of Cuba, 103 miles (166 km) south.

NORTH AMERICA
UNITED STATES

Florida Keys

Why? The Florida Keys are everything that's wonderful about the red, white, and blue. Despite being small in size (Key West is only 2 mi/3.2 km wide), the Keys are larger than life. Big characters. Big trucks. Fifteen-page breakfast menus. And more history than you can imagine crammed into 200-plus years.

The Keys are also a natural stunner: The 2,900-square-nautical-mile (9,947 sq km) Florida Keys National Marine Sanctuary encompasses a turquoise wonderland rich with mangroves, seagrass beds, and North America's only living coral barrier reef. Key Largo's John Pennekamp Coral Reef State Park was the United States' first designated undersea park (established 1963), recognizing the love Americans have for outdoor recreation and the importance of protecting these natural treasures for generations to come.

And perhaps best of all, the Keys collect a diverse population of renegades.

We split our time between Key Largo and Key West, two of the Keys' five main regions, traveling the 113-mile-long (182 km) Florida Keys Overseas Highway to get from one to the other. Any time of year is a good time for this journey. Pack up and hit this remarkable road. ■

John Pennekamp Coral Reef State Park has more than 50 miles (80 km) of mangrove wilderness trails to explore by kayak or canoe.

Key Largo is the first link in the island chain, and it's no surprise it's a favorite with divers of all levels: Key Largo is encompassed by Florida Keys National Marine Sanctuary and John Pennekamp Coral Reef State Park.

Molasses Reef is an underwater kingdom with more than 30 dive sites, ideal for new divers (and snorkelers). This shallow reef system is home to a booming population of fish, turtles, and rays. All areas in the Florida Reef Tract are under pressure: It's estimated the region has lost 95 to 97 percent of its coral cover in the past 40 years, which makes it difficult for new divers, especially, to understand what a healthy baseline looks like. However, Molasses Reef's coral is still in relatively good condition, and it's a great introduction into what makes the reef world so special.

Key Largo's wrecks are better suited for divers with more experience (and deep-dive certifica- tion; currents can be strong here). There are plenty to choose from, but the purposefully sunk **U.S.S. Spiegel Grove** is one of the most impressive. This landing craft stretches more than 510 feet (155 m) in length, resting at a depth that ranges from 63 feet (19 m) to 141 feet (43 m). Barracuda, moray eels, goliath grouper, schools of fish, and sharks share the site with you, so between the plethora of marine life, and the staggering size of the wreck, you'll need multiple dives to see it properly.

Don't be so enchanted with the underwater world that you forget topside: **John Pennekamp Coral Reef State Park** is as impressive on land, and well worth a visit. The visitors center is a good place to start, with exhibits on the environment and a list of recent wildlife observations. Snorkel trips, glass-bottom boat rides, and kayak rentals are available, but we enjoyed wandering a few of the trails, like the 0.3-mile (0.5 km) Wild Tamarind Trail, a forest trail canopied by mahogany, gumbo-limbo, the do-not-touch poisonwood, and tamarind, the preferred shade tree of Keys' locals. (Tip: The far- ther into the park you travel, the thinner the crowds.)

For a truly special experience, pair your visit to John Pennekamp with a canal cruise on the original **African Queen,** the steamboat that starred in the movie of the same name alongside Katharine Hepburn and Humphrey Bogart. She's been restored to her original 1912 splendor and is now based in Marina Del Mar (3 mi/4.8 km south of the park). Advance bookings are essential, as it takes an hour to get the old boiler going.

We departed Key Largo, driving the Florida Keys Overseas Highway south to Key West. This has to be one of the world's best highways, with more than 40 bridges spanning the Florida Bay, the Gulf

A French angelfish explores the U.S.N.S. *Vandenberg,* a large, deep Key West wreck that is a drawing card for experienced divers.

Make a Difference

A visit to the **Coral Restoration Foundation** (CRF) *(coralrestoration.org)*, the world's largest coral restoration organization, should be a must for any Key Largo visitor. Since 2007, CRF has planted more than 100,000 corals (primarily endangered elkhorn and staghorn) onto the Florida Reef Tract. Their visitors center has a wealth of information about how critical coral reefs are. Reefs generate half the Earth's oxygen, absorb nearly one-third of the carbon dioxide generated by burning fossil fuels, and provide a critical habitat for more than a quarter of all marine life. Snorkelers and scuba divers can join CRF for a day of hands-on coral restoration, helping outplant corals at one of their seven coral nurseries. Presentations can be arranged for families or dive groups with advance notice.

of Mexico, and the Atlantic Ocean. The highway is raised a few feet above the water, and pelicans paced us at car-window height, soaring over the green-and-blue ocean.

During the 1980s war on drugs, the U.S. government put a checkpoint on this road, grinding tourism (the Keys' lifeblood) to a halt. The Keys responded by declaring themselves an independent nation called the Conch Republic. They seceded from the Union, declared war on the United States, then promptly surrendered and requested one billion dollars in aid. The clever gambit worked. The checkpoint was removed and a new motto was born: "We seceded where others failed."

The Keys may need to draw on that renegade spirit again soon. There seems to be a vast discrepancy between the future Florida residents want and the one their state government is steering them toward. In recent years, Florida's cities and communities (including the Keys) have attempted to ban plastic straws and sunscreen containing reef-harming chemicals (like oxybenzone and octinoxate) in an attempt to protect their environment—and their tourism-based livelihood. The Florida Senate responded by *banning* the ban of non-reef-safe sunscreen and plastic straws (despite the fact that 500 million straws are used in the United States every day). When faced with public outcry, Florida's governor responded: Vote for someone else if you don't like it.

Getting to the Keys is half the fun, and the Seven Mile Bridge is an iconic section of the 113-mile-long (182 km) Overseas Highway.

It's good advice. We as individuals can do a lot, but unless the overarching system (governments and large corporations) changes, too, our reach is limited. This is why it's important to vote in every election (local and national) and with every dollar you spend.

Individual spirit is what makes Key West such a delightfully quirky place. One of the best ways to see Key West is on a **city tour with Key Lime Bike Tours.** This 2.5-hour cycle tour (covering about 5 mi/8 km) took us from iconic Mallory Square, where we learned about the Keys pirates (past and present), to mahogany tree–lined Caroline Street,

SOMETHING SPECIAL

Don't miss a day trip to 19th-century Fort Jefferson in the Dry Tortugas, located about 70 miles (113 km) west of Key West. This trip is part history lesson, part nature tour, and epic snorkeling. *(Tip: There is no shade on-island!).*

once home to Robert Frost, Tennessee Williams, Shel Silverstein, and Jimmy Buffett. Caroline Street was also home to Pan Am's first office, selling tickets for the Prohibition-era "Highball Express" from Key West to Havana, Cuba.

Weaving around Key West's local population of chickens, we continued our tour past the (theoretical) southernmost point in the continental United States (the southernmost point is on a Navy base, so this is a placeholder for tourists), eventually winding up in a (blissfully) air-conditioned diner for a complimentary piece of iconic key lime pie.

(Tip: Do this tour early in your visit. By the end, you'll have a long list of places you'll want to return to, like **Ernest Hemingway's house** *and the* **Key West Lighthouse Museum,** *and good swimming spots, like* **Fort Zachary Taylor Historic State Park.***)*

Diving here is just as delicious: Key West offers plenty of reef diving (and snorkeling) to thrill beginners, including a shallower inner reef and an outer bar that's known for its sea fans and striking coral formations. Most divers, however, come here for the wrecks, including the world-class **U.S.N.S. Vandenberg.** This 524-foot (160 m) wreck had a notable career, serving as a troop carrier during World War II and a tracking ship of the Mercury, Gemini, and Apollo capsules, before she was sunk to be an artificial reef, attracting a large amount of marine life. (Fish school around the large radar dishes.) This is a deep wreck: Her deck is around 95 feet (29 m), and she's exposed in a stiff current, so it's not a dive for beginners.

You could spend a lifetime exploring the Florida Keys. Don't be surprised if your visit slips by in a green flash (a famous Key West phenomenon).

Key West's stately Ernest Hemingway Home and Museum, which was the residence of the legendary writer in the 1930s

NEED TO KNOW

GETTING HERE: Miami International Airport is the closest gateway, but it is a nightmare to navigate. Keys' residents told us they travel out of their way to fly in and out of Fort Lauderdale, as it's a better experience.

GETTING AROUND: Driving the Overseas Highway is an amazing experience. Leave time to stop off at spots that catch your eye, like the History of Diving Museum on Islamorada and the amazing Florida Keys Eco-Discovery Center in Key West.

PACKING TIPS: Sporty and fun, with comfortable footwear for exploring.

WEATHER: Summer averages 89°F (31.6°C), with winter dipping to a pleasant 70°F (21°C). The hurricane season runs June through November, with August through October having the most potential for storms.

IN ADDITION: Freshwater is liquid gold here. The Keys' drinking water is pumped 130 miles (209 km) from Florida City to Key West, so use it sparingly.

Diving

OVERVIEW: Wreck and reef diving on an awesome road trip. The Keys have more dive sites then you can explore in a lifetime, including North America's only living coral barrier reef, a marine sanctuary, and a Shipwreck Trail comprising nine historic underwater wrecks and artificial reefs stretching from Key Largo to Key West. There's plenty on offer for beginner through advanced divers.

- Visibility: From 26 to 99 feet (8 to 30 m)
- Water Temp: 70°F (21°C) in winter / 88°F (31°C) in summer
- Depth Range: From 10 to 100 feet (3 to 30 m)

MARINE LIFE: Coral (elkhorn, staghorn, brain, boulder), fish (jacks, barracuda, grouper), sharks (Caribbean reef, nurse, bull, tiger), rays, and turtles (loggerhead, green, hawksbill, Kemp's ridley, and leatherback)

SHOP INFO: We dove with **Rainbow Reef Dive Center** in Key Largo. This is a popular, busy shop operating eight boats. They are Blue Star certified in their commitment to protecting reefs, and are a knowledgeable and professional shop. (Great to learn with!) In Key West, we dove with **Dive Key West,** a smaller shop that is incredibly experienced with great local knowledge. They have a custom-built dive boat and offer courses and Nitrox.

Accommodations

HIGH-END: Kimpton Key West's Winslow's Bungalows captures that Key West vibe: Think cool, spacious rooms, wraparound porches, and a turquoise pool. Located on quiet, historic Truman Street, it's an easy walk to the hustle and bustle of Duval Street. ~$712 USD

MID-RANGE: Ocean Pointe Suites in Key Largo has 170 apartment-style suites, set on a 60-acre (24 ha) oceanfront sanctuary. Great for families. ~$339 USD

BUDGET: Boyd's Key West Campground has been a family-run institution since 1963. There are more than 260 basic sites for RVs and tents, with pool, laundry facilities, and bathhouses on-site. ~$65 USD

Food & Drink

The **Stoned Crab** in Key West is what seafood dining should be: great food, lively atmosphere, waterside dining, and sustainably sourced. The Stoned Crab works with Three Hands Fish, which connects local fishermen with Key West restaurants. Your seafood is wild-caught by fishermen who are mindful of environmental pressures, and sold directly to the restaurant. The restaurant serves your meal accompanied by baseball cards featuring information on the fisherman who caught it.

Mrs. Mac's Kitchen in Key Largo is an eclectic, fun diner with a huge and varied menu, including a page of staff and customer favorites should you feel stunned by choice. (Tip: Try the chili.)

Garbo's Grill serves up delicious street food out of a silver airstream trailer on Caroline Street in Key West. There are tasty tacos, burgers, BBQ, and hot dogs, served with a Caribbean and Korean flair.

KO SAMUI

Beauty, the Beast, and Balance

Ko Samui is a dreamy island in the Gulf of Thailand, sharing the Chumphon Archipelago with its beautiful sister islands, Ko Phangan and Ko Tao.

This is the epitome of paradise. Ko Samui's lush green interior is encircled by white-sand beaches that are shaded by palm trees and lapped by warm, translucent seas. It swiftly became one of Asia's most popular travel destinations, and therefore an island of extremes. Here you can find quiet coves and touristed beaches, relaxing retreats and parties by the light of the full moon, budget backpacker bungalows and luxury resorts.

This polarity even applies to diving: The area has a reputation as a dive course factory, churning out one of the highest numbers of Open Water certifications on the planet. Yet experienced divers still flock here for the irresistible mix of pelagic and macro, fringing reef and open ocean pinnacles.

But appearances can be deceiving. Ko Samui is a surprising place of balance—sea and land, beauty and beast—and it was one of the most soulfully fulfilling locations on our journey. Ko Samui has a lot to teach those who are eager to learn.

This is a good destination for divers traveling with non-divers. We split forces here, spending most of the day apart, joining up in the late afternoons. Chris went diving, while I spent my time at a Muay Thai training camp and a world-class wellness retreat. ∎

Ko Samui is one of the world's most popular places to learn to dive, but it also holds surprises for divers with some experience.

It's easy to understand Ko Samui's attraction to snorkelers and divers of all levels. Its turquoise waters average balmy temperatures of 84°F (29°C). Seas tend to be calm, thanks to geographical protection from the Gulf of Thailand. Most of the diving is on shallow reefs, speckled with brightly colored reef fish. However, the area also holds submerged pinnacles and rocky seamounts attracting schooling barracuda and jacks. Whale sharks are year-round visitors, favoring April and May when plankton levels are higher.

Ko Samui is a great base that gives divers the best of both worlds: spend the day at sea, returning in time to relax on the beach in the afternoon, or to join an evening Muay Thai or yoga class. Dive trips depart from Petcherat Marina in the morning aboard swift, comfortable speedboats, usually to sites around Ko Tao or Ko Phangan (about an hour's travel time).

Ko Tao's **Twins** is a sheltered, shallow spot for all levels. There are two large rock bommies here, resting on a sandy bottom cruised by bluespotted ribbontail rays. Nudibranchs and pipefish tuck themselves away, waiting to delight macro lovers, while titan triggerfish keep divers on their toes. (This is a known nesting area for them.)

Attending a traditional Muay Thai fight is a great cultural experience and opportunity to see this ancient art form. There are several stadiums in Samui, with fights most nights (around $50 USD). Many of the camp crew attend—and some fight.

Nearby is **Buoyancy World,** an artificial dive site used to teach and test divers' abilities. (This helps keep new divers away from fragile reefs as they learn control.) It features hoops, tunnels, and an underwater obstacle course that will challenge even the Jedi Masters of buoyancy.

Shark Island is a small island just off Ko Tao's coast. Diving is slightly deeper and often in current, but this site is aptly named. Blacktip reef sharks, whale sharks, and leopard sharks are often spotted here. It also has hard and soft coral, from big brains to branching gorgonians. Keep an eye out for turtles riding the current.

Sail Rock is the jewel in the Gulf's crown, a striking granite pinnacle located between Ko Phangan and Ko Tao. Divers enter a vertical chimney at 16 feet (5 m) and descend single-file to the exit at 59 feet (18 m), following the rock as it eventually slopes away beyond 131 feet (40 m).

Since Sail Rock stands alone, it's a magnet for marine life. This is the spot for large schooling fish: chevron barracuda, trevally, fusiliers, and tuna, with great barracuda and sometimes even a sailfish patrolling the deeper water. Whale sharks and manta rays also like Sail Rock, and the pinnacle ledges are covered in macro, moray eels, coral, and reef fish. You'll spot a lot of mesmerized-looking divers drifting around the rock, marveling at the marine life.

If marine life is one form of beauty, **Muay Thai** is another. Thailand's national sport of kickboxing is

A colorful sea anemone thrives on one of Ko Tao's reefs.

ancient, steeped in ritual, and reminiscent of a striking snake.

Ko Samui has a wide variety of Muay Thai training camps for the curious to the hard-core. **Superpro Samui** in Chaweng is the best of both.

Fighters stay in spartan rooms overlooking the camp, an urban jungle of covered, open-air rings and spaces lined with boxing bags. Days begin with a two-hour morning training session. Campers who attend this session (overseen by Superpro's team of nearly a dozen trainers) tend to be more serious about their training, but fear not: The camp is more accessible, the camaraderie more enjoyable, than you could imagine. Most of Superpro's camp dwellers aren't here to train for a fight— they're curious or want to get fitter. But being around the fighters (women and men) is infectious, and we all want what they have: focus and strength.

Each session involves stretching, jogging, skipping, pad work, and fighting techniques, and there is a lot to learn: Muay Thai utilizes every muscle in your body, including ones you never knew you

Kamalaya is a serene sanctuary, an East-meets-West wellness retreat that takes holistic health (mental, emotional, and physical) seriously.

---

had. Tanned legs are covered in bruises, and everyone wears a sheen of sweat.

Class breaks during the midday heat. Some people head to the beach; others retreat to their rooms for a shower and a nap.

The evening session (two to three hours) attracts a lot of locals and walk-ins, and there is more of a group feel to the class. As a former amateur boxer, I reveled in being back in my happy place. To me, this is what's beautiful about fight training: It's pure, stripping away everything else until you're entirely, utterly awake.

(Tip: A good level of base fitness is essential to handle daily training. All ages/abilities welcome. You don't need to stay on-site, but it adds to the experience. Chris stayed with me here and at Kamalaya, and went diving while I trained.)

Farther down Ko Samui's east coast, **Kamalaya** is a different type of training center. The phrase "wellness retreat" can be as nebulous as "eco-resort," but Kamalaya is the real deal. This East-meets-West establishment takes holistic health (mental, emotional, and physical) seriously, with a team of top specialists and visiting practitioners from around the world bringing together diverse traditions of healing and culture.

Kamalaya is a sanctuary: Open-air yoga pavilions are perched hillside with sweeping sea views, and accommodations, treatment rooms, and class-rooms are connected by jungle-fringed, winding pathways. This is a place to breathe deeply.

Each visit begins with a consultation to measure key health markers and set up a program customized to address your goals—often the goal guests arrive with isn't the one they end up focusing on.

From there, you embark on a personal journey within a community setting, utilizing as much or little support as you need from Kamalaya's skilled team. Along with meditation and breathing techniques to help with de-stressing, I had treatments such as Chi Nei Tsang (a Taoist abdominal massage designed to release tension) and a massage inspired by Korean hand acupuncture (ideal for desk workers, soothing nerves in arms and hands).

Kamalaya exhausted me more than the Muay Thai camp, which is why I nicknamed it the Beast. We all develop coping mechanisms to get through our days, and those compound day after day until we don't realize the weight we've taken onto our

Kebabs pop with color and flavor at one of Ko Samui's night markets.

own shoulders. This is the place to confront it head on, to be aware, and to reset.

All of us are familiar with fatigue. If we're out of balance, we don't have the energy for anything else. Spending time at Kamalaya—and on.

All of us are familiar with fatigue. If we're out of balance, we don't have the energy for anything else. Spending time at Kamalaya—and on Ko Samui—is the best gift you can give yourself.

Make a Difference

Climate fatigue is real, and it is the biggest threat to our future. When we feel overwhelmed or afraid, we tend to shut down. When we don't know what to do, we tend to do nothing. It happens to all of us. In this chapter, we touch on fighting and recharging, and both serve a purpose. To use an airplane analogy, you have to put on your own oxygen mask first before helping others. Sometimes that means unyoking from the weight of the world and allowing ourselves to experience joy, hope, and optimism. Those feelings are powerful motivators. What keeps us going is knowing we're not alone, and knowing that we want to be a part of this fight, however it might end. What can you do? Something. Anything. Most important, keep talking about what's happening in our world—don't shy away from the conversation.

NEED TO KNOW

GETTING HERE: Most flights transit through Bangkok, but there are some direct flights to Ko Samui from a number of international destinations.

GETTING AROUND: Transfers, taxis, and scooter rentals are how most people get around Ko Samui, rather than renting a car (also available).

PACKING TIPS: Casual clothes. You'll see a lot of yoga apparel, loose dresses and pants, and sarongs in vibrant colors.

WEATHER: Warm and humid most of the year. February tends to be driest, with late October through November the usual rainy season (which can reduce visibility).

IN ADDITION: If your baggage is not checked all the way through from point of origin to Ko Samui on a single ticket, allow at least an hour in Bangkok Airport to collect your bags and recheck them.

Diving

OVERVIEW: A mesmerizing mix of pelagic and macro, colorful coral reefs and lively pinnacles in the Gulf of Thailand, all within easy reach of a popular island base.

- Visibility: From 33 to 100 feet (10 to 30 m)
- Water Temp: 79°F (26°C) in winter / 88°F (31°C) in summer
- Depth Range: 20 to 112 feet (6 to 34 m)

MARINE LIFE: Whale sharks (year-round), titan triggerfish, barracuda, bluespotted ribbontail ray, blacktip reef sharks, turtles (hawksbill and green), abundant reef fish, Durban dancing shrimp, and nudibranchs

SHOP INFO: **Silent Divers** is run by ex-military expats (with an all-Thai crew), and is therefore run very efficiently, with safety and comfort being paramount. (They provide some of the best and most detailed briefings Chris has ever had!) Silent Divers is one of the few shops on the island that run their own boats (swift speedboats, which significantly reduce travel time), so you might be joined by groups from other dive shops. They also offer courses, snorkel trips, and private charters.

Accommodations

HIGH-END: Kamalaya is sublime, with a wonderfully warm and attentive team. There are 76 rooms, offering sea and garden views, some with their own plunge pools, all spacious with relaxing and comfortable interiors. The resort also features an architecturally striking pool, a pristine slip of beach, and a centuries-old Buddhist monks' cave, all surrounded by lush greenery. *~$244 USD (wellness programs are an additional cost)*

MID-RANGE: Amari Palm Reef Ko Samui is near central Chaweng (and, conveniently, the airport), set on the beach. This 188-room resort features a variety of accommodations. On-site restaurant and pool. *~$115 USD*

BUDGET: Superpro Samui offers spartan accommodations, which is just as it should be and just what you want. There are a variety of rooms (from shared-bath singles to apartments) with AC/fans, decks, and mini-fridges. Packages available. *~$32 USD including training*

Food & Drink

The **Cliff Bar & Restaurant** is one big charismatic rock with a restaurant perched on it, in full view of the sea and moon (when it's up). The dishes are a delectable mix of Thai, Portuguese, Italian, and Spanish cuisine—like tiger prawns with spicy Portuguese *piri piri* sauce and deep-fried snapper with a spicy Thai fruit medley. The service is excellent, and the atmosphere sparkles.

Soma, Kamalaya's main restaurant, is an open-air pavilion serving breakfast and dinner. The food is exquisite: fresh, local ingredients combined to create bursts of flavors, all designed to nurture both body and senses. (Think dishes like banana flower salad and Thai pumpkin soup.) There is a community table if you feel like company (great for solo travelers).

Chaweng Night Market is an open-air food market surrounding a cluster of tables and chairs. Authentic, local Thai food is served here, and it's delicious.

KOMODO

Here Be Dragons

Komodo dragons, known locally as *ora*, are as charismatic and spine-tingling as you hope they will be.

They are the largest living lizards in the world, averaging six to 10 feet (2 to 3 m) in length, and they are found only in Komodo National Park, a UNESCO World Heritage site that includes the islands of Komodo, Rinca, and Padar.

We came here to seek out these endangered and arresting animals, which not only spike a sense of wonder at our crazy, marvelous planet, but also remind us—quietly and firmly—about where we sit in the food chain. (Hint: It's not very high.)

And find them we did, trekking across Komodo's savanna-like hillsides, which curve around turquoise waters holding other marvels, like manta rays riding surging currents that wash over coral reefs. Komodo sits in the Coral Triangle, and there are innumerable dive sites (accessed by day boat or liveaboard) showcasing the area's impressive biodiversity.

Our base was the town of Labuan Bajo—the City of Sunsets—on the western tip of the island of Flores in the East Nusa Tenggara province of Indonesia. Komodo, Padar, and Rinca lie in the channel between East and West Nusa Tenggara, and if you keep island-hopping west, you'll hit Lombok and Bali.

This is a rugged place for adventurous nature lovers, a dragon-populated pocket in a world where frontiers are becoming few and far between. Are you ready to sail off the edge? ■

Komodo dragons, the largest living lizards in the world, are endangered: It's estimated that fewer than 3,380 dragons remain in the wild.

We wish we'd had more time to explore Flores. Like most travelers, we spent our time in Labuan Bajo ("Bajo"), the seaside base for dragon and diving expeditions. Bajo is a former fishing village that has taken on an upmarket backpacker mantle: The restaurants are good, getting around is easy, and there is a bright, affable energy about town.

If you have time, venture farther afield, exploring the serpentine **Trans-Flores Highway,** the island's main road. Along the way are caves and waterfalls, rice fields laid out like spiderwebs, dozens of traditional villages, and the color-changing lakes at **Kelimutu National Park.**

(Tip: Get travel advice in Bajo before setting off; tours are available, buses run regularly, and it's possible to self-drive, although roads can be rough.)

A day trip to see Komodo dragons, however, was one of the things we were most looking forward to on our entire journey, and it didn't disappoint.

Komodo National Park was established in 1980 mainly to conserve the dragons, but also to protect their unique habitat and its biodiversity. It takes about three hours by boat to get from Bajo to Komodo, and all visitors need to purchase tickets and hire a guide from the main office at Loh Liang upon arrival, choosing from several different trekking options. We chose a two-hour trek, a moderate hike that gets you away from the crowds.

NEARBY

Divers should speak with Uber Scuba Komodo about their liveaboard (three to six nights, pairing uncrowded diving with a Komodo dragon trek) or add a visit to remote Kalimaya Dive Resort, the only dive resort on East Sumbawa (west of Komodo).

Komodo is a wild place. We wound our way through dry forest, up hills with views of beaches and bays, and past the location where, in the olden days of tourism, dragons used to be fed in front of spellbound crowds.

We kept our eyes peeled for birds, water buffaloes, Timor deer, and, of course, dragons. "Sometimes we see; sometimes we're just walking," Agus Suyanto, our guide, explained. As we walked, Agus talked about the dragons he loves and is continually learning about ("They always create a new question"), casually carrying the long, forked stick that is our dragon protection.

These solitary animals are keepers of the island and lords of their domain. They are large enough to make you feel small, armed with lethal claws and teeth, powerful legs, and venom so deadly even a nip can be fatal, rendering victims too weak to fight. Dragons will calmly track bitten prey for miles.

And yet we know very little about them; they are shy creatures that keep to themselves.

We spotted our first dragon lounging by a water hole. The dragons are so well suited to their environment, it was difficult to see them unless they moved. And that, Agus told us, is part of the game. "There are three dragons here, do you see?" he said, pointing out two more dragons on the other side of the track. "And I am always looking for one more than I am seeing. He is here, and he can come from anywhere."

Manta Point, a shallow and swift drift dive, is a cleaning and feeding station for manta rays.

Komodo National Park, a UNESCO World Heritage site since 1991, is a wild and natural beauty, with a savanna-like interior and stunning bays.

It's estimated that fewer than 3,380 of these lizard kings and queens remain in the wild. (Their conservation status was upgraded to endangered in 2021.) Humans are encroaching on their space, poaching their prey, and poaching the dragons themselves, selling them for illegal pets or to zoos. In addition, rising sea levels are threatening to submerge the dragons' habitat. Time is running out to save them, and what a terrible loss that would be for the world if our dragons disappeared.

And so it is with manta rays, the other creature we came here to see. Like Komodo dragons, manta rays are vulnerable to extinction due to human-induced pressures. They have been protected in Indonesia since 2014, but that doesn't mean they aren't fished.

Manta rays use this area as a cleaning and feeding station, attracted by the nutrient-rich convergence of currents, where cold upswells clash with warm seas.

(Tip: These currents are unique—choose your operator carefully, make sure their day boat comes equipped with a small, fast boat that can pick up any separated divers quickly, and carry a PLB. Also, BYO towel and warm diving and topside layers, as the currents can be cold.)

Siaba Besar is commonly chosen as the shakedown dive, due to its shallow and protected location, and it's a good one. Bannerfish, leaf scorpionfish, painted frogfish, and flamboyant cuttlefish can be spotted among exceptionally robust beds of hard and soft coral. Keep a weather eye out: You'll soon see that coral move. Resting on top (remarkably camouflaged) or tucked underneath overhangs are turtles: dozens of large, healthy green turtles. This is a site for slowing down and taking a good look.

Karang Makassar (Manta Point) is something else entirely. This is one of the area's most famous sites, and you'll get an idea of what you're in for watching ripples on the surface of the water from the invisible boil of currents below.

This is a shallow drift dive, around 33 feet (10 m) deep, traveling about 1.5 miles (2.5 km) at speed. We dropped in in small groups, the current immediately whisking us along. We dodged coral bommies patrolled by titan triggerfish, keeping an eye out for manta rays. If someone spotted a manta, the group tried to stop, grabbing rocks on the rubble-strewn ocean floor to hold ourselves in place. If a diver lost their grip, the entire group let go to travel together.

When we did pause, the view was worth everything. Manta rays hovered effortlessly on the same currents that sent us tumbling. At one stop, we counted 12 individual reef mantas. We also spotted sharks, turtles, and barramundi, but the mantas stole the show, and our hearts. We wanted to take the ride again and again.

Komodo dragons and manta rays are caught in that conservation catch-22: Their popularity both protects and threatens them. Of course it would be best for the animals if they were left undisturbed, their habitats untouched. But that opens doors to smugglers and illegal activities. Tourism—responsible, sustainable tourism—places an economic value on these creatures that incentivizes protecting them and their fragile environment.

It also makes people care. Having seen Komodo dragons ruling their domain, and manta rays soar-

Komodo sits in the Coral Triangle. The convergence of cold-water currents helps protect the area's 260-plus species of coral from warming seas.

ing in their underwater amphitheaters, you can't help but feel invested in wanting to help them survive and thrive. The world is a better place with them in it.

This is a complicated conundrum. The answer involves education and activism, careful management, and mindful travel, especially here—keep your eyes wide open, ask questions, and make travel decisions with this query in mind: What impact does my being here have?

Make a Difference

Trash Hero Komodo (facebook.com/trashherokomodo) is a volunteer organization that holds cleanups every Friday afternoon in Labuan Bajo. These fun outings are open to everyone and are a great way to meet some of the community, make a positive difference locally, and learn how waste and recycling is handled in a different country. Trash Hero Komodo is one chapter of **Trash Hero World** (trashhero.org), a global network that brings together businesses, communities, schools, and travelers to take positive action on waste. At the time of writing, they have more than 150 active chapters and have collected more than 4.4 million pounds (2 million kg) of trash. Other ways to get involved: sponsor their distinctive yellow T-shirts (gifted to regular volunteers), donate money, or treat the crew to a post-cleanup meal.

NEED TO KNOW

GETTING HERE: Denpasar, Bali, is the main connection hub to Komodo airport, which is located about two miles (3 km) outside of Labuan Bajo. Garuda Indonesia offers 50.7 pounds (23 kg) of free sporting gear (i.e., dive gear) on top of a 44-pound (20 kg) checked bag, which is included in the fare. (International checked limits are higher than domestic; pack with domestic limits in mind.)

GETTING AROUND: It's easy to walk around town. Car, bike, and scooter rentals available; there are plenty of taxis and guide-driver options available.

PACKING TIPS: Fast-drying and lightweight clothes. Outside Labuan Bajo, it's respectful to cover shoulders and knees. Also: good walking shoes, a warm layer, hat, sunglasses, a reusable water bottle, and daypack.

WEATHER: Diving is year-round in this Southern Hemisphere destination. The wet season is usually January to March, with February the low season for visitors (some places close). The wet season can bring rougher conditions at some sites, but it also brings fewer crowds. The dragons are also year-round but are seen less during their mating and nesting months (July through November).

IN ADDITION: Check out the Dive Operators Community of Komodo (DOCK). This group of around 15 tourism organizations operates to agreed standards of safety, professionalism, and environmental and social sustainability that are in line with international best practice.

Diving

OVERVIEW: Exciting diving for all levels in the land of dragons, from swift drift dives with manta rays to shallow reef dives with turtles.

- **Visibility:** From 16 to 82 feet (5 to 25 m)
- **Water Temp:** 75°F (24°C) in winter / 82°F (28°C) in summer
- **Depth Range:** 33 to 115 feet (10 to 35 m)

MARINE LIFE: Manta rays (oceanic and reef), turtles (green and hawksbill), sharks (gray reef, blacktip reef, and whitetip reef), moray eels, grouper, barramundi, whales, dugongs, dolphins, and more than 260 species of coral

SHOP INFO: We dove with **Uber Scuba Komodo Dive Center,** the premier shop in Labuan Bajo. Uber Scuba offers day trips, liveaboards, and dive training, operating small groups from modified traditional wooden boats with a focus on safety. Their multinational and energetic team infuses every dive with passion, fun, and local knowledge. Dive plans in this area can be tide- and weather-dependent, so a flexible attitude comes in handy.

Accommodations

HIGH-END: **AYANA Komodo Resort** is a large resort (205 guest rooms and suites) located on secluded Waecicu Beach, north of Labuan Bajo. ~*$279 USD*

MID-RANGE: The 19-room **Bayview Gardens Hotel** is close to town. Rooms have ocean views, private terraces, and casual but elegant furnishings. ~*$50 USD*

BUDGET: **Seaesta Komodo Hostel and Hotel** was designed by travelers *for* travelers (and divers). They offer private rooms to liveaboard-style dorms, and clever touches abound such as secure lockers with charging stations in them. Seaesta is a five-minute walk from town, and features a rooftop restaurant and pool with ocean views. ~*$13 USD*

Food & Drink

MadeInItaly is Italian fine dining in Flores. This contemporary restaurant imports some ingredients from Italy and sources the rest from their own farms to create dishes like thin-crust pizza, pumpkin risotto, and organic chard and ricotta ravioli. (Ask about the culinary boat trip.)

The Uber Scuba dive crew introduced us to **Artomoro Restaurant and Grill.** This upstairs, airy establishment has long wooden tables (perfect for groups) and serves affordable local dishes, like *ayam goreng atm* (spicy fried chicken).

Deli Point is a well-stocked shop with everything from fresh veggies to Vegemite.

HAWAI'I

A Remarkable Work in Progress

The Hawaiian Islands are a seamount chain stretching across more than 1,500 miles (2,414 km). Comprising reefs, atolls, shoals, and more than 132 islands, Hawai'i is best known for eight main islands: Hawai'i, Oahu, Kauai, Lanai, Maui, Molokai, Kaho'olawe, and Ni'ihau.

Despite the familiarity we have with the name, it's mind-bending to think the Hawaiian archipelago is one of the most remote in the world, located approximately 2,400 miles (3,862 km) from a continental landmass. These islands contain nearly every climatic zone on the planet, and a staggering proportion of endemic species (nearly 25 percent).

And it's just getting started.

The Hawaiian Islands were created by hot spot volcanism, and the Earth, apparently, considers them a work in progress. Hawai'i (also known as the Big Island, and our base for this visit), for example, was constructed by five volcanoes, and several are still busy.

In May 2018, Kilauea, currently one of the most productive volcanoes on the planet, erupted, forcing the evacuation of nearly 2,000 people.

The Big Island's volcanic nature is evident everywhere you look. On land, black-and-red rubble fields are brightened by yellow flowers, and black- and green-sand beaches sparkle in the sun. Underwater ancient lava flows, twisted and tortured, are home to coral gardens and diverse marine life.

You can feel the transience of time here: These islands are constantly transforming, both geologically and culturally. This multicultural hot spot is currently experiencing a resurgence of pride in its identity and a feeling of fierce protection for its environment. Make your way, and be part of Hawai'i's journey. ■

As it is on land, so it's mirrored underwater: Hawai'i's volcanic landscape extends to its dive sites, a playground of arches and caverns.

The Big Island, larger than all the other Hawaiian Islands combined, is both a geologic baby (less than a million years old) and a grandfather of history (the Polynesians first landed at the island's southern tip, and the Big Island is where Kamehameha, unifier of the Hawaiian Islands, established his kingdom). There is legroom to burn on the Big Island, and a different view around every curve, from popular Kailua-Kona (with its mighty banyan and fragrant frangipani trees), to dry and golden Kohala, to the emerald cliffs threaded with waterfalls on the eastern side.

Getting a bird's-eye view of the island on a **helicopter tour with Paradise Helicopters** is an eyeopener of the Big Island's vastness and diversity. We chose a two-hour circumnavigation of the island, lifting off from Kona International Airport (the island's western tip) and heading south. We passed over verdant coffee plantations and sapphire Kealakekua Bay, where Captain Cook was killed on Valentine's Day 1779. Now a marine preserve popular with snorkelers and kayakers, it was slightly unsettling to see where the mighty captain met his fate.

As we rose up over the remnants of Kilauea's red crater, the smell of sulfur seeped in through the helicopter's windows, and steam billowed from unseen vents. We followed the lava trail down what used to be the main streets of Leilani Estates, a neighborhood segmented and consumed by rivers of lava.

Our pilot kept up an informative banter throughout, answering questions on everything from history to geology to real estate prices and dinner recommendations. As we traveled north up the east coast, the lush windward side, we felt like we were seeing an entirely different island. Waterfalls plunged 2,000 feet (610 m) down sheer cliffs, sometimes spilling directly into the sea. Heading back down the west coast, we had a fantastic aerial view of the offshore reef system, and Chris and I felt restless: We couldn't wait to get into the water to explore. *(Tip: Heli trips can often be delayed a day or two due to weather, so don't schedule them for the very end of your trip; factor in flexibility.)*

Big Island diving lives up to its reputation: There are dives for all levels here (brand-new to experienced), and the diving is delightfully varied.

Kohala, on the northwest side of the island, is not as well known as the more popular area around Kona, and is therefore quieter. We departed Kawaihae Harbor, cruising the clear indigo water accompanied by a pod of spinner dolphins and some flying fish before reaching an aptly named site called **Turtle Spa.** Here, six green turtles were suspended in the water as dozens of blue and yellow tang cleaned the algae from their shells. The turtles

A scenic helicopter tour provides a bird's-eye view of the verdant valley and black-sand beaches of Hawai'i's Pololu Valley.

Make a Difference

One of Hawai'i's biggest battles is with an invisible enemy: ghost nets. Ghost nets are abandoned fishing gear that continue to do what they were designed to do: trap and kill everything in their path, including sea turtles, dolphins, whales, birds, and more. Mostly made from nylon and plastic, ghost nets last forever, unless physically removed from the ocean, making up 10 percent of all marine litter and 46 percent of the Great Pacific Garbage Patch, eventually breaking down into harmful microplastics. How can you help? Locally, **Hawai'i Pacific University's Center for Marine Debris Research** *(hpu.edu/cncs/cmdr)* is investigating the sources of plastic marine debris. The **World Wildlife Fund** *(worldwildlife.org)* is tackling the problem of ghost nets globally. (Donations welcome at both.)

radiated contentment that was contagious to divers; we, too, were suspended and motionless, watching from a respectful distance, taking part in one of those unforgettable underwater moments.

While most diving on the Big Island is from boats, there is some shore diving available. We dove the beach next to **Kona Harbor,** renowned for tiger sharks, and straightaway spotted a 13-foot (4 m) female, beautifully patterned and slowly heading out into deeper water. Mesmerized, we followed her, and it was only after she disappeared that we realized we were under a gaggle of snorkelers frolicking with a pod of curious spinner dolphins, manta rays flanking us on either side. *(Tip: This was a relatively shallow and easy dive. Some of the coastal areas can get gnarly with current and surf; go with an experienced operator who knows the area.)*

Feel like something completely out of this world? Try Jack's Diving Locker's legendary **Pelagic Magic dive.** This black-water night dive suspends divers by 33-foot (10 m) drop-lines over 5,000 feet (1,524 m) of open ocean, miles off the Kona coast. Although initially spooky, the dive transforms into a meditative experience, an opportunity to see all the tiny deep-sea creatures that venture up to the surface at night to feed. Once our eyes adjusted, we saw we were surrounded by bioluminescence and flashing colors, an underwater, nighttime disco that's a privilege to behold.

A ctenophore (also known as a comb jelly) lights up a black-water night dive called Pelagic Magic off the Kona coast.

Back on land, for another out-of-this-world view, head to the **Mauna Kea Observatory.** *(Tip: The observatory visitors center sits at 9,200 ft/2,804 m, so factor in a deco day if you've been diving. Our recommendation:* ***coffee-tasting at Greenwell Farms,*** *a working farm on the 30-mile-long/48-km Kona coffee belt that's been in operation since 1850. It offers free tours and tastings, from a beautiful—and fragrant—setting: Think ocean views and orchids.)*

The observatory itself is about an hour's drive from Waikoloa Beach. The road cuts through

Night dive or snorkel with manta rays with **Kona Diving Company** or **Jack's Diving Locker.** The Kona Coast has a resident population of more than 100 mantas, which visit a specific site to feed on plankton, putting on a nightly underwater ballet.

Serengeti-esque plains of lion-colored grass and black lava rocks, slowly snaking upward in an ear-popping drive. I'm a human altimeter: I can always feel when I hit 6,000 feet (1,829 m), and that's not even reaching the visitors center.

Mauna Kea measures more than 33,000 feet (10,058 m) from the ocean floor, a landmark for ancient navigators and a laboratory for modern-day astronomers. The visitors center has rangers available to answer questions, free stargazing some evenings, and plenty of information. The summit is far more serious business: 12 telescopes are set at 13,796 feet (4,205 m); there's 40 percent less atmospheric pressure up here than at sea level, and the weather can strand travelers year-round.

No matter how you choose to visit Mauna Kea, do so with respect. At the time of writing, Hawaiians are opposing the construction of a new telescope on Mauna Kea, a place they consider to be sacred. Hawai'i has always been a melting pot of cultures—Polynesian, Asian, European, etc.—and Hawaiians take pride in their diversity. They also take pride in welcoming visitors, but not at the expense of their culture or their land. In 2021, Hawai'i became the first U.S. state to ban sunscreens harmful to coral reefs. (Up to 14,000 tons of sunscreen end up in coral reef areas every year, and chemicals like octinoxate and oxybenzone contribute to reef degradation.) There is a wave of cultural renewal and care, which creates exciting opportunities for Hawaiians and visitors alike. Travel like a guest, and you will find a home in Hawai'i, welcomed back with open arms any time your journey takes you this way.

Mauna Kea is one of the world's premier observatories. Twelve telescopes sit at the 13,796-foot (4,205 m) summit of this dormant volcano.

NEED TO KNOW

GETTING HERE: Honolulu on the island of Oahu is the main gateway; from there, it's an easy interisland flight to the Big Island (which also gets some direct flights from major hubs like San Francisco and Los Angeles).

GETTING AROUND: Having a rental car provides the most flexibility (book before you arrive), but there is a free bus service called Hele On (Let's Go).

PACKING TIPS: Casual is the look, and traditional aloha shirts and sundresses suit most occasions. Good walking shoes and a light jacket or sweater also come in handy.

WEATHER: Hawai'i has two main seasons: Summer is May to October, with temperatures averaging 85°F (29.4°C) and possible hurricanes July to September. Winter is November to April, cooling down to 78°F (25.6°C) and bringing localized rain—and humpback whales!

IN ADDITION: Don't forget the reef-friendly sunscreen! We use **Stream2Sea** products. Their mineral-based sunscreen has been tested and proven safe for fresh- and saltwater fish and coral larvae. It's also received HEL Labs' Protect Land + Sea certification.

Diving

OVERVIEW: Spectacular marine life and a wide variety of dives for all levels, from ancient lava beds to coral reefs to otherworldly night dives.

- **Visibility:** 60-plus feet (18+ m)
- **Water Temp:** 75°F (23.9°C) in winter / 82°F (27.8°C) in summer
- **Depth Range:** 56 to 82 feet (17 to 25 m)

MARINE LIFE: Manta rays, turtles, sharks (tiger, silky, nurse, hammerhead, whitetip reef, gray reef, blacktip reef), dolphins, whales, fish (blue and yellow tang, Picasso triggerfish, peacock grouper, frogfish), and pelagic seahorses (also known as Fisher's seahorse)

SHOP INFO: Kohala Divers is a wonderful operation with a well-set-up boat, comprehensive briefings, and small group sizes that rotate around dive sites to avoid crowding. This is a great shop for new divers and snorkelers. **Jack's Diving Locker** is a professional outfit in the heart of Kona. They know what they're doing, and they do it well, running multiple boats for divers and snorkelers. Jack's offers a variety of dive excursions (including Pelagic Magic), and they have a large staff that lives and breathes diving. **Ohana Shore Divers** is a smaller operation offering boutique shore diving experiences from different locations. They can tailor dives to suit your schedule, and set up a canopy on the beach, with snacks and seats for surface intervals.

Accommodations

HIGH-END: Waikoloa Beach Marriott Resort & Spa is a beachside hotel on the northwest coast of Waikoloa, a quieter base than Kona, but still central. All the Marriott amenities are on offer: a variety of rooms, three outdoor pools, golf, and on-site dining. *~$510 USD*

MID-RANGE: Holualoa Inn is an elegant bed-and-breakfast located on Mount Hualalai, just outside of Kona. This boutique inn features four guest rooms, two suites, and two cabins, each individually decorated, on 30 acres (12 ha) overlooking the coastline. *~$435 USD*

BUDGET: The **Kona Tiki Hotel** is located oceanside in the heart of Kona at a price that doesn't break the bank. This casual, 16-room hotel is a favorite with return guests: a comfortable, friendly place to stay in a convenient location with great views. *~$269 USD*

Food & Drink

Kona Brewing Company is a local institution—pizza and beer at its best—that's great for group lunches or dinners with indoor-outdoor casual dining inspired by a traditional Hawaiian canoe house.

Kona's **Tea:Licious Café** is a tucked-away, cozy spot with delightfully mismatched decor, serving all kinds of delectable treats.

Kohala Burger & Taco is a great post-dive lunch stop, serving up the basics (burgers, tacos, fries, and shakes) that hit the spot after being in the ocean.

LAGUNA BEACH

Once Is Never Enough

I n California's plethora of playgrounds, it's easy to overlook Laguna Beach, a seaside enclave tucked halfway between Los Angeles and San Diego.

This seven-mile (11 km) stretch of scalloped coastal coves, tide pools, sea caves, and sandy beaches seems designed for days spent on the shore—diving, kayaking, surfing, walking, exploring—and tailor-made for watching the sun set. In fact, it's only after the last orange-pink glow fades from the horizon that Laguna Beach residents finally decide to call it a day and head indoors.

Divers will find plenty of shore diving in temperate kelp forests. If you can turn your back to the beach and cast your eyes to the coastal hills, you'll find more than 20,000 acres (8,090 ha) of protected wilderness filled with hiking and biking trails. (Some of the best mountain bikers in the world call Laguna Beach home because of this spectacular backyard.)

In between the beach and hills is a very walkable seaside community featuring a collection of local businesses. Thanks to a pleasant, Mediterranean-style microclimate, Laguna Beach is a year-round town favored by artists and photographers. It also has a passion for festivals, cramming the calendar with as many events as it can.

And it isn't just locals who fall in love with Laguna. On average, most visitors return several times, which is fair warning: Count on the fact that you'll want to come back. ∎

Located between Los Angeles and San Diego, Laguna Beach boasts hiking and biking trails, tide pools, and secluded coves, shops, and eateries.

Laguna Beach's coastline extends from protected, golden-sand coves to rocky outcrops frothed with white surf. Beyond that is the wild Pacific Ocean. It's the type of coastline shore divers dream of, and it's the center of attention in a community that loves its outdoor lifestyle.

There are innumerable dive sites within a short drive of Laguna Beach, most of which fall within the protected no-take area of Laguna Beach State Marine Reserve, one of three marine protected areas within city limits.

Most dives are shallow shore dives next to craggy rock formations that mimic Laguna's terrestrial landscape. Thanks to the marine reserve, fish are plentiful—sheepshead, sea bass (white and giant black), and garibaldi, a bright orange and fearless damselfish that is California's state fish.

Divers might also receive visits from dolphins and seals. Swells can spoil the party (and visibility), making for tricky entries and exits. Otherwise, most diving is relatively easy and suitable for divers (and snorkelers) of all levels.

(Tip: Always dive with a buddy here. You can hire a guide and rent gear from the area's one shop, **Beach Cities Scuba,** *as well as get valuable intel if self-guiding. For added safety, dive with a surface marker buoy [SMB], a flashlight, and a knife.)*

Shaw's Cove is one of the most popular shore (and training) dives in the area. Once beyond the breakers, you'll discover a reef that's home to spiny lobster, bat rays, sand bass, and garibaldi. Along with kelp beds, there are plenty of underwater formations to explore, including crevices, archways, and swim-throughs. Spend time nosing around the rocks.

Diver's Cove, farther south, lives up to its name. This is one of the more protected coves, a shallow and diverse site frequented by bat rays, with reef ridges and kelp beds. Kelp forests are reminiscent of taking a stroll through a forest—awesome yet serene, full of life, and plenty to see if you slow down and take the time to look. The shoreline kelp has been decimated by storms and purple sea urchins (often spotted here), but efforts are being made by local organizations to remove the urchins and replant kelp to restore the forests to their former, sun-filtered glory.

Fisherman's Cove is home to some of the area's healthier kelp beds. Mind the rocky entry—and your navigation, otherwise you'll end up in Shaw's Cove or Diver's Cove. Look for the deep hole in the reef known as Mermaid's Grotto, a good place to take a breather from the surge and explore some cracks and crevices crowned with sea fans.

Although seemingly close to shore, **Deadman's**

A chorus of elephant seal pups at the Pacific Marine Mammal Center, which has rescued, rehabilitated, and released more than 10,000 animals

Make a Difference

Rising ocean temperatures are causing more than 80 percent of marine life to migrate to different places and/or change their breeding and feeding patterns. Here, that often results in seal pups being abandoned by mothers having to travel farther to hunt. Located on the outskirts of Laguna Beach, the **Pacific Marine Mammal Center** (*pacificmmc.org*) has been doing great work for more than 50 years. They've rescued, rehabilitated, and released more than 10,000 animals since their inception, including Pacific harbor seals, Guadalupe fur seals, and elephant seals. Visitors to the area can take a free, self-guided tour of the facility (docents available), and the website is a gold mine, including donation opportunities, ingenious options for environmentally conscious kids, and day-brightening animal release videos.

Reef is best dived from a boat to avoid a long surface swim. Rocky bommies and channels are enclosed by kelp forests, and schooling fish (like sargo and yellowtail barracuda) abound.

Although the shore diving in Laguna is spectacular, boat dives offer the opportunity to explore reefs along the edges of the marine protected areas. Kelp forests here are healthier and thicker: Kelp can grow a staggering two feet (0.6 m) per day in rich waters. Look for horn sharks, as well as pelagics, like blue or thresher sharks.

Back on land, **hiking and mountain biking** are the sports of choice, and there are more than 40 miles (64 km) of trails to choose from in this coastal wilderness preserve. This is the California of old, a mix of rolling hills, rocky bluffs, and canyon floors, with old-growth oak, sycamore, and sage. (*Tip: Bring cash for parking and carry plenty of water. This area is home to mountain lions and rattlesnakes, so don't hike alone and stay on the trails.*)

And, of course, there's golfing. Until Laguna, we had never felt any urge to swing a club, but **Ben Brown's Golf Course at The Ranch at Laguna Beach** is so cool (that's really the only suitable adjective), it's a mind-changer. This nine-hole, par 32 course is legendary among those who love the game, and locals have been playing here for more than 40 years. The Ranch has an almost 1970s vibe, holding regular events like Vino and Vinyl evenings or Three-Club Barefoot Golf Tournaments (exactly as advertised).

Author Chris Taylor explores Laguna's temperate kelp forests. This area is renowned for its shore diving.

The vibe might be retro, but The Ranch is fully present. Sharp-eyed instructors know their game. (I struck a 200-yd/183-m shot on my first drive.) The course is also GEO Certified, with programs like Bottles to Bunkers, which crushes glass bottles into sand that's used to fill golf bunkers.

Along with outdoor activities, Laguna Beach is also made for wandering. There are more than 100 independently owned shops and galleries to nose around, crisscrossing sunny streets that hug the coastline. Start by the whale mural on Legion Street and walk toward town. You won't go far before the mouthwatering smells from **La Rue du Chocolate** on Peppertree Lane entice you in for a fresh chocolate-dipped strawberry.

After your tasty treat, it's a short walk to the **Narrative Gallery with the Art of Dr. Seuss Collection,** featuring paintings, statues, and sketches by or inspired by Dr. Seuss. Continue on to the **National Geographic Fine Art Gallery,** which features exhibits and exclusive limited editions of the photography that made the magazine a legend.

Don't miss stopping by **Tuvalu,** a rustically elegant shop which is packed with eclectic, exquisite homewares (and souvenirs).

Follow Forest Avenue until it T-bones 3rd Street: There's a lovely adobe-looking fire station adjacent to a peaceful garden fronting the Laguna Beach County Water District. Both are well worth a look and a deep breath.

Opposite is **Lumberyard,** a Normandy-looking restaurant built in 1919 on the site of Laguna's for-

---

Author Carrie Miller strikes a 200-yard (183 m) shot on her first drive, thanks to instructor Ryan Sheffer's tutelage.

Santa Catalina Island is an easy day trip from Laguna Beach (via the ferry from Dana Point, 7.6 mi/12.2 km south). Part of the Channel Islands, Catalina's shore diving is legendary: kelp forests, wrecks, and plenty of marine life.

---

mer lumberyard. It serves down-home favorites like tomato bisque soup and meat loaf.

Walk off lunch exploring Laguna's lovely coastline, which rises up on bluffs that overlook the ocean, and drops down to a network of fascinating tide pools, natural aquariums filled with marine life such as sea stars, sea anemones, crabs, and gobies.

Stay for the spectacular Laguna Beach sunsets, a nightly work of art. The sky is a canvas of oranges, pinks, and fire reds, blending together before slowly dropping into the sea.

No wonder locals love living here, and visitors keep coming back.

NEED TO KNOW

GETTING HERE: John Wayne Airport (about 16 mi/25.7 km north) is the closest airport, or drive California's iconic Pacific Coast Highway from San Diego (72 mi/116 km south) or Los Angeles (50 mi/80.5 km north).

GETTING AROUND: This walkable city has ride-sharing and public transportation options, including a free weekend trolley. Rental cars come in handy for exploring, but be aware of the toll roads. (Usually handled in rental agreements, but do ask.)

PACKING TIPS: A mix of light layers, activewear, and individual style (think statement jewelry or scarves). The sea breeze can be chilly, so a jacket or sweater comes in handy, as does a pair of good walking shoes.

WEATHER: Mild year-round, with temperatures ranging from 65°F (18.3°C) in winter to 85°F (29.4°C) in summer. January through March has more rainfall. Diving visibility is better in winter, but winter can bring swells that make shore entries impossible.

IN ADDITION: If taking an Uber or Lyft from the airport or nearby city, use the code VISITLAGUNABEACH (Uber) and your first ride will be free up to $20, or VISITLAGUNA (Lyft) and receive up to $50 off your first ride.

Diving

OVERVIEW: World-class shore diving in a temperate kelp forest, a stone's throw from a lively coastal community.

- **Visibility:** From 10 to 20 feet (3 to 6 m)
- **Water Temp:** 55°F (12.7°C) in winter / 75°F (24°C) in summer
- **Depth Range:** Around 45 feet (13.7 m)

MARINE LIFE: Sharks (horn, leopard, the occasional blue or thresher), sea lions, harbor seals, kelp forests, sheepshead, Garibaldi damselfish, and sea bass

SHOP INFO: Beach Cities Scuba is the only dive shop in Laguna. This small, helpful shop can arrange gear rental, shore dives, guides, boat dives, and dive instruction. It's staffed by locals who know their backyard (and changeable dive conditions) well.

Accommodations

HIGH-END: Montage Laguna Beach is a sprawling (200-plus rooms) five-star resort located 2.5 miles (4 km) outside of Laguna Beach, perched on a coastal bluff overlooking the Pacific Ocean. ~$1,030 USD

MID-RANGE: We had so much fun staying at **The Ranch at Laguna Beach,** which is tucked away on 87 acres (35 ha). It's encircled by a canyon and located a few hundred yards from the beach and a few miles from Laguna Beach township. The Ranch is elegant and laid-back, West Coast style. The staff are relaxed, helpful, and welcoming, the rooms are spacious and comfortable, and it's a great place for families with kids. Mule deer wander the golf course with impunity. ~$429 USD

BUDGET: La Casa Del Camino is the quirky grande dame of Laguna Beach. Built in 1929, this Spanish-style, storied hotel features a collection of rooms and cottages (all styled a bit differently), and a rooftop bar. Located less than a mile (1.6 km) from town. ~$135 USD

Food & Drink

Cool and elegant, **Selanne Steak Tavern** is a classical-style restaurant in a historic 1934 home. Side dishes (like Broccolini with chilies, garlic confit, and Meyer lemon) are made to be shared. Try the Hat Trick cocktail: vodka, fresh grapefruit, St.-Germain, and agave.

The Ranch knows where everything on your plate comes from: herbs and vegetables from its own sustainable garden, single-line fish caught by local fishermen, etc. Guests can do a garden walk-through and/or arrange to go out with the fishermen (or to the market with the chef) if you'd like to source your entire meal. Delectable, delicious dining (paired with an enviable wine cellar).

La Sirena Grill serves up quality Mexican-style cuisine in a casual, almost fast-food manner: made-from-scratch taquitos, fajitas, tortas, and more, sourced sustainably and served in eco-friendly materials. A great spot for groups of friends and families.

LIZARD ISLAND

A Lesson in Endurance

Lizard Island

AUSTRALIA

The Great Barrier Reef is exactly as billed: a maze of more than 3,000 coral reefs stretching 1,429 miles (2,300 km) along Australia's eastern coast in a breathtaking palette of turquoise, gold, and emerald.

Lizard Island—a windswept collection of scrub-coated rocks, scalloped by 24 gleaming white-sand beaches—is one of the jewels in this natural crown. This three-square-mile (7.8 sq km) island is home to a luxury lodge and the Lizard Island Research Station (ground zero for coral research since 1973), an incongruous but harmonious pairing that is oddly reflective of the island itself.

The weather dictates everything here. Lizard became an island when sea levels rose 9,000 years ago, flooding the coastal plains and separating it from the Australian mainland. The 1,000-foot (305 m) hills kept the island from being submerged; they also helped Captain James Cook espy a passage out of the Great Barrier Reef, where he and the HMS *Endeavour* had become trapped. In 2014 and 2015, two tropical cyclones passed directly over the island. What the first cyclone missed, the second demolished. On the heels of this devastation, 2016 and 2017 heralded the worst cases of coral bleaching the world had ever seen, with Lizard Island at the epicenter.

But the island is a testament to nature finding a way. It is a privilege to visit this plucky place, unrivaled in her private and natural beauty. Go now. ∎

Lizard Island is scalloped by white-sand beaches and secluded bays, like the Blue Lagoon.

Relaxing on a remote tropical island can be surprisingly time-consuming, so dive straight into what's important.

A visit to the **Lizard Island Research Station** (LIRC), available to any lodge guest, should be the first stop: It will help inform everything you're seeing on the Great Barrier Reef.

This world-class facility, owned and operated by the Australian Museum, studies what makes the reef tick, and they're in a unique position to understand the sustained damage of climate change—the reef's greatest threat, confirmed by the Great Barrier Reef Marine Park Authority (GBRMPA), the government agency that manages the Great Barrier Reef Marine Park. In 2019, the GBRMPA published its five-year outlook report, downgrading the health of the Great Barrier Reef from poor to very poor.

The problem is the cumulative effect of pressures on the reef. Bleaching events, cyclones, and mass aggregations of crown of thorns sea stars have happened before, but not this fast, one after the other, giving the reef no quarter, no time to recover. This is the effect of human-made climate change: cyclones increasing in intensity; mass bleaching events caused by elevated water temperatures brought about by global warming (there

_____ SOMETHING SPECIAL _____

Lizard Island's seven-course degustation dinner (wine-paired), served in a private beach pavilion, was one of the most memorable meals of our year. (*Tip: Mind the generously served wine. One couple happily snoozed off dinner in the shrubbery.*)

have been three since 2016, and it is estimated the Great Barrier Reef has lost more than half its coral population); increased coastal runoff (the 35 catchments that drain into the Great Barrier Reef lagoon carry at least four times the sediment inflow compared to 150 years ago); and unexplained outbreaks of crown of thorns, a large sea star that can eat its way through 108 square feet (10 sq m) of coral a year.

People used to believe the world's largest coral reef system was too big to fail, but it is failing. This complex ecosystem is incredibly fragile, and it needs our help. While tourism does put pressure on an environment, scientists at the LIRC told us that pressure is outweighed by the urgency for people to see what's happening. "Apathy is one of the biggest problems the reef faces," said Dr. Penny Berents, a senior research fellow with the Australian Museum who's been visiting Lizard Island since 1975. "The best thing for the reef is if everyone sees it and says: 'No, this is too important to lose.' Having seen the reef, people are much more likely to care about it and to do something."

After visiting the LIRC, we couldn't wait to get in the water to see the Great Barrier Reef for ourselves. Even in its precarious state, it's a showstopper.

Most of the dives from Lizard Island are guided boat dives, with a number of sites to choose from within a 10- to 60-minute boat ride. The outer reef can be subject to strong currents and is better

A green turtle swims the shallows of Casuarina Beach, a popular snorkel spot with visitors.

suited to divers with more experience, but the inner reef is lazy diving: slow, no rush, plenty to see. It's ideal for learning to dive or less-experienced divers. *(Tip: Prebook all diving before arrival.)*

From walls, to sandy bottoms studded with coral bommies the size of hatchbacks, to channels cutting through barrier reef, there is always a corner to poke your head around or a crevice to shine your flashlight into. Both the inner and outer reefs are a hive of life—barramundi, octopuses, garden eels, reef fish, barracuda—guaranteeing you'll run out of air before you run out of things to look at.

The **Cod Hole** is one of the most legendary sites in this area for both divers and snorkelers, famous for its potato cod-feeding sessions. The **MV Serranidae** (the Latin name for grouper, an homage to the resident fish, a member of the grouper family) takes a mix of divers and snorkelers on a 6.5-hour day trip to the Cod Hole. Divers descend through

Lizard Island is one of the few places (apart from liveaboards) that has access to both the inner and outer Great Barrier Reef.

the surface chop and are immediately approached by the large, prettily patterned cod. The guide slowly feeds the cod, which brings in other big fish: titan triggerfish, red sea bass with tiny vampire teeth, whitetip reef sharks, and gray reef sharks.

Snorkelers hang on to a rope stretched out behind the boat, floating over a topographic map of coral cliffs and trenches and watching the activity from the surface, a rare opportunity to see some of the bigger fish usually observed only by divers.

Snorkelers should also explore house reef options, a short walk from the rooms at Lizard Island Resort. The **Clam Gardens,** for example, rivals many exclusive dive sites. We finned out over a reef filled with the iridescent greens, purples, and shocking pinks of giant clams, *Tridacna gigas,* that grow more than 4.5 feet (1.4 m) in length, the stuff of childhood Jules Verne dreams. It was encouraging to see bright blue points of staghorn coral growth, something we had learned to look for. (Thanks to our research station tour, already we were seeing the reef differently, better understanding how everything fits together.)

(Tip: Stinger suits or wet suits are recommended year-round for protection against blue bottles [Portuguese man-of-war].)

Although the Great Barrier Reef takes center stage, there are a surprising number of land-based activities to choose from on the island, including oceanside yoga in a shaded pavilion and a multitude of hikes. **Cook's Look** is the one not to miss. This steep 2.5-mile (4 km) return track is a scramble up sticky granite slopes along a mildly formed trail marked by white paint, with stunning views of the reef below.

It's easy to understand why, in 1770, Captain Cook twice hiked up to this 1,178-foot (359 m) vantage point to find a way out of the Great Barrier Reef for the **HMS *Endeavour.*** From here, the maze of the reef is decoded, a path materializing through the submerged barriers.

(Tip: Take this extraordinary hike seriously. It's three to four hours to return, and an early start is necessary to avoid the heat—and to get back in time for breakfast. Recommended: hiking boots, sun-protective clothing, plenty of water, and a

Lizard Island has a number of hiking trails, like Cook's Look, which leads to a vantage point used by Captain Cook in 1770.

backpack to keep hands free for scrambling. If you don't go with a guide, tell the resort staff your plans: This path is an ankle-turner, and there is one variety of venomous snake on the island.)

Make a Difference

Help support the critical research being done at the **Lizard Island Research Station** by donating your money or time. Direct donations can be made through the **Lizard Island Reef Research Foundation** website *(lirrf.org).* Any amount is welcome, and donors can choose to receive regular email updates about ongoing research (which is fascinating). Or apply to be a station or research volunteer, working a set number of hours per week over a 10-day to two-week period to help with maintenance or, if qualified, research. Application information is on the Lizard Island Research Station website *(lizardisland.com.au).* Download the comprehensive Lizard Island Field Guide from the website prior to visiting (island Wi-Fi is poor); it has photographs and information for more than 2,000 local species.

GETTING HERE: The one-hour, twice-daily flight from Cairns to Lizard Island gives a sense of the Great Barrier Reef's scale—and importance. The resort team will help organize everything. Bag limits (55 pounds/25 kilograms) are strictly enforced.

GETTING AROUND: Walk (the lodge is surrounded by trails), take a boat (dinghies are available to explore secluded beaches), or hitch a ride in the staff truck to the research station.

PACKING TIPS: The lodge is relaxed, but this is the perfect place to take your resort wear out for a spin. Hiking boots and a small backpack come in handy for the many trails, some of which are rugged.

WEATHER: The rainy season is December through March, but "rainy" usually means one week of heavy rain with clear weather for the remainder—and without the trade winds that blow steadily the rest of the year in this Southern Hemisphere spot. Cyclones are possible during this time.

IN ADDITION: The lodge provides reusable water bottles and free drinking water to minimize plastic usage. Wi-Fi is limited on the island.

Diving

OVERVIEW: The Great Barrier Reef is bucket list diving, and Lizard Island is one of the few places that have access to both the inner and outer reefs.

- **Visibility:** From 65 to 100 feet (20 to 30 m)
- **Water Temp:** 72°F (22°C) in winter / 80°F (27°C) in summer
- **Depth Range:** 20 to 66 feet (6 to 20 m)

MARINE LIFE: The area around Lizard Island, protected in the Great Barrier Reef World Heritage Area, is home to a staggering diversity of coral (600-plus species, including staghorn, boulder, plate, sea fans) and marine life (1,625-plus species of fish, such as potato cod and oriental sweetlips).

SHOP INFO: The resort is the only shop on the island,

and they run a good one, with high-quality gear. Diving is available to lodge guests only.

Accommodations

HIGH-END: Lizard Island was the most luxurious place we stayed of all 50 destinations—not in cost but in service: The professional, friendly staff didn't miss a beat. And Lizard really does feel like your own private island—there are so many places to seek solitude here that you don't realize how many guests fill up the 40 rooms until everyone gathers for dinner. The resort is the only one on the island, offering several accommodation options. The prime room is the **Pavilion,** a private residence perched on a ridge with sweeping ocean views and a secluded plunge pool. ~$4,060 USD

MID-RANGE: The **Oceanview Villas** are dressed to complement the impressive environment. Our room came with a resident, under-bungalow, yellow-spotted monitor lizard, which lends the island its name. (We called him Mitch.) ~$2,127 USD

BUDGET: The **Gardenview Rooms and Suites** are the place to get in touch with nature, with private decks surrounded by the landscape and nothing but birdsong, wind, and waves as background noise. ~$1,570 USD

Food & Drink

We couldn't wait for mealtimes at the resort (one of two spots to dine on the island, the other being The Marlin Bar). The **Salt Water Restaurant's** changing daily menu was a delight, with fresh, light meals (like fish with pickled fennel, grapefruit, olives, and lemon dressing) served in just-right portions. Don't miss the daily breakfast juice concoctions, such as a pineapple, ginger, mint, and apple mix.

Located next to Salt Water, the **Driftwood Bar** is the spot for pre-dinner cocktails.

The **Marlin Bar** is a rustic open-air restaurant frequented by boaties and the staff. It's open Mondays, Wednesdays (pizza night), and Fridays (tapas night).

SAINT-MALO

Tides and Time

Bretons have saltwater for blood. Brittany is bordered on three sides by the Atlantic Ocean and the English Channel, and Bretons grow up cockle-hunting at low tide, wading into the chilly surf, accompanied by the sound of gull cries. "When you are really young and really old, you swim here," one local woman told us, "otherwise it is too cold." Most Bretons have fishermen, sailors, or pirates in the family tree and proudly wear traditional blue-and-white-striped garments as a show of allegiance to their maritime past and present.

You can't escape the sea here. The walled city of Saint-Malo, our base on the Brittany coast, sees some of the highest tides in Europe, which ebb and flow 42 feet (13 m) every six hours, exposing more than a mile (1.6 km) of glistening, blushing sand. When the tide comes in, it comes in fast, frequently catching inexperienced beachcombers unaware.

There is much to see and do in Brittany and the neighboring region of Normandy. Wander the narrow streets of the medieval Corsair city of Saint-Malo. Dive the dramatic wreck-littered Brittany coastline and the macro-filled Rance estuary. Take part in a centuries-old pilgrimage to Mont-Saint-Michel. Pay homage at the lonely beaches of Utah and Omaha.

Although we spent more time on land in Brittany than in other locations, we never felt far removed from the presence of the sea. Let the tides sweep you to Brittany—and soon. ∎

The mighty, medieval seaward fortress of Saint-Malo is wrapped within thick walls and witnesses some of the highest tides in Europe.

The seaward fortress of **Saint-Malo,** the setting of Anthony Doerr's best-selling novel *All the Light We Cannot See,* is rebellious and romantic. Walls nearly 10 feet (3 m) thick, with wide city gates set at intervals, wrap around this medieval city like an embrace. Its interior is a warren of narrow and winding cobblestone streets crowded with hotels, shops, restaurants selling oysters and crepes, and pubs serving cider and beer.

Although 80 percent of the city was destroyed in World War II, a few original half-timbered buildings with resplendent stained-glass windows still stand. The rest were painstakingly rebuilt: Stones were numbered, cleaned, and replaced, one by one.

Wide battlements provide views of the sea and two nearby islands: **Petit Bé,** crowned with a fort, and **Grand Bé,** which holds the tomb of writer René de Chateaubriand. Both can be reached at low tide. A castle **(Château de St-Malo)** sits to one side of the walled city, built in the 15th century by the Duchy of Brittany who, sniffing rebellion, wanted to keep an eye on Saint-Malo's population (known as Malouins). They had good reason to be nervous:

From 1590 to 1594, Saint-Malo gained a brief spell of independence it's never forgotten. "Our motto is: 'I am Malouin. Malouin for sure. Breton, maybe. French if there is something left over,'" one local told us.

(Tip: Self-exploring is fun and easy, although guided tours are worthwhile.)

Don't miss the opportunity to see the splendor of Saint-Malo from the perspective of a traditional, **horse-drawn carriage ride with Les Chevaux De La Mer.** This hour-long outing at low tide is a magical way to slow down and take Saint-Malo in stride from the comfort of a covered wagon with a cheese platter, baguettes, and wine at the ready. Guided by Solene Lavenan and pulled by a content, dappled-gray Percheron ("I only do two trips a day to keep the horses happy," Solene said), we learned about the area's past and present, watching the horse's big gray hindquarters move in rhythm, like the tides. "The sea is everything to us, but we can no longer rely on it," Solene told us. "In the last 10 years or so, the weather has turned upside down: warm when it's supposed to be cold, and cold when it's supposed to be warm."

Those changing weather patterns are affecting Brittany's seabirds: As the water warms, fish are moving north, which means the birds are having to travel farther to find food.

Cap Fréhel, an hour's drive west of Saint-Malo, is a special (and protected) nesting area for maritime birds, which makes it an ideal spot for an easy wander and a bit of bird-watching. Heather-lined walkways wind along pink sandstone cliffs, which drop suddenly into an energetic sea, punctuated by towering sea stacks that house resting and nesting native and migratory birds, like cormorants, petrels, gannets, gulls, oystercatchers, and the strangely goth-looking razorbill penguins.

The Benedictine abbey and UNESCO World Heritage wonder of Normandy's Mont-Saint-Michel rises from milky floodplains.

Make a Difference

Carbon offsetting (compensating for your carbon dioxide emissions) is both confusing and essential. Tourism's contribution to global carbon dioxide emissions is smaller than other industries, but difficult to quantify accurately. Air travel, which is challenging to decarbonize, makes up the largest proportion of travel emissions. We were determined to carbon offset our travel for this book. We researched options and offset more than 75 percent of our travel using a carbon offset program. However, during our fieldwork, we realized we wanted to do things differently—perhaps targeting a habitat (like mangroves) we know needs help or looking into carbon capture versus offsets. We're working on finding the best solution for us. If you're struggling with this, too, keep trying—doing something is better than doing nothing.

(Tip: Birding is best from February to mid-July; don't forget your binoculars and stick to marked paths in this fragile environment.)

Looking out over the expanse of the English Channel, flecked by the wings of swooping seabirds, it's easy to contemplate the maritime history this place has seen, and the hidden wrecks that attract divers to this cold-water coast. It is rumored there are more than 400 wrecks in the area, with more still being discovered. Many are from World War II, and diving them is an all-day affair, with travel times to sites ranging from 40 minutes to 1.5 hours. Depths extend beyond 66 feet (20 m), requiring longer surface intervals between dives.

There are German patrol boats, sunken planes, and the **Walter Darré** and **Hey Hinrich,** torpedoed on the same night in 1944 while escorting a convoy. They are now home to lobster, conger eels, and other macro life. The **S.S. Hilda** is a passenger steamship that sank in bad weather in 1905. She now lies in 82 feet (25 m) of water and is a popular dive site, as well as a memorial—most of her passengers never made it to shore.

(Tip: Wreck diving is very tide dependent. Speak to a dive shop before booking your trip to get the timing right.)

Shore-diving the Rance estuary is a different experience. Also known as Reince, home of the oldest tidal power station in the world, the estuary extends inland on the left-hand side of Saint-Malo.

Gray seals are right at home in the cold waters off the Brittany coast.

This dive reminded us strongly of pier diving: a shore entry, low visibility, and slow-paced. It's all about taking your time and appreciating the area's unique marine life: spiny lobster, octopuses, spider crabs, conger eels, and John Dory. Diving the Rance gave us a better feel and understanding for the English Channel environment—you come away with a strong sense of this place.

(Tip: Although new divers are welcome, Brittany is more suited for divers with some experience, due to the currents, low visibility, depths, and cold water.)

Neighboring Normandy is also worth visiting. Take part in a centuries-old pilgrimage to the Benedictine abbey and UNESCO World Heritage wonder of **Mont-Saint-Michel,** about one hour's drive east of Saint-Malo. Its iconic pyramidal shape, surrounded by milky floodplains, is spine-tingling. Mont-Saint-Michel is crowded and touristy: People jostle along narrow, winding streets, spill out of busy cafés and taverns, pay for guided tours, and dodge vendors hawking souvenirs. But the fun thing is, this is the way it's been for centuries—it's easy to imagine pilgrims doing the exact same thing, only without Instagram.

From Mont-Saint-Michel, it's a 2.5-hour drive northeast to the beaches of **Omaha** and **Utah,** the stage of D-Day, one of the greatest amphibious assaults the world has ever known. In early June 1944, this now peaceful place would have been pandemonium and purgatory.

Utah Beach and the seaside **Utah Beach D-Day Museum** got under our skins. The museum is a fascinating place to spend time, featuring 22,600 square feet (2,100 sq m) of interactive exhibits, artifacts, and equipment (including a B-26 Marauder). There's even a dis-

___ WISH WE KNEW_____

Saint-Malo has some of the highest tides in Europe: 42 feet (13 m) every six hours. Tide tables, which determine dive opportunities, are mapped out months in advance. Research before you plan your trip. (Beachcombers: Tides come in *fast.*)

play about *Band of Brothers'* Easy Company.

However, nothing compares to the feeling of standing on that lonely stretch of red-tinged sand, speckled with the long shells of razor clams and crowned by high dunes with waving grasses. Utah Beach holds the weight of its history. Whatever you learned at school or have seen in movies, it doesn't hold a candle to standing on the sand of Utah with your own two feet, experiencing this place for yourself.

Tides and time—you're never far from either here.

A diver shines a flashlight on a lobster. Brittany is a mix of unique estuary diving combined with WWII wrecks in the English Channel.

NEED TO KNOW

GETTING HERE: Great Britain and Ireland are hubs for Brittany's regional airports (and ferries). We took the train from Paris to Saint-Malo (around 3.5 hours), which was inexpensive and pleasant.

GETTING AROUND: A rental car is useful for day trips. Otherwise, walking and cycling are great ways to get around Saint-Malo.

PACKING TIPS: Brittany is colder than expected: The wind yanks the heat from the sun. Layers are the way to go. Don't forget good walking shoes and reusable bags.

WEATHER: This is an oceanic climate, so summers are cool (around 70°F/21°C). Autumn is still mild, but growing windier and rainier as winter approaches. Winter is cold, damp, and delightfully moody.

IN ADDITION: In Saint-Malo, Cap Fréhel, Mont Saint-Michel, and Utah and Omaha Beaches, guided tours are available. Book in advance, especially in summer.

Diving

OVERVIEW: World War II wrecks and unique estuary diving around the Brittany coast, which has some of the highest and most dramatic tides in Europe. This cold-water destination is best suited to divers with a little more experience.

- **Visibility:** 20 feet on average (6 m)
- **Water Temp:** 46°F (8°C) in winter / 64°F (18°C) in summer
- **Depth Range:** 66 to 197 feet (20 to 60 m)

MARINE LIFE: Brittany is big on macro and smaller critters: seahorses, pipefish, conger eels, octopuses, cuttlefish, nudibranchs, spider crabs, spiny lobster, cockles, razor clams, lesser spotted dogfish, and John Dory.

SHOP INFO: We dove with **Nautilus Plongée** (based in Dinard, a short drive from Saint-Malo). This boutique, family-owned shop tailors diving to your schedule, desires, and level. Training and private dives are available. They're open year-round, have their own boat, and run a good operation. Although we didn't dive with them, **Saint Malo Plongée Émeraude** (Saint-Malo Emerald Diving Club) also has a good reputation. They offer courses and guided dives; open year-round, they also have their own boat and on-site pool for training.

Accommodations

HIGH-END: You can stay *in* Mont-Saint-Michel. There are a few hotels on this rocky islet (all overpriced—it is what it is), and **La Mère Poulard** is a historic inn (1888) in the heart of the medieval village. Rooms are simple, and the restaurant is renowned for its omelets. ~$200 USD

MID-RANGE: **Hôtel France & Chateaubriand** is an elegant, oh-so-French establishment in Saint-Malo. Twenty of its 80 rooms have a dramatic view of the tidal plains that's worth splurging for. This 19th-century hotel's character and location can't be beat. ~$100 USD

BUDGET: **Hôtel Les Charmettes** offers charming accommodations right on the sea, a 20-minute walk along the promenade to Saint-Malo. This comfortable 16-room hotel feels more like a guesthouse, with unfussy hospitality and a mix of snug garden- and sea-view rooms. A lovely and convenient place to stay. ~$83 USD

Food & Drink

Brasserie du Sillon is a classic seafood restaurant located right on the seawall. We dined watching the tide come in, until the waves were striking our second-story window. The taste is straight from the sea and classical, the ambiance casual elegant (one or two diners even brought their dogs along). *(Tip: Not unexpectedly, everything is in French.)*

Hôtel Les Charmettes has an on-site bistro (indoors or seaside on a wooden terrace sprinkled with sand) serving simple, fresh food: homemade sandwiches, casseroles, kebabs, and desserts.

Crêperie Grand Mère Alice is a cozy restaurant located within the walls of Saint-Malo, serving up Breton specialties: gourmet crepes and pancakes, both sweet and savory, sourced locally.

MARLBOROUGH SOUNDS

The Sound of Nature

Queen Charlotte Sound (Tōtaranui) is the easternmost of the Marlborough Sounds, the fragmented northern tip of New Zealand's South Island. This massive series of sunken river valleys has more than 932 miles (1,500 km) of coastline, with ridgebacks and forested coves sheltering the deep, cool waterways that wind from the rowdy Cook Strait to the mainland. Every bay beckons, replete with native forest, birds, and marine life, including dolphins, stingrays, orcas, and New Zealand fur seals.

Queen Charlotte Sound was an important place to Māori (the *tangata whenua* or Indigenous people of New Zealand) who inhabited the area around 500 years before Europeans arrived. The Māori used it as a place to fish and gather food. It was also an important place to British explorer Captain James Cook, who spent 168 days here between 1770 and 1777—more time than he spent anywhere else in New Zealand. Cook favored the area's sheltered anchorages as a place for rest and repairs, taking on supplies, and tending to the wounded.

Queen Charlotte Sound's reputation as a place of relaxation and rejuvenation hasn't changed. It is popular with holidaymakers and famous for the Queen Charlotte Track, a 44-mile (70 km) coastal trail that can be hiked, mountain biked, or kayaked over three to five days.

These sunken river valleys are also one of New Zealand's lesser-known dive destinations, which is surprising, given that one of the world's biggest and best diveable shipwrecks—the 577-foot (176 m) *Mikhail Lermontov*—lurks nearby.

Follow in the footsteps of those who have already fallen in love with this restorative pocket of nature. ∎

View from the swimming pool of the *Mikhail Lermontov*, one of the world's biggest and best diveable shipwrecks

NEW ZEALAND
Marlborough Sounds

The **Queen Charlotte Track (QCT),** which runs between Anakiwa and Ship Cove, is one of our favorite hikes. New Zealand's walkways are renowned for their beauty, but no other walk has the QCT's flexibility, which makes it a truly enjoyable and unique experience.

The track is accessed by boat from the gateway town of Picton and can be tackled from either direction. You can hike, mountain bike, kayak, or mix and match approaches (for example, hike the first day, bike the second, and kayak the third). Or you can walk shorter segments of the track, getting dropped off and picked up by water taxis that transfer your luggage from one overnight stop to the next (which means you only need to carry a daypack).

(Tip: This flexible approach means the QCT is ideal for multigenerational families and those with young kids.)

Along the route, there are a number of overnight options, ranging from campsites to luxury lodges, as well as shelters, toilets, and picnic stops. You can make your own plans or have a company make all the arrangements for you. We always use **Wilderness Guides,** owned and operated by two New Zealanders who grew up in the region. They offer a variety of trips—guided or independent with support. Our preference is to hike the first two days of the track and kayak the last leg.

This area is known for its seafood, like these greenshell mussels, and its wine—it's part of New Zealand's largest Sauvignon Blanc region.

SOMETHING SPECIAL

Hop on the Mail Boat Cruise with **Beachcomber Cruises** in Picton, a half-day excursion that is part of a 150-year-old tradition delivering mail, groceries, and schoolwork to families living in remote bays. Great sightseeing and people-meeting!

(Tip: The QCT is made possible thanks to private landowners. Please stick to the track, close gates, and pack out all trash, including toilet paper and food scraps. Even organic scraps like apple cores and banana peels are harmful to wildlife.)

The QCT follows a raised ridgeline, the ocean winking in and out of view on either side. As most overnight stops are located down on the coast, days begin with an uphill push to rejoin the ridge, a wake-up call that gets the muscles singing.

Along the track, conveniently placed picnic tables and benches overlook sublime vistas. During lunch stops, you're likely to meet a New Zealand native: the weka, a flightless, chicken-size brown bird with ruby red eyes that materializes out of the undergrowth to brazenly stare you down for scraps. (Don't feed them.)

Birds love it here. Mornings begin with the metallic notes of bellbirds and tuis (which have a jaunty cravat of white feathers at their throats). Listen for the velvet *whoosh* that comes from the wingbeats of the kererū (New Zealand's native pigeon) and the high-pitched squeaks of pīwakawakas, also known as fantails. These cheeky, cotton-ball-size birds are our favorites and they love hikers. Fantails will flit along with you, spreading their black-and-white tails and dancing on branches. (Hikers kick up the insects they like to feed on; try squeaking back to them for a lively conversation.)

Much of the track is enclosed in forest: manuka,

native beech, silver ferns (New Zealand's native emblem; gently turn over fronds to see the silver-white underside), and ramrod-straight rimu, many of which were growing during the time Cook visited the area.

These forests, like all forests, are magic. They sequester carbon, produce oxygen, protect the soil, and provide homes for countless species, safeguarding biodiversity. Spending time in the woods also has a profound and well-documented benefit on our physical and mental health, which is instantly apparent here.

Yet we tend to treat forests as commodities. Humans have cut down half the planet's trees since the beginning of civilization, and more than half the land on Earth has been transformed into farms or pastures. New Zealand isn't immune. Before people arrived here, 80 percent of New Zealand's land was covered in dense native forest; now it's around 30 percent.

The area's magic continues underwater, as well. The Queen Charlotte Sound (QCS) is not well known

The quiet, sheltered coves of Queen Charlotte Sound have long been favored by sailors—from Māori to Captain James Cook to holidaymakers.

as a dive destination, but it's diveable year-round, thanks to protection from the inlets. All diving is from boats departing from the Picton Marina. Dive sites are peppered along the sound, all the way to the mouth of the Cook Strait. (It's common to spot dolphins, New Zealand fur seals, little blue penguins, and occasionally orcas on boat travel to and from sites.)

Just out of Picton is **Double Cove,** a nice little reef that is home to the **S.S. Koi,** a purpose-sunk, iron-hulled former passenger ferry resting upright in 39 feet (12 m) of water. The *Koi* has a penetrable engine room and holds, and is a good wreck for new divers and night dives. Visibility usually isn't great, but the macro is—decorator crabs, seahorses, blennies, and nudibranchs. Gently swaying kelp forests offer cover to crayfish (Kiwi-speak for rock lobster) and carpet sharks, while the Cook Strait currents bring in larger fish like blue cod, yellow-eyed mullet, and leatherjackets.

At the opening of the QCS, across from Ship Cove, is **Long Island-Kokomohua Marine Reserve.** This site is protected from sharp southerly winds, and the dives here are shallow, around 49 feet (15 m). Kelp beds obscure the rocky outcrops on this submerged reef, which collects schools of fish like kingfish, tarakihi, blue cod, and butterfly perch.

Logistics-wise, because diving is based out of Picton, dive trips should be scheduled before or after tackling the QCT. (*Tip: If you're traveling with a non-diver, you can arrange to meet them mid-track—just hop on a water taxi.*)

For those interested in diving the **Mikhail Lermontov**—a Russian cruise ship that is one of the biggest diveable ships in the world (577 ft/ 176 m)—dive trips, again, should be scheduled before or after tackling the QCT. Because the *Lermontov* rests in one of the less accessible areas of the Marlborough Sounds, divers base themselves at the remote Lermontov Lodge in Port Gore. From there, it's a five-minute boat ride to the wreck site.

The *Lermontov* is a 20,000-plus-gross-ton gargantuan that sank in 1986 after a nasty close encounter with the reef, coming to rest on her starboard side. Although hundreds of people were on board, there was only one fatality; experienced local skippers saw the ship foundering and rushed to her aid.

Guided dives range from 39 to 118 feet (12 to 36 m), both on the outside of the wreck and penetration and decompression dives for more expe-

Punga People, an art installation featuring punga trees carved into faces with paua shell eyes, keep watch at eclectic Lochmara Lodge.

rienced divers. (The *Lermontov* is a candy store for tech divers!) Outside the hull, a kelp forest shelters moki, cod, dogfish, carpet sharks, and octopuses. Inside, there are staircases, chandeliers, a swimming pool, and more.

From weka to wrecks, this place is something special, and there are many ways—from diving to hiking to kayaking—to experience it.

Make a Difference

Trees That Count (*treesthatcount.co.nz*) is a national project delivered by **Project Crimson Trust** (*project crimson.org.nz*) in partnership with New Zealand's Department of Conservation. They mobilize New Zealanders to plant native trees (such as the rimu and beech seen on the Queen Charlotte Track) to restore the environment, mitigate climate change, and protect biodiversity. So far, they have planted nearly one million native trees. Here's how it works: You can fund or gift a tree via the website, which purchases a native tree to be planted and cared for by one of the community-based planting projects around New Zealand. You can also volunteer your time or land (if in New Zealand), or get involved as a business or family.

NEED TO KNOW

GETTING HERE: Marlborough Airport is located just outside Blenheim; it's a 30-minute drive to Picton. (Taxis and shuttles available.) There are also two ferry companies (Interislander and Bluebridge) running regular and picturesque services between Wellington and Picton.

GETTING AROUND: You don't need a rental car in Picton unless you want to explore the wider area. Beachcomber Cruises in Picton is the way to get around on water, offering transfers and water taxis.

PACKING TIPS: All-weather outdoor clothes. If walking the track, have a daypack with park pass, map, warm layers, swimsuit, plenty of water, basic first-aid supplies (including flashlight and sunscreen), snacks, and small bags to pack out trash and toilet paper. Pack a rain jacket and rain pants, and wear sturdy boots. We always carry a small thermos of tea, as well.

WEATHER: Picton's climate is mild and temperate, ranging from 42°F (5.5°C) to 70°F (21°C). During Southern Hemisphere summer months and public holidays, book well in advance. Diving is year-round, with September to November having the best visibility.

IN ADDITION: This area is New Zealand's largest Sauvignon Blanc region. Wine-tasting tours are a highlight. Another must-visit is the Omaka Aviation Heritage Centre in Blenheim, with WWI and WWII exhibitions, as well as joy flights.

Diving

OVERVIEW: A series of sunken river valleys containing reefs, reserves, and wrecks. This is an off-the-radar dive destination in a stunning natural environment.

- Visibility: From 16 to 82 feet (5 to 25 m)
- Water Temp: 54°F (12°C) in winter / 65°F (18°C) in summer
- Depth Range: 39 to 118 feet (12 to 36 m)

MARINE LIFE: Spiny dogfish, crayfish (Kiwi-speak for rock lobster), kingfish, blue and red cod, blennies, triplefins, terakihi, carpet sharks, octopuses, and sea perch

SHOP INFO: Go Dive Pacific is a well-set-up, customer-focused shop, offering small half-day and day trips for recreational and tech divers within the sounds, as well as expeditions to the *Mikhail Lermontov*. Open Water to technical training offered.

Accommodations

HIGH-END: Bay of Many Coves is a jewel, a luxury five-star resort with apartments and suites. It has a touch of 1950s resort charm, modernized and nestled into a lush hillside (they've planted more than 13,000 native trees within their 247-acre/100-ha site). It also has beaches, a heated outdoor pool, and a restaurant. ~$642 USD

MID-RANGE: Punga Cove is a popular stopover on the track, with a range of cozy accommodations (hillside suites, chalets, and base camp facilities for travelers on a budget) tucked into a hillside of punga ferns overlooking a stunning bay. ~$60 USD (base camp) and $200 USD (chalet)

BUDGET: We saw kids throw tantrums when forced to leave **Lochmara Lodge.** This eclectic 14-room lodge on Lochmara Bay is located on an 11-acre (4.5 ha) property filled with artwork, games, and hammocks. Hand-feed eels, stingrays, pigs, and Kākāriki parakeets, and visit the glowworm grotto after dark. ~$72 USD

Food & Drink

The **Foredeck,** Bay of Many Coves' signature restaurant, is fine dining by candlelight with views overlooking the bay. Specialties are crafted using local and seasonal produce accompanied by award-winning wines. Open to non-guests; reservations essential.

Punga Cove's atmospheric **Punga Fern Restaurant and Bar** has à la carte dining featuring dishes with Marlborough seafood, produce, and wild game. Down on the jetty, the **Boatshed Café & Bar** has more casual fare and is a popular happy hour venue.

In Picton, **Le Café** is a restaurant, bar, and live music venue with sweeping views of the marina.

MILFORD SOUND

The Lost World

Milford Sound (Piopiotahi) is a prime-val, prehistoric place. Sharp, teethlike granite mountains rise 5,551 feet (1,692 m) directly from the ocean floor, neck-craners and jaw-droppers, framing a fjord holding oily-looking jade green water.

Tucked away in the southwest corner of New Zealand's South Island, Milford Sound is part of Fiord-land National Park, New Zealand's largest national park (2.9 million acres/1.2 million ha), a wild area in the heart of Te Wāhipounamu-South West New Zealand, a UNESCO World Heritage site.

It rains 25 feet (7.6 m) a year here, and that rainfall is the key ingredient in the amplified alchemy of this otherworldly landscape. It's critical to the lush flora that stubbornly clings to impossibly steep rock faces coursing with silver threads of waterfalls. It's also critical to the bizarre marine life. The rain strips tannins from the soil, layering tinted freshwater 30 feet (9 m) thick on the fjord's saltwater, choking off light, tricking creatures of the deep into thinking they're in hundreds of feet of water when they're actually in 50 feet (15 m).

This area is home to the Milford Track, a 32-mile (53.5 km) trail known as the Finest Walk in the World. It is also a popular destination for day trips and overnight cruises. For divers, Milford Sound is somewhat of a fond secret. This marine reserve is off the beaten recreational dive track, but beloved by those in the know. It is a unique area, filled with life (from black coral forests to sevengill sharks to Fiordland crested penguins), making for unforgettable diving. ∎

NEW ZEALAND
Milford Sound □

Neck-craners and jaw-droppers: The granite mountains framing Milford Sound add a wild, remote feel to this special place.

Milford Sound stretches roughly 10 miles (16 km) from Freshwater Basin to the Tasman Sea. It's actually a fjord, rather than a sound (having been carved by glaciers, not rivers), that is nearly two miles (3 km) across at its widest point. The fjord runs more than 882 feet (269 m) deep, hemmed in by jagged peaks that are still being born. The Alpine Fault, one of the world's major plate boundary faults, crosses the mouth of Milford Sound, shifting around two to three centimeters every year.

This is the wettest inhabited place in New Zealand, and one of the wettest on Earth. It rains an average of 182 days per year, which keeps the towering Lady Bowen Falls (531 feet/162 m), one of Milford's two permanent waterfalls, in business.

Milford Sound is located at the end of an adventurous road that winds through the Eglinton Valley (a golden tussock carpet flanked by mountains) before siphoning vehicles through the Homer Tunnel, a 0.8-mile (1.3 km) wormhole hewed largely by hand from solid granite.

(Tip: You might be lucky enough to spot kea en route. These intelligent birds are the only alpine parrots in the world, with brilliant orange coloring under their wings and curved beaks. You may catch them calmly dismantling your car or removing

The Milford Sound road is 3,084 feet (940 m) above sea level at its highest point. Divers need to plan for the altitude, perhaps booking an overnight cruise or lodge stay after diving (especially tech dives). **Descend Scuba** can help advise.

anything left unattended; do not feed them.)

There is plenty of hiking in this area, which is as hard as you want it to be. (Bear in mind that help can be difficult to come by in this remote place.) Day cruises are also popular and efficient ways to explore Milford Sound, like **Southern Discoveries' Encounter Nature Cruise** on the *Lady Bowen*. This two- to three-hour trip takes place on one of the smaller boats running in the area, with an indoor seated area, outdoor viewing deck, and café serving up warming soup, coffee, and sandwiches (bring cash).

On board, we slowly cruise out into the sound, pausing to admire some snoozing New Zealand fur seals, or to crane our necks at waterfalls that seem to descend from the sky itself. During the trip, we learn about the area's flora and fauna, history and legends, some of which go hand in hand—sandflies, for example, the blight on this otherwise brilliant location, were dubbed the "most mischievous animal" by Captain Cook in 1773. According to Māori legend, the underworld goddess Hine-nui-te-pō was fearful humans would not want to leave the paradise of Fiordland so she created sandflies as a most effective reminder that we shouldn't linger too long.

Hine-nui-te-pō was wise to be worried: Milford Sound has long cast a spell over travelers. Tourism was already booming here back in the 1890s as legend of the region's wild beauty attracted walkers by the droves. Before the 2020 pandemic,

Milford Sound has unforgettable, otherworldly diving, with marine life ranging from octopuses to black coral forests to sevengill sharks.

Overnight cruises aboard vessels like the *Milford Wanderer* are a memorable way to experience Milford Sound.

Milford Sound was reaching critical mass: 500,000 visitors in 2012 soared to more than 900,000 in 2018, 90 percent of whom came from overseas. (Many Kiwis haven't been to Milford, deeming it "too touristy.")

The combination of Milford's remote location, coupled with its fragile ecosystem, means that something needs to give. There was a plan: Back in 2007, the Fiordland National Park management proposed capping the daily limit of tourists to 4,000, but that was never enforced. At the time of writing, restricting visitor numbers is being reconsidered, but that approach isn't popular with everyone. And therein lies the rub: weighing the incalculable benefits of travel against its very real cost. There is no easy answer, no silver-bullet solution.

The day cruise wraps up with two special activities: a 45-minute **kayak,** gently paddling around protected Harrison Cove, before visiting the **Underwater Observatory.** This is New Zealand's only floating underwater observatory, a circular viewing room located 33 feet (10 m) below the surface, giving non-divers a literal window into the area's deepwater emergence in action: the tannin-rich layer of freshwater convincing dark-loving marine life to thrive near the surface.

And this is why Milford Sound is so special to divers. Divers descend through the cold and disorienting cloud of freshwater to reach the warmer, clearer saltwater below, revealing gently sloping rock reefs and walls. The walls are carpeted in yellow zoanthids and bright red coral, a protected species that can be found around 59 feet (18 m). In some areas, the walls plunge downward beyond sight—one reason why this relatively unexplored area is so attractive to tech divers.

On our first dive, we followed a wall with an abundance of nudibranchs, sponges, and gorgonians. More than 150 species of fish can be found here, and we shared the water with schooling kingfish, blue cod, girdled wrasse, and spiny dogfish. A New Zealand fur seal and a couple of sevengill sharks also turned up to have a look at us.

Our second dive was deeper, with more spiny dogfish and large crayfish (Kiwi-speak for rock lobster). We also explored the area's black coral forests, a deep-sea coral usually found at depths below 262.5 feet (80 m). Here, it can be found at 26 feet (8 m). Fiordland is believed to have the world's highest concentration of black coral trees, which have feathery white branches and are often wrapped in striped snake stars. (These echinoderms have a symbiotic relationship with the coral.) Black coral grows very slowly (around 1 to 2 cm per year), and the colonies here are believed to be hundreds of years old, reaching heights of 16.4 feet (5 m).

This area is a marine reserve, established in 1993. Dive sites (which don't have names) are chosen based on what the weather is doing. Most days are two dives, kept on the shallow side (82 ft/25 m) due to the high-altitude road. A hot drink and snacks are ready and waiting on the boat between dives. (Sometimes the surface interval includes a short walk to a secluded waterfall, as well.)

Do not leave Milford Sound without embarking on an **overnight cruise,** like Real Journeys' *Milford Mariner* or sister ship *Milford Wanderer*. Designed to replicate traditional trading scows, these voyages depart around 4:30 p.m., cruising the sound

Fiordland's wild beauty has attracted hikers since the 1890s. The most popular walk is the 33.2-mile (53.5 km) Milford Track.

with weather-dependent activities on offer (kayaking, a tender boat cruise, even swimming) before mooring up in Harrison Cove for the evening.

After a delicious buffet dinner, the stars pop out in a sky free from light pollution and the sound settles down to sleep. Even more spectacular is the quiet of the morning, like dawn crowning the very first day, waking up to a still beauty and all the promise morning and this remarkable place bring.

Make a Difference

There are two Māori values every traveler should be familiar with: *manaakitanga* ("hospitality," a culture of looking after one another) and *kaitiakitanga* ("guardianship"—a culture of looking after the environment). We can all practice being better travelers, better stewards, looking after each other and the places we visit. A few tips from our travel colleagues on how to leave the world a little *better* for wear: (1) **Slow down and savor:** Spend more time in one place rather than speeding through; (2) **Take the road (or season) less traveled:** Visit lesser-known destinations or travel at off-peak times; (3) **Travel for the future:** Think long term—is your travel experience (choices, activities, etc.) leaving this place as good as or better than you found it?

GETTING HERE: Driving takes roughly five hours (one way) from Queenstown and three hours from Te Anau, with no fuel stops between Te Anau and Milford Sound. Research the route and leave plenty of time. Bus trips from Te Anau and Queenstown available.

GETTING AROUND: You will need transportation (rental car or bus reservations).

PACKING TIPS: Wet-weather gear (jackets, pants, bags) and layers (for a change of clothes and changing weather). Anti-itch cream comes in handy.

WEATHER: Year-round rain with some stunning, sunny days. New Zealand's Southern Hemisphere summer (December through February, around 64°F/18°C) is busy, with pressure on bookings and increased road traffic. Winter (May to September, 41°F/5°C) is beautiful, but with more challenging road conditions.

IN ADDITION: Sandflies are tiny insects with a bite that lasts for days. Wear environmentally friendly repellent on exposed skin. (Whatever you put on ends up in nature, and 900,000-plus visitors a year have an impact.)

Diving

OVERVIEW: Dive one of the most otherworldly and unique places on the planet, where deepwater creatures thrive at shallow depths. Diving Milford Sound is easy, but cold, and it can be spooky for inexperienced divers.

- **Visibility:** 0 at the surface; 10 to 25 feet (3 to 7.6 m) below the freshwater level
- **Water Temp:** Freshwater layer: 36 to 46°F (2 to 8°C); saltwater layer: 52 to 59°F (11 to 15°C)
- **Depth Range:** 66 to 82 feet (20 to 25 m)

MARINE LIFE: Black coral forests, red coral, sea pens, glass sponges, rock lobster, sharks (spiny dogfish, carpet, sevengill, sixgill), conger eels, octopuses, New Zealand fur seals, spiny sea dragons, dolphins (dusky and bottlenose), and Fiordland crested penguins

SHOP INFO: Descend Scuba is the only dive operation in Milford Sound. The experienced team offers guided dives and courses for recreational and tech divers (Open Water to rebreather). Diving is year-round and prior bookings essential. Trips depart from the Milford Marina, which has basic facilities and is the launch point for their two small but stocked vessels. Note the departure point—Deepwater Basin Boat Ramp—is in a different location from the main tourism operations.

Accommodations

HIGH-END: The 60-person *Milford Mariner* is snug and comfortable, with private cabins, viewing decks, an observation lounge, and dining saloon (serving a three-course buffet dinner and cooked breakfast). *~$175 USD*

MID-RANGE: Milford Sound Lodge is the only accommodation in Milford Sound, with secluded chalets and suites. There is also an adjoining campervan site. *~$39 USD* (campervan) and *$225 USD* (lodge)

BUDGET: Eglinton Valley Camp is located roughly halfway between Te Anau and Milford and is a good budget/overflow option, with views of the Eglinton Valley. There are six simple units of various configurations with small kitchens (bring your own food; staples like tea and sugar provided). There is also a small campground. *~$13 USD* (campground) and *$100 USD* (unit)

Food & Drink

Pio Pio Restaurant at Milford Sound Lodge is open for lunch and dinner for guests and day visitors, serving locally sourced food and drink, like Fiordland wild venison and craft beers.

The **Fat Duck Gastropub** in Te Anau is a popular stop pre- or post–Milford Sound, serving casual meals (including vegan options). It often has live music or rugby on the big screen.

If traveling through Queenstown, head to **Tanoshi Teppan and Sake Bar** on Cow Lane for authentic Japanese cuisine in an intimate setting. This is one of our favorites: Chris can eat his weight in the spicy fried chicken wings. It's small and popular—book in advance!

RAJA AMPAT

Fit for Four Kings

B est diving (and snorkeling) of our entire journey.

    There. We said it.

This is the richest coral reef in the world, with more than 1,300 species of reef fish and 70 percent of the world's known coral species.

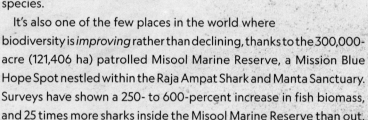

It's also one of the few places in the world where biodiversity is *improving* rather than declining, thanks to the 300,000-acre (121,406 ha) patrolled Misool Marine Reserve, a Mission Blue Hope Spot nestled within the Raja Ampat Shark and Manta Sanctuary. Surveys have shown a 250- to 600-percent increase in fish biomass, and 25 times more sharks inside the Misool Marine Reserve than out.

What does that look like to divers and snorkelers? Thick schools of diverse species of fish. Manta rays swooping over vibrant and varied coral reefs. No wonder the name Raja Ampat translates to the "Four Kings."

Located in the northwest corner of Indonesia's West Papua province, the Raja Ampat archipelago sits in the Coral Triangle. It is popular with liveaboards, but Misool Resort, an honest-to-goodness eco-resort in the deep south of Raja Ampat, is the jewel in these four kings' crowns.

You will leave your heart here, in the care of thumbnail-size pink pygmy seahorses; with the baby blacktip reef sharks that boldly cruise the shallows at low tide; and with the amazing people who make Misool what it is. ∎

Baby blacktip reef sharks share Misool Resort's protected North Lagoon with a snorkeler.

Misool Resort is hidden in a maze of islands, 103 miles (165 km) from the nearest port and 12 miles (20 km) from the closest village. The area is spiked with spires of karst covered in green vegetation, rising from surrounding lagoons that fade from crystal to the deep blue of drop-offs.

The elegantly rustic Misool Resort is on one of these islands—Batbitim. Eight stilted water cottages and the restaurant circle the North Lagoon, a protected snorkeler's paradise. Over the hill are seven more beachfront villas, reached by a short, steep walk or by water taxi. We stayed on the South Beach, and the evening water taxi rides under an inky, star-studded sky, trailing our hands in the ocean to create green sparks of bioluminescence, were peace-filled moments we still treasure.

The resort's origin story is a remarkable tale best heard in full during one of the evening presentations, complete with photos that bring the herculean effort home. In brief, Misool is the vision of two broke dive instructors, Marit and Andrew Miners, who stumbled across paradisiacal Batbitim Island (and a recently abandoned shark-finning camp)

during a surface interval. It spurred them to action. They contacted the local villages who were battling with outside fishermen plundering their traditional fishing territories. A partnership was formed, and Misool was born, the eco-resort that would fund conservation work in the area.

Since its inception, Misool has trained and funded a local 18-person Ranger Patrol to maintain constant vigilance on the marine reserve. They've also set up job and recycling programs, all while developing one of the best dive and snorkeling lodges on the planet.

If you ever doubt a handful of passionate and determined people can make a difference in this world, Misool is the place to find your faith. And we say that with a sweeping gesture—Misool is a team effort: the founders, the village partners, the staff.

This small resort (max 40 guests) runs on a relaxed schedule that guests can participate in, or not. (Many choose to kayak or read in overwater hammocks.) Divers are split into small groups and have the option of joining several daily guided boat dives. A special touch: Dive groups rotate around different sites (there are more than 60 within a one-hour radius) so that no site receives too much pressure or crowding.

Here's another special touch: Snorkelers are treated like divers, with twice-daily guided trips, taking them to different places in the reserve. Misool is the only place we've been that does that and, given the number of snorkelers staying at the resort with us, word is deservedly getting around.

As for the diving, every descent was exceptional and different. This ecosystem of fringing reefs, mangroves, and seamounts has been referred to as a "species factory," and the amount and diversity of marine life here is staggering.

A Moorish idol enjoys a cleaning over a barrel sponge. Biodiversity is actually improving inside the patrolled Misool Marine Reserve.

Make a Difference

Misool Resort exists to fund the **Misool Foundation** *(misoolfoundation.org),* which tasks itself with safeguarding this biodiverse area and empowering local communities. The resort donates a portion of profits to the foundation, as well as $100 USD per visitor, inviting guests to match that. In 2019, the resort donated $358,950 USD to the foundation—your visit *does* make a difference. Projects include the Ranger Patrol; education programs; community recycling (the foundation purchases rubbish from communities and ships it to be recycled—they collected 700 metric tons [more than 770 U.S. tons] of rubbish in 2019); and creating sustainable jobs for local people. Many staff started as dishwashers and worked their way to dive guides. Guests can help by paying for dive courses; speak to Misool if interested. You can also donate directly.

Most dives are gentle drifts (depths around 76 ft/23 m) along walls with branching coral and gorgonians, where you're likely to spot moray eels, electric clams, and pygmy seahorses. Turn out to the blue, and you'll see schools of bumphead parrotfish and barracuda. Safety stops are over beds of plate and staghorn coral clouded by fish schooling in the thousands.

Certain sites like **Yillet** and **Boo Windows** have striking topography. The island of Yillet is undercut with time and currents, creating overhangs and mini-caves (bring a flashlight to nose into dark corners). Boo Windows has two namesake, swimthrough windows that look spectacular when illuminated by sunlight.

And then there's **Magic Mountain,** a submerged ridge in the open ocean that is a magnet for marine life. Wobbegong sharks rest on bright beds of coral in ambers and pinks, and there are so many fish it can be difficult to spot your dive buddy: triggerfish, tuna, batfish, and grouper.

There are two year-round manta ray cleaning stations here: one at the pinnacle around 23 feet (7 m) and one farther down the ridge at around 82 feet (25 m). This is one of the few places you'll find both species of mantas (oceanic and reef), and it's the genesis for the Misool Manta Project, which gathers information on vulnerable manta populations to better protect them.

The magic doesn't stop at the mountain. Even

Manta rays soar over seascapes. Raja Ampat is one of the few places where both species of mantas (oceanic and reef) can be found.

Misool's **House Reef** is enchanting, from fish-filled, self-guided shore dives, to dusk and night dives searching for mandarin fish that wow divers with their sunset courtship rituals, and Raja Ampat "walking" sharks. These endemic epaulette sharks were discovered in 2006 and use modified pectoral fins to walk over the shallow reef.

Topside, there are a surprising number of experiences on offer, including **day trips** cruising the maze of karst islands, spotting wild orchids, carnivorous plants, and birds like hornbills and sea eagles; **spa treatments;** and **cooking classes.**

If the opportunity is available, don't miss the chance to spend time with Misool's **Ranger Patrol,** visiting one of their stations, checking on turtle

──── FOR FAMILIES ────

Misool is a natural, wondrous paradise for kids, with a sheltered lagoon to snorkel, diving from age 10, islands to explore, and cultural immersion. There is no "kids club" here, though—families spend time together, but it is quality time.

nests, and more. On their watch, fish life on the reef doubled in six years. That success, however, has attracted more illegal fishing pressure.

While overtourism is definitely an issue, under-tourism is equally problematic. In 2020, when the pandemic brought travel to a screeching halt, well-equipped illegal fishermen targeted Magic Mountain. They knew the dive boats wouldn't be around to keep watch on the area. The Ranger Patrol caught them and confiscated 330 pounds (150 kg) of ecologically sensitive fish—but the damage was done, the fish long dead.

Tourism is a complex balancing act, but it remains the only juggernaut powerful enough to challenge unsustainable, extractive practices like mining, logging, and overfishing. Sustainable tourism (done in the right way) places an economic value on protecting places and species, and it supports community-based conservation. No one is shark finning or dynamite fishing for fun—it's to feed families or to fill a demand (and usually not one created locally). If there was another way to make a better living (being paid to breed and raise giant clams, for example, another Misool initiative that employs 32 former fishermen), most people would consider it.

For now, the interim solution seems to lie in supporting places that are striving to do the right thing and to use the privilege of travel to gather experience, knowledge, and inspiration.

Doubt that you can make a difference, or feel the world is too far gone to save? Come here. The Four Kings will restore your faith.

Raja Ampat is a maze of lush karst spires, rising from lagoons that fade from crystal to turquoise to the deep blue of drop-offs.

NEED TO KNOW

GETTING HERE: Transit through Jakarta and fly Garuda Indonesia to Sorong Airport. Misool's team will meet guests at the airport, and transfer to the resort is via private speedboat, taking around four hours. Review Misool's FAQ page and follow up if you have questions.

GETTING AROUND: Getting from the North Lagoon to South Beach is a hike over the hill or a water taxi transfer. Both are beautiful.

PACKING TIPS: Casual, quick-drying clothes in light colors (fewer mosquitoes), with warm layers. Misool's FAQ page has a checklist of what to bring, including some much needed extras if you have space.

WEATHER: This Southern Hemisphere spot is tropical year-round. Misool Resort is closed July through mid-September (rougher weather).

IN ADDITION: The internet is snail-slow, so prepare to unplug while you're here. Don't miss the evening presentations—each one was fascinating and inspirational.

Diving

OVERVIEW: Possibly the best coral reef diving and snorkeling in the world, in a patrolled, protected area in the Coral Triangle that's increasing in biodiversity. Snorkelers are treated like divers, and there is diving for all levels on walls, reefs, and pinnacles.

- Visibility: 65-plus feet (20+ m)
- Water Temp: Around 79°F to 82°F (26°C to 28°C)
- Depth Range: 49 to 98 feet (15 to 30 m)

MARINE LIFE: Sharks (gray reef, blacktip reef, wobbegong, and Raja Ampat "walking" shark), pygmy seahorses, electric clams, mandarin fish, hawksbill turtles, bumphead parrotfish, and healthy coral (plate, staghorn, gorgonians, and more). Manta rays (oceanic and reef) turn up year-round, but sightings have peaks and valleys.

SHOP INFO: The **Misool Dive Centre** is the resort shop. This spacious center has wet and dry areas, workstations for camera gear, and a veranda for warming up between trips. Groups are small and the guides are skilled. Diving is non-deco, due to the remote location, and free Nitrox is available. Book all diving, snorkeling, courses, private guides, and rental equipment well in advance; wet suits are not available for rent.

Accommodations

HIGH-END: Misool has all-inclusive packages for seven, nine, or 12 nights, including an additional night in Sorong. Speedboat transfers, diving, and snorkeling are extra. Rooms are designed for dreamy, casual comfort, utilizing natural materials. There are several larger villas overlooking North Lagoon or South Beach that are perfect for families or groups of friends, with separate bedrooms and shared common areas. ~$3,720 USD pp/7 nights

MID-RANGE: Eight **Water Cottages** circle the North Lagoon. They are built on stilts over the water, with hammocks built into the verandas. These cottages are close to the restaurant and dive center. ~$3,100 USD pp/7 nights

BUDGET: The seven **South Beach Villas** are quieter, bordering a beach. These villas are a short walk or water taxi ride from the action, but have a more secluded feel. ~$3,100 USD pp/7 nights

Food & Drink

Misool's restaurant overlooks the North Lagoon, and room rates include four meals a day. Meals are a delectable mix of local and Western fare, sourced as naturally and sustainably as possible. A **mini-breakfast** is offered before the day's first dive, followed by a generous cooked **second breakfast** afterward.

Lunch is a family-style buffet showcasing a variety of dishes like gado gado (an Indonesian salad served with peanut sauce), corn fritters, and fruit salads.

Dinner is plate service: two choices (beef rendang, for example) with a set appetizer and dessert, plus an à la carte menu if you don't fancy either option. This meal is a communal affair: Guests gather to talk about their day and choose tomorrow's activities.

MOOREA

A Redemption Song

Moorea has long held sway over starry-eyed honeymooners who compare the island's shape to that of a heart. (We see a three-toed dinosaur footprint.) Even Charles Darwin was infected, describing Moorea as "a picture in a frame." The comely island also helped shape Darwin's theory on how coral islands form, but that's another story.

Despite Moorea's obvious charms, we were warned away from her while researching this book. Moorea's trashed, we were told; hit the Tuamotus instead—the diving is still pristine there.

That rubbed us the wrong way, and we dug a little deeper. Yes, the conscience-free travel years took its toll on Moorea, and reckless treatment of the reefs (careless anchor drops, seashells sold by the seashore, overfishing) left scars. But travel (and diving) should never be parasitic: ravaging one destination before dismissing it as "trashed" and moving on to the next. We have a responsibility to repair damage we've wrought.

And that's what's happening in Moorea. Quietly, without fanfare or much resource, Moorea is experiencing a resurgence of conservation initiatives from locals determined to save their beautiful home. It's working. We found reefs teeming with smaller fish, turtles, and a surprisingly healthy population of sharks (blacktip reef, lemon, and gray reef).

Add your own note to Moorea's redemption song—now's the time to visit. ∎

Moorea
FRENCH POLYNESIA

A blacktip reef shark patrols the coral gardens of the Fakarava Atoll in the Tuamotu Islands.
This is how Moorea was, and could be again, with our help.

Moorea's jagged profile, with jade green mountains spiking to 3,960 feet (1,207 m), is a breath-catcher, and it's just as beautiful underwater. The naysayers who warned us not to dive here can eat their words: The water was clear and warm, with surge but minimal current, holding an abundance of hard coral, brightly colored reef fish, turtles, and a multitude of sharks. Although the inner lagoon has been affected by bleaching, there is evidence of recovery, and the outer lagoons are in a good state, with about 20 percent in a marine protected area.

Most dives are a 10-minute boat ride past the breakers on sloping reefs with hard coral beds, cut through by channels. The channels tend to be deeper and are especially conducive to spotting sharks. This is one of Moorea's appeals: There is something for more experienced divers as well as for new, novice, or out-of-practice divers.

Tiki holds robust hard coral gardens. We descended through a cloud of vampire triggerfish,

circled by blacktip reef sharks, to around 62 feet (19 m) on the fringing reef. Gray reef sharks cruised the deeper water, while farther up the sloping reef we found plenty of fish—paddletail snapper, peacock grouper, and (my new favorite) lemonpeel angelfish.

Taotoi has a series of coral ridges you can swim up and over, often surprising sleeping hawksbill and green turtles that have nestled in for a rest. In between are sandy channels, so depth fluctuates from 33 feet (10 m) to 62 feet (19 m), making for a fun, swoopy dive.

One of the main channels leading into the lagoon is **Lemonshark Valley.** As the name suggests, this spot is a favorite with lemon sharks. At the top of the trench is a sloping reef with more resting turtles.

There are even wall dives, like **Coral Wall,** which has plenty of overhangs and holes for macro life and more turtles.

The landscape is just as riveting topside, and there are a variety of hiking trails to explore this 51-square-mile (132 sq km) island, leading to picture-in-a-frame vistas. The **Pass of Three Coconuts** is popular, but not to be taken lightly, with an elevation gain of 850 feet (259 m) to panoramic views. The **Pass of Three Pines** is easier, winding through forests and past 13th-century structures to a lookout point: three pine trees outlining a magnificent view of Cook's Bay.

(Tip: Expect rain, wear mosquito repellent and closed-toe shoes, and prepare for a complete lack of toilet facilities. Both hikes are around four hours round-trip; guided treks available.)

Visitors can also take part in Moorea's cultural resurgence. **Moorea Maori Tours' History and**

Moorea's iconic, pointed profile. Hiking is extremely popular here, and the island has trails suitable for all levels, with sweeping views.

Make a Difference

The **Coral Gardeners** (*coralgardeners.org*) began as a passionate grassroots project run out of founder Titouan Bernicot's parents' basement. They've now evolved into a revolution, a team of mobilized young men and women adept at harnessing social media and driven to make a difference. Along with raising awareness (they aim to reach one billion people by 2025), the Coral Gardeners are growing and planting more resilient corals called "super corals," working with experts, and experimenting with cutting-edge techniques. This crew is going places. What can you do? Join the movement and spread the word about what's happening in the ocean. Visit the team on Moorea. Adopt a coral. Donate. (Committed, ongoing funding—especially—would be a huge help to them.) This is a worthwhile project.

Legends Tour is a full-day, small-group activity (max four people) led by a local couple that can be tailored to the group's interest. We chose to learn more about traditional sports, trying our hands at javelin throwing and fruit carrying.

However, the real story here (and our favorite activity) is the conservation work being done throughout the island, and there are wonderful ways to get involved.

We joined Dr. Michael Poole on one of his three-hour **dolphin- and whale-watching ecotours,** watching a pod of spinner dolphins put on an aerial display as Dr. Poole shared information about the dolphins' behavior and environment. Dr. Poole spent a decade lobbying for a whale and dolphin sanctuary that is more than 2.1 million square miles (5.5 million sq km), roughly half the size of the continental United States. Around one-third of the world's population of whales and dolphins visit Moorea—humpback whales migrate through from July through November, while the dolphins are permanent residents.

(Tip: Moorea has several swim with dolphin or stingray experiences on offer, where animals are handled, usually for photographs, but that's not best practice. "Dolphins can't say whether or not they want to be touched," Dr. Poole said. "In the wild, you may or may not see one, but it's on their terms and therefore it's a much better experience.")

Dr. Cécile Gaspar, founder of sea turtle protection agency Te Mana o Te Moana, examines an injured sea turtle.

We also joined Dr. Cécile Gaspar, president of **Te Mana o Te Moana** ("spirit of the ocean"), a sea turtle protection agency. Te Mana o Te Moana is based out of the former InterContinental Resort and Spa, which had kindly set aside part of their lagoon as a recovery area for turtles, many of which have been severely injured by spearguns, fishing gear, and plastic ingestion. We joined one of the twice-weekly, 1.5-hour guided tours through the sea turtle care center to learn more about turtle species, the threats they face, and current rehabilitation.

Te Mana o Te Moana's work is paying off. In 2004, they documented 25 tracks of nesting turtles. In 2018, they documented 1,300 tracks, and 50,000 empty shells. "Poachers know we're monitoring the nest sites," Dr. Gaspar says. "The main issue is

⸺ NEARBY⸺

Divers shouldn't pass up the opportunity to island hop from Moorea to the Tuamotus, with sites ranging from lazy lagoons to roaring, shark-filled drifts. Check out Air Tahiti's island-hopping "passes."

poaching for meat, which is a cultural issue, but we are starting to see a shift in attitude. We started educating kids [120,000-plus at the time of writing] when they were 10 years old. Now some of those kids have become marine biologists."

Moorea's youth seem to be growing up with a passion to protect their island. The **Coral Gardeners** are an inspirational group of local young men and women who grew up surfing the waters surrounding Moorea. "In 2014, when I was 16 years old, I noticed our surf breaks were changing," said founder and president Titouan Bernicot. "We started free diving to take a look and see what's happening, and we noticed the reefs were damaged. So, we decided to do something about it."

We have lost half of the world's coral reefs since the 1950s. Reefs are lifeblood: They are home to 25 percent of all marine animals and plants. They absorb 97 percent of a wave's energy, buffering coastlines. More than 500 million people rely on reefs for food, income, and coastal protection. Without healthy reefs, we don't have a healthy ocean—and bear in mind 70 percent of the oxygen we breathe comes from the sea.

At the time of writing, the Coral Gardeners have transplanted more than 15,700 corals around Moorea. Their goal? Plant one million corals around the world by 2025. Visitors can stop by the Gardeners' headquarters to meet the team and learn more about the project. They can also adopt a coral and watch it grow via livestream through the Gardeners' AI platform, ReefOS, a network of cameras and sensors collecting crucial data about the reef.

"Hopefully one day soon we'll be out of a job," Titouan laughed. "When the reefs are healthy, and the ocean is valued and protected. I'm not going to stop until I help make that happen."

The Coral Gardeners are an inspirational group of young people who noticed their reefs were deteriorating and decided to take action.

NEED TO KNOW

GETTING HERE: International flights arrive at Tahiti's Faa'a International Airport. It's a 15-minute flight or 30-minute ferry crossing to Moorea.

GETTING AROUND: Self-driving is the best way to explore. With one road circling the island, it's difficult to get lost—difficult but not impossible. There are no street names on Moorea: Kilometer signs indicate the distance from the ferry terminal and which side of the island (ocean or mountain) the road is on. For example, "KM 22 on the ocean side." It can be more cost-effective to rent a car on Tahiti and take it across on the ferry.

PACKING TIPS: Moorea is an island for showing off your resort wear. Dressy casual is the look here.

WEATHER: This is the Southern Hemisphere climate we dream about on dreary winter days: a daily average of 80°F (26.6°C) and plenty of sun, cooled by steadily blowing trade winds. November to March has regular tropical showers, with the heaviest in February.

IN ADDITION: Avoid cruise ship season (February through April).

Diving

OVERVIEW: This is a diver's honeymoon: warm, clear water, sharks and turtles, coral gardens, and a fringing reef cut through by channels. Great spot for new divers. Plus, your diving makes a difference here.

- **Visibility:** 100-plus feet (30+ m)
- **Water Temp:** 77°F (25°C) in winter / 82°F (28°C) in summer
- **Depth Range:** 82 feet (25 m)

MARINE LIFE: Sharks (blacktip reef, gray reef, sicklefin lemon, occasional tiger and hammerhead), turtles (hawksbill and green), reef fish (clownfish, angelfish, vampire triggerfish), and 25 species of dolphins and whales (humpbacks visit July through November)

SHOP INFO: We dove with **TOPDIVE,** located at the former InterContinental Resort and Spa (pickups at other hotels arranged). TOPDIVE has good facilities, with in-depth briefings in English and French. Most important, they always have a skipper on the boat, as well as a guide in the water. (Be aware: Several shops on Moorea have the skipper guiding the group, leaving the boat unattended. This may cut their costs, but it also cuts your safety margin.) TOPDIVE is unique in that all of their dives are on Nitrox, requiring Nitrox certification. (The shop can organize an internal Nitrox certification on-site. Don't worry, new divers: It's easy.)

Accommodations

HIGH-END: The **Hilton Moorea Lagoon Resort and Spa** has 106 rooms ranging from overwater suites to garden rooms with private pools. It has a beach, a pool, and an overwater restaurant that receives nightly visits from blacktip reef sharks. ~$716 USD

MID-RANGE: **Manava Beach Resort and Spa Moorea** has 90 accommodation units (including overwater bungalows) and lagoons and pools aplenty, but it still maintains the personality and feel of a smaller, local hotel. Good central location. ~$332 USD

BUDGET: The **Moorea Beach Lodge's** off-the-beaten-track location (around the left side of the island, near Haapiti) means it's a quieter place to stay. This collection of 12 beachfront bungalows is centered around a shared living area. ~$172 USD

Food & Drink

Rudy's Moorea is relaxed French cuisine (think pepper sauce beef tenderloin) spiced with island influences. This is the spot for family and friends who enjoy a good meal.

The Hilton's **Toatea Crêperie & Bar** is dinner and a shark show: sweet and savory French crepes served at overwater tables visited by blacktip reef sharks every evening. (We counted 18.) (Tip: Request a lagoonside table.)

The Coral Gardeners took us to the lively **Manuia Grill,** an under-cover outdoor patio near Manava Beach Resort. Their specialty is barbecue skewers, served with two sides and a sauce.

TANZANIA

ZANZIBAR

Seduction of the Spice Island

Dhows still ply these opal-tinted waters, their creamy wakes temporarily obscuring the hints of purple-pink reefs that seem to lie just out of reach under the water. The scent of cloves mixes with sea air, tropical flowers, smoke, and the occasional whiff of something less savory to create an intoxicating perfume inhaled by centuries of travelers.

AFRICA

Zanzibar
TANZANIA

The Zanzibar archipelago is located 22 miles (36 km) off the east coast of Tanzania, slightly north of Dar es Salaam and south of Mombasa. Its location made it a hotbed of trading—spices and enslaved people, primarily. For centuries, the Sultanate of Oman ruled over this colorful mishmash of cultures: Persian, Arabic, Indian, and the interior of the African continent. Hundreds of years of comingling and intermarrying forged an independent island (although part of Tanzania, most islanders consider themselves Zanzibari) that is tolerant of others. Although primarily Muslim, Stone Town also houses cathedrals and Hindu and Buddhist temples.

Zanzibar also has a legacy of piracy, cholera epidemics, and royal scandals worthy of a novel or two (like Princess Salme's extraordinary *Memoirs of an Arabian Princess from Zanzibar* and *Trade Wind* by M. M. Kaye). In Stone Town, the carved wooden doors are still studded with large bronze nail heads, relics from a time when homes needed protection from the assaults of war elephants.

There is much to explore here, from Zanzibar's storied history, to its blindingly white beaches, to warm turquoise waters, which beckon snorkelers and divers of all levels.

The charms of the Spice Island are impossible to resist. ◼

Zanzibar has attracted travelers for thousands of years, thanks to its beauty and location (22 mi/36 km off Tanzania's east coast).

For travelers who seek out strong cultures, and who enjoy things not going entirely to plan, Zanzibar is the island for you. The northern beach-town resort of Nungwi is the best base for diving and snorkeling, but spend a couple of days in Stone Town at the beginning or end of your trip.

Stone Town is an ancient Swahili trading town and UNESCO World Heritage site on the westernmost spur of Zanzibar's coast, reaching out toward Tanzania. Lorded over by the **Old Fort,** an imposing sunset-tinted structure that overlooks the sea, this mazelike city is fun to wander, and we looked forward to getting lost: "Wrong" turns led to spectacular finds and memorable interactions.

(Tip: Zanzibaris acknowledge strangers—greetings aren't laden with intent. Have a few words of Swahili at the ready, like asante sana, *which means "thank you very much," or* habari, *a formal greeting, or* jambo, *an informal greeting. Women should wear headscarves, and shoulders and knees should be covered. Tourists in tank tops are conspicuous in conservatively dressed Stone Town.)*

Not-to-be-missed Stone Town spots include the **Palace Museum,** formerly a residence for the sultan's family and stocked with memorabilia, including insights into the life of Princess Salme, who has her own small museum—the **Princess Salme Museum**—nearby. The memoir-writing princess was a sultan's daughter and sister to warring brothers Barghash and Majid; she scandalized Zanzibar

___ WISH WE KNEW _____

Outside of Stone Town and the airport, ATMs are few and far between, especially in the north part of the island, and few places accept credit cards. Check what your hotel and dive shop accept before arrival. Cash is king, so plan in advance.

by eloping with a German merchant, living out the rest of her life in Hamburg.

It was Sultan Barghash who built the **Hamamni Baths,** the first public baths in Zanzibar (worth a visit, although no longer functioning). The baths are located across the road from the **Cultural Arts Centre,** which features works by local artists using locally sourced materials—paper bead jewelry, notebooks, paintings, and more. (Keep an eye out for workshops on offer.)

The northern town of **Nungwi** is a jarring contrast to Stone Town. It is famous (and rightly so) for its powder-white-sand beaches and translucent turquoise seas. In Nungwi, bikinis and hijabs comingle on the beach, and florid, chain-smoking travelers exchange greetings with local fishermen prepping their dhows for a day at sea. *(Tip: Beach areas are relaxed, but follow cultural protocols in the community and don't take pictures without permission.)*

A special way to experience the village—or beaches—is to take a ride with the **Zanzibar Horse Club** (ZHC), located behind the Z Hotel. I am cautious recommending riding stables, but at the time of writing, ZHC had a small stable of well-cared-for horses in a difficult landscape. (They have a lovely British-style barn, but shade, food, and basic care items are difficult to come by here.)

These Arab/Somali crosses (mostly rescues) are small in stature with large personalities. Most people choose a beach ride, but we opted for a village

A sea star in one of Zanzibar's coral gardens. This is a terrific spot for snorkelers and divers of all levels, with great vis and warm seas.

ride (children ran after us yelling *"Farasi, farasi!"* the Swahili word for horse), followed by a swim. Riding out into the warm aquamarine ocean, bareback, letting the water lap our legs as the horses dipped their noses and pawed at the sea, dhows gliding past on the horizon, was one of those travel moments that sear into memory.

(Tip: Rides are limited to minimize the impact on the horses, so book early; they are also subject to tide times and weight limits apply for adults.)

Once you slip into Zanzibar's seas, you don't ever want to emerge. This is a great place for snorkelers and new divers: Most of the sites are shallow, with excellent visibility, warm water, and a mix of coral gardens and bommies. More experienced divers can spice things up with drift dives over open ocean seamounts and night dives.

The majority of sites are located around Nungwi, the spear tip of Zanzibar, flanked by two islands:

Children play in an alleyway in Stone Town, an ancient Swahili trading town and UNESCO World Heritage site.

larger Tumbatu on the west coast, and microscopic Mnemba Island, a marine conservation area, on the east. Most sites are within a 30- to 90-minute dhow ride.

On the Tumbatu side, **Shetani** is a shallow sloping reef with some of the most robust hard and soft coral gardens in Zanzibar. Turtles and macro life abound here.

Leven Bank, off the northern tip of Nungwi, is a seamount sloping from 39 to 180 feet (12 to 55 m). Best suited to experienced divers due to strong currents, this is one of the few spots to see the larger stuff: barracuda, grouper, tuna, and kingfish.

Mnemba Island, a popular dive and snorkel spot, is about an hour's boat ride along the wilder east coast of Zanzibar. Two popular sites for all levels include **Kichuani,** a gentle drift dive along a sloping wall, and **Wattabomi,** a sandy bottom filled with bommies and a large area of plate coral. Both sites have multitudes of life, including angelfish, Moorish idols, sergeant majors, bluespotted ribbontail rays, moray eels, mantis shrimp, frogfish, flounder, stonefish, and scorpionfish.

(Tip: Sun cover comes in handy on boats. Mnemba is crowded: Keep an eye on your dive group or you might go home with another.)

Mnemba isn't a "paper park" (a conservation area that largely exists in name only), but it is a work in progress. The intent is good, and there has been collaboration between dive shops, tourism operators, the Zanzibar Department of Fisheries, and Zanzibari fishermen. The agreement includes recreational fees and specific areas for diving, snorkeling, and fishing, but Mnemba could be so much more.

More than three billion people rely on the oceans as their primary source of protein, and in places like Zanzibar, where the average daily wage is less than $4 USD, fishing is a necessity.

However, no-take marine parks—that are enforced and managed—benefit everyone: They restore and preserve biodiversity, they create jobs and income through eco- and dive tourism, and they benefit fishermen. In no-take marine reserves, where fishing is prohibited, fish populations rebound, spilling over invisible reserve boundar-

Author Carrie Miller takes Crumble, one of the Zanzibar Horse Club's horses, for a swim in the Indian Ocean.

ies. (Fishermen, on average, catch four times more fish near no-take reserves than near unprotected areas nearby.) It is estimated that establishing no-take zones across one-third of our coastal seas would provide the world with all the fish it needs.

The Spice Island has all the right ingredients to support its population while transitioning into a world-class dive and snorkel destination. All it needs is a little love and protection.

Make a Difference

The Dr. Sylvia Earle–led **Mission Blue** *(mission-blue.org)* is one of our favorite organizations. Their goal? Ignite public support for a global network of marine protected areas "large enough to restore the ocean, the blue heart of the planet." These are Hope Spots, special places that have been scientifically identified as critically important to the health of the ocean. Local on-the-ground organizations (NGOS, dive shops, scientists, etc.) can champion Hope Spots, with support from Mission Blue. (Zanzibar's Mnemba Island is a perfect example of an area that could benefit from a Hope Spot.) Mission Blue also offers expeditions, and donations are gratefully accepted via their website. Check out their website to learn more, and for tips on how everyday folk can become ocean-supporting superheroes.

NEED TO KNOW

GETTING HERE: Karume International Airport on the west coast is the arrival point in Zanzibar.

GETTING AROUND: It takes about one hour to travel to Nungwi. Taxis and shuttles are available (some hotels can help with arrangements); there is also a local bus.

PACKING TIPS: The majority of Zanzibar residents practice the Islamic faith; outside of the beaches, respect the conservative dress code (trousers, skirts that cover the knees, shoulders covered), which also comes in handy for sun cover.

WEATHER: The sun is intense in this Southern Hemisphere spot, and the average temperature is a humid 80°F (27°C), cooled by trade winds. There are two rainy seasons: March to May and October to December; ironically, these are the best seasons for diving (no wind, calm seas, good vis).

IN ADDITION: When transiting in Africa, look into Ethiopian Airlines via Addis Ababa. At the time of writing, they offered cheaper flights, with two 50-pound (23 kg) bags per person included. Also, if there are more than 10 hours between connecting flights (with no other available flight and departure ticket booked), the airline will arrange a transit visa, overnight hotel, and transport to and from the hotel free of charge. It's a great (and cost-saving) perk. Fair warning: The hotels—while comfortable—aren't flashy, and the process is a bit chaotic. We did this five times during our fieldwork, and it always worked out.

Diving

OVERVIEW: Exotic diving in opalescent waters of the Spice Island. This is a great spot for beginners, with a few spicy dives for the more experienced, ranging from coral gardens to open seamounts with strong currents.

- Visibility: 65-plus feet (20+ m)
- Water Temp: 77°F (25°C) in winter / 86°F (30°C) in summer
- Depth Range: Average 52 feet (16 m), with some deeper sites

MARINE LIFE: Bluespotted ribbontail rays, turtles, frogfish, leaf fish, crocodilefish, mantis shrimp, dragon moray eels, octopuses, and an abundance of reef fish. Humpbacks migrate through in August and September.

SHOP INFO: We dove with **Spanish Dancer Divers,** one of the first dive centers in Zanzibar, located on Nungwi Beach. This is a fun, multicultural team: They're professional and love sharing Zanzibar with visitors. Boats are traditional wooden dhows with some sun cover, holding up to 14 divers. The shop offers free refresher courses and drinking water, and can help with travel advice.

Accommodations

HIGH-END: &Beyond Mnemba Island is a private luxury paradise on an atoll near the Mnemba Island Marine Conservation Area, which they helped to establish. It has 12 rustic yet elegant bungalows, along with an on-site restaurant and dive center. ~$1,320 USD

MID-RANGE: Swahili-style and Nungwi-based **Atii Garden Bungalows** is a small, quiet hotel surrounded by gardens and located a short walk from the beach. Spacious, comfortable rooms and on-site restaurant. ~$77 USD

BUDGET: Located next to Spanish Dancer Divers (on the beach), **Nungwi Inn Hotel** offers a cheerful collection of 28 rooms with an on-site restaurant and bar. ~$75 USD

Food & Drink

The oceanside restaurant at **Langi Langi Beach Bungalows** (also called Marhaba) is excellent for atmosphere and food (Indian, Italian, and traditional Zanzibari).

For a post-dive meal, you can't beat **Mangi's Bar and Restaurant,** located next door to Spanish Dancer Divers. Good selection of food (although it can be a wait), milkshakes, and prime sundowner spot.

At night, the **Nungwi roundabout** is the place for authentic street food. It's encircled by stands selling delectable dishes like *mishkaki* (chicken or beef skewers) or *chipsi mayai* (an omelet with french fries).

NHA TRANG

A Macro Delight in a Modern City

Nha Trang is known as the Riviera of the South China Sea, a high-rise city with equally high energy, lining a nearly four-mile (6 km) stretch of golden beach.

It's located on the southeast coast of Vietnam, about 278 miles (448 km) northeast of Ho Chi Minh City. Here, the coastline gets fragmented, with several offshore islands having broken away into Nha Trang Bay. Hon Mun is one of these islands, a marine protected area favored by divers and snorkelers. Hon Tre is another, home to the incongruent Vinpearl Land amusement complex, with its mini–Eiffel Tower pylons holding up cable cars full of eager tourists, heading out to the water parks, Ferris wheels, and fairy-tale castles.

Even with its 2,026 miles (3,260 km) of coastline, Vietnam is a relatively new destination for divers, and Nha Trang offers some macro delights for divers and snorkelers of all levels. You just need to time your visit to avoid monsoon season, which can wreak havoc with visibility.

Topside, this energetic city is a mix of the old (ancient temples and traditional street food), the natural (rivers, hot springs, and waterfalls), and the new (rooftop bars and a forward-thinking approach to growing the city).

Nha Trang is a delight to visit, infectious with its energy, and easy to explore, with day and night offering two completely different sides to this vibrant city. It's time to put this hot spot on your travel radar. ■

ASIA

VIETNAM

Nha Trang

Nha Trang has elevated street food to haute cuisine. Many experienced vendors sell out their signature dishes in the blink of an eye.

During the day, beachgoers flock to Nha Trang's golden strip of beach, which is separated from the city by a single road. At night, that road lights up electric, and the same beachgoers—now dressed to impress—hop from one nightspot to the next, reveling in the humid night air.

There is an atmosphere of possibility in Nha Trang that visitors latch on to almost immediately. This is a lively, growing city, full of young entrepreneurs, while still maintaining its strong Vietnamese heritage.

Not only is Nha Trang growing, but it's trying to grow in a sustainable direction, thanks to the efforts of a dedicated local community group. **Visit Nha Trang** comprises several hotels, restaurants, attractions, and dive shops with two primary goals: First, showcase the best the city has to offer; second, and perhaps more important, grow Nha Trang sustainably, to preserve the ocean, beach, and unique environment that make this city special. Smart travelers are the key to making that happen. If the city attracts visitors who are interested in marine parks and places that prioritize a green economy, it might just ignite something forward-thinking and fabulous.

In Nha Trang, you're never far from an ocean that is beginning to gain a reputation as a macro destination, and the bay is one of Vietnam's best diving and snorkeling spots. Most dive trips are a full-day outing and take place in **Hon Mun Marine Park,** which is about five miles (8 km) offshore and a short ride from the harbor.

Hon Mun was the first marine conservation project in Vietnam, established in 2001 to protect the area's internationally ranked coral reefs. There are 350 species of hard coral here, 230 species of fish, 112 species of crustaceans, seven seaweed species, and much more—a lot of biodiversity is packed into this little park.

Hon Mun is a mix of deepwater pinnacles and shallow, sandy beds (ideal for dive training). **Fisherman Bay** (59 ft/18 m) is home to hard and soft coral favored by clownfish and damselfish, with nudibranchs tucked away in coral crevices, while **Moray Beach** is the preferred spot of its namesake residents. (There are several giants here.) **Mamahan Beach** has striking topography and plenty of critters (scorpionfish, frogfish, cuttlefish, lionfish, nudibranchs), while **Madonna Rock** is pocked with caves tightly packed with schools of fish. (This spot is beloved by photographers: The streaming sunlight creates mystery.)

This dive area has huge possibilities and is a great place for macro lovers, but it also has work to do—the coral is healthy, but even with protec-

A golden anemone fish peers out from its protection. Nha Trang is home to Vietnam's first marine park, and it is a great spot for macro lovers.

The angular clay structures of Po Nagar Cham Towers, built between the eighth and 11th centuries, seem to glow, as if lit from within.

tion, overfishing is an issue here. And anything in the Cai River empties right into the bay. A steady stream of dive travelers can help draw attention to Nha Trang's potential, and with a little more patrolled protection, this area could rebound quickly.

It's also worth spending a few days exploring the city on foot. A few blocks back from the beach, the Riviera feel fades and the city reveals another side: Clothing stores display intricately hand-embroidered linen shirts and pants, scooters zoom past carrying impossibly large or improbable loads, and café chatter carries.

XQ Hand Embroiderers features extraordinary silk thread paintings that shimmer with life: The leaves in forest scenes seem to flicker without wind; the water underneath boats rolls without tides. The embroidery is a handcraft that has existed in Vietnam for centuries, the silk thread dyed with yam, indigo, and Indian almond. (Paintings are for sale, from small frames to room-separating screens; this is a unique souvenir worth splurging on.)

Po Nagar Cham Towers' angular clay structures, built between the eighth and 11th centuries, are architectural marvels, and this complex—though crowded—is a place of peace and meditation. Across the Cai River, **Long Son Pagoda,** built in the late 19th century, is crowned with a 79-foot-tall (24 m) white Buddha seated on a lotus throne, serenely watching over the city below. (Tip: These sites are still actively used for worship; dress respectfully. There is historical signage throughout; guided tours are also available.)

Our favorite experience was a two-hour **street-food tour with local restaurant Lanterns.** Nha Trang has elevated street food to haute cuisine. Many vendors (perched on corners and tucked down alleyways) have decades of experience, selling out signature dishes in the blink of an eye.

Our walking tour featured seven stops. Sitting on minuscule plastic chairs next to tiny plastic tables, we'd watch culinary wizards work their magic. One delectable dish followed another, like *banh can* (cooked in smoking hot clay cups) or grilled rice paper tacos with black sesame cut up with scissors and served in a bowl with tamarind dipping sauce, washed down with iced tamarind juice. One of the sell-out spots had sweet pink bananas coated in tapioca and sprinkled with raw peanuts. People waited patiently on scooters and motorcycles for this dish, sitting with money in hand.

(Tip: Tour itineraries are created and led by staff members who handle transactions, answer questions, and assist with ordering. This is especially useful if, like me, you have food allergies.)

The best way to see Nha Trang, however, is from one of its rooftop bars, with an ice-cold drink in hand, watching the hazy sun set behind the hills. And **Skylight Nha Trang** is the belle of the high-rise ball.

Owned by young entrepreneur and Visit Nha Trang member TK Nguyen, who has a local reputation as the city's "vibe director," this world-class and crazy venue has 360-degree views of the city, a wonderful restaurant serving Pan-Asian cuisine, three bars (the one gallon/3.5 L Strawberry Mule-Vodka Punchbowl is a must-order), four event

Nights come to life on Nha Trang's rooftops, where bars like Skylight Nha Trang serve up vibes and cocktails with 360-degree views of the city.

spaces (often featuring live local music), a swimming pool, and a glass-covered skywalk on the 43rd floor. There's even a lighthouse, a beacon that can be spotted throughout Nha Trang, beckoning residents, expats, and travelers to come join the city's biggest party.

Make a Difference

Most of us know about the harm caused by plastic bags (we use 500 billion every year) and plastic straws (500 million used daily in the United States alone), but did you know that cigarette butts are the world's most littered plastic item? Cigarette filters are plastic and are easily disposed and forgotten about with a flick—it's the last socially acceptable form of littering. Eventually they wash into the sea, where they break into microplastics, unless marine life mistakes them for food first. Nearly 6.5 trillion cigarettes are purchased by smokers around the world every year, roughly 18 billion every day. That's trillions of plastic cigarette filters thrown away every year. (E-cigarettes/vaping is no better—it generates a lot of plastic and battery waste.) Have to smoke? Rolling your own is best.

NEED TO KNOW

GETTING HERE: Cam Ranh International Airport handles domestic and international flights to Nha Trang. The airport is located about 22 miles (35 km) outside the city; taxis, buses, and transfers available.

GETTING AROUND: Nha Trang is easy to walk around, and taxis are readily available. You can rent a car or scooter, but traffic here has a chaotic rhythm—it works, but you have to be confident.

PACKING TIPS: Daytime: Good walking shoes and loose clothing (it is hot and humid). Nighttime: Nha Trang turns it on. This is a great place to dress up.

WEATHER: Nha Trang has one of the best climates in Vietnam. Monsoon season (September to December) is short; July and August are the hottest; February to May is the best time to visit. Diving is year-round, but aim for when rainfall is at its lowest for best vis (April to August).

IN ADDITION: Two tips: Keep your bag tags handy (you'll need them to exit the airport), and fly with Vietnam Airlines, which does a great job. (VietJet Air, on the other hand, wins our award for "airline with most room for improvement.")

Diving

OVERVIEW: Macro madness in Vietnam's first marine protected area, a short distance from a vibrant beachside city. This is a great destination for divers of all levels (especially underwater photographers), and a good chance to promote dive tourism in a relatively new area.

- **Visibility:** 33 feet (10 m), except during monsoon season (6.6 ft/2 m)
- **Water Temp:** 70°F (21°C) in winter / 84°F (29°C) in summer
- **Depth Range:** 54 feet average (16 m)

MARINE LIFE: Lionfish, clownfish, frogfish, small reef fish, moray eels, staghorn coral, pipefish, nudibranchs; turtles are starting to return to the area.

SHOP INFO: We dove with **Sailing Club Divers,** based on the main beach at the Sailing Club restaurant. Established in 1999, Sailing Club offers regular small-group diving and snorkeling trips under the guidance of a highly experienced and multicultural team (French and Vietnamese). They know and love their area and are active leaders in shaping Nha Trang's future. Courses offered.

Accommodations

HIGH-END: Amiana Resort and Villas overlooks Nha Trang Bay, with 153 spacious rooms and villas, two pools, and a private beach. ~$254 USD

MID-RANGE: Sheraton Nha Trang Hotel & Spa is a centrally located, 280-room hotel that outdoes itself in friendly customer service. The views from the upper rooms of this 30-floor hotel are like staring out from a ship: nothing but ocean filling the expansive view. There are six delicious restaurants and a pool. ~$120 USD

BUDGET: Azura Hotel is in the center of town, close to the beach (and Sailing Club Divers). The rooms are basic but clean and comfortable, and the staff go out of their way to be helpful. Great value for money. ~$17 USD

Food & Drink

The **Sailing Club** transforms itself depending on the time of day. Daytime, it's a beach club, serving up light meals and coffees. Evenings, it's an elegant restaurant. Nighttime, it becomes a lively nightclub, complete with dance floor.

Lanterns is lovely. This second-story, open-air restaurant serves up succulent local dishes (including hot pots and clay pots) as traffic bustles about below and its trademark red lanterns cast a glow on the floor. Along with offering cooking classes and a street-food tour, Lanterns also supports local orphanages with scholarships and free weekly lunches.

MIX Restaurant was a strange and delightful find: an authentic Greek restaurant in the heart of Nha Trang with a unique historical decor. The owner regularly does the rounds, checking on customers, and it's such a popular spot you need reservations for dinner.

NOSY AMBARIOVATO

Welcome to Madagascar

Imagine David Attenborough colliding with Dr. Seuss. That is Madagascar, where nature is taken to extremes. This place is home to towering, smooth-skinned baobab trees, saucer-eyed lemurs, chary chameleons, and beeping earthworms that add their calls to the cacophony of night sounds: wind and thunder, cicadas, and roaring ceiling fans. This is a brutal, beautiful place, bursting with life.

Madagascar is the fourth largest island in the world (roughly the size of Texas), located off the east coast of Mozambique (page 40). Due to its long separation from Africa, the vast majority of Madagascar's flora and fauna is found nowhere else on the planet. It is a biodiversity hot spot.

That continues underwater, too. The topaz waters and coral forests of this up-and-coming dive destination teem with life, including 34 species of whales and dolphins, 1,300 species of fish (like frogfish and crocodilefish), five of the seven species of sea turtles, and 56 species of sharks (including whale sharks).

Despite abundant natural resources, life in Madagascar is desperately hard. Most of the population exists on less than $1.90 USD per day. Its natural resources are under constant threat from climate change and exploitation (both legal and illegal). Ecotourism, when done properly, is lifeblood here.

We based ourselves at Tsara Komba Luxury Beach & Forest Lodge on Nosy Ambariovato, more commonly referred to as Nosy Komba, also known as the island of lemurs. This small island is tucked between the northwestern mainland coast and the larger island of Nosy Be. It's the perfect spot to settle in, relax, and drink in Madagascar's marvelous madness. ■

Color fills the view from Tsara Komba Luxury Beach & Forest Lodge, located on Nosy Komba, the island of lemurs.

Nosy Komba is a dormant volcano covered in dense tropical forest that is home to wildlife straight out of our childhood picture books. There are no roads here: The handful of villages that dot the island are connected by red-dirt footpaths, and most travel is by boat or pirogue (a traditional dugout canoe).

It's tempting to spend your stay island-hopping on the numerous excursions offered by Tsara Komba, but wonder can be found in the backyard. **Tour the lodge's tropical botanic garden,** which pulses with color and contains more than 200 endemic species, as well as baby baobab trees, papaya, lime, and vanilla. The lodge has developed ingenious environmentally friendly solutions to care for its leafy charges: Herbs are planted on triangular bamboo towers (the design keeps the slugs at bay, no pesticides required); ill or damaged plants are tended to in a separate plant hospital; and the gravity-fed irrigation system reduces water waste and energy consumption.

Feeling adventurous? **Hike up and over the 2,040-foot (622 m) spine of the island,** from the lodge to the craft village of Ampangorinana on the opposite coast. Guides from the neighboring village led us up faint footpaths under the forest's thick canopy, passing motionless chameleons, Malagasy ground boas, and black-and-yellow giant hognose snakes (endemic to Madagascar). Our guides knew the vegetation like the backs of their hands—tree bark that is helpful in treating burns and plants with leaves that are "good for eating with a little salt," but with roots that can kill you. Occasionally, we came across a grouping of two or three huts nestled in a clearing, home to families who work the banana, pepper, and coffee plantations in the forest.

The five-hour hike culminated in a park filled with macaco lemurs, Madagascar's best known ambassadors. It was a delight to see lemurs gracefully roaming the treetops, some with babies perched on their backs, watching us with wide, expressive eyes. Pay the admission to support the park, but decline to feed the wild animals. (Just because you can doesn't mean you should; it's up to each of us to exhibit best practice, especially in places where it isn't enforced.) It's enjoyment enough to see these marvelous and critically endangered creatures.

(Tip: This is a hot, humid hike—take plenty of water and sun protection. Carry a little cash for the tiny café at the summit, where you can purchase juice and water, and for Ampangorinana, which sells local crafts. Return is by boat, with a snorkeling excursion en route.)

Even though Madagascar is an island, and a large one at that (more than 3,107 mi/5,000 km of Indian Ocean and Mozambique Channel coastline), its

Down the garden path: Tsara Komba is lush with trees and plants like papaya, passion fruit, and vanilla, which find their way into meals.

Make a Difference

Speak to dive shops about sponsoring a local dive guide. Seventy-five percent of Madagascar's population live on less than $1.90 USD per day, so saving up for a dive course is nearly impossible. Paying course fees for a member of the local community who wants to learn to dive not only opens up a career path, but it involves (and invests) the community in ocean conservation and protection. (This is a win-win opportunity in many poorer countries.) The **Madagascar Whale Shark Project** *(madagascarwhalesharks.org)* has a dual mission of whale shark research and raising awareness and empowering local communities. They're also doing important work confirming the importance of sustainable whale shark tourism to Madagascar's economy. There are many ways to get involved, from volunteering to donations.

underwater landscapes aren't as well known as its terrestrial ones. Therefore it's a water baby's delight, prime for exploration.

There is varied diving for all levels here, and it's also a great destination for snorkelers. **Sugar Loaf Reef** is popular with both, located inside the Nosy Tanikely nature reserve and marine park. Day-trippers wander around the white-sand islet, pointing at the Indo-Pacific bottlenose dolphins patrolling the perimeter, while snorkelers fin over the sloping reef, gliding through crystal clear water that illuminates layered coral gardens. Divers, however, have the best view, gently drifting with the current that flows around the edges of the island. We floated past purple vase sponges large enough to sit in, golden table coral that lives up to its name, and enormous and delicate branching sea fans in bright reds, eclipsing the table coral in size. Crocodilefish lie hidden in the sand while lavender-colored frogfish cling motionless to bommies bustling with clownfish and anemones.

Although highly touristed, the amount of life in this small park shows that the reserve is working. It's a positive example of how Madagascar could thrive with more protected areas like this.

Open Water sites, like **Rosario** and **Two Sisters,** have similar, if not superior, spectacular coral formations, although the visibility is dimmed by nutrient-rich currents. Large schools of trevally and tuna more than compensate, surrounding divers

A humpback whale breaches off the coast of Nosy Komba. More than 34 species of whales and dolphins visit the area, along with whale sharks.

in dizzying tornados before disappearing with astonishing speed.

The **Mitsiu Wreck,** a small fishing boat resting at 89 feet (27 m), is home to a plethora of marine life, including clouds of lionfish (native to the area) and large schools of trevally, which also attracts the local fishing fleet, long-lining by hand out of their dugout pirogues. *(Tip: Carrying a dive knife is a good precaution at this site, due to its popularity with fishermen.)*

As this is still a relatively new dive destination, divers should bear in mind that the diving is a little rough-and-ready here. But this is also an area that benefits massively from dive tourism, and that alone—coupled with great diving—makes it worth a visit.

WISH WE KNEW

This was the only country where we were approached for a bribe (at the airport on departure)—"Do you have a gift for me?" The U.S. Embassy's advice is to not pay bribes and report incidents, but it's unsettling when it happens. Be prepared.

(Tip: There is one shop on Nosy Komba, and more on neighboring Nosy Be. Book in advance, and the shops arrange to pick up divers and snorkelers at their hotels by boat in the morning, dropping them off in the afternoon.)

If it's whale shark season (mid-October to mid-December), dive shops will combine diving with a **whale shark snorkel.** If a whale shark is spotted, snorkelers gear up and slip softly into the water to swim alongside the spotted gentle giants as they suck up plankton through wide mouths. Although these filter feeders are the largest fish in the sea (reaching city bus lengths), whale sharks are shy; they reminded us of gargantuan tadpoles, with sweet, almost surprised, expressions. Whale sharks are also surprisingly swift swimmers: They move like white sharks, and we were finning full out to keep pace with even leisurely moving juveniles.

(Tip: Support operators who follow best practices like keeping snorkelers a minimum 10 ft/3 m distance from the animal, and definitely no touching. Let the whale shark dictate the experience.)

Establishing formal protections for whale sharks is a wonderful opportunity for Madagascar. The three-month whale-shark tourism season in Nosy Be brings in more than $1.5 million USD, with a 2021 study confirming Madagascar is a hot spot for whale sharks. More than 400 individuals have been identified so far. Protecting whale sharks is an overwhelmingly popular initiative (supported by more than 90 percent of tourists and operators), and hopefully Madagascar can transform whale shark research and protection into a long-term, sustainable industry, one befitting of such a magical place.

Snorkelers and divers of all levels will love this area, which has nutrient-rich currents, colorful coral gardens, and fish-filled wrecks.

NEED TO KNOW

GETTING HERE: Multiple European and African hubs fly to Madagascar. (Check out our tip about Ethiopian Airlines via Addis Ababa on page 201.) Fascene Airport on Nosy Be is the best entry point for Nosy Komba.

GETTING AROUND: It's a 20-minute taxi ride from the airport to the port, and 10 minutes by boat to Nosy Komba. Speak to lodges about transfers.

PACKING TIPS: It's humid and the mosquitoes are voracious. Casual, covering, breathable, and quick-drying clothes are best, with sturdy footwear.

WEATHER: Temps average 86°F (30°C) in this Southern Hemisphere spot. May through December is the best time to visit; October through December is best for diving; January through March is cyclone season.

IN ADDITION: You will be approached at every turn with offers to help carry your bags. A simple *"non, merci"* suffices if you want to carry your own; otherwise, carry small amounts of cash for tipping.

Diving

OVERVIEW: Madagascar is an up-and-coming, year-round dive destination where the underwater world is as diverse and wonder-filled as the terrestrial, with reef, wreck, wall, and drift dives for all levels. Dive tourism is especially beneficial to this area.

- **Visibility:** Around 49 feet (15 m)
- **Water Temp:** 79°F (26°C) in winter / 84°F (29°C) in summer
- **Depth Range:** 59 to 89 feet (18 to 27 m)

MARINE LIFE: Trevally, batfish, (native) lionfish, scorpionfish, giant clams, frogfish, Malabar grouper, Klunzinger's wrasse, whale sharks (mid-October–mid-December), manta rays (September), Indo-Pacific bottlenose dolphins, humpback whales, turtles, sponges, and good coral (sea fans, table, and more)

SHOP INFO: We dove with **Nosy Komba Plongée**, a small shop and dive school located in Ampangorinana Village on Nosy Komba. They know their area well, are

invested in it, and have a great staff. They have good boats and do water pickups at hotels around the island for a (usual) half day of diving. During whale shark season, they'll combine dives with whale shark snorkels.

Accommodations

HIGH-END: Tsara Komba Luxury Beach & Forest Lodge is perched on a hillside with spectacular views. This four-star lodge radiates local charm, from its sumptuously simple decor (crafted by Madagascan artists), to its sustainability initiatives, to its welcoming staff, most of whom live in two neighboring villages. Eight bungalows (max 18 guests at the lodge) flank the main building, which holds the restaurant and lounge. ~$348 USD

MID-RANGE: Coco Komba Lodge is located on the western side of the island near a small village. This secluded five-bungalow spot has a family feel and an on-site restaurant. ~$76 USD

BUDGET: Auberge Le Maki Lodge is perched on a rock overlooking the sea, near Ampangorinana Village. It has five simple bungalows, a restaurant, and utilizes solar energy for water heating. ~$60 USD

Food & Drink

Most lodges are isolated, so meals are lodge-based. **Dinner at Tsara Komba** is a sensual experience. Menus favor "slow food"–style cuisine made from the lodge's organic garden and locally sourced fish. For example, barracuda marinated in berries and mango, with a wild dill filling and served with green citrus vinaigrette.

Breakfast is simple (eggs, yogurt, and cereal), served with fresh fruit, tea, and coffee. Every morning we were joined by brightly colored gold dust day geckos, ever hopeful for a drop of honey or jam. Their presence made breakfast our favorite meal of the day.

Thanks to an abundance of natural fruit, vanilla, and cocoa, **desserts** here are divine. Think roasted pineapple, served with mango and coconut, and a scoop of freshly made papaya sorbet.

NIUE

Punching Above Its Weight

Niue is one of the world's smallest countries situated on one of the world's largest raised coral atolls. It might be small, but as far as conservation goes, Niue is a heavyweight.

It was the first country to become a dark sky sanctuary. It's preserved its largest remaining forest area (the Huvalu Forest Conservation Area, covering 23 percent of the island). Niue also established an enormous marine reserve, the Moana Mahu Marine Protected Area (49,035 sq mi/127,000 sq km), constituting 40 percent of the country's exclusive economic zone.

Located 1,491 miles (2,400 km) northeast of New Zealand, Niue is a self-governing nation in close alliance with New Zealand (all Niueans have dual citizenship). There are approximately 1,700 residents living in 14 villages around Niue, and the land belongs to their families, cultivating a strong connection to the island they call home.

Niue is a quirky place with its own rhythm, and that's just how Niueans prefer it. This place is made for self-exploration, with a wealth of natural attractions to enjoy: There are sheltered rocky coves to swim in, scenic forest walks to wander, dolphins and whales to watch, and snorkeling and diving in remarkable visibility, with a healthy population of endemic sea snakes. Niue is laid back, but not for sitting still.

Niue quickly became one of our favorite places on the planet, and it's another spot Chris wants to move us to. (I was told good-naturedly that I was "too effervescent" for island life, so there's that.)

Come see why we love it; we have a feeling you will, too. ■

Niue is an explorer's dream. Its coastline is riddled with caves, rock pools, and surprising finds, like the oasis of Togo Chasm (pictured).

This wild drop of an island is located in the middle of an ocean triangle formed by Tonga, Samoa, and the Cook Islands. From the air, it resembles a flat green muffin top: Niue's highest peak is 223 feet (68 m) above sea level, and rocks (rock pools, rock chasms, rock pinnacles) dominate the landscape; white-sand beaches are thin on the ground.

Niue is believed to have been settled more than a thousand years ago by voyagers from Polynesia. Similar to Rarotonga (page 256), visitors are absorbed into the island's daily rhythms rather than set apart in tourist areas. Niue is Niue, and you're welcome to come along. Strike up a conversation while picking up some homemade coconut bread from a café, or browse the thrice-weekly *makete* (market) for handicrafts and fresh fruit, or to ogle at live *uga* (coconut crab) for sale. This fearsome-looking crab is a culturally important delicacy that is now protected: Uga can be consumed on Niue, but export is prohibited, to keep harvest rates within sustainable levels.

Mostly, though, visitors are given their own space to explore, and driving tours of the island never disappoint.

(Tip: Pack your swimsuit, towel, reef shoes [not flip-flops], reusable water bottle, and snacks, like locally made coconut and plantain chips. There is good signage and natural paths with wooden guardrails, but that's about it. **Explore Niue** offers guided tours, including an orientation tour that is a great introduction to Niue.)

Starting from Alofi town center and traveling counterclockwise, drive to **Avatele Beach** (a good snorkel/swim spot) and **Washaway Café,** a real-deal beach café with an "honesty bar" that is open Sundays from 11 a.m. until late.

Along the southeast coast, a long flight of stairs leads to **Anapala Chasm,** a cold, dark freshwater pool. Farther along the coast in the Huvalu Forest Conservation Area is **Togo Chasm.** Follow the coastal forest path as it winds through razor-sharp pinnacles, past waves thundering against the coastline, and descend a ladder into an unlikely find: a protected inland oasis, with white sand, palm trees, and an algae-choked lagoon.

Within the Huvalu Forest Conservation Area are forest tracks like **Vinivini Bush Road,** an old 4WD trail through mature rainforest that can be walked or cycled. (The complete loop is around 8.4 mi/13.5 km; stop off at the **Hikulagi Sculpture Park.**)

The northwest coast is dotted with secluded caves and chasms (**Matapa, Limu,** and **Vaila,** for example), some with sheltered rock pools for swimming. **Avaiki Cave** was our favorite, and one of the most magical experiences of our entire journey. Soaring cathedral ceilings arc over an opalescent pool of blues, popping pinks, and glowing purples, with views straight out to sea. It was heaven on earth, and it's easy to understand the cultural importance of these places. These caves are Niue's history. They were freshwater sources and homes for early

National Geographic Explorer Dr. Jessica Cramp calls Niue "one of my favorite places on the planet." Sharks Pacific (page 259) conducts research here.

Make a Difference

Just by visiting Niue you're supporting a destination that is making an effort to create a long-term, sustainable future for itself. Pay attention to the **Niue Ocean Wide Project** (NOW) *(niueoceanwide.com)*, a partnership between Niue's government and Tofia Niue, a local nonprofit that aims to ensure the long-term sustainability of Niue's ocean resources. NOW has created a vast no-take marine reserve around Beveridge Reef (a partially submerged atoll in its waters) and reinvigorated community-managed marine areas, which helps maintain cultural heritage and healthy fish stocks for food. They are also working with neighboring South Pacific countries on sustainable fishing practices for pelagic migratory species, including sharks with Dr. Jessica Cramp and tuna with Dr. Alan Friedlander of Pristine Seas.

settlers. They are places of ancient burials and the wellspring of legends.

(Tip: Pools can be "forbidden" for traditional reasons—for example, during the kaloma *[juvenile goatfish] spawning season, an authentic Niuean tradition, which takes place sometime between January and April, and lasts an unpredictable length of time. Please adhere to closures. Also, don't walk on coral and avoid wearing lotions and repellents in the pools.)*

Underwater, Niue's rocky landscape continues, with the same caverns, canyons, and arches found topside. (The limestone filters rainwater, resulting in remarkable visibility.) This is another spot for exploratory diving: Along with a dozen or so established dive sites, more are being discovered all the time.

The **Tunnel** is an easy dive. Deep channels cut through twisted topography, leading to a coral garden where propagation efforts are under way. In 2017, Niue lost around 60 percent of its coral in a major bleaching event, and the island's isolation means the reef is vulnerable. In addition, Drupella snails are attacking the weakened coral. (Divers can assist dive guides in removing the snails to help preserve coral. Thousands have been taken off the reef so far.)

Other spots like **Chimney** (a dark cave with a vertical chimney exit onto a reef) and **Bubble Cave** (a small cave where the air pressure changes with

Niue's endemic katuali (flat-tail sea snake) are often spotted by divers. Katuali lay their eggs in dry crevices in sea caves.

the surge) offer a little more excitement with their intriguing landscapes.

The **Dome Cave** is a place of dreams—wondrous and spooky in equal measures. Timing it with the surge, we entered a short, dark tunnel. (It easily fits four abreast and eyes quickly adjust.) We emerged into an open chamber with thousands of ancient stalactites, stalagmites, and fluted columns, removing our gear and climbing up onto the rocks for a good look around. But we weren't alone in the cave.

The Dome Cave is a favorite with katuali, a flat-tail sea snake endemic to Niue. These lithe black-and-white creatures are highly venomous and remarkably placid and curious. The cave was filled with them: Dozens joined us entering and exiting the cave and a ball of mating katuali were writhing on a

Upon arrival, all visitors who intend to drive (necessary for getting around Niue) have to report to the police station and purchase a Niuean driver's license (around $20 USD). It's an unapologetic shakedown, but you get a great souvenir.

nearby rock ledge. I accidentally stood on one's tail (it bumped against my bare leg to let me know, but it wasn't aggressive), and I watched another swim through the gap between Chris's BCD and his chest, entering through one armhole and exiting through the other, as we timed our exit with the surge. We emerged into a canyon-walled maze, navigating it with our katuali companions.

If you visit during July through October, you might have the opportunity to **snorkel with humpback whales.** (Niue respects the whales' privacy, and strict regulations are enforced, such as going out with a licensed operator.)

For Niueans, the massive conservation efforts are a way of honoring their ancestors, while protecting their future—not just spiritually but financially as well. Niue's wonders, like all nature, are valuable assets. Conservation experts estimate that natural capital—forests, wetlands, soil, water, air, all living things (from mammals to microbes)—contribute more than $125 trillion USD to the global economy every year. (Not to mention we're dependent on natural capital for our survival.) However, up until now, societies have valued the *depletion* of these resources—take now and pay later—rather than seeing the overwhelming value in protecting our irreplaceable natural wealth.

Niue is making that transition. And that alone should be reason to visit. But from glittering rock pools to katuali, whales to uga, and dark skies shimmering with thousands of bright stars, Niue makes a bold impression.

Limu Pools is one of many sheltered, natural rock pools to be discovered along Niue's coastline.

NEED TO KNOW

GETTING HERE: Air New Zealand has direct flights from Auckland to Niue twice a week. (Niue is on the eastern side of the international dateline from New Zealand.) When departing Niue, check in and drop off your bags around 9 a.m. and return around noon.

GETTING AROUND: Renting a car is best and driving explorations are a ball. You can drive around the island in about two hours.

PACKING TIPS: Casual dress for warm weather. Pack good reef shoes (rocks are slippery and sharp) and walking shoes, plus a wind jacket and warmer layer.

WEATHER: Niue has warm temperatures (averaging 77°F/25°C) that cool in the evenings. Many Niueans visit with family and friends during Southern Hemisphere summer (November through March), and tourism businesses may or may not be open (check and prebook accommodations). There are yacht crowds May through November, whale-watching season is July through October, and diving is year-round (conditions tend to be a little rougher December through April).

IN ADDITION: Sundays are closed for rest and worship. There are no ATMs on Niue: Bring New Zealand dollars or withdraw cash from the island's one bank.

Diving

OVERVIEW: An enormous marine reserve, twisted rock formations (tunnels, caves, chimneys), spectacular visibility, visiting whales, and endemic sea snakes. This is a special place with unique diving, suitable for divers of all levels, although a little experience is helpful.

- **Visibility:** Beyond 98 feet (30 m)
- **Water Temp:** 73°F (23°C) in winter / 82°F (28°C) in summer
- **Depth Range:** Up to 98 feet (30 m)

MARINE LIFE: Katuali (flat-tail sea snake), green turtles, whitetip reef sharks, reef fish, trevally, eagle rays, honeycomb grouper, yellowstripe goatfish, dolphins, and seasonal humpback whales

SHOP INFO: After our visit, and due to the pandemic, Niue's two dive shops were purchased by a single new dive operator and merged into the island's only shop—**Niue Blue.** This isn't their first rodeo: The new owners have 20 years' experience operating a dive business in New Zealand and previous dive experience in Niue. They also received strong endorsement from the previous dive shop that we dove with on-island—a shop we rated highly. Located next to the Scenic Matavai Resort, Niue Blue offers diving and dive courses, snorkeling, and whale tours. Prebooking before arrival is essential.

Accommodations

HIGH-END: Stone Villas in Alofi is surrounded by forest, yet close to the main town. There are two one-bedroom, stand-alone, and self-contained villas, and rentals come with a private car to use. ~$140 USD

MID-RANGE: Scenic Matavai Resort Niue is the only full-service resort on Niue, with an on-site restaurant, pool, ocean-view deck, and a variety of accommodation options. ~$120 USD

BUDGET: Taloa Heights is a centrally located collection of eight free-standing, self-catering, studio-style cabins, each featuring a small kitchen, snug interior, and deck with views. Town is a short walk away. ~$90 USD

Food & Drink

Have at least one meal at Scenic Matavai's **Dolphin Restaurant,** which has ocean views and dishes that are a blend of Niuean and European cuisine.

Falala Fa Café & Bar is a local favorite, sourcing fresh ingredients to create delicious dishes with an island twist, like coconut crab and crayfish chowder, or fish parcels wrapped in banana leaves infused with coconut cream, island ginger, and lemon.

Hio Café is a tiny eatery with an ocean-view deck. This lively spot serves up burgers, nachos, and fish tacos, and they make some of the best smoothies we've ever had (the papaya mint on a hot day hits the spot!).

OKINAWA

A Cultural Stronghold in Subtropical Islands

f Japan is shaped like a dragon, Okinawa is the dragon's tail, stretching out between the East China Sea and the Philippine Sea until it almost touches Taiwan. The Okinawa Prefecture comprises more than 160 islands, 47 of which are inhabited. Naha is the capital, located on the long and narrow main island, which looks as though it's been chipped away at the edges by time.

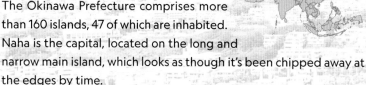

The striking Shuri Castle is a good emblem for Okinawa. The red wooden palace was the cultural heart of the Ryukyu Kingdom, which flourished from 1429 to 1879. The Ryukyu Kingdom was an independent center of politics, art, trade, and diplomacy, where all were welcome. Flanking either side of its main hall were two guesthouses, one designed in the Japanese architectural style, the other in Chinese. Their purpose was to make the visiting guests of major trade partners feel at home, as they often stayed for long periods of time following arduous journeys. It was a deft and thoughtful touch.

Shuri Castle has been torn to its foundations many times by war and fire, most recently in 2019. That, too, is representative of Okinawa. Japan took full control of Okinawa in 1879; it was also under U.S. administration for a time after WWII, all of which shaped its unique culture.

Today, Okinawa is a modern place with strong, distinctive roots. There are nine UNESCO World Heritage sites here. The food and art are amazing, and the diving even more so: Okinawa is known as the "Hawai'i of Japan" thanks to its rich coral reefs and warm, clear water.

This is a place that stays with you. Any visit will spark a desire to return, because any visit barely scratches the surface. ■

Capital city Naha's neighborhoods encircle Shuri Castle, which is emblematic of Okinawa: resilient, diplomatic, and unique.

Most of Okinawa's action happens in the southern half of the main island. There are beaches, castles, and quirky neighborhoods, including Chatan, home to the **American Village,** a fun Japanese replication of American culture. *(Tip: Visit the **Akara/Bokunen Art Museum,** featuring prints from Okinawan artist Bokunen Naka, and go for a soak in the natural hot springs complex of **Terme Villa Chula-U.**)*

Naha's neighborhoods encircle **Shuri Castle,** marching almost to its gates. This UNESCO World Heritage site, in whatever state it's in, should be one of your first stops. For 450 years, this was where the king lived and government officials worked. Some areas, like the throne room, are red and gold and opulent. Other areas have a *ryokan* feel, with tatami-matted rooms and delicate artwork. Visitors can hire a guide or self-guide, following a circular route through informative exhibits outlining the history and culture of the Ryukyu Kingdom, viewing artifacts on display.

(Tip: At the time of writing, the plan was to rebuild the castle by 2026. Travelers are encouraged to visit during the reconstruction.)

Located about 17 miles (28 km) north of Naha is **Murasaki Mura,** a re-creation of a traditional village complex that is home to more than 30 artisan workshops. Visitors can try their hands at traditional pottery making and glassblowing, and participate in cultural arts like dance, music, and karate.

Whale-watching is growing in popularity in Japan, thanks to groups like the Zamami Village Whale Watching Association (Kerama Islands).

NEARBY

Yonaguni Jima, Japan's westernmost point, is closer to Taiwan than Okinawa. Divers flock to its underwater monolith, still debated as to whether it's a natural formation or the submerged ruins of an ancient city. (Flights available from Naha.)

Okinawa is the birthplace of karate. Its origins are believed to have traveled here with Chinese martial arts practitioners when they visited Okinawa in the 1300s. We couldn't pass up the opportunity to **take a class at the International Karate Study Centre** (IKSC). This dojo complex welcomes all ages and abilities, from first-timers like us, to travelers who come to stay on-site and immerse themselves in the art.

In a large, unadorned training room, our instructor guided us through basic patterns of movements. It reinforced the maxim that what is simple isn't easy. As with practicing yoga, the challenge lies in perfecting the building blocks, maintaining fluidity, and focusing within, not on the external (attack).

(Tip: Classes are available in Japanese and English, are one-hour long, and are tailored to the student. Extended sessions and courses available. Book in advance.)

Karate classes are a worthwhile experience for divers, reinforcing self-reliance and calm problem-solving. The precision and attention to detail found in the dojo is often replicated in Okinawa's enthusiastic diving community. Both shore and boat diving are popular here, with most dives taking place on shallow, sloping coral reefs.

The **Sunabe Seawall,** just north of Chatan, stretches for around three miles (5 km) and is home to several shallow sites (around 59 ft/18 m deep) renowned for bright, soft coral. It can be accessed

by shore or boat, and there are plenty of reef fish, turtles, sea snakes, shrimp, and anemone crabs. (This is also a top night-diving spot.) One of the sites, a no-fishing area called the **Water Treatment Plant,** has two coral-encrusted, human-made structures that are a refuge for all manner of fish, including a patrolling school of barracuda.

Shore diving is popular on Okinawa, with sloping reefs renowned for soft coral in bright colors.

Cape Manzamo, also known as Cape Manza, near Onna Village (17 mi/27 km north of Chatan), is another popular spot. This collection of dive sites sports fascinating topography and marine life, from the maze of passages and swim-throughs at **Onna Point** to the **Toilet Bowl,** filled with fish, turtles, coral, and sharks. This horseshoe-shaped site gets its name from the frequent surge that flushes in and out, so enter and exit with care.

The **Kerama Islands** are located about 22 miles (35 km) west of Naha. There are more than 20 startlingly green islands, with emerald waters and creamy beaches. We dove near **Aka Island** during a storm, and the visibility was still crystal clear.

Here, coral bommies stud a snow white seafloor. As we finned from bommie to bommie, circling these mini-worlds bustling with marine life, we often found ourselves accompanied by sea snakes and turtles. We also saw a lot of WWII debris, like bundles of 50-caliber bullets, half-coated with sand. We were told that every time a typhoon comes through, something new is revealed, reminders of the United States' amphibious invasion of Okinawa during WWII.

If visiting December through April, stay on Zamami Island in the Kerama Islands and go out **whale-watching with the Zamami Village Whale Watching Association** (ZWWA). The organization was established in 1991 to protect the humpback whales that visit Okinawa every year. A next to nil population of whales in the 1960s has increased to more than 1,300 individuals, with an average of 250 returning yearly. "We are the hometowns of these whales," Hirokazu Otsubo, secretary-general of the ZWWA told us. "They deserve our protection."

Japan is synonymous with whale hunting and, worryingly, pulled out of the International Whaling Commission (IWC) in late 2018, arguing that whale hunting is part of their culture. However, the sign of a strong culture is its ability to evolve, and data shows whale-watching in Japan is on the rise. There are ways to honor the past while adapting for the future.

This lesson is on display at the **Okinawa Prefectural Peace Memorial Museum,** on the southeastern tip of the main island. This peaceful park overlooks stunning sea cliffs and has row upon row of granite blocks inscribed with the names of the more than 200,000 people who lost their lives here during WWII. The names are irrespective of nationality—Japanese, American, and more than 25 percent of Okinawa's civilian population.

In one of those serendipitous travel moments, the taxi driver who brought us to the memorial took us to visit the grave of his father, an Okinawan killed by an American soldier. "But my mother and I would have starved if it hadn't been for the kindness of the Americans after the battles. [My father] would be happy to have you visit him," he added.

We—an Okinawan, an American, and a German—stood by his father's grave 75 years after D-Day, remembering his father and our grandfathers (all

Known as the "Hawai'i of Japan," Okinawa has a subtropical climate with rich coral reefs and warm, clear water.

four fought in the war, for four different countries), and memories turned to laughter, coloring that pensive place like sunshine.

The diplomacy of the Ryukyu Kingdom. The nonaggressive art of karate. The persistent patience of coral reefs, weathering storms and currents. The kindness of strangers and the promise that time brings healing and change. Okinawa is generous with her gifts, and a wise and welcoming teacher to travelers.

Make a Difference

The **Zamami Village Whale Watching Association** (*zwwa.okinawa*) was founded by a collective of 15 companies to promote whale-watching and conservation. December through April, they offer twice daily whale-watching tours, following an agreed set of self-imposed, best-practice rules. You have to be staying on island to go on a tour, due to the unpredictability of weather and wildlife, but it's a wonderful local experience and a great way to place an economic value on living whales. If visiting on a day trip or out of season, visit their office in Zamami's port. They have interesting informational displays and souvenirs for sale. To learn more about the fascinating world of whale societies and their importance, check out Brian Skerry's book and Emmy-winning television series *Secrets of the Whales*.

NEED TO KNOW

GETTING HERE: Naha Airport receives direct flights from most major Japanese cities, as well as some international flights.

GETTING AROUND: You can walk around Chatan. For the rest of the island, rent a car or use buses or taxis.

PACKING TIPS: Dressy-casual layers and a daypack come in handy. The most important packing tip is good socks (many establishments require the removal of shoes) and shoes that slip on/off, rather than lace.

WEATHER: Okinawa is warm and comfortable year-round, with temps ranging from 63°F (17°C) in winter to 82°F (28°C) in summer. Summer is busy and also typhoon season. Winter is cooler with rougher conditions. Diving is year-round, but June and July are prime time.

IN ADDITION: Although Japanese is the main language in Okinawa, many businesses and people speak English, a nod to the United States' enduring presence here since WWII.

Diving

OVERVIEW: Tropical, diverse diving in Japan, from South Pacific–looking islands with coral gardens in great visibility, to main island shore-diving over reefs renowned for soft coral and epic night dives, to caves and WWII wreckage. Suitable for all levels.

- **Visibility:** 66-plus feet (20+ m) average
- **Water Temp:** 68°F (20°C) in winter / 84°F (29°C) in summer
- **Depth Range:** Less than 66 feet (20 m) on average

MARINE LIFE: Okinawa is known for its soft coral. There are also turtles, sea snakes, lionfish, puffer fish, nudibranchs, octopuses, jacks, barracuda, and reef fish. Humpback whales December through April.

SHOP INFO: We dove with **Reef Encounters,** the premier dive shop specializing in international (and English-speaking) divers visiting Okinawa. They offer boat and shore dives based out of Chatan, and offer free pickups from most hotels in Chatan and the American Village. This is a well-set-up shop with a focus on small groups (max six divers per guide); they also offer courses and gear rental. In the Kerama Islands, we dove with **Zamami Sailing,** a father-son operation that offers dive trips off a sailing yacht moored in Zamami. English is more limited, but the diving is safety-focused and spot-on. They close shop for a few weeks in January and February, and summer can be booked out months in advance. (They have a lot of repeat customers.) Divers can come over from the main island for a one-dive day trip or stay on Zamami to do multiple dives.

Accommodations

HIGH-END: Rinken's Hotel is located in Chatan, easy walking distance to the beach and the American Village. It has 25 basic rooms with ocean views, a restaurant, and weekly live performances of Okinawan music. ~$129 USD

MID-RANGE: Okinawa Green Lodge is a trailer-style, one-bedroom, self-contained villa with living room and kitchen near Araha Beach. ~$105 USD

BUDGET: The high-rise **Beach Tower Okinawa** has wonderful staff and is situated in the same great location as Rinken's Hotel. The 280 rooms are spacious and comfortable, some with sweeping ocean views, and they offer an amazing buffet dinner. ~$80 USD

Food & Drink

Ryukyu Sabo Ashibiuna is located near Shuri Castle and is open for lunch. The indoor restaurant overlooks a peaceful outdoor garden, and the food is top-notch traditional Okinawan cuisine, like *rafute* (pork simmered in soy sauce) and soba topped with spare ribs.

We went to **Ajijiman** (close to the American Village) a lot for dishes like *mozuku* (seaweed) tempura, chicken wings, and edamame. It had a great, almost pub-style atmosphere.

Gajimaru Shokudo in Chatan is a locals' lunch spot, serving classics like *chanpurū* stir fry, miso soup, and crispy white fish with pickled radish and cabbage.

ORKNEY ISLANDS

An Ocean of Time

Orkney is shaped by two things: the sea and time.

This archipelago of 70 islands, 20 of which are inhabited, lies in the North Sea, 10 miles (16 km) north of mainland Scotland. Orkney's 570 miles (917 km) of coastline features grim lances of sea stacks and weather-worn cliffs. Its interior bears a striking lack of trees, which can't withstand the winds. Instead, rolling green hills are studded with round bales, grazed by dappled horses with heavy manes, and cut through with stone walls.

Orkney is a place that wears time. It's seen more than 5,000 years of human habitation, as evidenced by standing stones and the remnants of Neolithic homes. (The island is a UNESCO World Heritage site.)

More than a thousand years ago, Vikings discovered the attraction that draws divers today: a strategic and vast natural harbor. Accessible by a maze of narrow channels, it is the ideal place to shelter or hide a fleet of ships. Viking earls—some wise, some wicked—ruled over Orkney until the islands were handed over to Scotland as part of a marriage settlement in 1468.

Changing hands, however, was merely logistics. Orcadians, forged by storms and isolation, are a friendly, independent, and resourceful people. (The islands have produced a surfeit of explorers.)

This place forced us to confront two very difficult questions: Why haven't we been here before, and how soon can we return? ■

A diver shines a light on history. Scapa Flow harbor has been used since Viking times and is filled with wrecks, including WWI battleships.

The Mainland, Orkney's main island, was our base. The picturesque stone village of Stromness, nestled along the protected bay of Hamnavoe, is one of the Mainland's two main townships (the other being Kirkwall, an ancient Norse town and Orkney's capital).

Stromness has always welcomed visitors with a safe port. Sleek cats camp out in sunny spots along the town's precariously narrow flagstone streets and the cries of seabirds are ever present. Grab a coffee at the **Bayleaf Delicatessen** and nose around art galleries and bookstores. Stop by **Login's Well** (now sealed), once a freshwater source for renowned ships like *Resolution, Discovery, Erebus,* and *Terror.*

The **Stromness Museum** (established 1837) is a labyrinth and treasure trove crammed with artifacts from strange and faraway countries that seafaring Orcadians sent home to their families. This delightful collection has no rhyme or reason—a taxidermy Jamaican hummingbird sits next to a brick from a Babylon palace. Every glance reveals something new.

There is also an exhibit on **Scapa Flow,** a 120-square-mile (310 sq km) area that has been a

harbor since Viking times and bore witness to the maritime golden age. It is said that no wind can harm ships in this naturally protected anchorage; man, on the other hand, has done plenty of damage.

Scapa Flow played a critical role in both World Wars. In 1918, it was the holding pen for the German High Seas Fleet following armistice. While terms were being debated, Admiral Ludwig von Reuter decided he would rather see his fleet of 74 ships at the bottom of the sea than in British hands and scuttled them, incurring some of the last casualties of the Great War. Many ships were later salvaged, but three battleships and four light cruisers remained, contributing to one of the greatest wreck diving sites in the world. It is unusual to dive an area with lots of large wrecks in close proximity; diving an area with multiple WWI wrecks is unicorn-rare.

Dives begin with a checkout shore dive in the shallower (36 ft/11 m) World War II area of Scapa Flow called the **Churchill Barriers.** These blockaded passages were built to protect the harboring British fleet from marauding German U-boats. Although there are some small critters (sea stars, crabs, and flapper skates), like all of Scapa Flow, the drawing cards are the wrecks rather than marine life.

From there, it's on to the show-stealers: the wrecks of the High Seas Fleet, resting in 52 to 151 feet of water (16 to 46 m). Divers descend along a shot line through cold, murky, green-tinged water. Visibility is low, which adds to the atmosphere.

Conger in the cannon! A conger eel takes shelter in a Scapa Flow wreck, which now houses marine life like crabs, sea stars, and sponges.

Dawn comes to the Ring of Brodgar, a Neolithic circle of angular standing stones.

It's eerie, watching the huge ships slowly take shape. The wrecks are covered in more than 100 years' worth of growth—seaweed and small barnacles—that gives them an encrusted look, blurring their lines. Once your eyes adapt, there is always something to catch your attention: anchor chains, looming gun turrets, and empty frames where the lifeboats once hung.

(Tip: Although the wrecks have become more penetrable as they age, do so with caution, as the structures are old, visibility is low, and it's easy to kick up silt.)

The **S.M.S. *Dresden*** is one of the smaller cruisers, surprisingly intact and resting on its port side on an incline. It is often used as the starter wreck, thanks to its shallower bow section (82 ft/25 m). Look for plentiful feather stars, and the rare feather star shrimp. The **S.M.S. *Karlsruhe,*** another light cruiser, is more damaged but provides greater penetration opportunities. It is also home to a bed of horse mussels.

The **S.M.S. *Markgraf,*** though, is the grand-daddy wreck. The 479-foot-long (146 m) König-class battleship was involved in most of the World War I fleet actions. Despite resting upturned on her starboard side in 148 feet (45 m) of water for over a century, she's still in good condition, wowing divers (who return again and again) with her immensity and presence.

Diving Scapa Flow is usually an all-day outing on converted fishing boats, with warm drinks during surface intervals to relieve the Orkney chill. These intervals give you plenty of time to reflect on your proximity to history. Scapa Flow has harbored warships since the days of the Vikings, which is heady to think about. We're just passing through.

(Tip: Advanced Open Water, deep dive, and dry suit certifications are useful here. Orkney is a great place to do further training or tech diving courses. Make sure you're familiar with British diving rules.)

That just-passing-through feeling is something you'll experience on land, as well. It's not uncommon to drive past a standing stone or Neolithic settlement, tucked among the pink-purple blooms of heather, easily accessible and explorable.

Skara Brae is a preserved Stone Age settlement uncovered on the west coast during an 1850 storm. Skara Brae dates back to 3100 B.C. and was inhabited before the Pyramids at Giza and Stonehenge were built. This UNESCO World Heritage site is a subterranean, seaside maze of interconnected homes, complete with stone furniture (beds and cupboards that are remarkably similar to furniture today). Some 5,000 years ago, life played out here: For around 600 years people were born, they hunted and farmed, they sheltered together, they died. It is a thought-provoking place.

(Tip: Visit nearby **Skaill House,** *a 17th-century manor with a fascinating history and filled with extraordinary artifacts like Captain Cook's dinner service, brought here by his crew after his death in Hawai'i [page 148].)*

The **Ring of Brodgar**—a circle 341 feet (104 m) in diameter, bordered by thin, angular red sandstone standing stones—keeps watch on a field of pink and purple heather between the Lochs of Stenness and Harray, an important bird reserve. It predates Stonehenge by 500 years.

In comparison, **Highland Park** whisky is a drop in the time bucket. They've been distilling whisky since 1798 at the same Kirkwall site where their founder, a Viking descendant by the name of Magnus Eunson, used to run an illicit still.

Skara Brae is a subterranean, seaside settlement that was inhabited before the Pyramids at Giza and Stonehenge were built.

The tradition hasn't changed much over time. Barley is smoked over 4,000-year-old heathery peat taken from their own moor on the shores of Scapa Flow in one of the distillery's two kilns: the Old Kiln (the original) or the New Kiln (1907).

(Tip: Tours are available. Book in advance. Highland Park is usually closed mid-July to mid-August.)

Their golden whisky is Orkney in a glass: the land, the sea, the time—a taste that is both sweet and complex, and rich beyond measure.

Make a Difference

The Orkney Islands have taken their future into their own hands. They invested heavily in renewable resources, and in 2020, all of the islands' yearly electricity demands were met by solar, wind (the islands are home to more than 700 micro wind turbines), and marine energy. Since 2003, Orkney has been home to leaders in the deployment of marine energy services. And with 62-foot (19 m) waves and strong tides, Orkney is the ideal place to test marine energy converters, which generate electricity by harnessing the power of the ocean. Recently, Orkney announced a multimillion-dollar investment in "smart energy." The goal is to eventually eliminate the need for fossil fuels. Think we can't science our way out of the mess we've created? Let Orkney be your inspiration.

GETTING HERE: Loganair flies to the Mainland from major Scottish hubs including Glasgow and Edinburgh. Ferry transport is also available.

GETTING AROUND: Orkney is ideal for self-exploration: Country roads are scenic, slow, and two-laned. There are several car agencies on the Mainland. Buses, taxis, interisland ferries, and bike rentals are also available.

PACKING TIPS: Scarves. Everyone wears scarves here—men, women, children. Pack outdoorsy, casual layers and a good pair of hiking boots.

WEATHER: Surprisingly temperate but windy. Summer (June through September) is the best time for diving, with temperatures around 60°F (15.5°C), and it is light until late in the day. Winter is around 41°F (5°C), and light during the middle of the day.

IN ADDITION: We can't imagine a better holiday destination for adventurous couples, solo travelers, or families with young children. The cost is in getting here. Once here, Orkney is inexpensive, fascinating, friendly, outdoorsy, and easy to get around.

Diving

OVERVIEW: One of the best wreck diving destinations in the world, and one of the few places with diveable World War I shipwrecks.

- **Visibility:** From 16 to 30 feet (5 to 9 m)
- **Water Temp:** 44.6°F (7°C) in winter / 55.4°F (13°C) in summer
- **Depth Range:** 75-plus feet (22.9+ m)

MARINE LIFE: Scapa Flow is all about the wrecks rather than marine life, but you might see conger eels, sponges, crabs, jellyfish, flapper skates, warbonnet fish, sea stars, brittle stars, and sea urchins.

SHOP INFO: **Kraken Diving** in Stromness is the only operator offering guided dives of Scapa Flow, as well as diving courses. Kraken has experienced instructors who have dived Scapa Flow thousands of times. Safety is their top priority. (Book in advance.)

Accommodations

HIGH-END: The **Merkister Hotel** has an alone-on-the-moors feel, located in the middle of the Mainland on the shores of Harray Loch (roughly 15 minutes' drive from Kirkwall or Stromness). This small, family-run hotel is peaceful, with an on-site restaurant. ~$241 USD

MID-RANGE: The **Ferry Inn,** located on the Stromness waterfront, is wonderfully Orcadian. This family-run hotel has simple, comfortable rooms located upstairs from a sociable pub that's a local favorite. It's central, surprisingly quiet, and bursting with personality. We loved our stay here. ~$174 USD

BUDGET: The **Orkney Hotel** dates back to 1670. It's had a few modern touches since then (like Wi-Fi), but still maintains its original charm. This 30-room hotel is located near the center of Kirkwall, the former home of a local merchant. (Look for the 17th-century love message he left his wife near the entrance.) ~$139 USD

Food & Drink

The **Ferry Inn** offers traditional fare that's locally sourced (from farmers, butchers, and a sustainable fishing cooperative) and done right. For example: a roasted-vegetable-and-Orkney-farmhouse-cheese tart, steak-and-ale casserole, or freshly caught haddock and chips. Booking in advance is advised—this place is popular!

The 1890s Kirkwall Hotel's **Harbour View Restaurant & Highland Park Bar** serves up a traditional weekend brunch (10 a.m.–2 p.m.) that's worth partaking in: Orkney roast (lamb or beef), gravy, roast potatoes, market veggies, and Yorkshire pudding (plus more than 100 Highland Park whiskies at the ready).

Located about 15 minutes' drive from Stromness, the Orcadian-owned **Orkney Brewery** is housed in a former schoolhouse (which was attended by the owner's father), with tasting flights of award-winning, hand-crafted beer paired with delicious meals. Tours (including a special kids' tour with Victorian costumes) available.

UNITED STATES

OUTER BANKS

Shifting Sands

The Outer Banks (OBX) is a chain of barrier islands, as thin and fine as the sketch of an artist's pencil, separating the Atlantic Ocean from the North Carolina mainland coast. The islands extend more than 130 miles (209 km) south from the North Carolina–Virginia border, cradling a series of shallow sounds. You can sit on an OBX beach reading a book and be 30 miles (48 km) out to sea.

This dynamic seaside environment is home to a surprising number of firsts: the United States' first national seashore (Cape Hatteras, established 1953); the first motor-operated flight (Orville and Wilbur Wright took to the skies here in December 1903); America's first English colony (settlers arrived on Roanoke Island in 1587); and America's first great mystery (those same settlers disappeared in 1590).

Weather-worn towns with picturesque names like Kitty Hawk and Kill Devil Hills are home to resilient residents. The natural rhythm and beauty of this place appeals to writers, artists, photographers, and pirates—Blackbeard himself plied these waters 300 years ago. This is also where he met his fate: He was killed by British naval forces in a bloody battle on Ocracoke in 1718.

OBX is a dangerous place for sailors, pirate or not: Since 1526, there have been more than 2,000 shipwrecks along the North Carolina coast, thanks to unseen, ever shifting sandbars that sway with every storm. This wreck-filled and sharky ribbon of coastline carries the nickname the Graveyard of the Atlantic. A terror for sailors, perhaps, but a haven for divers and visitors looking for someplace truly special. ∎

An aerial view captures the beauty and fragility of the Outer Banks, a chain of barrier islands on the east coast of the United States.

Sand dunes shimmer in sea haze. The sharp smells of pine trees, cedar, and ocean air mingle in an invigorating perfume. Ghostly surf rumbles rhythmically in the background; if you listen closely, it's almost always within earshot. We breathe deeply in OBX.

The popular swath between Kill Devil Hills and Nags Head is the perfect place to start, and the **Wright Brothers National Memorial**—the site of the world's first motor-operated flight—should be one of your first stops. Wilbur and Orville Wright selected this spot because of its incessant wind. After four years of experimentation, they lifted our collective dreams airborne on December 17, 1903. The entire first flight only lasted 12 seconds and could have taken place in the cargo hold of a 747. Visitors can follow boulder markers on a grassy field charting the 120-foot (36.5 m) course of the initial flight and subsequent trials. There is also a monument (a pleasant walk up Kill Devil Hill), a reconstructed hangar of their 1903 living quarters and workshop, and an informative visitors center that tells the Wright brothers' story, a lesson in

tenacity: Flight didn't just happen—they had to work for it. (Tip: Park ranger talks take place every hour, and don't forget to turn your eyes skyward and marvel that you're standing on the ground where flight began, as planes soar overhead. It makes the neck tingle.)

Visiting the Wright Brothers National Memorial gave us itchy wings of our own, so we headed just over four miles (7 km) south to Jockey's Ridge State Park to **go fly a kite with Kitty Hawk Kites.** This sea of sand is the tallest living sand dune on the Atlantic coast, and it brings out the barefoot kid in all of us. In a one-hour lesson, we rediscovered the unbridled, uncomplicated joy of flying kites, guiding two-handed, colorful sports kites through a stiff wind that snapped at the lines. (Tip: Kitty Hawk Kites also offers hang-gliding lessons—even for kids! For something truly special, fly a rare, museum-quality reproduction of the Wright brothers' 1902 glider.)

Hatteras—63 miles (101 km) south of Jockey's Ridge—has an entirely different feel: lusher and calmer, with quaint communities of large, pointed houses, usually hitched up on stilts, most with a sundowner platform at roof level.

(Tip: En route to Hatteras, stop at the **Pea Island National Refuge Visitor Center.** On the sound side there's amazing bird-watching; on the beach side lies the **Oriental, a Civil War wreck** that was part of the Burnside Expedition. You can still see the ship's boiler poking out of the surf.)

The drawing card here is the iconic black-and-white-striped **Cape Hatteras Lighthouse.** At 198.5 feet (60.5 m), it's the tallest brick lighthouse in America, erected in 1870. There are different tours available. We chose to climb the winding cast-iron staircase to the top: 257 steps, the equivalent of 12

The North Carolina Aquarium on Roanoke Island is a great place for kids to learn more about the area's marine life, like this seahorse.

Make a Difference

The **North Carolina Aquarium on Roanoke Island's** (ncaquariums.com/roanoke-island) on-site Sea Turtle Assistance and Rehabilitation (STAR) Center is a working hospital that is open to the public, who can watch staff in action and learn more about threats sea turtles face. (Six of the seven sea turtle species are classified as threatened to critically endangered, due to climate change, hunting, and pollution.) The aquarium also has a cool kids' area. At Operation Sea Turtle Rescue, kids don lab coats and take their (replica) turtle through a diagnostic center before treating it and placing it in the recovery pool. STAR works with their all-volunteer local partner, NEST (Network for Endangered Sea Turtles—nestonline.org) to rescue, release, and educate. Visits and donations welcome.

stories, with eight landings along the way. The view from the gusty lookout is worth the effort: a green, marshy, inland forest, and the ghostly sea, obscuring the Graveyard of the Atlantic.

Full disclosure: OBX is one of two places we didn't get to dive on our 14-month journey. In Taiwan (page 112), we both had bad colds. Here, we were weathered out by massive storms that made diving impossible. However, we gathered as much on-the-ground research as we could.

The coastal geography of shallow, shifting sandbars and the treacherous collision of the warm Gulf Stream slamming into the cold Labrador Current has resulted in a wealth of shipwrecks scattered from Nags Head down to Wilmington, North Carolina. This is a diving tour of maritime history, including World War I and II wrecks (like the **U.S.S. Schurz,** a German gunship that collided with another ship in 1918, and the **U-532,** a German U-boat that picked the wrong fight while cruising OBX in 1942). The only diveable American submarine in the United States can also be found here— the **U.S.S. Tarpon,** a WWII sub that sank in 1957.

Other ships, including the **U.S.C.G. Cutter Spar** and the **Aeolus,** were purpose-sunk as artificial reef projects, lending their hulls to North Carolina's marine life. Sand tiger sharks, in particular, seem to enjoy the area's wrecks as much as divers do, and these big, toothy beauties (reaching lengths of 10.5 ft/3.2 m and 350 lb/159 kg) can often be found

The black-and-white Cape Hatteras Lighthouse is an icon, and the views from the top are worth the 12-story climb.

aggregating around wrecks, delighting divers with their quiet and inquisitive companionship.

Most dives are full-day boat trips, although beach dives are available. Wreck sites tend to be slightly deeper than usual, around the 100-foot (30 m) mark. There are dives for all levels here, but divers with more experience will probably enjoy the action more.

(Tip: Currents can be strong on these open-ocean wrecks, and visibility varied. Many sites are dived on the buddy system: A topside crew provides advice and support, but dives are self-guided. In the excitement of sharks and ships, it's easy to forget that many wrecks are also graveyards. Treat these memorials with respect.)

___FOR FAMILIES_____

Hop on a two-hour, 4WD experience with **Corolla Outback Adventures** to see herds of wild horses roaming the beaches and maritime forests in Corolla (road's end in northern OBX). This area is untamed and beautiful, just like its horses.

Whether on land or underwater, it's easy to see that the Outer Banks are remarkably resilient: Its ever shifting sands flex under onslaughts of wind and sea. If left to its own devices, OBX would ride out every storm, as it's always done.

It is our involvement with these islands that is fragile. Locals joke that "if you buy a house soundside, eventually you'll have ocean-front property." Storms sweep the legs out from stilted houses. Land erodes from underneath bridges and roads. We are trying to be permanent on an impermanent place.

It's a fallacy to think it's just low-lying Pacific and Caribbean islands that will be affected by rising sea levels and worsening, more frequent storms. At the time of writing, approximately 100 million people live within 3.3 feet (1 m) of the current tide levels, and it's estimated that sea levels will rise more than 10 inches in the next 80 years if we simply manage to *stay the course,* keeping within the 3.6°F (2°C) target set in the Paris Agreement. Millions of people could be displaced, and that includes people in Boston, New York City, and New Jersey, all of which are already investing heavily in the search for preventative solutions.

The Outer Banks, too, is trying to keep the tides at bay, investing millions of dollars in renourishment projects, which involve dumping eroded sand back onto OBX beaches.

One way or another, OBX will weather the storm; hopefully we can weather the storm along with it, because this is a special and remarkable place—one worth returning to.

A sand tiger shark swims over one of the area's plentiful wrecks.

GETTING HERE: Norfolk International Airport (82 mi/132 km) and Raleigh-Durham International Airport (192 mi/309 km) are both gateways to OBX.

GETTING AROUND: Rental cars are ideal for exploring, and driving is easy and scenic: Take your time. Don't tackle 4WD-only beaches unless you have the proper vehicle and know what you're doing.

PACKING TIPS: OBX is windy, sunny, and sandy—casual layers are the norm here.

WEATHER: Summer is busy. Nags Head's population swells from approximately 2,900 to 40,000 during the summer months, due to glorious weather (in the low 80s°F/26.6°C) and school holidays; water clarity is best during this time, too. Spring and fall are locals' favorites, with pleasant weather perfect for outdoor activities. Many places close in winter, but you'll have long, empty stretches of beach all to yourself.

IN ADDITION: The sound side of OBX is as beautiful and often quieter than the ocean side. Be mindful of riptides in the Atlantic. Ask a ranger if you're unfamiliar with the area before wading in.

Diving

OVERVIEW: OBX is a wreck-filled chain of barrier islands that's not a well-known diving destination, but divers familiar with the area are passionate about diving here. This Mission Blue Hope Spot has some of the highest biodiversity and density of marine life on the American East Coast, including more than 80 species of fish.

- **Visibility:** Averages around 50 feet (15 m)
- **Water Temp:** 63°F (12°C) in winter / 82°F (28°C) in summer
- **Depth Range:** Offshore wrecks usually lie around 100 feet (30.5 m)

MARINE LIFE: Sharks (sand tiger, dusky, great hammerhead), turtles (Kemp's ridley, hawksbill, loggerhead, green, leatherback), amberjacks, and schooling fish

SHOP INFO: There are a few dive shops in Hatteras, and in Morehead City and Beaufort City on the mainland. **Roanoke Island Outfitters** in Manteo (near Nags Head) is the most central to OBX, and we sat through several storms at their shop, discussing diving in the area. This is a small shop with extensive local knowledge and a loyal clientele. They do dive courses, shore dives, and dive charters.

Accommodations

HIGH-END: First Colony Inn, located south of Jockey's Ridge State Park and a short walk to the beach, was built in 1932 and is listed on the National Register of Historic Places. This 27-room bed-and-breakfast is classic OBX style: wraparound porches, an angular roof wreathed in weathered shingles, with weather-watch windows peering from the top of the building. ~$220 USD

MID-RANGE: Down Hatteras way, the **Inn on Pamlico Sound** is a boutique waterfront spot with a pool and on-site restaurant, located on the banks of one of North America's largest estuaries. ~$180 USD

BUDGET: The **Oregon Inlet Campground** is the most northerly of four campgrounds in Cape Hatteras National Seashore, located near Nags Head. Facilities include tent campsites, RV hookups, flush toilets, drinking water, and heated outdoor showers. ~$30 USD

Food & Drink

The **Lifesaving Station** (located in a historic lifesaving station in Duck) is an elegant restaurant serving up southern comfort food such as okra, fried chicken and biscuits, and corn chowder.

Fishheads Bar & Grill is a family-friendly spot, located at the Outer Banks fishing pier. They have 33 craft brews on tap to accompany burgers, tacos, and sandwiches.

The **Orange Blossom Bakery and Café** on Hatteras is beloved for their signature pastry, Apple Uglies. These clumps of deep-fried dough are stuffed with apples and glazed with sugar. They also do excellent breakfast sandwiches. Open until 11 a.m. seasonally.

PETIT ST. VINCENT

Home Sweet Home

You know that dream about buying an island and living out carefree days in paradise? This is that island.

Petit St. Vincent (colloquially known as PSV) is a privately owned, 115-acre (47 ha) island in the Lesser Antilles chain, the southernmost dot of land in St. Vincent and the Grenadines. Two miles (3.2 km) of white-sand beaches encircle an interior filled with tropical woodlands that rise up to a natural lookout called Marni Hill (275 ft/84 m).

The only thing on PSV is an exclusive resort—the Petit St. Vincent Private Island Resort. It boasts 22 cottages scattered across the island, homey places with lofty, airy ceilings and wooden decks with sweeping views of an emerald-colored sea. Temperatures hover around 85°F (29.4°C) year-round, cooled by trade winds.

Relaxing here is harder than you think. PSV is big on outdoor activities and is ideal for families with kids. Guests can choose to go kayaking, sailing, tortoise-spotting, snorkeling, or cycling (a paved track runs around half the island). They can tackle the 20-station fitness trail (which runs around the other half), take a yoga class, or hike to the top of Marni Hill. But diving is what PSV does best, with consistently good conditions, easy reef explorations for newbies, and feistier, deeper drift dives for the more experienced.

Fair warning: You will not want to leave. We met one couple who have spent two weeks here every year for the past 20 years. To them, this is home, and every visit is a reunion. We can easily understand why. ∎

NORTH AMERICA

Petit St. Vincent

ST. VINCENT & THE GRENADINES

Petit St. Vincent is designed to help you unwind. The island has one resort, featuring 22 secluded, ocean-view cottages.

Island life has a rhythm, and it's remarkably easy to adapt to it.

Keen to relax and unwind? There are more than a **dozen secluded beach areas** on the west side (Caribbean Beach) and northwest side (West End Beach) of Petite St. Vincent. Beaches are first claimed, first served, and a typical area has a hammock shaded by a thatched roof, lawn chairs and table, and a jug of iced water at the ready. White sand slips into a turquoise sea, and while neighbors are nearby, discreet groves of trees act as screens. You feel you have a sliver of paradise all to yourself, listening to the sound of waves and birdsong. It's the easiest thing in the world to while away a day on the sand, armed with a good book.

Feeling peckish? Communication on PSV takes place by semaphore: Different-colored flags alert guests' needs to the attentive staff (the staff-to-guest-ratio is 3:1, so there's always someone on flag-spotting duty). If you're hungry, simply peruse the menu at a nearby flag station, fill in your preferred lunch (or cocktail) selection, pop it into the

bamboo holder, and raise the yellow flag. Staff circle the island every 15 to 20 minutes and, depending on the timing of their last pass, voilà! Lunch is delivered about a half hour later.

(Tip: This flag system is also used at the cottages. Yellow flags indicate you'd like something; red is do not disturb. It's also worth noting that PSV seems to go out of its way to employ friendly people. Return guests told us that long-standing friendships with staff members are one of the reasons they keep coming back.)

Fun with flags aside, we found it difficult to sit still on an island filled with possibilities. Our mornings began with a circuit of the island's **20-station fitness trail,** a self-guided dirt and sand track circling one-half of the island and featuring different exercise stations en route. Or we partook in a **yoga class** at one of two outdoor pavilions. The 30-minute **Marni Hill walk** also gets the blood pumping: A rock-and-dirt path winds through the inland forest to the island's natural lookout, a flat-topped hill overlooking many shades of blue, cooled by a steady breeze.

Keep an eye out for the island's population of **red-footed tortoises.** The larger ones wander freely, but the resort holds youngsters in an enclosure near the Main Pavilion until they are large enough for land crabs to leave alone. (We found a half-dollar-size tortoise we named Winnebago. If you see him, please give him our love!)

Although PSV offers plenty of reasons to stay put, off-island excursions are a joy. On a **sailing trip** aboard the 49-foot (15 m) cutter-rig sloop *Beauty* we explored **Tobago Cays Marine Park,** a collection of five uninhabited cays and one inhabited island along a 2.5-mile (4 km) horseshoe-shaped reef. It takes about 90 minutes of sailing to reach

Sometimes we simply want a *vacation.* Choosing responsible operators (like Petit St. Vincent Resort) lets you leave your worries at home.

Make a Difference

Sometimes we just need a *vacation*. Doing your homework and choosing places that are doing the right thing allows you to leave your cares at home and shelve any fretting about environmental impacts. Look for places that are committed to protecting their corner of the planet and are actively investing in it, like PSV. For example: The lodge has installed a desalination plant to turn ocean water into drinkable tap water (avoiding importing plastic bottled water). They also employ people from local communities (one employee just celebrated 50 years) and run a scholarship fund to help finance education for their employees' children. Simply visiting PSV makes a difference. As our colleague Dr. Andrea Marshall likes to say: "If everyone chooses responsible operators, pretty soon there would only *be* responsible operators."

this 19-square-mile (50 sq km) marine protected area.

Once at the marine park, rangers approached our vessel to collect the required park fees, which are around $10 per person and are used toward the park's protection and preservation. Although this is a popular dive destination, we opted to hike and snorkel the area, and continued in a dinghy to **Horse Shoe Reef.** This is a swift drift snorkel from a deep sapphire wall to a shallow reef. The current carried us on a marvelous ride over brilliantly colored coral, nurse sharks, schools of blue tang, huge cow and parrot fish, and purple and gold sea fans.

(Tip: Once in the water, you're moving, so it helps to be comfortable with your gear before jumping in.)

Our next stop was the **Baradal Turtle Sanctuary,** a small cay with a protected seagrass-filled lagoon. We snorkeled with dozens of grazing green and hawksbill turtles, as stingrays circled lazily. We wrapped up our Tobago Cays trip with a short walk on land to look for iguanas before returning to the boat for a cooked lunch and a little rum punch. This is a full day out, but it's a good one.

PSV (along with surrounding islands Mayreau, Tobago Cays, and Union Island) offers a wide variety of dive sites. It's a popular area for turtles, as well as more than 20 species of whales and dolphins. PSV is a Marine Conservation Area that is adjacent to the St. Vincent and the Grenadines

Petit St. Vincent is enjoyable for all divers, but it's the ideal place to learn to dive, with warm, clear water and plenty of marine life.

Mission Blue Hope Spot. More than a decade of fishing and anchor restrictions has seen a steady increase in biomass.

For new divers, you couldn't find a better place to give scuba a try than PSV's surrounding house reef. These easy, shallow, sandy-bottomed dives are filled with fish like juvenile, adolescent, and adult drum fish; schools of blue tang; cowfish; and unicorn fish. There is even a wreck—the **Puruni,** a 1918 English gunship—resting in 40 feet (12 m) of water that is suitable for beginners. During our visit, we volunteered to share a Discover Scuba

Personalized, handwritten invitations are delivered to guests at breakfast for special resort functions. The most memorable was outdoor movie night, when we watched *Cool Runnings* on a screen at the Beach Restaurant.

Dive with two sisters, ages 12 and 13, since their father was stuck topside with a cold: Their delight at the underwater world was infectious and a wonderful reminder why we dive.

(Tip: PSV is the perfect place to learn to dive, and they offer courses and activities for kids ages five years old and up. Groups are small so the instructor can spend time with divers.)

More experienced divers have even more choices within an hour's boat travel, including deeper wall and drift dives. Mayreau, a small island and marine protected area, has an array of dive sites like the **Mayreau Gardens,** a drift dive over coral gardens frequented by rays and schooling fish. Two diver favorites are the **Hot Springs,** which bubble out of the sand thanks to an underwater volcano, and **Sail Rock,** a seamount that attracts a plethora of life, including schools of fish, stingrays, and sharks—even the occasional tiger. (This site is very weather dependent and strong currents can kick up.)

(Tip: Exploratory diving is also on offer for experienced divers who are keen to check out new sites. Speak to the shop if interested.)

As always, paradise has its problems. Whaling still takes place in the area. Fish populations are taking a hit from invading lionfish and illegal fishing, and hard and branching coral are struggling here. In an effort to help, PSV has constructed a coral nursery that will be used to repopulate reefs around the island.

As Jean-Michel Cousteau, son of ocean explorer Jacques-Yves Cousteau, has said: "It is our hope that by encouraging and enabling divers to explore the waters around PSV, we will be raising awareness of the importance of protecting our water planet."

It is, after all, our home.

Accessible only by boat, Petit St. Vincent has more than a dozen beach areas to choose from, some with views of neighboring islands.

NEED TO KNOW

GETTING HERE: Petit St. Vincent (PSV) can only be accessed by boat. It's a 20-minute boat ride (arranged by the lodge) from Union Island, which is part of St. Vincent and the Grenadines. Barbados, Grenada, and St. Lucia are all gateways to Union Island.

GETTING AROUND: This is an easy island to walk around. The lodge also offers bikes to guests and features golf cart–style service cars as needed.

PACKING TIPS: Relaxed resort wear. Don't forget to pack activewear for the fitness trail and yoga classes.

WEATHER: The average temperature is blissful, hovering around 85°F (29.4°C) year-round.

IN ADDITION: The lodge is closed from August through October. There are very limited Wi-Fi areas on the island; plan to be out of touch (a great perk for families looking to unplug together).

Diving

OVERVIEW: PSV is resort diving: warm water, a wide variety of dive sites to choose from, and visibility is good year-round. This is an ideal place for divers of all levels, and it is a feast for macro photographers.

- **Visibility:** Around 65 feet (20 m)
- **Water Temp:** 75°F (23.8°C) in winter / 88°F (31°C) in summer
- **Depth Range:** 26 to 100 feet (8 to 30 m)

MARINE LIFE: Drum fish, cowfish, unicorn fish, spiny lobster, stingrays, flying gurnard, barracuda, and nudibranchs. This area is popular for dolphins (Atlantic spinner, pan-tropical, clymene, bottlenose, and more) and whales (sperm, short-finned pilot, pygmy sperm, and melon-headed). Orcas can be seen year-round; humpbacks arrive January to May.

SHOP INFO: We dove with the on-island shop, **Jean-Michel Cousteau Diving Caribbean.** This is one of only two dive shops bearing the legendary Cousteau name, and—although Jean-Michel himself is not permanently on-site—he established the shop and oversees operations. The day-to-day running is left to the experienced staff. Due to the nature of the luxury resort, diving is conducted in small groups with multiple dive boats available. Let the shop know in advance if you're interested in taking a course.

Accommodations

HIGH-END: Petit St. Vincent is the only resort on the island, featuring 22 ocean-view luxury one- and two-bedroom cottages scattered across beaches, hills, and bluffs. Despite the elegant details (stone and hardwood, Italian linens, and plenty of space), the cottages feel homey, with plenty of nooks and crannies to tuck away belongings. You'll feel moved in and ready to relax in no time. Keen for something special? If you can swing it, you can rent out the entire island (up to 44 guests) for a special occasion at around *$30,000 USD.*

MID-RANGE: There are six two-bedroom **beachfront villas** that are ideal for families. Rates include all meals, nonalcoholic beverages, butler service, and all non-motorized water sports. *~$1,900 USD*

BUDGET: There are 16 one-bedroom **cottages** scattered across the island, each with a unique advantage, whether it's sweeping views of the Atlantic, or the perfect spot to watch the sunset. The same amenities apply. *~$1,350 USD*

Food & Drink

The **Main Pavilion** offers refined island dining: three-course meals and a cellar stocked with more than 5,000 bottles of wine. The real show-stealer, though, is the perched hilltop position.

The other dining option is the toes-in-the-sand **Beach Restaurant,** located by the sea and serving Mediterranean-style salads and Caribbean tapas. (Great for lunch or a lighter dinner.)

We're still dreaming of PSV's **breakfasts:** homemade banana and papaya jam (sourced and made on the island), lime yogurt, and breakfast beans.

PORT LINCOLN

Welcome to the Wild (Great White) West

Located across the bight from Adelaide in South Australia, Port Lincoln is a fascinating dichotomy of the old (sailors still reference charts made by Matthew Flinders in 1802) and the new (this aquaculture gold mine produces millions of dollars in largely sustainable farmed seafood). Although this harbor town is evolving, Port Lincoln hasn't lost its rough-and-ready character, or its wild beauty. The area is surrounded by a harsh landscape of scrub green, rust orange, and eye-blasting whites.

AUSTRALIA

Port Lincoln

If there is one thing Port Lincoln is known for besides seafood, it's sharks—specifically great white sharks, *Carcharodon carcharias,* "the ragged-tooth one." This is where shark-cage diving was pioneered by Rodney Fox, a great white shark attack survivor turned shark activist. Rodney had a hand in most of the early great white shark research, working with the likes of Jacques Cousteau and National Geographic, and coordinating the live shark footage for Steven Spielberg's *Jaws.*

Rodney's son, Andrew, now runs Rodney Fox Shark Expeditions (RFSE), the only place in the world with an ocean-floor cage, which offers divers the rare opportunity to see great white sharks from below. (There is also a surface cage for non-divers.)

If you want to see one of the world's most charismatic creatures, Port Lincoln is the place. Prepare to be spellbound. ■

A great white shark swims past the surface cage. Seeing one of these sharks up close is an extraordinary and unforgettable experience.

The moment a great white shark materializes out of the blue, you'll realize why you're here.

Great white sharks are some of the most awesome predators on the planet—powerful and charismatic. Yet due to their underwater domain and migratory nature, great whites remain a much maligned mystery. Their torpedo-shaped form is hauntingly familiar, their behavior an enigma. Spending (controlled) time in the water with them is a privilege, and RFSE is the only shark operator that allows divers to see them from a 360-degree vantage point as they cruise the seagrass beds and rocky reefs of the protected Neptune Islands.

This three- to 10-night expedition-style trip is for people who love sharks and want to learn more about them. It's an old-school voyage: educational, adventurous, and downright fun. The good thing about a multiday liveaboard is that everyone gets to participate and enjoy sharks in their own way and in their own time. This is a great experience for non-divers and divers of all levels, from newbies to experts, an opportunity to eat, sleep, and breathe sharks.

The dive plan is formed when the day begins, depending on weather and shark activity. The team puts out berley, a natural tuna mix, to attract

NEARBY

Tumby Bay Jetty (30 mi/48.3 km from Port Lincoln) is a good dive site for spotting the phantasmagorical leafy sea dragons. Whyalla, three hours from Port Lincoln, is the mating aggregation point for Australian giant cuttlefish (May to August).

sharks to the boat. (The sharks are around, but they aren't naturally interested in boats. The berley keeps them intrigued.)

There are two cages on the boat: a surface cage, holding four people, submerged a few feet under the surface, and an ocean-floor cage, holding three divers and a dive supervisor (or cage captain), lowered to a depth of 82 feet (25 m).

Surface cage divers descend a ladder through the top of the cage, breathing through a regulator attached to a hookah system. It's as easy as snorkeling: No dive certification is required, and kids as young as eight years old have fallen in love with great white sharks from this very vantage point.

Divers enter the **ocean-floor cage** from the main deck. The cage captain controls the rate of descent so all divers are able to equalize, coming to a stop about a foot (0.3 m) above the ocean floor.

Down here, the sharks are more relaxed (they tend to be more alert on the surface) and are usually found in greater numbers. They nose up to the cage, circling repeatedly. Divers might also spot massive smooth stingrays cruising the seagrass beds, fish (leatherjackets, trevally, and kingfish), and occasionally other species of sharks, like bronze whalers.

Due to the small group size and enclosed space, the cage captain can easily keep track of no-deco limits and air consumption, and the confined nature of the cage (no buoyancy to control or fins required)

Many shark-diving trips include a visit to Hopkins Island, to snorkel with playful, curious (and endangered) Australian sea lions.

means that Open Water certified divers are allowed to dive at slightly greater depths than normal.

Although more than 1,000 individual great whites have been identified in Neptune Islands Group (Ron and Valerie Taylor) Marine Park, sharks are wild, migratory creatures in a vast ocean, and they don't always come when they're called. It's essential to have the "roll with it" attitude of explorers and enjoy the experience for what it is.

When the sharks aren't around, excursions are often organized. Guests cruise the shorelines of the Neptune Islands—a pair known as North and South—in a small craft, spotting birds (like white-breasted sea eagles and albatross) and helping to monitor the seal population. The Neptunes are home to Australia's largest colony of New Zealand fur seals, and healthy seals mean healthy sharks.

At certain times of the year, while traveling between Port Lincoln and the Neptunes, RFSE will stop by Hopkins Island so guests can **swim with endangered Australian sea lions.** This is a special experience. These liquid-eyed, agile animals are

Aerial view of North Neptune, a scrub-coated granite island that is home to birds, reptiles, and Australia's largest colony of fur seals

as curious and playful as puppies, spinning around snorkelers in underwater acrobatics.

On some evenings, Andrew Fox will give a not-to-be-missed shark talk about biology and behavior, individual personalities (many sharks return to the Neptunes annually, year after year, and Andrew knows them well), and the latest research on these critically important apex predators. (The Fox Shark Research Foundation is involved in data collection, genetic studies, and researching the human impact on great white sharks—including a hard look at the cage diving industry).

Berleying, which is highly regulated in South Australia, can be a controversial subject. With highly migratory species (like great whites), there is no conclusive evidence that using berley affects their behavior long-term. What we do know is there has been a staggering drop in the population of oceanic sharks and rays—71 percent since 1970, mainly due to overfishing. This should be our flash point.

It's past time to flip the switch: We need to stop harping on how dangerous sharks are, and start thinking of them as endangered. And anyone who is fortunate enough to see these incredible sharks for themselves can't fail to become their champion. That's what we need right now.

Rodney Fox once told us: "The mornings and nights out here, you realize you're alone in a wilderness, on the edge of a huge ocean, and you've been allowed a glimpse of something otherworldly. Sharks are our monsters—ours to protect and ours to love."

(Tip: If you can't swing a multiday expedition, head out on a day trip to the Neptune Islands with **Calypso Star Charters** *to experience great whites from a surface cage. Sea lion swims offered, as well.)*

After returning to shore, the quirky township of **Port Lincoln** is well worth exploring. Don't miss the **Axel Stenross Maritime Museum,** which is a 20-minute walk from the Port Lincoln Hotel along the seaside **Parnkalla Trail.** This eclectic museum is crammed ceiling to floor with maritime memorabilia and—best of all—stories.

Goin' Off Safaris offers tailor-made guided excursions through Port Lincoln, **Mikkira Station** (an 1842 European homestead with resident koalas), **Glen Forest Tourist Park** (ideal for kids—it has kangaroos, wombats, and koalas), and **Coffin Bay** (a coastal town famous for oysters).

The area around Port Lincoln township is beautiful, desolate, and perfect for day drives. Keep your eyes peeled for emus and kangaroos.

The area surrounding Port Lincoln township makes for some stunning day drives. The **Eyre Peninsula** is a beautiful and desolate wilderness flanked by two national parks—**Lincoln National Park** and **Coffin Bay National Park.** Look for emus and kangaroos, and check out the dramatic red-cliff coastline and topaz shallows of **Fisheries Bay** and **Whaler's Way.**

(Tip: Read the informational signs: This area saw a lot of history. Look out for wildlife while driving. Oh, and mind the swimming—this is shark territory.)

Make a Difference

Established in 2001, the **Fox Shark Research Foundation** *(rodneyfox.com.au)* aims to give "great white sharks a voice"—dispelling misconceptions and gathering data to build up what little we know about these amazing creatures. The foundation has compiled a database of more than 1,000 individual great whites, deploying noninvasive tracking tags, monitoring feeding and migration habits, and researching any impact humans might be having on great whites (including the cage-diving industry). Diving with RFSE means you're contributing to the foundation's work, and guests are invited to assist with research. Want to help further? Financial donations to the foundation are always valued. If you have time in Adelaide, stop by the **Rodney Fox Shark Museum & Learning Centre.**

NEED TO KNOW

GETTING HERE: Qantas and Regional Express operate multiple daily flights from Adelaide to Port Lincoln. It's a four-hour boat ride to the Neptune Islands, where the ship shelters until its return to Port Lincoln.

GETTING AROUND: Self-driving is a great way to explore Port Lincoln before or after your liveaboard trip.

PACKING TIPS: Quick-drying shoes with grip for the decks (not flip-flops) and a pair of warm slippers with rubber soles for the interior. (Diver-dampened carpets are a terror on socks.) Dive gear (regulators, wet suits, etc.) can be rented on board or bring your own (personal mask strongly recommended). Towels provided. Seasickness medication advised (just in case).

WEATHER: Australia's southern coast can get wild, especially in Southern Hemisphere winter (June through September). RFSE has had a 95 percent success rate of shark sightings in the past 20 years.

IN ADDITION: Large reusable water bottles come in handy; it's important to stay hydrated on the ship.

Diving

OVERVIEW: This is the *only* place in the world to ocean-floor cage-dive with great white sharks, viewing one of the world's most powerful predators in its natural habitat.

- **Visibility:** Around 59 feet (18 m), with the clearest water August to October
- **Water Temp:** 59°F (15°C) in early spring / 66°F (19°C) in mid-autumn
- **Depth Range:** 0 to 82 feet (up to 25 m)

MARINE LIFE: Sharks (great white, bronze whaler, mako, blue, epaulette), New Zealand fur seals, Australian sea lions, horseshoe leatherjackets, trevally, kingfish, and smooth stingrays

SHOP INFO: RFSE is the pioneer operator with decades of experience, and one of three shark-cage operators in South Australia. (The other two are day-trip operators offering surface-cage experiences.) The shark diving industry is heavily regulated: Only two operators (RFSE and Calypso Star Charters) have been granted licenses to berley, and all operators meet strict safety regulations and observe non-activity days, which is a good thing for the sharks, visitors, and the industry.

Accommodations

HIGH-END: The *Rodney Fox* sleeps up to 18 passengers in nine differently configured cabins on a standard trip (sole occupancy available). The ship has plenty of hot showers and a welcoming lounge area lined with Andrew Fox's peerless photographs of great whites. The observation decks are great places to do a little stargazing at night, or shark-spotting during the day. Standby specials are available for flexible travelers. ~ *$1,435 USD for three nights/two days; longer trips available*

MID-RANGE: The **Marina Hotel** is situated outside the main township but within walking distance to the marina where the day-trip boats depart. ~ *$110 USD*

BUDGET: Conveniently located in town with sweeping views of Boston Bay, the **Port Lincoln Hotel** will surprise you with how quickly you feel at home here. Best town base for *Rodney Fox* departures. ~*$95 USD*

Food & Drink

Line & Label (attached to Peter Teakle's winery) is one of the restaurants elevating Port Lincoln's culinary game. Friendly staff helped us choose nannygai (a local fish) with slow potatoes for Chris, and a beet and carrot salad with local peach for me. (I loved it—and I dislike beets and carrots.) Book in advance.

Meals on the *Rodney Fox* (included) are simple, hot, and exactly what you're craving after a big day on the sea: potatoes, pasta, salads, and scrumptious desserts. (Drinks available for purchase.)

The **Fresh Fish Place** is a find, and a great spot for lunch. The fresh catch of the day and chips (french fries) costs around $10 USD. Check out the adjacent market selling salt, olive oil, and fresh fish.

KO LANTA

Divine Diving and Laid-Back Island Life

ASIA

THAILAND Ko Lanta

Ko Lanta is a group of 50-plus islands in the Andaman Sea, off the west coast of southern Thailand. The largest and best known island—Ko Lanta Yai, often referred to as Ko Lanta—is the preferred base. A variety of accommodations pepper the white-sand beaches on the west coast, with its enviable and uninterrupted sunset views. Mangroves and reefs surround the island, while a spine of rainforest plumps out its interior. Ko Lanta National Marine Park in the south protects a swath of these landscapes, along with many of the surrounding islands.

Ko Lanta is not flying under the radar: It shares the warm, aquamarine Andaman waters with hot spots Ko Phi Phi and Phuket. However, Ko Lanta retains an undiscovered, relaxed feel. Perhaps that's because it takes a little extra effort to get here. Mostly, though, we think Ko Lanta just can't be bothered. There are parties here: full-moon, half-moon, hey-it's-a-Tuesday parties. However, most evenings find travelers enjoying a delicious meal while watching the sun go down; later, they might stroll on an empty beach, or stargaze from a hammock, dreaming about tomorrow's diving. Rousing oneself for a rager slides into the too-hard basket. It's easier—and more pleasant—to simply be.

Because of this laid-back atmosphere, Ko Lanta is a wonderful destination for families or adventurous couples who don't want to be slowed down by hangovers. The diving is divine, the snorkeling spectacular, and there's a wide variety of activities from authentic Thai cooking classes to kayaking through mangroves to choose from.

Ko Lanta: You really should be here now. ■

Lanterns catch the breeze while hanging from one of the over-water restaurants in Ko Lanta's Old Town.

Ko Lanta has some of the most diverse diving in the world on its doorstep. The warm green waters of the Andaman hold vividly colored coral, a wide array of marine life (from manta rays to tiger tail seahorses), and a large number of sites to roll with the conditions.

Divers (and snorkelers) come to Ko Lanta for its marine world, and we'll wager you'll be spending most of your day on or under the water. Most of the diving is from boats departing from various parts of the island, including the long floating jetty in Kantiang Bay, and most of the diving is a full-day outing, as the sites are a one- to three-hour trip out to sea.

Ko Haa is a favorite. This marine park holds five islands (Ko Haa means "five islands"), those iconic pink-gray karst formations Thailand is famous for, clustered around an emerald-colored lagoon. This is a spot for snorkelers, swimmers, and divers of all levels, featuring about 12 sites, with depths reaching around 60 feet (18 m). It can get busy, but dive groups make an effort to give each other space and often a group will have an area all to itself.

We had a three-dive day here, beginning with the **Lagoon,** which is ideal for beginner divers (crystal clear water and good reference points).

Pimalai offers a Muay Thai boxing academy (beginner to advanced) that's fun and accessible, rather than hard-core. (Small group sizes; kids welcome!) There is also an aerial yoga class to take your practice to new heights.

The sandy bay is smattered with soft and hard coral, and there is plenty of marine life to marvel at: hawksbill turtles, curious longfin batfish, brown-marbled grouper, and porcupinefish.

The **Chimney** kicks things up a notch with its topography: Divers descend a tall, vertical chimney through clouds of schooling fish, opting to explore side tunnels that open into different chambers filled with lionfish, banded sea krait, and macro life. The pinnacle itself is covered in purple and pink coral, and it is washed by current, which brings in larger schools of snapper and barracuda. (We saw barracuda play a fascinating game of keep-away with a severed cobia head.) This spot is also home to a large number of the biggest, healthiest moray eels we've ever seen.

The caverns at the **Cathedral** are one of Ko Haa's highlights. The first two high-ceilinged chambers are connected by a shallow swim-through, providing a spectacular backdrop for a silhouette photo. On exiting, the rocky landscape is alive with squid, octopuses, beautiful lemon yellow tiger tail seahorses, brightly colored sponges, and large titan triggerfish, guarding their invisible Cones of Death. For those unfamiliar with titans, Thailand is instructive. Titan triggerfish are the fish most feared by dive guides. They aggressively guard their territory, which extends upward in the shape of a cone—swimming away horizontally is your best escape route.

Fish school around a colorful coral bommie in Ko Haa, a marine park that is a favorite with divers and snorkelers.

Authors Chris Taylor and Carrie Miller take a cooking class at Pimalai Resort and Spa, making dishes like red curry and *miang kham.*

This marine park is in pretty good shape, due to the number of dive boats that monitor it daily (during the months it's open). Fishermen aren't allowed within 1.9 miles (3 km) of the area, but their ghost nets are a real issue, especially at the beginning of the dive season. (The shops hold cleanups.)

(Tip: Ko Haa is closed between May and October, but not to worry: There are plenty of alternate sites to enjoy. During the low season, the departure point can change, too, as the boats are moored in different areas; check with the dive shop.)

Farther off the coast are two advanced and world-renowned dive sites: **Hin Daeng** and **Hin Muang** (Red Rock and Purple Rock, respectively, named for the coral that light up their landscapes). They are deeper dives on two open ocean pinnacles with unpredictable currents and less visibility, but they attract the marine life that likes those conditions: gorgonian fans, carpets of anemones, manta rays coming in for a clean, schooling fish, and occasionally sharks (whale, leopard, and gray reef).

When the Andaman releases you from her siren song, Ko Lanta is the perfect place to wake up and see where the day takes you, offering up caves, waterfalls, and mangroves to explore. With few roads, it's easy to rent a car or scooter for a leisurely look-round. *(Tip: People often try scooters for the first time on holiday, which is a great way to end your vacation quickly. Practice at home first, where the roads are familiar, before giving it a try someplace new.)*

Visit **Sala Dan,** Ko Lanta's main town, on the northern tip of the island; it has a high concentration of shops, restaurants, and cafés, some built on pylons over the channel that runs between Ko Lanta's two main islands. Ko Lanta's **Old Town** (also called Old Lanta Port), on the southeast coast of the island, is even more lovely—quiet (even when bustling) and timeless. Teak buildings—a mix of homes, restaurants, and shops, some more than 100 years old—are built on stilts over the water. The tide laps beneath the boards under your feet as you sip an iced coffee, or examine linen shirts and pants, hand-made rice jars, or colorful hammocks for sale.

You won't have a bad meal on Ko Lanta, and one not-to-be-missed island activity is to take a **traditional Thai cooking class.** We opted for Pimalai Resort and Spa's two-hour experience.

We began with the ingredients, browsing Pimalai's organic garden for items we needed, some of which we had never heard of—sweet basil, lemongrass, kaffir lime, butterfly-pea, Thai eggplants (which look a little like figs), and galangal.

Clad in our souvenir aprons, we headed to Pimalai's stunning Seven Seas restaurant, with its distracting views of Kantiang Bay, and set about preparing a three-course meal for our lunch. The menu included *miang kham* (a traditional snack of peanuts, lime, ginger, and raw coconut wrapped in a betel leaf, delivering a powerful punch of taste in one bite), *tom kha gai* soup, and red curry, cooked up with coconut milk we made from scratch. This is a fun and insightful glimpse into Thai culture, taught by a patient and encouraging chef. The resulting meal was one of the best of our entire trip.

We still cook the recipes from time to time, when we're feeling travel-sick. As the lemon-spicy smell wafts through the kitchen, it conjures up memories of showstopper sunsets fading into lantern-lit

Pimalai Resort and Spa's infinity pool has sweeping views of Kantiang.

beachside bars, humming with laughter and the clink of bottlenecks as friends cheer a day well spent. Karst formations rise up out of turquoise seas teeming with life, and Ko Lanta comes back to us. This is one of those places that sneaks up on you: In Ko Lanta, you're so present and relaxed in the moment, you don't realize how wonderful the travel experience is until you return home . . . and begin making plans to return.

Make a Difference

Depending on your bank, your money may be financing projects you don't support—like fossil fuel extraction. Since the 2016 Paris Agreement, major banks have provided $3.8 trillion of financing for fossil fuel industries with your money. (At the time of writing, JP Morgan Chase, Wells Fargo, Citigroup, and Bank of America are four of the largest financiers.) Do your research, make sure your bank's values align with your own, and pull your money if need be. In 2019, Norway's Government Pension Fund Global, the world's largest sovereign wealth fund, did just that, dealing a seismic blow to the fossil fuel industry by announcing it was going to get rid of its fossil fuel stocks and invest directly in renewable energy going forward. If people start moving their money to ethical options, banks will have to take notice.

NEED TO KNOW

GETTING HERE: Krabi airport is the closest to Ko Lanta. The two-hour journey is a mix of driving, car ferries, more driving, and possibly a speedboat. The trip is easier than it appears on paper, and many hotels will help with travel arrangements, so do ask.

GETTING AROUND: Unless you're based far from the dive shops, you won't need a rental car. Car and scooter rentals are offered by the day; taxis are also plentiful.

PACKING TIPS: Relaxed and casual. Ko Lanta is more traditional than some of the party islands.

WEATHER: The average temperature here is 86°F (30°C). November to April is hot and dry (high season), while May to October (green season) has periods of stormy weather, but the rain comes and goes—it's not monsoon season in the traditional sense.

IN ADDITION: Green season is a great time to visit Ko Lanta. There are significantly fewer visitors and hotel prices are a fraction of what they are during the high season. Ko Haa will be closed and the diving may operate differently, but green season is one of the best times to dive Ko Lanta.

Diving

OVERVIEW: World-class diving in the Andaman Sea from a quiet island base.

- **Visibility:** From 33 to 98-plus feet (10 to 30+ m), depending on location and time of year
- **Water Temp:** 81°F (27°C) in winter / 84°F (29°C) in summer
- **Depth Range:** 60 to 82 feet (18 to 25 m)

MARINE LIFE: Colorful hard and soft coral, manta rays, whale sharks, longfin batfish, moray eels, squid, octopuses, seahorses, triggerfish, porcupinefish, barracuda, pipefish, and nudibranchs

SHOP INFO: We dove with **Scubafish**, which has several locations on Ko Lanta, including at Pimalai. This shop knows diving. They keep group sizes small and offer training, and non-divers/snorkelers are welcome. They have two comfortable, purpose-built dive boats, which are important in an area with longer travel times. They also walk the talk, from ghost net cleanups to good briefings (on sunscreen, reef care, and wildlife interactions), and offer recycling/reusable cups on their boats.

Accommodations

HIGH-END: Pimalai Resort and Spa in Kantiang Bay is something special. This 120-room hotel has two sections: beachside and hillside, set in a lush 100 acres (40 ha). Pimalai has multiple restaurants, pools, a spa, and all the trimmings, but it's comfortable, not glitzy. And it has soul: Pimalai has set ambitious environmental targets, both for itself and Ko Lanta, and is leading the charge on reducing waste and saving water and energy, working with schools and the wider community. Complimentary round-trip transfers to Krabi Airport. ~$166 USD

MID-RANGE: The adults-only **Houben Hotel** (also in Kantiang Bay) is a 15-room boutique hotel with a European feel and flair, and a focus on tranquility. On-site bar and restaurant. ~$80 USD

BUDGET: Narima Bungalow Resort is located 2.5 miles (4 km) north of Kantiang Bay, offering cozy bungalow accommodations in a natural setting, featuring a terraced pool and on-site restaurant and bar. ~$45 USD

Food & Drink

Pimalai Resort and Spa has several restaurants to choose from: the high-end Seven Seas, with exquisite views of the bay; Spice and Rice, serving traditional Thai cuisine; and Rak Talay Beach Bar and Restaurant, perfect for light snacks and seafood.

Everyone eventually finds themselves at **Drunken Sailors,** a kicked-back hangout (with Wi-Fi, a book exchange, hammocks, beanbags, and tables) offering Thai and Western food, and spectacular coffees and fruit shakes.

Beachside **Aqua Bar** is the dive guides' watering hole—"always has been, always will be." You'll find drinks, food, and good music in a relaxed atmosphere.

RAROTONGA

Paradise Found

The Cook Islands are inhabited by approximately 15,000 people scattered across 15 individual islands covering a territory the size of Western Europe. More than half the population is settled on the main island of Rarotonga.

Rarotonga
COOK
ISLANDS

Cook Islanders have always been a voyaging people, undertaking ambitious open ocean journeys centuries ahead of other cultures. "The Vikings should have been called the Polynesians of the north; our ancestors were just that good," one proud local told us. It was through a gap in the fringing reef on the east side of Rarotonga that 20 massive *vaka* (voyaging canoes) set forth around the fifth century, seeking what they always sought: new lands and new beginnings. Ten were never heard from again. One made it to Easter Island, another to the Society Islands, one returned home, and seven arrived in New Zealand, believed to be the foundations of Māori culture.

Despite—or perhaps because of—their seagoing nature, land is precious to Cook Islanders; it can never be bought or sold (foreigners can only lease land). It is passed down through blood, with families taking the extra precaution of entombing ancestors on their closely cropped front lawns to make ownership claims irrefutable.

This place has personality. There is plenty to do. And it is blue-green beautiful.

Love yourself a little paradise. We'd return in a heartbeat. ■

By air, land, or sea, Rarotonga is a stunner, with a rugged interior, golden beaches, and fringing reefs cut through by channels.

Our days were full and never long enough here.

The diving in Rarotonga is spectacular, with underwater landscapes straight out of a Grimm's fairy tale: enchanted forests of giant, mushroom-shaped hard coral formations, both eerie and mesmerizing. Most dives are boat dives on the fringing reef that encircles the island. The easy conditions (clear, warm water) make it a good location for new divers, while the exceptional visibility and bounty of natural light makes this place ideal for underwater photography.

Nga Tipa is one of the fabled forests, a maze of channels winding through porites, a type of stony coral that looks like burgeoning mushrooms. This is an easy dive around 50 feet (15 m), with plenty of marine life (lemonpeel and flame angelfish, fire dartfish, and whitetip reef sharks) seeking cover under coral overhangs.

Coral Gardens is similar but with flourishes of fanned-out montipora coral colonies and coral bommies lining sandy trenches. These trenches are a favorite with whitetip reef sharks and we also spotted a hefty yellow-edged moray eel.

There are more than 30 sites around the island, and each side of the island has its own personality, from good coral coverage to shallow lagoons to steep drop-offs. The fringing reef slopes to around 100 feet (30 m) before plunging into the open ocean, and these drop-offs offer opportunities to spot elusive fish species, like Pitcairn and peppermint angelfish. Passages like **Tupapa** and **Avana** cut through the reef. These sand rivers are flanked by coral reefs and are frequented by turtles, sharks, plenty of butterflyfish (threadfin, Meyer's, and teardrop), and squadrons of eagle rays.

The Cook Islands have a 733,594-square-mile (1.9 million sq km) multiple-use marine park known as the **Marae Moana.** Formally established in 2017, it covers the country's exclusive economic zone and bans industrial fishing (long-liners and trawlers) within 50 nautical miles (93 km) of each island. However, more work is needed to complete the zoning of the park.

At the time of writing, deep-sea mining within the park is still a contentious subject. Environmentalists want a 10-year moratorium on seabed mining to collect baseline data and to conduct sufficient research to understand any potential environmental impacts. Scientists are concerned that we know too little about the deep ocean and how it supports life both above and below water, and even less about the impacts of mining it.

The Cook Islands government, however, is interested in exploratory mining now, believing it could diversify the country's revenue streams and contribute toward clean energy.

Balancing protection with sustainable development is difficult. In the Cook Islands, which has a total land area of 93 square miles (240 sq km), the surrounding ocean is a precious resource to local

A squadron of ocellated eagle rays glide over a sand channel in Rarotonga.

Make a Difference

Sharks Pacific *(sharkspacific.org)* is on a mission to protect sharks and the people and places they rely on by undertaking scientific field research, advocating for sharks in politics, and balancing conservation goals with the needs, history, and culture of local communities. Founder and National Geographic Explorer Dr. Jessica Cramp understands that marine reserves, while important, aren't enough to reduce mortality rates of sharks and rays: Fishing limits, community buy-in, active government support that includes training and enforcement, and continued science and education are also essential. This is an honest-to-goodness organization doing the research and liaising directly with fishermen and governments. How can you help? Follow along and provide funding (ongoing and one-off donations via the website).

people, and its health will play a significant role in the islands' future.

Cook Islanders are a modern Pacific culture, a blend of strong Polynesian heritage infused with the bits of Western influence they liked and decided to keep. Rarotonga is unique to most small islands in that visitors are part of the ebb and flow of daily life, rather than tucked away in a resort somewhere.

Everyone goes to market. The **Punanga Nui Cultural Market** is the come-together place on Saturday mornings. Located on the waterfront next to Avarua, Rarotonga's main township, it bustles with souvenir-seeking tourists, grocery shoppers, and vendors who are more interested in catching up with one another than pushing sales.

(Tip: The market opens early and closes around lunchtime; don't forget to carry cash.)

The **Muri Night Market** is a cash-only, BYOB market open several nights a week, serving ripping good local food (salt-and-pepper squid with chili and lime glaze, or marinated pulled pork) at cheap-as-chips prices. Share a table, share a laugh, but get here early: Food favorites run out quickly.

There is plenty of hiking around the island to work off all the good food. The half-day **Cross Island Trek** (also known as Pa's Trek) is a strenuous hike requiring a moderate level of fitness and an adventurous attitude, but it's worth every drop of

Rarotonga has a strong cultural heartbeat, and visitors are encouraged to take part in the ebb and flow of daily life here.

sweat. This 3.7-mile (6 km) hike climbs up and over the spine of the island, an elevation gain of 1,300 feet (396 m).

We followed an ancient trail past wavy trunks of banyan trees, the roots of which make excellent handholds on the slippery clay trail. The pinnacle is the base of the 1,312-foot (400 m) Needle, an "energy point" for Polynesian people, with near-360-degree views from the top. The hike wraps up at **Wigmore Falls,** where a packed lunch (and a swim, for those who bring their bathing suits) is waiting.

WISH WE KNEW

Wi-Fi can break the bank. Camera enthusiasts: Don't expect to upload any footage on island. Bring plenty of storage and tackle the uploading post-trip. Also, cash comes in handy, so carry some with you.

(Tip: Guided trips available. Bring a backpack, plenty of water, snacks, and sturdy footwear.)

If hiking isn't your bailiwick, or if traveling with a family, hop on a 3.5-hour **Koka Lagoon Cruise** for a snorkel at a marine reserve, followed by a stop at a *motu* (islet) for a barbecue lunch. This locally owned and operated business runs large glass-bottomed boats topped with thatched roofs and staffed by a high-energy crew.

Cultural experiences are a great way to engage with Rarotonga. **Te Vara Nui** presents a historical village tour with a buffet dinner and an overwater choreographed show, which can be viewed from chairs or a horseshoe-shaped platform that encircles the lake. It's a four-hour experience that is lively, enjoyable, and entertaining.

Te Ara—The Cook Islands Museum of Cultural Enterprise has fascinating exhibits on Cook Island history, navigation, settlement, and reef health. It's also a sustainable cultural business incubator supporting local businesses to develop locally made products, which are sold on-site.

For something truly special, island hop to **Aitutaki** for the Aitutaki Day Tour, operated by Air Rarotonga. A 45-minute flight landed us on a small island (population 2,000) with a lagoon the likes of which we've never seen. There are more shades of blue here than we thought possible, from the color of Bob Dylan's eyes, to tempest, to tourmaline. Silhouettes of palms rise up from the white beaches of motus, the water creaming in crystal turquoise along the edge of the comfortable, catamaran-style boat.

We stopped at three motus (mostly uninhabited except for hermit crabs) for short walks. There are also snorkeling opportunities with giant clams and the bulky, brutish giant trevally that hunt the lagoon. This is a full day out but a special one. Those shades of blue still haunt our memories.

There are plenty of opportunities for hiking in Rarotonga, ranging from easy wanders to half-day treks over the spine of the island.

NEED TO KNOW

GETTING HERE: Auckland, New Zealand, is the main hub to Rarotonga. Air New Zealand also has direct weekly flights from Sydney and Los Angeles.

GETTING AROUND: Although wizards on the water, Cook Islanders keep things simple on land. Rarotonga is encircled by a 20-mile (32 km) ring road. (Buses simply read "clockwise" or "anticlockwise.") Car and scooter rentals are common ways to get around; mind the 31-mile-per-hour (50 kph) speed limit.

PACKING TIPS: Sporty days, dressy casual nights sum up Rarotonga. Keep things light and comfortable. Pack a pair of hiking boots.

WEATHER: This Southern Hemisphere destination has a warm and sunny climate year-round, with a warmer and more humid season (and occasional tropical showers) November through March.

IN ADDITION: Although the Cook Islands manages its own affairs, it is technically a New Zealand colony, and much of its population (an estimated 60,000) makes use of their New Zealand passports to seek opportunities overseas. ("If everyone came home at once, the islands would probably sink," a Cook Islander joked.)

Diving

OVERVIEW: Rarotonga is a destination to dive for, with all types of sites (wrecks, coral gardens, sand rivers, caves, channels, drop-offs) for all levels of divers around the island, which is surrounded by a reef-fringed lagoon, sloping gently into deeper water.

- **Visibility:** From 65 to 100 feet (20 to 30 m) and beyond
- **Water Temp:** 72°F (22°C) in winter / 82°F (28°C) in summer
- **Depth Range:** Shallow to 100 feet (30 m)

MARINE LIFE: A riot of colorful reef fish, including Moorish idols, angelfish (lemonpeel, emperor, flame), grouper (peacock and honeycomb), triggerfish (titan, blackpatch, orangelined), whitetip reef sharks, eagle rays, moray eels, and fairy-tale hard coral formations

SHOP INFO: Rarotonga has two shops with stellar reputations. **Pacific Divers** is an experienced and conservation-minded shop that runs daily dive excursions from the island's southeast side (near Muri Beach). **Adventure Cook Islands Diving Centre** offers diving, free-diving, and snorkeling trips from the southwest (near Aroa Beach). Both offer one- and two-tank dives and courses. Booking in advance is recommended.

Accommodations

HIGH-END: Te Vakaroa is a beachfront collection of six villas that are a curious mix of rustic luxury and quirky charm. These two-floor apartments have open-air patios overlooking a swimming pool. Complete kitchens make it easy to dine in, and the Muri Night Market is close by. No children under 12. ~$602 USD

MID-RANGE: We consistently heard the same two phrases about the **Muri Beach Club Hotel:** "great location" and "friendly staff." This adults-only hotel is your typical beachfront resort, a 30-room sparkly oasis with a pool and lagoon to choose from. ~$355 USD

BUDGET: Dorothy's Muri Beach Bungalows is one of those rare finds—four self-contained bungalows located in the heart of popular Muri Beach. Dorothy's is island living made simple, for travelers who prefer to spend most of their time exploring. ~$129 USD

Food & Drink

The **Waterline Restaurant and Beach Bar** is oceanside deck dining under the soft light of wind-flickered candles. Boutique and favored by locals, this is a special spot, not just the spot to celebrate something special.

Bamboo Jacks is an indoor-outdoor restaurant serving up Asian cuisine with an island twist (like Cantonese-style ginger and spring onion crayfish).

21.3 Vaiana Bistro & Bar is the after-work hangout. On offer: live music, $10 meals (burgers and fries, chicken, fish wraps), beachside picnic tables, and a lagoon for the kids to splash in.

SABA

The Little Island That Could

aba is the antithesis of a Caribbean island. Everything about this rugged green jewel is improbable, from the wandering beach that appears occasionally in the rocky coastline, to the 330-foot-high (100 m) sea cliffs that culminate in a cloud forest.

There are four villages on this five-square-mile (13 sq km) island: the Bottom (the capital), St. John's (residential), Windwardside (tourism hub), and Zion's Hill/Hell's Gate (residential). By law, these quaint communities must have red roofs, white exteriors, and green or red latticework shutters.

Saba has two directions—down or up—and two main activities that seem to complement that: diving and hiking. Both are best described as spectacular and unexpected, from the underwater pinnacles rising from depths of 1,000 feet (305 m) a half mile (1 km) offshore, to the 2,877-foot (877 m) summit of Mount Scenery, covered in orchids and mountain mahogany. (As Saba is a Dutch municipality, this is the highest official point in the Netherlands.)

But it's the Sabans themselves that make this place special. Sabans are tolerant. Independent. Ingenious. They're fiercely proud of their island and love showing it off.

With a population of 2,000 and an average of 100 visitors on the island at any given time, you will soon be one of the "sinners amongst the saints"—an island joke: Saba's closest neighbors are Saint Eustatius and Sint Maarten.

This place instantly, strangely felt like home to us. So much so that Chris still wants us to move here. (Or Byron Bay, Niue, or Cocos, pages 52, 214, and 310—his top four preferred places for us to live post-trip.)

We loved Saba; we think you will, too. ∎

The Harry L. Johnson Museum in Windwardside holds a collection of Saba's heritage and culture in a 160-year-old sea captain's cottage.

It's helpful to understand a little of Saba's can-do history before exploring. Ingenuity is at the heart of both the people and the island.

Saba was a seafaring society out of necessity, but the skill of Saban sea captains was so legendary it attracted pirates. The pirates would hire Saban sailors to upskill their crews in seacraft and resource gathering. (We haven't heard of any other place that offered continuing education for pirates.)

During the mid-1800s, with most of the male population at sea, Saba became known as the Island of Women, and life was hard. Out of desperation, Saban women taught themselves an intricate form of drawn threadwork known as Saba Lace. They obtained U.S. postal addresses and used them to send samples to customers abroad, developing a thriving mail-order business that fed their children and put many through school.

Until the 1950s, all goods arrived by ship, which meant that everything—food, pianos, housing materials—had to be carried up 900 stairs from Ladder Bay, the first landing place, to the Bottom.

The Sabans understandably grew tired of this and asked the Netherlands to build them a road. The Dutch declared a road impossible. So, Saban local Josephus Lambert Hassell ("Lambee") studied engineering via correspondence school, and—with no formal training—built Saba's nine-mile (14.5 km) road connecting Fort Bay Road to Flat Point. It took 20 years using wheelbarrows and manpower; they had no machinery.

The road was completed in 1963, in time for the opening of Saba's airport, also declared by the Dutch to be an impossible task, and once again built by hand by the Saban people.

This resourcefulness forged a quirky culture that is continuously carving its own path. Saba is in the process of transitioning to solar power. There are no franchises here, and there are as many bars as churches.

Visitors find themselves a curiosity and solo travelers, especially, will never feel alone. So dive in, starting with a historical tour of **Windwardside,** visiting the **Saba Heritage Center** and **Harry L. Johnson Museum** and their collections of Saba's heritage and culture. Near **Lambee's Point,** Josephus Lambert Hassell's former home, there is an interesting display on the "Road That Couldn't Be Built."

The **Saba Lace Ladies** still meet every Thursday afternoon at the **Eugenius Johnson Center** to work on pieces and keep the tradition alive. Visitors are most welcome to stop by—to chat, to watch and learn, or to try their hand at the craft.

Hiking is another way to experience Saba's history. There are 15 main trails on the island, adding up to more than 20 miles (32 km) of hiking. Your first stop should be the **Trail Shop** in Windwardside: It sells maps and merchandise, which help fund trail upkeep, but the advice is free, and there's plenty of it.

Saba lace is a needlecraft practiced for 150-plus years. The Saba Lace Ladies meet Thursdays (visitors welcome) to keep the tradition alive.

Make a Difference

The **Saba Conservation Foundation,** or SCF *(sabapark.org),* was established in 1987 to be a caretaker of Saba's marine and terrestrial environment. Sabans have always been very protective of their natural and cultural heritage, and the SCF acts as a nonprofit nature management organization, with a focus on education, monitoring, enforcement, and scientific research. Saba National Marine Park, for example, is one of the world's few self-sustaining marine parks, thanks to a $3-per-dive fee that contributes to park upkeep. Want to get involved? Become a Friend of the SCF for a minimum annual fee ($25 per year at the time of writing); individual donations are also gratefully accepted. The SCF often lists activities on its website, or contact them if you'd like more information.

Most of the trails are historic, from the **Ladder Trail,** which retraces the old steps where everything was carried up by hand, to the **Spring Bay Trail,** past the ruins of old homes and sugar cane plantations.

(Tip: The red-bellied racer snakes are harmless, and the iguanas plentiful.)

Guided hikes are available to the abandoned **Sulphur Mines** in lower Hell's Gate, where the remains of an old sulfur oven are perched on the edge of a sea cliff. The entrance of the mine starts at a balmy 115°F/46°C and grows hotter the farther in you go. It's a treacherous place: The narrow walls glitter with purple gypsum and bright yellow sulfur, and mummified iguanas cling to their surface.

(Tip: It's easy to get lost here; don't attempt it without a guide.)

The most popular hike is, of course, to the highest point in the Netherlands, the **Mount Scenery Trail.** This trail takes around three hours round-trip (1,064 steps), climbing from the sea grape– and mountain palm–populated lower slopes, to the dense vegetation and cloud forest that cover the upper reaches. The temperature drops steadily the higher you hike, and clouds shred and swirl around the summit, often obscuring the three viewpoints near the top.

(Tip: Sign in and out at the Trail Shop; they'll also hand you a certificate on completion.)

The view from the summit of the 2,910-foot (887 m) Mount Scenery, the highest point in Saba and the Netherlands

Diving rivals hiking for popularity and is a huge part of island culture. Many Sabans scuba dive, and this love of their ocean gave them the foresight to establish Saba National Marine Park in 1987, in an effort to preserve their unique underwater environment *before* it needed protection. (Divers will see a ton of medium-size fish in Saba's waters, which is increasingly rare, especially in the Caribbean.) The park circles the entire island to a depth of 197 feet (60 m), covering about 3,212 acres (1,300 ha) and utilizing permanent moorings to prevent coral damage.

Saba's volcanic origins created spectacular underwater topography and structural diversity, from seagrass fields to coral colonies to soaring pinnacles. Saba is best suited for divers with a little experience, given the depth and current on some sites. (Thanks to the local medical school, there is a hyperbaric facility on the island.)

Man O' War Shoals is one of the easier dive sites, a rock structure lying on a sandy bottom that can be circled twice (once at depth and once in the shallows). Keep your eyes peeled for octopuses and the rarely spotted banded jawfish.

Nearby is one of the fish-magnet pinnacles, **Diamond Rock.** This Saba icon is a guano-covered spire that pierces the surface and drops to 85 feet (26 m). Divers circumnavigating the steep walls might spot sharks, stingrays, horse-eye jacks, and barracuda, as well as smaller critters like hermit crabs, juvenile angelfish, and furry sea cucumbers.

Third Encounter is beloved by divers. This slightly menacing-looking pinnacle sits within a C-shaped wall. Divers will have plenty to look at, from the stunning topography to the multitudes of fish (barracuda, yellowtail snapper, grouper). Sharks (Caribbean reef and nurse), turtles, and occasionally manta rays turn up in the current, and the rocks hold plenty of macro life.

Currently no operators are going out to **Saba Bank,** an offshore submarine atoll rumored to have some of the richest marine life in the Caribbean (and a heavy ship traffic area), but the hope is dive tourism could be used to help protect the area. And if anyone can make that happen, Saba can.

The little island that could. Saba's spirit will remind you that anything is possible: All you need is tenacity and ingenuity. We just need to get on with it, removing one rock at a time. Eventually, that leads to a road—even one they said couldn't be built.

A flamingo tongue snail nibbles on a sea fan. Thanks to a marine park established in 1987, Saba has an abundance of marine life.

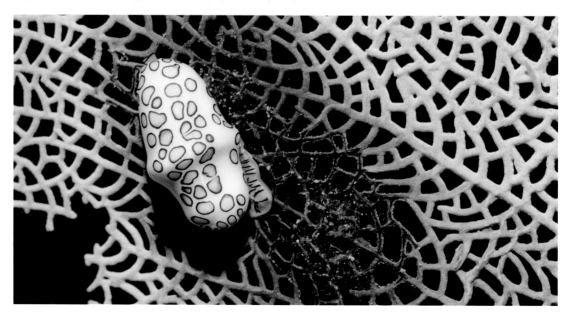

NEED TO KNOW

GETTING HERE: Arrival is an adventure: one of the world's shortest commercial flights (about 13 minutes from Sint Maarten) landing on one of the world's shortest commercial runways (1,300 ft/396 m). There are multiple flights a day between Sint Maarten and Saba aboard WinAir; there are also several 90-minute ferry crossings per week.

GETTING AROUND: Saba's one road—the "Road That Couldn't Be Built"—traverses the island, resembling a luge track. Taxis and car rentals are available.

PACKING TIPS: Saba is a place for hiking. A small backpack and reusable water bottle come in handy. Tap water is drinkable, but all water is rain catchment: Sabans call it "liquid gold"—use it sparingly.

WEATHER: The average temperature is 80°F (27°C), and trade winds keep things cool. Saba is in the hurricane belt, with storms possible July to November.

IN ADDITION: Stop by the local tourism board office (one of the best we've encountered) to get a map, some advice, and to say hello. You'll be glad you did.

Diving

OVERVIEW: Spectacular underwater topography (from pinnacles to walls to coral colonies), with tons of schooling fish. The early establishment of a marine park (1987) means Saba has some of the healthiest marine life in the Caribbean and operators invested in protecting it.

- **Visibility:** Around 65 feet (19.8 m)
- **Water Temp:** 77°F (25°C) in winter / 83°F (28°C) in summer
- **Depth Range:** 60 to 80 feet (18 to 24 m)

MARINE LIFE: More than 150 species of fish have been recorded: great barracuda, wahoo, horse-eye jacks, tarpon, sharks (nurse, Caribbean reef, bull, hammerhead, and tiger), turtles, triggerfish, and parrotfish.

SHOP INFO: There are two operators on Saba, and both are good ones, adhering to strict safety standards, organizing pickups, offering courses and gear rental, and investing in conservation. **Saba Divers** is based in the harbor (Fort Bay), operating one boat with small groups (maximum four divers per dive guide). **Sea Saba** is based in Windwardside, operating two customized boats (maximum 10 divers per boat) for greater flexibility.

Accommodations

HIGH-END: The **Queen's Gardens Resort** reigns from a hillside perch in the Bottom. This elegant complex features 12 suites, a spa, swimming pool, and delicious dining. (Even if you're not staying here, stop by for cocktail hour: it's magical.) ~$300 USD

MID-RANGE: **Juliana's Hotel** is the most popular girl at the party, the hub of Windwardside activity. The on-site Tropics Café and Tipsy Goat Bar ("What happens here we laugh about all week!") are watering holes for locals and visitors alike. There are 12 rooms offering a variety of accommodations, from budget to private cottage. Great base for solo travelers. ~$140 USD

BUDGET: The **Cottage Club Hotel** is the only Saban-owned hotel on the island, perched on a Windwardside hill. This hotel is a world apart from gregarious Juliana's: Guests come here for peaceful relaxation. Each of the 10 self-contained cottages has a private balcony, perfect for tea and biscuits in the morning and a glass of wine in the evening. ~$110 USD

Food & Drink

Windwardside's **Chez Bubba Bistro** is a locals' spot, a relaxed but elegant French bistro. Cash only.

Brigadoon is a romantic restaurant tucked away in an old Saban home in Windwardside. It offers a wide variety of dishes, from traditional Caribbean to Mediterranean to French, and the atmosphere is low-lit and heavenly.

Family-owned **Saba Snack** (also in Windwardside) is a great lunch spot, with a full menu of reasonably priced sandwiches, snacks, and meals, made fresh daily. This roadside spot has covered deck seating, great for watching Saba stroll by.

LORD HOWE ISLAND

One of a Kind

ord Howe Island is a wonderland. This beguiling beauty is located 485 miles (780 km) northeast of Sydney. It has the world's southernmost tropical coral reef, two 2,460-plus-foot (750+ m) mountains (each with a cloud forest), and the world's tallest sea stack, the diveable Ball's Pyramid, a basalt fang that looks like a Bond villain's lair. This island is the remnant of a large shield volcano, home to endemic species and a population of roughly 380 people, many of whom are fifth- and sixth-generation islanders.

No more than 400 visitors are allowed on the island at any given time. There are few locks (the honor system is strong here) and even fewer cars—most people cycle the eight miles (13 km) of roads, past trees with fluffy white tern chicks perched precariously on branches, in a fuzzed-out, perpetual state of static cling.

This isolated UNESCO World Heritage site is a place of weird and wonderful things: 241 species of indigenous plants, nearly 50 percent of which are found nowhere else on Earth; more than 500 fish species; 207 species of birds, including the threatened Lord Howe Island woodhen; and around 1,600 species of insects, including the world's rarest—the Lord Howe Island phasmid—a cigar-size creature that was believed to be extinct in 1935, only to be rediscovered in 2001. (Guess where they found it? The Bond lair of Ball's Pyramid.)

If you come here—to snorkel and dive, hike, and spend time with loved ones—you'll wonder why you haven't visited sooner, and you'll never want to leave. ∎

Luxury retreat Capella Lodge has spectacular views of everything that makes this extraordinary island special.

With its abundance of golden, uncrowded beaches curving around green-and-sapphire lagoons, Lord Howe attracts water babies; it's an ideal spot for surfers, snorkelers, and divers. There are no rivers draining into the bays and no nearby commercial fishing, just that marine artery, the East Australian Current, sweeping past Lord Howe Island, which has a marine park extending 12 nautical miles (22 km) around the island.

Ned's Beach is one of the best snorkel spots, with kingfish, wrasse, and spangled emperors. Hawksbill and green turtles also migrate through the area, feeding on seagrass. Masks, snorkels, and fins are stored in a shed on the beach and can be rented by leaving money in the honesty box. (Guided snorkel and glass-bottom boat tours are on offer.)

Diving still has an exploratory feel here, probably due to the lack of dive traffic. Small-group guided dives are offered three times per day (morning double dives, single-afternoon dives, and night dives on request), with more than 100 sites to choose from, depending on conditions.

The **Admiralty Islands** are just 15 minutes by boat, a grouping of small offshore volcanic islands with more than 24 dive sites between them. Fish flit

The endemic Lord Howe Island woodhen is one of the island's many conservation success stories, with numbers rebounding from 20 to 220.

FOR FAMILIES

It's not cheap to get a family to Lord Howe Island, but it's worth it. This natural island paradise is perfect for kids: They can ride bikes, snorkel with turtles, picnic, and learn about conservation and some amazing, crazy creatures.

around coral- and algae-covered boulders, and the dives are shallow enough (56 ft/17 m) to roll with the surge and glance up to see waves crashing against the rocks. Small Galápagos sharks zip around, darting between the boulders and the open ocean. There are at least 12 species of rays and sharks found in Lord Howe's marine park, the most common being the Galápagos shark, which are rare elsewhere in Australian waters. (On one dive, we had more than 20 Galápagos sharks cruising around us.)

Malabar is a shallow playground for divers, with easy lava-tube swim-throughs and arches to explore. This seems to be a favorite spot for macro, although we also spotted doubleheader wrasse, kingfish, Lord Howe moray eels, and more Galápagos sharks.

There is a little something for everyone here, from the shallow **Lagoon** for beginner divers (with its abundance of coral and fish life), to **Ball's Pyramid** for more experienced divers (due to current and its open ocean location).

Divers like to joke that Ball's is the "pinnacle of dive excellence" in the area. It's about 1.5 hours by boat and trips cannot be planned in advance. Certain weather requirements and diver numbers need to be in place to dive it. (Unfortunately we were weathered out.)

Ball's Pyramid is the place to see schools (trevally and kingfish), pelagics (marlin and sharks), and the world's rarest angelfish, the Ballina angelfish, a

Gorgonians and soft coral light up a site called Tenth of June Deep in the Admiralty Islands, a small group of offshore volcanic islands.

deepwater angel that usually stays below 328 feet (100 m) but can be seen here at recreational limits (most dives are around 82 ft/25 m).

Lord Howe Island gives off the feeling that there's always something more to explore, whether you're underwater or on land. More than 85 percent of the island is still covered in native forest, and 70 percent is protected in park reserves. **Bird-watching** is a hugely popular activity here, with more than 170 species of land and sea birds either visiting the island or calling it home. (The endemic Lord Howe Island woodhen can be spotted year-round; this bird is one of the island's many conservation success stories, with numbers rebounding from 20 to around 220.)

Hiking is also a popular pastime, with ribbons of trails winding through forests and along coastlines and sea cliffs. (There are tracks, and loops for all levels; just ask the islanders for advice.)

For the fit and adventurous, don't miss a guided hike up **Mount Gower with Lord Howe Environ-mental Tours.** This strenuous eight- to 10-hour trek (8.7 mi/14 km round-trip) is one of Australia's best day walks, leading up to the 2,871-foot (875 m) cloud forest on Mount Gower's summit, the highest peak on the island. The track snakes along an exposed cliff face (ropes are there for safety, and helmets are worn on this section to protect from rockfall), and other steep sections have fixed ropes to help hikers pull themselves up.

The payoff? Along the route, you'll traverse through lush forest, with views of most of the island unfolding below you. At the summit, a 67-acre (27 ha) plateau contains a mythical cloud forest clad in ferns, mosses, and flowering plants, 86 percent of which are found nowhere else on Earth.

(Tip: Book in advance: There are limited spaces on hikes, which are held only on certain days. Speak to

the tour office if you have any questions about the hike; they can provide a comprehensive briefing.)

It's sobering to think that all this weird and wonderful diversity came within a whisker of being lost. Islands hold around 5 percent of the world's land area, but 28 percent of its biodiversity, including 40 percent of the world's threatened species. They are home to some of the world's greatest conservation success stories, yet more than half of all extinctions have occurred on islands. It is a balance as fine as a fish scale, and all it took was a sinking ship to upset the ecological apple cart.

In 1918, the **S.S. *Makambo*** grounded on the reef, and black rats escaped the ship to lay siege to the island. They swiftly caused the extinction of at least 13 invertebrates, five land birds, and two plants, bringing the Lord Howe Island woodhen and the Lord Howe Island phasmid (a 6-in/15-cm stick insect) to the brink of extinction.

Dead as a dodo. We've all heard the phrase because the dodo was a cautionary tale of human-induced extinction. It wasn't too long ago that extinction was unthinkable. Now we're getting acclimatized to it, which is dangerous. Species (animals, insects, and plants) are going extinct 1,000 times faster than ever before, and numbers are plummeting. In the last 100 years, we've lost 90 percent of the ocean's large fish. In the last 50 years, we've lost 60 percent of wildlife populations. We can't let ourselves shrug it off. We have to fight back.

Lord Howe Island is fighting back. It's the largest

Hard hats are required for this exposed section of the Mount Gower hike, an 8.7-mile (14 km) round-trip trek up to a cloud forest on the summit.

populated island to undertake a full-scale eradication of an estimated 360,000 unwanted rodents, a project that began in 2019, which could protect more than 70 threatened species if successful.

Wrap up your visit to this extraordinary island by cycling to the **Lord Howe Island Museum** to learn more. Spend a few hours perusing collections and displays about the island's history, environment, and conservation efforts. You'll come away marveling at how truly special this island is.

Make a Difference

Become a **Friend of Lord Howe Island** (FLHI) (*lordhowe-tours.com.au*). An annual subscription of around $15 USD helps fund conservation initiatives and support the community group working to protect and conserve Lord Howe Island. (FLHIs also receive a quarterly newsletter with updates.) In addition, volunteer programs are offered throughout the year, usually during the winter period. These week-long tours are a combination of a half day of hands-on work (i.e., weeding, surveying the marine park, beach cleanups, land bird surveys, and more), followed by a half-day nature tour with evening lectures. It's a great opportunity to help preserve this unique World Heritage site while meeting like-minded citizen scientists.

NEED TO KNOW

GETTING HERE: QantasLink operates daily two-hour flights from Sydney to Lord Howe Island. *(Tip: This is a value-for-money route to use Qantas points!)* There are strict weight limits: one 15.4-pound (7 kg) carry-on and one 30.8-pound (14 kg) checked bag. You are allowed a second checked bag, but there's no guarantee it will make the flight.

GETTING AROUND: Wilson's Hire Service has bikes and a handful of cars for rent; some lodges provide bikes, as well. Cycling and walking are the preferred (and easiest) modes of transport.

PACKING TIPS: Casual outdoor clothes, with a few smarter options for dinner. Sun (hat, reef-friendly sunscreen) and rain/wind protection, hiking boots, and beach shoes. A flashlight is useful (the island is dark at night); so is a daypack and water bottle. Divers should pack computers and masks, and rent other equipment on-island.

WEATHER: Southern Hemisphere summers (November to February) are booked out well in advance, with temps around 77°F (25°C); winters are mild (63°F/17°C) and a pleasant time to visit. Lord Howe is diveable year-round, with September through May being best. Winds pick up in July and August (Pro Dive usually closes during this time).

IN ADDITION: Certain restaurants open certain days. When you arrive, choose which places you want to eat at and make reservations in advance for your entire stay. There is no mobile phone reception on the island.

Diving

OVERVIEW: The southernmost coral reef in the world, turquoise lagoons, the world's tallest sea stack, and a thriving marine park—Lord Howe Island is a unique, target-rich environment for divers of all levels.

- **Visibility:** From 33 to 131-plus feet (10 to 40+ m)
- **Water Temp:** 64°F (18°C) in winter / 79°F (26°C) in summer
- **Depth Range:** 20 to 131 feet (6 to 40 m)

MARINE LIFE: Galápagos sharks, wrasse (double-header and greenblock), opal eye cod, flame snapper, yellowtail kingfish, Spanish dancers, Ballina angelfish, spangled emperors, turtles (green and hawksbill), occasionally whales, dolphins, manta rays, and whale sharks

SHOP INFO: Pro Dive Lord Howe Island is the only dive operator on the island, and they run a good shop, staffed by a great team. They offer snorkel tours and dive training, and have quality rental gear and a comfortable dive boat. Prebook dive packages prior to arrival.

Accommodations

HIGH-END: Capella Lodge is a luxury retreat on the outskirts of town, with spectacular views of the ocean and rolling pastures. Nine suites sleep 22 guests. On-site restaurant; usually closes in July. ~$650 USD

MID-RANGE: Beachcomber Lodge is owned by the Payten family (seventh-generation islanders), one of the original island homesteads, surrounded by gardens and a short walk to beaches and cafés. They have six cozy self-contained apartments. ~$217 USD

BUDGET: Ocean View Apartments is another original homestead run by fifth- and sixth-generation descendants of the Wilson family. There are 15 basic studio units with kitchenettes, a game room, pool, and tennis court. Located a short walk to the jetty and cafés. ~$90 USD

Food & Drink

Meals at **Capella Lodge** are an occasion: Think garlic beef with roast pumpkin, rosemary custard, capers, and hand-cut potatoes. They have a stunning deck for sunset cocktails.

Earl's Anchorage is a popular spot on the lagoon waterfront serving breakfast, lunch, and dinner (like Parma ham with honey-roasted figs, arugula, and goat cheese). Great food at a great venue.

The island's social centers are the **Bowling Club Kitchen** and the **Golf Club,** both of which offer simple dinners (pizza and pub food) and a great opportunity to mingle with the islanders.

TAVEUNI ISLAND

The Warmest Welcome in the World

Taveuni Island

FIJI

ula! This greeting is the word you'll hear most often in Fiji. However you hear it, however you say it in return, *bula* will always make you smile: The Fijian welcome is that genuine.

Fiji has a communal culture that naturally spills over to visitors: Solo travelers are invited into the fold, children are fawned over, courting couples are teased. That culture strengthens when you travel off Viti Levu (the largest and most touristed of Fiji's 333 islands) to other islands. People often mistakenly believe that this South Pacific paradise is nothing but white-sand, layabout beaches shaded by palm trees. It is that, but so much more, with thick tropical forests, rugged mountainous interiors, swift-flowing rivers, underwater walls, and thriving reefs.

Each island has its own personality. Taveuni Island, for example, is known as the Garden Isle—a verdant breadbasket producing copra, taro, and kava. A large swath of the island's western side (40,000 acres/16,187 ha) makes up Bouma National Heritage Park, an impossibly green canopy threaded with white ribbons of waterfalls. This is an island of wild beauty, cut through by the 180th meridian—part of the world's timekeeping system, which is ironic, given the fluid relationship Fijians have with time.

Fiji Time is a very real thing: Schedules are suggestions here. It's a cultural quirk that takes some getting used to, but go with the flow and enjoy! ■

Fiji is known as the "soft coral capital of the world," offering up some of the best tropical reef diving in the Pacific.

Fijian culture has three pillars: the village (family and extended community), the church, and rugby. To get a true feel for Fiji, try to incorporate as many of these into your trip as possible. Many regions are poor, and there is a persistent resort culture that looks to separate visitors from the realities of Fiji rather than connecting the two, so it's important to choose your home base wisely: Find one that acts as a bridge rather than widens the gap.

A guided visit to the **Holy Cross Church and Wairiki Catholic Mission** is a good first stop. This noble-looking red-and-white building overlooks a rugby pitch, home field of the First Light Taveuni rugby team (catch a game if you can). The origin of this parish began in a battle more than 150 years ago, when warriors from Taveuni defeated Tongan invaders. According to legend, the Taveuni warriors credited their victory to a small cross presented to them by a French Catholic priest before the battle, which they believed protected them. (That cross is still housed in the church.) Legend also tells how the slain Tongan enemies were cooked in a *lovo* (earthen oven) and eaten with breadfruit in celebration of the victory.

There are many opportunities for **village visits,** which can feel awkward (for both parties) at the beginning, but you get out what you put in. Paradise Taveuni organized a two-hour visit to the village of Duivosavosa for us. Viliame Seru was our guide—his grandfather owned and cultivated the 383 acres (155 ha) where 50 people live in seven family groups. We learned about weaving palm frond baskets, producing tapa (bark cloth), and the importance of coconut trees. "We plant them wherever we want water," Viliame told us. "When we're working the land, especially on hot sunny days, there's no need to take a meal with you. We drink from the coconut and we eat copra [dried coconut meat]."

Asking questions about what you're seeing and learning is a great way to break the ice. Before long, we're being peppered by questions from the community in return.

"We like sharing our culture," Viliame said. Visits like this extend beyond a friendly exchange, too— the fee is used to support the village, primarily by putting children through school.

(Tip: Dress modestly, and ask advice about specific protocols prior to visiting villages.)

Waitabu Marine Park is a combination of village visit and marine conservation. The 30-family community of Waitabu noticed a certain area of their reef was being overfished, so they made fishing *tabu,* or forbidden, and in turn developed a successful and flourishing no-take marine park, which is surveyed regularly by the community and NGOs working with the park. The Waitabu community proudly shows visitors through their marine park

Church and rugby are two of Fiji's passions. Here, the Holy Cross Church and Wairiki Catholic Mission overlooks a rugby pitch.

Make a Difference

Sponsor a shark through Beqa (pronounced *Benga*) Adventure Divers' (BAD) conservation initiative, **My Fiji Shark** (*myfijishark.com*). Shark lovers can "adopt" a well-known resident shark, with profits going to scientific research and initiatives benefiting the local shark population including habitat conservation, fishery management, and assisting the Fijian government in standing by its conservation commitments. (Direct donations are also gratefully accepted.) BAD and Aqua-Trek run shark dives out of Pacific Harbour on Viti Levu in the nearby Shark Reef Marine Reserve, Fiji's first national marine park, home to at least eight species of sharks, including bull, tiger, sicklefin lemon, silvertip, tawny nurse, gray reef, whitetip reef, and blacktip reef. (The financial revenue brought in by shark diving led to the marine park's establishment.)

on a snorkeling tour from a *bilibili* (a handmade raft), which can also be combined with a cultural experience (spending time with the community, learning a Fijian dance, etc.).

(Tip: Call and arrange your visit a few days in advance, as it needs to be coordinated with the community and—if snorkeling—the tides. Allow half a day.)

Bouma National Heritage Park is another example of Taveuni's conservation work. This 168-square-mile (435 km) patch of protected rainforest conceals three stunning waterfalls, plunging into swimmable jade pools. It was an easy, flat 10-minute walk to the first waterfall, a further 40 minutes uphill through a leafy forest to the second, and the same again to the third. Paradise Taveuni organized a half-day guided excursion to the park for us, which can also be turned into an all-day outing when combined with a visit to a natural waterslide, the Holy Cross Church, and the 180th meridian, standing with a foot in today and a foot in yesterday.

The beauty of Bouma is its cascading waterfalls. The beauty of the Somosomo Strait is its movement: Most dives here are shallow drift dives over flat or sloping sand reefs populated with bright soft and hard coral (there is some damage from the 2016 cyclone), thousands of reef fish, large schools of yellowtail fusiliers and Spanish mackerel, and whitetip reef sharks.

Taveuni's protected Bouma National Heritage Park is known for its plunging waterfalls, lush rainforest, and secluded swimming pools.

(Tip: Although Fiji is a great place to learn to dive, some Somosomo sites have strong currents. Divers with a few dives under their weight belts should be fine. Make sure you can nail your buoyancy before diving here and listen to local advice.)

The **Fish Factory** is a fun, flat reef filled with schools of yellowtail fusiliers and reef fish, while sloping **Nuku Reef** is more about the macro. Hawksbill turtles float over coral bommies chock-full of nudibranchs, shrimp, crabs, and anemones. **Terry's Jelly** is a swift drift over hard and soft coral, with an abundance of whitetip reef sharks. Every dive destination has a **Cabbage Patch,** and so it is

Fiji Time was described to us like this: *Sometimes early. Never on time. Always late.* Your bus might depart 10 minutes early or your dive charter 40 minutes late. You're on Fiji Time!

in the Somosomo, a large collection of cabbage coral ideal for nosing around with a flashlight.

The **Great White Wall** was something special, partly because we were fortunate enough to dive it at dawn. The Wall needs to be dived on slack low tide, and on our dive that happened to be dawn, so it was just us and our guide diving what can otherwise be a crowded site.

(Tip: This is a deeper dive—105 ft/32 m. Keep an eye on your depth: It's easy to get distracted.)

We jumped in the water as the sun started to rise. It was eerie descending through a little cre-vasse and coming out on a vertical wall at about 65 feet (20 m) in near dark. We descended farther to 105 feet (32 m) and drifted slowly along the wall, which soon turned on its party trick. When the tide hits it just right, the Great White Wall glows white, like ice, as the coral start feeding in the nutrient-rich current. This was magic, gliding along, nearly alone in the semidark, against a white wall with a few moray eels for company. We ascended through a crevasse to the top of the wall, dropped back down, and drifted past it again. All dives are memorable, but every now and again, the ocean gives you a gift: This is one we'll remember.

Vinaka vakalevu (thank you very much), Fiji.

A diver marvels at the Great White Wall, which glows white, like ice, when the tide hits it just right.

NEED TO KNOW

GETTING HERE: Nonstop flights are available from Los Angeles. From there, it's a 60- to 90-minute flight from Suva or Nadi to Taveuni. Nail your weight requirements on interisland flights: Tipping the scales is costly. There are no overhead compartments and limited room for hand luggage; carry on the absolute essentials.

GETTING AROUND: Most of the resorts and dive sites are on the west side of the island. Resorts usually arrange transfers, as well as activities. There are a couple of car rental agencies on the island.

PACKING TIPS: Dress modestly and conservatively, especially when away from the resort. Women should cover their knees and shoulders (T-shirts are fine).

WEATHER: Most days bring a brief shower. The official cyclone season in this Southern Hemisphere spot is from November through April, although that—as for everywhere—is changing. Travel insurance is recommended.

IN ADDITION: Mild repellent will keep mosquitoes at bay. Dengue fever is present. Don't wear hats in villages or touch anyone's head (it's considered disrespectful).

Diving

OVERVIEW: Fiji is known as the soft coral capital of the world, and the legendary Somosomo Strait—a nutrient-rich channel running between Taveuni Island and Vanau Levu—offers up some of the best tropical reef diving in the Pacific.

- **Visibility:** Around 75 feet (23 m), best April through October
- **Water Temp:** 78°F (26°C) in winter / 84°F (29°C) in summer
- **Depth Range:** Up to 100 feet (30+ m)

MARINE LIFE: More than 390 species of coral (including gorgonians and staghorn) and 1,200 species of fish (whitetip reef sharks, yellowtail fusiliers, clownfish, lionfish)

SHOP INFO: There are multiple dive shops and resorts on Taveuni. We went with Paradise Taveuni's dive center, Rainbow Reef. This well-set-up shop has good boats (most dives are boat dives), free shore diving and snorkeling on the house reef, and a separate locked camera cleaning and storage room. Nitrox is available.

Accommodations

HIGH-END: Tides Reach is a five-star beachfront resort. Each guest is assigned a personal staff member (available 24/7). Meals (included) utilize organic ingredients selected from the resort's garden. *~$875 USD*

MID-RANGE: Paradise Taveuni is a "gentle adventure" diving lodge and a welcoming spot for families and solo travelers. It overlooks the ocean, and wooden steps and coral paths wind through bright green lawns bursting with flowers. The friendly staff can arrange activities, and there's a restaurant and dive shop on site. The 16 rooms (38 guests max) have drinkable tap water (pack your reusable bottle), and hosts that put their everything into this place. It says a lot that, after Cyclone Winston leveled Paradise in 2016, former guests volunteered to help rebuild the lodge. *~$305 USD*

BUDGET: Maravu is a former five-star resort that has aged into a relaxed, humbler property—a great find for budget-conscious travelers. Maravu features 21 cottages and an on-site restaurant. *~$45 USD*

Food & Drink

Eating out is tricky in Fiji (restaurants can be hard to get to), so resort food packages are good investments.

Paradise Taveuni has a varied and changing menu, offering weekly themed nights, like **Lovo Night.** Enjoy an evening of performances and traditional fare: taro and cassava cooked in an earthen oven, paired with *waki poki* (fried eggplant wrapped in spinach leaves) and coconut bread.

Try **kava,** a root-based drink with a strong place in Fijian culture. Small amounts have small effects—a slight numbing of the tongue and a relaxed feeling. The taste is best described as muddy river water.

MEXICO

TULUM

Indiana Jones and the Temple of Bohemia

The original Mayan name for Tulum was *Zamá*, which means "dawn." It's a fitting name for a place that is one of the first to see the day break in Mexico.

Tulum is located on the Yucatán Peninsula, a spur of land straddling the Gulf of Mexico and the Caribbean, part of the glittering Riviera Maya. Elegant gray-stone Maya ruins maintain a cliffside watch over a six-mile (9.7 km) sugary stretch of beach, washed by the Caribbean Sea.

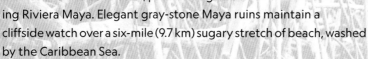

The ship has sailed on Tulum being an off-the-beaten-track destination, but its relaxed bohemian flair hasn't been ousted (yet) by growing tourism numbers. Most people travel here with purpose, practicing yoga by the sea in the morning before indulging their inner Indiana Jones in the afternoon.

Travelers can wander through ancient Maya cities or drift-snorkel through Sian Ka'an Biosphere Reserve, a UNESCO World Heritage site and one of Mexico's largest protected areas.

Divers, however, come here seeking cenotes (ancient sinkholes).

The Yucatán Peninsula holds three of the world's longest underground water systems, which created the largest cave system in the world. Where cave ceilings have collapsed, cenotes appear, emerald-and-brown drops surrounded by lush forest. And these attract divers like bees to honey: clear water flooded with striking beams of light and fascinating rock formations.

Is it any wonder Tulum brings out the explorer in all of us? ■

A path winds through a mangrove in Sian Ka'an Biosphere Reserve, one of Mexico's largest protected areas and one of the world's lungs.

Cenotes are mysterious things. Some look like jungle-enclosed sapphires, perfect circular pools surrounded by overhanging trees; others look like mud puddles. None of them willingly reveal what lies beneath, and that is the siren song of cenotes: Every descent is an adventure.

Dives usually begin with a sweaty trek along a jungle path, lugging gear. The entrance depends on the private land owner: Some facilities are well maintained, with solid stairs and wooden platforms. Other entries involve a scramble and giant stride into a tiny hole you'd never imagine would open up into an otherworldly, soaring cavern.

This is where knowing your limits comes in: There is a cenote for every level of diver. Hard-core cave divers can explore their fill, from vertical sinkholes to tunnel systems. Open-Water-certified divers are allowed to "cavern dive" in cenotes that have natural light. *(Tip: Bring a flashlight when diving cenotes.)*

Dos Ojos is often used as the shakedown dive. These two shallow, connected cenotes are part of a larger cave section and suitable for divers of all levels. Dos Ojos is busy, but it has well-established facilities, lots of natural light, clear water, and stunning formations. *(Tip: This is also a good cenote for snorkelers.)*

Temple of Doom is well named, as this cenote makes every diver feel like an underwater Indiana Jones. The entry is a seven-foot (2 m) leap of faith into a hole. Inside the cenote, there is a chink in the cavern roof that lets in a single beam of light, which falls directly on a stone plinth. It's not too difficult to imagine a gold statue resting there. *(Tip: Heed the underwater signposted warnings guarding entrances to deep cave systems here. The exit for this cenote is a slippery, steep ladder.)*

Archaeological finds are still being made in cenotes. Divers have discovered the ancient remains of mammoths, giant jaguars, and a 10,000-year-old human skeleton. Freshwater from rainfall forms a layer at the top of some cenotes, a lid isolating salt water from atmospheric oxygen. The layer between the fresh and salt water is called a halocline, a hazy blend that distorts visibility. In other cenotes, toxic hydrogen sulfide caused by trapped and rotting vegetation creates a mysterious white mist, drifting like an autumn fog.

The Pit has both. A steep stair entry leads to a small pool surrounded by rainforest cover. Divers descend through the halocline around 40 feet (12 m) and reach wisps of hydrogen sulfide, which waft around overhangs and rock formations, at around 100 feet (30 m).

Cenotes are strangely personal: Every diver has a favorite. Chris's favorite was **Angelita.** *(Tip: Angelita is considered an intermediate-level cenote and not suitable for new divers like me.)* This cenote is all atmosphere. The first seven feet (2 m) are murky,

The Yucatán Peninsula has the largest cave system in the world, and cenotes (ancient sinkholes) attract divers with a yen to explore.

Make a Difference

It's rare to be in possession of a treasure like Sian Ka'an Biosphere Reserve. Like all great tracts of untouched land, Sian Ka'an is threatened by development—and once that door is opened, we can never go back. The World Economic Forum ranks biodiversity loss as one of the top five risks for the coming decade. We've already lost more than a third of all wetlands and more than 32 percent of the world's forest area. **Amigos de Sian Ka'an** (amigosdesiankaan.org) is an NGO founded in 1986 to protect Sian Ka'an. It works in conjunction with federal and state governments to pair sustainable development with conservation. Donations can be made via their website. And give feedback: Email the Riviera Maya Tourism Board, and speak to your hotels and guides about the importance of preserving this unique reserve.

giving way to crystal clear water. Below that, at about 100 feet (30 m), there's a thick layer of hydrogen sulfide. When the roof of this former cavern caved in, it left a pile of debris and trees on the floor. Sunken tree limbs protrude through the sulfide layer, the mist curling around the limbs, reminiscent of a nightmare. Below the sulfide layer, it is pitch black, but the water is crystal clear. This is a place to take your time and soak in the mood.

The Riviera Maya is part of the Mesoamerican Reef system, a Mission Blue Hope Spot encompassing 11 kinds of coastal and marine wetlands, punctuated with 16 marine protected areas. The gem in its crown is **Sian Ka'an Biosphere Reserve,** 1.3 million acres (528,148 ha) of mangroves, tropical forests, coastal and inland lagoons, marshes, and a barrier reef, supporting thousands of species of birds, insects, mammals, plants, and marine life, including howler and spider monkeys, jaguars, manatees, toucans, and tapirs.

The Maya people named it "origin of the sky"; today, we know it as one of the world's lungs—one of the few remaining untouched pockets of life, essential to the Earth's health and well-being, right on Tulum's doorstep.

We joined **Agua Clara Diving Tulum** on a day trip to this extraordinary area, which began with a boat journey through narrow waterways in the marshes and mangroves that flank jade- and tourmaline-colored lagoons. From there, we donned

The ancient Maya city of Ek Balam rises out of the jungle. Located about two hours from Tulum, much of Ek Balam remains unexcavated.

life jackets and masks for a cruisey drift-snorkel down ancient trading canals used by the Maya from around 350 to 300 B.C. to trade jade, quartz, and clay pots of pumpkin, honey, and seeds with civilizations around Guatemala and Belize. (Shards of those pots can still be seen in the white sand.)

We soared over history, carried by blue-green water, cool and refreshing, changing with the light. This is a special place—even scratching the surface will tell you that. Sian Ka'an is continuously staving off the threat of development, especially as Tulum grows, but its preservation and protection are paramount to the planet.

The ancient Maya city of **Ek Balam** is another wonder worth exploring. Located about two hours from Tulum, this city of 52 buildings sprawls across nine miles (14.5 km). It flourished around A.D. 700 as a bustling city center with roads and aqueducts (complete with algae-cleaning turtles). For more than 230 years, Ek Balam had control: It was so powerful, it used to extract income taxes from Chichén Itzá (today one of the most popular tourist attractions in Mexico).

There are 17 restored buildings to examine, each one decorated with hieroglyphics or symbols, made from stones that still contain the fossils of ancient shells. Circling the city is a shaded forest track past mounds of unexcavated ruins. "Much of Ek Balam is still hidden," our guide said. "There's no money to do the work." Guides are mandatory at

Ek Balam, and our guide used to walk this area with his grandfather—"But never after dark: I've seen strange things."

Wrap up your visit with a **half-day cycle tour of Tulum with Tulum Bike Tours.** These small-group tours travel about nine miles (15 km) around the city and are a great way to experience Tulum.

The tour includes plenty of stops along the way, like the coastal, cliffside **Tulum Archaeological Site** (the only Maya site built next to the Caribbean Sea) and a visit to the Melipona bee colony at **Don Diego de la Selva Hotel.** (These stingless bees are essential to the endemic plants of the Yucatán Peninsula and are under threat of extinction.)

We finished our ride—of course—at a cenote, slipping into the cool, clear water for a welcome swim, wondering at what hidden marvels might lie beneath us.

Bicycles are a great way to explore Tulum and the surrounding area. You can pedal from Maya ruins to cafés to cenotes for a swim.

GETTING HERE: Cancun International Airport is Tulum's gateway, receiving regular flights from around the world.

GETTING AROUND: Rental cars are useful. It's about a 90-minute drive from Cancun airport, and while driving is easy and the roads are good, don't skimp on insurance and do not drive at night. Tulum Beach, where many hotels and restaurants are located, is about four miles (6.5 km) from Tulum township.

PACKING TIPS: Tulum's style is barefoot-and-linen: Think earth-colored, flowing garments in natural fibers and permanent sunglasses. Throw in sturdy walking shoes and sun-protective hats and you're ready to go.

WEATHER: Tulum's temperature averages around 80°F (26.6°C). The dry season (and therefore high season) is December through April, with peak population during the holidays and spring break.

IN ADDITION: Tulum has been weathering a growth spurt and is scrambling to catch up. The city is working on addressing the single-use plastic issue, as well as rubbish and recycling. Non-reef-friendly sunscreen and repellent is restricted in some areas.

Diving

OVERVIEW: Cenote diving is a marvel for divers of all levels, from hard-core cave divers to first-time cavern divers. Think striking rock formations, crystal clear water, jungle entries, and transfixing turns of light. You'll be hooked.

- **Visibility:** 100-plus feet (30.5+ m)
- **Water Temp:** 78.8°F (26°C) year-round
- **Depth Range:** How long is a piece of string? Most range from 16.5 to 262.5-plus feet (5 to 80+ m), but in reality, unknown.

MARINE LIFE: Apart from the odd fish, cenotes don't hold much marine life. Divers come here for the atmosphere and rock formations. However, cenotes can hold archaeological finds, so keep your eyes peeled. And don't forget to bird-watch during your surface interval.

SHOP INFO: We dove with **Agua Clara Diving Tulum,** which also offers land-based tours for non-divers. Cenote diving can be dangerous, so dive with a reputable shop rather than hiring a random guide. Per regulation, all guides must be fully certified cave divers and are required to use full cave diving equipment.

Accommodations

HIGH-END: Maya Tulum Retreat & Spa stands out in a town that specializes in the mind, body, and spirit. Located on Tulum Beach, white-sand paths link a series of cabana-style, beachside bungalows. Yoga classes are offered twice daily, and the on-site spa offers traditional Maya treatments. ~*$390 USD*

MID-RANGE: Nueva Vida de Ramiro, also on Tulum Beach, has 33 bungalows, scattered along 18.5 acres (7.5 ha) of oceanside property. This hotel supports local conservation and community initiatives. ~*$114 USD*

BUDGET: Don Diego de la Selva, in Tulum township, is a collection of 12 rooms surrounded by a garden, featuring an on-site restaurant and pool. This is the home of the stingless Melipona bee colony, and it's a great base if you'd like to learn more about this endangered creature. (You can even sponsor a beehive.) ~*$66 USD*

Food & Drink

Maya Tulum's restaurant is a circular room with white limestone walls and windows thrown open to let in the ocean breeze. It serves vegetarian and seafood dishes that reflect its ethos: light, fresh, natural.

Mateo's Mexican Grill is a popular spot on the main drag of Tulum Beach, serving up favorites like fresh ceviche and tacos. Fun, casual, and good value for money.

Ah, **La Tia Restaurant**—this roadside diner is the real deal: *poc chuc* (marinated pork) served with tortillas, salsa, onion, lime, and bean soup, hot enough to blow your head off.

UMKOMAAS

Safari Diving

"Africa is not for sissies." So reads a wall mural in the small coastal town of Umkomaas, and so it is. Africa—and especially Aliwal Shoal, Umkomaas's offshore reef—favors the bold (and those with a sense of humor). This is cowboy diving, punching through the surf on Rigid Inflatable Boats (RIBs) to explore a fossilized sandstone reef buzzing with the big stuff.

Aliwal Shoal is a 3.1-mile-long (5 km) reef located about three miles (4.8 km) offshore from the Umkomaas River mouth. This marine protected area holds underwater amphitheaters and pinnacles, pockets and overhangs, set amid a vast, sandy plain. The ready-made shelter, swept by the Agulhas Current (transporting warm, tropical Indian Ocean water southward along the South African coastline), attracts a wealth of marine life to the Shoal. More than 1,200 species can be found here, from humpback whales to pineapple fish to sand tiger sharks (known as ragged-tooth or "raggies" around here).

Aliwal Shoal swings toward diving adventures. Non-divers are most welcome, however. Topside, the compact community of Umkomaas—a hillside town about 31 miles (50 km) south of Durban—is more of a functional town than a tourist one. If you want the best of both worlds, the best pairing with diving Aliwal is to add a multiday land safari to the end of your journey. That way, everyone gets their wildlife fix.

Are you ready for a wild ride? Be bold: Aliwal awaits. ◼

A baited drift dive brings in oceanic blacktip sharks. Aliwal Shoal is renowned for two things: sharks and the annual sardine run.

South Africa is surf-and-turf safariing. Above water, the country holds more than 20 national parks, including Kruger National Park, home of the Big Five (lion, leopard, elephant, Cape buffalo, and rhinoceros). Underwater, Aliwal Shoal is renowned for two things: sharks and the annual sardine run, a June–July event dubbed the "greatest shoal on Earth." This is the ocean equivalent of the great wildebeest migration: massive bait balls forming an all-you-can-eat seafood buffet that attracts whales, seabirds, game fish, dolphins—and, of course, sharks.

Although the annual sardine run takes things up to ludicrous mode, diving Aliwal Shoal at any other time of year is still a feast for the senses. As with any safari, you have to be in it to win it. The greater the investment (time spent in the environment), the greater the rewards. Therefore, the focus in quiet Umkomaas is diving, and it was some of the best diving we've ever done. This was a bucket-list destination that didn't disappoint Chris and was a big step up in skills for me. Intro dives and courses are offered here; however, this is open ocean diving in conditions where you have to have your wits about you. Aliwal is best suited to divers with some experience.

A typical day of diving begins early and hard: tiny RIBs packed with eight to 10 divers launch from the Umkomaas River mouth, punching through the

SOMETHING SPECIAL

The annual sardine run is suitable for divers, snorkelers, and free divers. Most dive shops offer packages and are based in the town of Port St. Johns, 196 miles (315 km) south of Umkomaas, for six weeks in June and July. Book well in advance.

surf in a cowboy entry over the sandbar. (The river mouth is rumored to be a favorite hangout for bull sharks, so don't fall in during the launch! It's all part of the adventure.)

Conditions vary wildly out here. On one day we dove in 10-foot (3 m) swells whipped up by 25-knot winds, on the ragged edge of what's considered acceptable risk. The next day, the conditions were what the guides call "Aliwal Lake": flat calm, with 66-foot (20 m) vis.

(Tip: If it's anything other than Aliwal Lake, wear the offered spray jacket: The wind and spray can chill you quickly, even on the short 15-minute trip out to the dive site, which isn't ideal before cool-water diving. Getting back into the boat after a dive involves hanging on to a rope, passing up your gear, and porpoise-ing onto the RIB, so some dexterity/fitness is required.)

Dives begin with a counted-down, collective back-roll entry, and as you descend (and your heart rate settles back down to normal), you begin to realize what makes this place special. Baby scalloped hammerheads skitter close to the surface, wary, no doubt, of the shadows that patrol the periphery of visibility. (Oceanic blacktip, tiger, bull, and fully grown hammerhead sharks are regularly spotted here.) Potato bass putter along in the surge, which washes over pink anemones and surprisingly colorful rock formations. Snowflake moray eels have multiple hidey-holes to choose from,

The fossilized sandstone reef of Aliwal Shoal buzzes with marine life, from crayfish to sand tiger sharks (known as "raggies" here).

while bluespotted ribbontail rays skim along the sandy seabed.

Between June and November, raggies are everywhere. These 10-foot (3 m), slightly hump-backed sharks hold a tangle of teeth that frightened people into hunting them to near extinction in the 1950s. Raggies are docile during the day, perking up at night (feeding time; they prefer fish and crustaceans), and they are the only known shark to gulp air at the surface, storing it in their stomachs to achieve neutral buoyancy that's useful for stalking prey.

Divers benefit from this party trick, too: You can get quite close to raggies if you're patient. (Swim toward them, and they'll move away with surprising speed, fixing you with a reproachful, side-eye stare.) At a site appropriately named **Raggie's Cave,** a horseshoe-shaped canyon curving around a raised sandy patch, we came across what our guide called a "raggie parking lot," 15 to 20 large sharks, drifting with the surge. I glanced up to watch some giant trevally carve through a bait ball, and when I turned to look for my dive buddy

In South Africa, as in most areas, it is a constant battle to balance wildlife preservation with urban expansion and agricultural demands.

(Chris), I spotted his yellow-and-black fins sticking out from under a cloud of raggies. Chris was lying on his back in the sand, unmoving, and these curious sharks couldn't get enough of him, slowly drifting over him, completely fascinated. (Raggies were the first animal Chris saw on his very first dive; he has a real soft spot for them.)

(Tip: If you want to kick things up a notch, baited shark dives bring divers into close proximity with bigger sharks, including large oceanic blacktip, tiger, and bull. Divers drift with baited drums, as the sharks materialize out of the edge of visibility, streaking past and circling around the dive group.)

The underwater world is a tough act to follow, but safaris—camping under the stars in a wild place and waking up in the cold dawn to go on a game drive, not knowing what you might see—are equally magical. They gift you the same love and wonder for an untamed place.

There are plenty of safari options to choose from, and if you can swing a multiday adventure, it's worth it. However, if you're short on time, spend a day or two at **PheZulu Safari Park,** about a half hour's drive inland from Durban. It's set up for day outings, with regularly scheduled activities such as game drives. There's no escaping the fact that PheZulu is touristy, rubbing elbows with suburbia. However, as you bump along rutted tracks in a covered 4×4, watching a herd of zebra drink from a watering hole or a month-old giraffe loping over to the safety of its mother, you dissolve into the beating heart of South Africa.

Many places in Africa—including South Africa—are still waging the long and mighty battle between wildlife preservation—critical to environmental health and the economy—and urban expansion and agricultural demands (both necessities).

That battle is being waged underwater as well, although the conflict (and casualties) is much less visible. Overfishing—from both commercial, and illegal, unreported, and unregulated (IUU) vessels—is a huge issue. Less than a decade ago, fishing fleets nearly wiped out the sardine run, which not only brings in valuable tourism revenue, but is an ecologically crucial event already threatened by climate change. A 66-year study of South Africa's sardine run published in 2019 showed that the sardines are arriving later every year due to warming ocean temperatures and increased cyclones.

Who's watching who? A pair of giraffes and a traveler eye each other up on a game drive. On land or underwater, South Africa is a safari.

This affects the food chain, as predators and prey are no longer in the same place at the same time.

We need wild places like Aliwal Shoal. Not only for the world's (and our) physical health, but our emotional well-being, too. The wild feeds the soul, and Aliwal is bold, big, and special.

Make a Difference

If the big issues are keeping you awake at night, **National Geographic's Pristine Seas** (nationalgeographic .org/projects/pristine-seas) is an organization that is getting results. Founded in 2008 by Dr. Enric Sala, Pristine Seas partners with local on-the-ground conservation groups and "combines exploration, research, and storytelling to inspire world leaders to protect the last wild places in the ocean." At the time of writing, Pristine Seas has completed expeditions in 31 places, 24 of which have since been protected. That's more than 2.3 million square miles (six million sq km) of protected ocean as a result of this collective effort, and they're determined to help protect at least 30 percent of the world's oceans by 2030. You can follow their work and donate online to support expeditions.

NEED TO KNOW

GETTING HERE: King Shaka International Airport is Durban's main airport (located 22 mi/35 km north of the city). It's about a one-hour drive from the airport to Umkomaas. The lodge can arrange transport (book in advance), or taxis and rental cars are available.

GETTING AROUND: We didn't need a rental car; it was cheaper and easier to organize transport.

PACKING TIPS: Although Umkomaas is warm, diving can chill you, so pack casual, warm layers. A hat or beanie is useful during surface intervals, and good moisturizer is a post-dive must (skin takes a hammering from wind, salt, and sun).

WEATHER: A warm and temperate Southern Hemisphere climate with regular rainfall. February is warmest (75°F/24°C), July is coolest (63°F/17°C), December and January are the busiest (with the best vis), and spring (August through November) can have swells.

IN ADDITION: This is a great place for solo travelers.

Diving

OVERVIEW: An offshore reef in a marine protected area that buzzes with big stuff: sharks, rays, whales, and game fish. This exciting, iconic dive destination has drift dives, interesting topography, wrecks, and hosts the annual sardine run.

- **Visibility:** From nil and 98 feet (0 to 30 m)
- **Water Temp:** 68°F (20°C) in winter / 82°F (28°C) in summer
- **Depth Range:** 52 to 89 feet (16 to 27 m)

MARINE LIFE: Sharks (raggies, bull, hammerhead, oceanic blacktip), dolphins, potato and brindle bass, pineapple fish, moray eels, stingrays, and giant trevally. Seasonal critters include: raggies (June to November), tiger sharks (summer), humpback whales (May to November), and the sardine run (June and July).

SHOP INFO: We dove with **Blue Ocean Dive Resort, a** friendly, experienced shop and convenient base with an integrated lodge and restaurant. (You become family very quickly here. It's difficult to leave.) All diving is off RIBs, with a dozen sites within a 15-minute boat ride and more farther afield if conditions are right. The shop has an instruction room and on-site pool for courses, with Nitrox and gear rental available. There's a large drying area, and all gear is secured overnight. Every diver should carry a surface signal device (whistle and/or surface marker buoy [SMB]) with them—if traveling light, pack that and your mask.

Accommodations

HIGH-END: We're definitely returning to **Blue Ocean Dive Resort:** You couldn't hope to meet a livelier and more welcoming group. It's great for solo travelers (no single fees), and families with kids are welcome, too. Casual and accommodating, there are 20 comfortable rooms, and the lodge is happy to create packages (diving, accommodations, and activities, including safaris) to suit your needs. ~$107 USD

MID-RANGE: PheZulu Safari Park has on-site one- and two-bedroom self-catering chalets, with a *braai* (barbecue) area and stunning views of the valley. ~$70 USD

BUDGET: Venti Dell'Est is a cozy three-room guesthouse in Westbrook (close to the airport and Durban), with views of the Indian Ocean and memorable hosts. This peaceful pocket is a great base for exploring Durban, or a pre-/post-flight stopover. ~$60 USD

Food & Drink

Blue Ocean Dive Resort has a casual on-site restaurant and bar that is popular with locals and guests. Their homemade wood-fired pizzas are delicious.

The **Boma Restaurant** at PheZulu Safari Park has valley views that can't be beat. Try the bunny chow, a traditional Durban dish of beef curry served in a hollowed-out quarter loaf of bread.

Grab a beer with your dive guides at **East Coast Brewing Company,** an indoor-outdoor meeting point in Umkomaas that has great live music.

VALDEZ

The Last Frontier

M other Nature plays favorites. Alaska's vast borders swell with the call of the wild. They're filled with a jumble of towering pinnacles (including 20,310-ft/6,190-m Denali, the highest mountain in North America); cold, rushing rivers; frozen, rippling tongues of glaciers; and forests glowing in coppers, jades, golds, and reds.

Alaska is the largest state in the United States (one-fifth the size of the lower 48 states, and bigger than California, Texas, and Montana combined) with the lowest population density. By area, more than half of America's national park lands are contained in Alaska's borders. There's more than 57 million acres (23 million ha) of designated wilderness, home to the wildlife of our dreams: bear, moose, Dall sheep, bald eagles, and caribou, to name a few.

And that's just topside.

Alaska doesn't leap to mind when people think about diving destinations, but it should: Its coastline stretches 6,640 miles (10,686 km), which is more than the rest of the United States' coastline combined. Orcas, humpback whales, harbor seals, and sea otters can be found here, and divers might be lucky enough to share the water with salmon, Pacific sleeper sharks, moon jellyfish blooms, Pacific octopuses, and speedy, elusive salmon sharks.

It's salmon sharks that we were after. We shared our time between Ravencroft Lodge in Prince William Sound, the only place you can reliably see salmon sharks (for now), and the harbor town of Valdez.

This is one of the last frontiers, drawing forth wanderlust from even the most road-weary traveler and demanding nothing less than an absolute commitment to adventure. ■

The call of the wild: Even Valdez's harbor, framed by mountains, whispers adventure and wanderlust.

Ravencroft Lodge is a rustic oceanside encampment on the Port Fidalgo arm of Prince William Sound. It's breathtakingly, wildly beautiful here, all senses amplified, with views of the Chugach mountain range framing the horizon.

The lodge sits on 240 acres (97 ha) of private land, accessible by boat or aircraft, and is hemmed in by forest on three sides. More than once we spotted a black bear turning over rocks along the shoreline near the dock. Bald eagles are frequent visitors, and we often spent our morning cuppa in the company of delicate rufous hummingbirds.

Ravencroft was the passion project of Daniel Boone Hodgin (known by his middle name), who, with his father, built the lodge by hand, transforming what used to be an old mine into a comfortable, seven-building lodge. When Boone married his biologist wife, Gina, a curious shift took place. Now Ravencroft's focus is understanding and protecting their special backyard. "Eighty percent of our clients now are divers," Boone said. "We've gone from being one of 400 hunting and fishing lodges in the area to being one of the only diving lodges."

Ravencroft's maximum 12 guests include a somewhat disparate mix of divers and fishermen: Wet gear is laid out to dry on every available railing, and stories are traded every evening in the shared dining hall and lounge. It works surprisingly well. We

_____ WISH WE KNEW _____

Valdez can get socked in by weather. The town's one rental car agency doesn't have capacity to send people to Anchorage one-way, so if flights are canceled and you don't have a rental car, you may have to stay put for a few days. Be flexible.

celebrated their successes, and the fishermen pored over our photos, marveling at an underwater world pulsating with soft white plumose anemones, lion's mane jellyfish, Pacific octopuses, and more.

Diving expeditions take place around the jetty (eelgrass beds and abandoned mining equipment) and the sloping rock walls of the sound, dropping to around 620 feet (189 m), home to nudibranchs, rockfish, and crabs.

Our favorite dive took place in a shallow river with spawning salmon. We took a small skiff to a river mouth, shouldering our gear for an upstream walk in what was definitely bear country: bear beds, bear scat, and salmon carcasses were strewn on both river banks. Armed with bear spray and yelling "Hey, bear!" as we walked upstream, I took up a lookout post on a fallen tree suspended over the river as Chris and Boone (in dry suits) donned tanks and slid in among a cloud of salmon, lying flat on their stomachs in stiff current, resembling sharks in a bait ball as the salmon parted around them.

Taking the skiff back to Ravencroft, we spotted a mother brown bear on the shoreline, her two cubs play-fighting in the ocean as a bald eagle floated overhead. This place is filled with moments like these, and the heart isn't big enough to hold them all.

The wildlife-watching is more than enough to keep non-divers busy, but most divers come here to see salmon sharks. These elusive speedsters

Rare salmon sharks, resembling pint-size great whites, congregate in Prince William Sound for a few weeks each summer.

Author Chris Taylor, kitted up in his dry suit and ready for a dive, takes in the view from the steps of rustic Ravencroft Lodge.

resemble pint-size great whites and move like makos. Ravencroft Lodge is the only operation in the world offering snorkel experiences with salmon sharks, and they have amassed years of knowledge about this rare species.

Salmon sharks are incredibly skittish—bubbles freak them out—so snorkeling is the best way to approach them. Boone has attached special handrails to his boat so snorkelers can hold as still as possible in the water.

We, unfortunately, missed the sharks by a week, which is not unusual. The salmon shark migration takes place between May and July, and often it takes a trip or two to time your visit. Encounters can be fleeting, but these sharks are as rare as polar bears—and becoming rarer.

"Their numbers used to be so thick I could have walked across their backs," Boone said. "Now their numbers seem to have plateaued around 30."

The reason for the sudden drop in numbers? Fishing. Apparently, these dynamic sharks are fun to catch, and they're also competing for the area's salmon, which doesn't endear them to fishermen.

Fishing is worth around $5.6 billion a year to Alaska. It's the state's biggest industry, supplying more than 60 percent of the United States' seafood supply and employing more than 58,000 workers. It's also an embedded tradition.

Boone regularly invites Valdez locals out to Ravencroft to talk to them about sharks around a dining table rather than the docks, and he's counting on divers like us to spread the word.

The commercial fishermen we spoke with acknowledged they're having to travel farther to catch fewer fish. There is a limit to what Mother Nature is willing to give, and we're catching more than the ocean can produce: 31 percent of the world's stocks of wild fish are overexploited, and 58 percent are at their limits. Climate change isn't helping matters, with warming ocean temperatures decimating fish stocks.

"We have a long way to go [to protect] the oceans," said Dr. Sylvia Earle. "People think of fish as seafood, rather than sea fish. We need to value the living system rather than the short-term sales version."

Our next stop, Valdez—a friendly, harborside town surrounded by forested mountains threaded with silvery waterfalls—has extracted itself from tight spots before, thanks to a fiercely independent and resilient population. In 1964, Valdez was the epicenter of the second largest earthquake ever measured, a 9.2. The town of Valdez had to be relocated to an entirely different area. (You can take a **guided or self-guided tour of Old Valdez.)**

In 1989, the *Exxon Valdez* struck Bligh Reef near Port Fidalgo, dumping between 10 and 38 million gallons (depending on who you ask) of crude oil into Prince William Sound, decimating wildlife and forever linking this disaster to the town.

A visit to the **Valdez Museum & Historical Archives** is a wonderful way to learn more about Valdez's boom-and-bust history, with informative exhibits and black-and-white photographs documenting the area's fascinating past. *(Tip: The museum has two buildings located a short walk apart; guided tours are available, and we loved the "please touch!" exhibits for children.)*

Wrap up your visit with a small-group **wildlife cruise with Lu-Lu Belle Glacier Wildlife Cruises.** Curious sea otters picked up their heads as we went

Authors Chris Taylor and Carrie Miller snorkel up to an iceberg calved by the Columbia Glacier, en route from Valdez to Ravencroft Lodge.

past, and we spotted humpback whales, orcas, Stellar sea lions, and Dall's porpoises as we nosed up to the impressive Columbia Glacier, the second largest tidewater glacier in North America.

Alaska is where wanderlust is born. Whatever you've seen or heard about this final frontier will be eclipsed in a moment of being here. Mother Nature has her favorites. Alaska will be one of yours.

Make a Difference

Salmon sharks need protection in Alaska. Alaska regulations allow sports fishermen to harvest up to two sharks per year, which is staggering, considering no one knows what the area's population of salmon sharks actually *is.* Research on numbers is more than two decades old, and proposed studies and conservation efforts have met with opposition, largely because the sharks are considered competition for salmon, even though their presence is essential for the balance of the area's ecosystem. Education and raising awareness are essential, but in the meantime, placing an economic value on live salmon sharks through dive tourism, encouraging the Alaskan government to establish protections, and banging the drum publicly for these sharks might help save them. *(alaskasharkconservation.com)*

GETTING HERE: Anchorage is the main hub into Valdez: From there it's either a 45-minute flight on RAVN Alaska or a five-hour drive, and both are stunning. Ravencroft Lodge is 35 miles (56 km) south of Valdez in a remote corner of Prince William Sound. The lodge will arrange a water taxi.

GETTING AROUND: In Valdez, taxis, rental cars, and bike rentals are available.

PACKING TIPS: Functional outdoor-wear and warm, weatherproof layers. At Ravencroft, indoors is a socks-only zone, so having a pair of slip-on/off boots with rubber soles, as well as a presentable pair of warm socks with tread, comes in handy.

WEATHER: Alaskan weather is changeable, with summer temperatures averaging 68°F (20°C). The salmon shark migration usually takes place between May and July. Spring and autumn are better for northern lights.

IN ADDITION: Ravencroft is open May through September. The lodge does not sell alcohol (BYOB if you want it) and there is limited Wi-Fi.

Diving

OVERVIEW: This is frontier diving, one of the few places in the world to get in the water with salmon sharks and spawning salmon.

- **Visibility:** From 30 to 50 feet (9 to 15 m)
- **Water Temp:** 50°F (10°C) at depth / 60°F (15.5°C) at the surface
- **Depth Range:** 65.6 feet (20 m) max—dive profiles are kept shallow due to the distance from medical help.

MARINE LIFE: Salmon sharks, jellyfish, spiny dogfish, Pacific sleeper shark, Pacific octopuses, plumose anemones, fish (salmon, halibut, rockfish), nudibranchs, crabs, and sea stars

SHOP INFO: Ravencroft Lodge is the only operator, and they know their business well. Dives are a mix of jetty and boat, a well-equipped 32-foot (10 m) catamaran with a heated cabin that can accommodate seven divers.

Boone and his team provide support and advice, but dives are self-guided with a buddy. Speak to Ravencroft about certifications required prior to arrival. Tanks and weights are supplied; divers need to bring any additional gear (rentals available in Anchorage).

Accommodations

HIGH-END: Rustic **Ravencroft Lodge** has a shared lounge and dining hall with million-dollar views of Port Fidalgo, and a forest-surrounded bunkhouse with eight private rooms for a maximum 12 guests. Bathrooms and showers (including flush toilets and hot water) are at the back of the bunkhouse. It's simple and comfortable, a great base for adventures. ~$4,000 USD per week

MID-RANGE: The **Totem Hotel & Suites** in Valdez is modern and friendly. There are 65 hotel rooms, 15 business suites, and 10 cabins to choose from, all within walking distance to town and the marina. ~$260 USD

BUDGET: Robe Lake Lodge is a family-owned lodge located a few minutes' drive from Valdez, with a mountain setting and lake views. There are a variety of accommodations, from cozy rooms in the main log cabin lodge, to cabins spaced across the property. ~$159 USD

Food & Drink

Dinners at **Ravencroft Lodge** are a fun, communal affair: The dinner bell calls lodgers to three shared tables for hearty fare like fresh-caught halibut, scalloped potatoes, corn bread, and coleslaw. (Breakfast is served at 7 a.m., and lunch is at your leisure.) Give advance notice of food allergies and intolerances.

The **Fat Mermaid** is the spot in Valdez for filling frontier breakfasts, like eggs, pancakes, and biscuits and gravy, with a side of reindeer sausage. It opens daily at 7 a.m.; lunch and dinner are also available.

The **Roadside Potatohead Too,** near Valdez harbor, serves up hot, affordable, handmade, potato-centered comfort food. This was heaven on earth for Chris, who worships potatoes.

ESPIRITU SANTO

Travelers Welcome

Vanuatu is a weird place, and that's absolutely wonderful. Its 83 islands have volcanoes, rainforests, and reefs, a surprisingly limited number of plant and animal species, and a rich culture with a long migratory history: Ni-Vanuatu (the Indigenous population) have been traveling for more than 3,000 years.

The Republic of Vanuatu is situated in the Coral Sea between Fiji, New Caledonia, and the Solomon Islands, and covers 4,706 square miles (12,189 sq km). Port Vila, on the island of Efate, is the capital, but Espiritu Santo (known as Santo) is Vanuatu's largest island.

In 1606, Portuguese explorer Pedro Fernández de Quirós mistook Vanuatu for Australia, which begs the eternal question: How much of exploration was an accident?

Less accidental was the Americans' decision to build their second largest World War II Pacific base in Luganville. At one point, there were close to 100 ships in the harbor and more than 100,000 troops on the island, compared to the local population of around 15,000.

One might expect Ni-Vanuatu to, understandably, harbor a distrust of foreigners, but this is an exceptionally friendly country to visit. Vanuatu gained its independence in 1980 and the young nation of old souls loves welcoming travelers.

On Santo, snorkeling and diving are favorite pastimes, which isn't surprising—Santo is home to one of the largest and most accessible shipwrecks in the world, the S.S. *President Coolidge*. World War II tours are riveting, and remarkable ribbons of road link beautiful beaches. ∎

Most travelers to Espiritu Santo come here to dive the wrecks left behind during WWII. (This was the United States' second largest Pacific base.)

Espiritu Santo
VANUATU

In his masterpiece *Tales of the South Pacific*, partially inspired by his time stationed on Espiritu Santo during World War II, James A. Michener wrote that, if we reject the food and customs, avoid the people, and fear the religion, we might as well not travel.

Vanuatu is a place worth traveling to. Here, many people believe in black magic. Lush gardens are filled with cassavas, noni, and bananas. The pastime of choice is enjoying a shell of kava (a root plant with a relaxing effect) at roadside **nakamals,** or kava bars. *(Tip: A light by the side of the road means the kava is ready. Kava is an important part of daily life and ceremonies here, and visitors are welcome at nakamals.)* To hail a taxi or bus, just wave vigorously (taxis have a T on their number-plate; buses have a B). As one driver informed us, there are "no poisonous snakes in Vanuatu—just poisonous politicians."

On Santo, Vanuatu's strong, unique culture thrives, along with a barefoot-traveler vibe of those drawn here by adventure, white-sand beaches shaded by coconut palms, snorkeling, and—especially—diving.

At the end of WWII, the Americans dumped their equipment into the sea. This snorkel/dive spot is known as Million Dollar Point.

___ WISH WE KNEW _____

Food and drink costs in Vanuatu are more expensive than you might expect, both dining out and buying groceries. A nice dinner costs around $30 USD per person. Just something to factor into your travel budget.

The majority of people who visit Santo come here to dive the **S.S. President Coolidge.** The 653-foot-long (199 m) *Coolidge* sailed for Vanuatu when WWII broke out, carrying everything from troops to howitzers to jeeps.

The one thing the *Coolidge* didn't have was accurate intel: No one informed the ship that Allied forces had set mines in the channel where the *Coolidge* was headed, and it struck two. The captain, knowing the ship was going to sink, went full throttle onto the reef, hoping to buy time to offload the crew and passengers. It worked: There were only two fatalities (one man died instantly, another died saving the lives of six others).

Divers can explore a variety of holds and decks on this intact wreck, which still contains equipment and items like a barber's chair and gas masks. They can also search for the Lady, a famous porcelain relief of a woman in a pink dress riding a unicorn.

Although the dive itself isn't necessarily difficult, you do have to have your wits about you, as it's easy to get lost and the wreck is deep. The ship rests on its side on a steep slope; the bow lies around 66 feet (20 m) and the stern around 236 feet (72 m). Reliable dive shops won't take divers beyond 131 feet (40 m) on a single tank of air. (Qualified tech divers can go farther.)

It's a shore entry and short swim following a line to the bow before descending along the sides, keeping an eye out for barracuda, lionfish, moray

Champagne Beach, with its sugary sand and warm water, is rightly considered one of the world's loveliest beaches.

eels, and other marine life. The sheer size of the *Coolidge* is a stunner, even for experienced wreck divers, and two dives isn't enough to see it all. Most divers recommend 10 to 15 dives just to get your head around this impressive ship.

The *Coolidge* is usually dived in conjunction with nearby **Million Dollar Point,** an underwater monument to the absurdity of war. After the war, the Americans knew they wouldn't be able to cart all their equipment—bulldozers, cranes, Willys jeeps, etc.—back to the United States, so they offered to sell it to the joint French-English government for a bargain price. In an expensive game of chicken, the French-English government turned down the offer, betting they would get the equipment for free when the Americans left the island. Rather than letting that happen, the Americans dumped the entire lot into the sea, creating an easy and rather bizarre shore dive and snorkel spot.

Santo also has lovely reefs for diving and snorkeling in warm, clear water. **Cindy's Reef** is a leisurely drift dive over impressive beds of bright coral. We spotted staghorn and plate coral, turtles, a whitetip reef shark, bumphead parrotfish, and trevally. (The fish are quite twitchy and shy; there is a lot of fishing in the area.)

Topside, there are any number of ways to explore the island. One must-do is a **WWII History Tour** with Santo Heritage Tours. Diving the *Coolidge* and Million Dollar Point are good introductions for travelers to understand the significant role Santo played during the war, but a three-hour guided driving tour of important sites (including the impressive **South Pacific WWII Museum**) provides so many more stories. For example, we visited the forest-encrusted wreckage of a B-17 plane that had crashed due to mechanical failure. Turns out the pilot was Lt. Eugene "Gene" Roddenberry, who—following a fascinating military history—went on to create *Star Trek*.

A ride with **Santo Horse Adventures** is another special experience. Owner Megan-Jane Lockyer purchases horses that are sick or need a new home, and she has made a good one for them in challenging conditions.

Around 10 of her horses are suitable for riding. Lockyer runs one trail ride per day, a slow-and-steady exploration of the 300 acres (121 ha) she leases from the local chief. Rides are done barefoot in shorts, using lightweight western saddles and hackamores, following the shade as the horses wind their way through forests and along palm plantations, the ocean winking into view. The horses are bright-eyed and alert (always good signs), and the ride wraps up through a remarkable mangrove tunnel to the open ocean, branches closing in over our heads, seawater lapping our thighs.

(Tip: Book in advance. If you have luggage space, contact Megan-Jane and ask if you can bring/ donate a few badly needed pieces of equipment, which are hard to source in Vanuatu.)

Don't depart Santo without renting a car and exploring the island's extraordinary beaches. There is one main road that threads and branches its way along the island's south and east coasts. The winding road is a pleasure to drive, flanked by palm trees and roadside villages, the beautiful countryside unfolding outside open windows.

Make your way to **Champagne Beach,** which rightfully holds the reputation as one of the world's loveliest, with trees shading champagne-colored beaches, local kids frolicking in the warm, still turquoise water, and a small bar standing by should you need refreshment.

(Tip: Public beaches in Santo charge a nominal

There are any number of ways to explore Espiritu Santo, from WWII history tours, to birding outings, to horseback-riding adventures.

entrance fee—around $5 to $15—per car, which goes to the landowner; bring cash.)

Continue on to **Port Olry,** a tiny town with thatched-roof bungalows and rustic, sand-floored restaurants set a short distance back from a picture-perfect beach. This is where you'll find **Chez Louis Restaurant and Bar;** bring your mask and fins and enjoy a post-snorkel lunch in the shade, with salt on your skin and sand under your toes, yarning with the locals and other travelers, and drinking in what a spectacular place this is.

Make a Difference

Pay attention to China's accelerating influence in the South Pacific. We encountered it everywhere: Fiji, the Solomons, Vanuatu. The region is important to China's Belt and Road Initiative, a trillion-dollar investment into establishing trade routes and industries in multiple countries. (Vanuatu has received hundreds of millions of dollars in grants and loans from China for things like a new convention center and wharf.) This largesse comes with pressure, as China seeks to extend its influence and territory, securing rights to natural resources and undermining diplomatic support for Taiwan. As other countries (like the United States) step back, especially regarding leadership around climate change, China is stepping in. Other countries have done worse in the past, but not during a global environmental crisis.

NEED TO KNOW

GETTING HERE: Air Vanuatu flies from Port Vila to Espiritu Santo daily and from Brisbane to Espiritu Santo weekly. Check in at least 90 minutes before all domestic flights or risk the flight closing. There is a departure tax of around $3.50 USD at each domestic airport after check-in. Baggage rates are expensive.

GETTING AROUND: Car and scooter rentals are available; buses and taxis run regularly. We rented a car for a day or two and used taxis and transfers for the rest, which worked well. Most hotels can help with plans.

PACKING TIPS: Casual and quick-drying clothing, with sun cover and reef shoes. Reef-friendly sunscreen and mosquito spray, a reusable water bottle, and daypack are useful. Bring a copy of James A. Michener's *Tales of the South Pacific* to read.

WEATHER: Vanuatu has a year-round tropical climate. Southern Hemisphere summer (November through March) is hot and humid, with temperatures averaging around 82°F (28°C). Winter (April to October) is drier and cooler, around 73°F (23°C).

IN ADDITION: Most shops close midday for two hours.

Diving

OVERVIEW: Along with great reefs, Vanuatu has one of the largest WWII wrecks, suitable for divers of all levels, but especially enjoyed by tech divers.

- **Visibility:** From 33 to 82 feet (10 to 25 m)
- **Water Temp:** 72°F (22°C) in winter / 82°F (28°C) in summer
- **Depth Range:** 131 feet (40 m) max recreational; 236 feet (72 m) to the *Coolidge's* rudder

MARINE LIFE: Giant trevally, barracuda, turtles (loggerhead, green, and hawksbill), dugongs, parrotfish, angelfish, whitetip reef sharks, lionfish, Spanish dancers, pygmy sea horses, and crayfish

SHOP INFO: We dove with **Pacific Dive** in Luganville for the wrecks, which is a good shop for recreational and tech divers. They have a solid reputation. For the reef dives, we dove with **Aore Adventure Sports,** located across the channel from Luganville (they offer pickups). This lodge/shop combo has a well-set-up boat and an experienced local crew.

Accommodations

HIGH-END: Aore Adventure Sports & Lodge is located on Aore Island. This self-contained beach house can sleep up to six adults. It's located on a private beach and five acres (2 ha) of garden, with a kitchen, BBQ area, and veranda, all a short boat ride from Santo's energy. *~$275 USD per night for the entire cottage*

MID-RANGE: Village de Santo Resort offers boutique accommodations with 15 open-plan, two-story suites encircling a gardened main pool and bar area. It caters to divers, offering an early breakfast from the on-site restaurant, as well as a wash-down and locked storage area for gear. Located a 15-minute walk from town and staffed by a great team. *~$135 USD*

BUDGET: Deco Stop Lodge is perched on a hill overlooking Luganville and the Segond Channel, a short walk (10 minutes) to town. There are 12 comfortable rooms, with on-site restaurant and pool. As the name suggests, this lodge also caters to divers, with a wash area for dive gear and secure storage facility. *~$105 USD*

Food & Drink

Village de Santo Resort's **Restaurant 1606** serves a wide range of delicious meals—tapas, Malaysian fusion, Mediterranean-inspired, and more.

Deco Stop Lodge's **Club Narcosis Restaurant & Bar** is a favorite watering hole for divers. Their popular menu has seafood, steaks, fresh fruits and vegetables, and a wide range of cocktails and beer.

You can't beat **Chez Louis Restaurant & Bar's** view. Located in the village of Port Olry, this beachside restaurant has a sand-coated floor, a thatched roof for shade, magnetic views of a turquoise bay, and ice-cold beer and fresh-caught seafood. It's just about perfect.

CURAÇAO

The Little Charmer

uraçao is alluring.
    Located in the south Caribbean Sea, about 37 miles (60 km) north of Venezuela, tucked in between sister islands Bonaire and Aruba, this little island is roughly twice the size of Washington, D.C., and seven miles (11.3 km) across at its widest point.

It's populated by roughly 160,000 inhabitants representing more than 50 different nationalities, a cultural mash-up that is apparent in the island's languages (Dutch and Papiamento, a mix of dialects dating back to the slavery era). It is also apparent in the country's history.

The Spanish wrested the island from the Arawak Indians around 1499; 135 years later, the Dutch West India Company seized it from the Spanish. Curaçao became a large slave depot, servicing all corners of the world. When the Netherlands abolished slavery in 1863, Curaçao's economy took a hit—until it started refining oil for Venezuela.

Now it's an autonomous country within the kingdom of the Netherlands, but one with a strong buccaneer feel: The trade winds still carry a waft of lawlessness, a knowing smile that makes Curaçao a fun, foreign-feeling port to explore, rather than an antiseptic Caribbean resort staffed by white-shirted waiters.

From the brightly painted buildings—shocking pinks, sunshine yellows, and turquoise blues—in the capital city of Willemstad, to the bonhomie of Curaçaoans, this little island will win you over, just as it did us. ∎

Curaçao's capital of Willemstad is known for its candy-colored waterfront row of historical Dutch buildings (a UNESCO World Heritage site).

Curaçao is geographically blessed with large, deep (984.3 ft/300 m), well-protected harbors. The colorful capital of Willemstad curves around Schottegat Harbor. The harbor connects to the Caribbean Sea via the Sint Anna Baai canal, which is spanned by the Queen Emma Bridge, a pontoon pedestrian bridge that opens at regular intervals to let ships pass. The bridge links Willemstad's two distinct neighborhoods—Otrobanda ("other side") and Punda ("the point").

A walking tour of the vibrant capital of **Willemstad** is a must (either guided or self-explored), beginning with the eye candy of **Handelskade,** a Punda-side waterfront row of historical Dutch buildings painted in eye-watering colors and a UNESCO World Heritage site. (The colors were a Dutch government decree: Apparently white reflected the intense sun, causing headaches and blindness. It led to a cultural passion for color.)

Turning corners takes you past the **Postal Museum** (the building dates from 1693), the yellow-and-green **Government House** (still with a few cannonballs inside its walls), **Keukenplein** (a mural-painted square surrounded by artisan shops like the **Nena Sanchez Gallery**), the **Mikvé Israel-Emanuel Synagogue** (the oldest Jewish synagogue in continuous use in the Western Hemisphere), and the **floating markets.** Operating for more than 100 years, small boats travel from Venezuela, bringing fish, fruits, and vegetables purchased by locals and restaurants.

Despite its proximity to Venezuela, Curaçao has an entirely different climate, which led to the creation of Curaçao liqueur. Shortly after the Spaniards arrived in 1499, they planted Valencia orange trees to stave off scurvy. The minerals in Curaçao's soil changed the properties of the orange, making it bitter. (Even the goats won't touch it.) Somewhere down the line, local firm Senior & Co. learned that, mixed with nine secret spices, the peel of this inedible orange made a tasty brew—and so the famous Blue Curaçao was born. (The color was added because Curaçaoans "think in color," we were told.)

The **Curaçao Liqueur Distillery,** housed in the 19th-century mansion **Landhuis Chobolobo,** is the only place in the world where Blue Curaçao is made—by hand, following a 120-year-old recipe. And here's the twist: The distillery brought some of the Valencia orange trees to Venezuela, in an attempt to expand production. Within three years, the oranges returned to normal. Curaçao liqueur can only be made in Curaçao.

Guided tours of the Curaçao Liqueur Distillery are a must-do, and there are different experiences to choose from, tastings and cocktails included.

Outside of Willemstad, outdoor adventure abounds. Try a lesson with **Windsurfing Curaçao** on quiet Spanish Bay, seven miles (11.3 km) to the

The Tugboat is a shallow wreck ideal for snorkelers and divers (especially beginners) that is home to a plethora of small marine life.

Make a Difference

In their native Indo-Pacific range, lionfish are in balance with their environment. In the Caribbean and Atlantic, lionfish—an introduced species—have no natural predators. They've decimated native fish populations by more than 65 percent and reproduce at an astonishing rate (one female can lay two million eggs per year). Killing lionfish is crucial to marine conservation. What can you do to help? **Hunt lionfish.** Many dive shops offer educational lionfish-hunting excursions. **Eat lionfish.** It's delicious! (And safe.) Many restaurants in Curaçao serve it. **Buy lionfish jewelry.** Lionfish Caribbean creates handmade jewelry from lionfish fins. **Support research.** The Smithsonian Institution in partnership with Substation Curaçao is studying lionfish at depths up to 800 feet (244 m).

south, suitable for all levels. To the north, hiking the 1,230-foot (375 m) **Mount Christoffel** in Christoffel National Park is a great way to experience Curaçao's desert-like vegetation.

The underwater landscape, however, is what attracts most travelers. Curaçao is a diving destination, particularly for shore diving, with rocky beaches extending to shallow reefs for around 160 feet (48.7 m) before plummeting to steep walls exceeding 1,970 feet (600 m). There is something for all levels of divers: Experts will find challenges, beginners will find good education and encouragement, and intermediate divers will be in heaven.

The west coast is quieter with calmer seas and a permanent jetty for shore dives, plus boat options. A five-minute boat trip took us to **Elvin's Plane,** a flat reef holding the wreck of a Fokker F27 airplane, scattered by storms across the reef. Wrecks attract life, and this area was filled with huge bait balls of blue runners, giant purple barrel sponges, and clouds of reef fish dining on surgeonfish eggs. The drift dive finished up at **Watamula,** another area of rolling bait balls and spectacular coral.

The south coast is more popular, offering reef, shore, night (check out Ocean Encounters' **fluorescent night dive** on their house reef), and wreck diving. Curaçao is home to the ***Superior Producer,*** a large, upright wreck sitting at 108 feet (33 m) near the cruise ship terminal. Certified divers can explore the exterior of the wreck on a guided

Pretty poison: Here, lionfish are an introduced species—and a plague. In Curaçao, there are ways travelers can help make a difference.

group dive, and wreck-certified divers can penetrate the cargo holds with a private guide.

Don't pass up the chance to be a deep-sea explorer. One of the highlights of our entire journey, a delight for divers and non-divers alike, was taking a 90-minute tour with **Substation Curaçao** in their minisub (CuraSub).

The CuraSub was purpose-built for scientific marine research, exploring the underwater "twilight zone" between 220 and 1,500 feet (67 to 457 m), one of the most under-researched places on the planet. This is a frontier few people have seen.

SOMETHING SPECIAL

Don't miss **Punda Vibes.** Every Thursday night, the pedestrian-only Punda area comes alive with a welcoming, lively, community-hosted street party, featuring salsa lessons, work from local artists, and cocktails, topped off with fireworks.

In between its research outings, the CuraSub takes visitors to depths of 1,000 feet (305 m), launching four times a day from its land-based port near Willemstad. It holds up to four passengers and one pilot, with the front two passengers lying on their stomachs on cushioned benches.

Within five minutes, we had descended farther than we had on the deepest dive of our trip and were in unknown territory. Marine snow (biological debris falling from higher in the water column) made it seem as if we were cruising through a snow globe, and scale was distorted. At one point, we spotted a brightly colored scorpionfish species discovered in 2016. (More than 50 species of fish, coral, and sponges have been discovered since 2011 by the Smithsonian Institute's Deep Reef Observation Project using CuraSub.)

Barbara van Bebber, our pilot, told us they've seen dolphins at 300 feet (91 m), hammerheads at 670 feet (204 m), and lionfish—sadly—everywhere. "They seem to be hanging around 400 feet (122 m), but the deepest we've ever seen them is 800 feet (244 m)," she said.

(Tip: Book in advance. Divers: It's safe to dive later in the day. Non-divers: This is an amazing way to see the sea. Some conditions apply and stringent safety measures are followed.)

Our CuraSub exploration highlighted how little we know about the ocean, even as divers; there is so much more to be discovered.

Chris and Carrie are all smiles in Substation Curaçao's minisub, which takes visitors to frontier depths of 1,000 feet (305 m).

NEED TO KNOW

GETTING HERE: Curaçao receives regular flights from North America, South America, and Europe.

GETTING AROUND: Walking and public transportation will get you most places in Willemstad. Rent a car for part of your stay: There is a lot to see outside the capital.

PACKING TIPS: Curaçaoans have a flair for fashion. We recommend loose-fitting clothes for two reasons: First, it's hot. Second, you can easily eat your weight in delicious food here—plan ahead waistband-wise.

WEATHER: Temperatures average 81°F (27.2°C), which doesn't reflect how scorching hot it can actually feel. November through March brings cruise ships; Willemstad can get crowded.

IN ADDITION: Strike up conversations: Curaçaoans are some of the friendliest, island-proud people you could ever hope to meet.

Diving

OVERVIEW: Curaçao has it all—reefs, walls, wrecks, night dives—but the island's real party trick is a seafloor that drops steeply a few hundred feet from shore, making shore diving accessible and popular. The northwest and southwest have different feels, and it's worth exploring both.

- **Visibility:** Around 82 feet (25 m)
- **Water Temp:** 73°F (23°C) in winter / 82°F (28°C) in summer
- **Depth Range:** 49 to 108 feet (15 to 33 m); the walls drop beyond 1,970 feet (600 m)

MARINE LIFE: Coral is in a relatively good state, especially for the Caribbean. Fishing pressure is high, but there is still plenty of life (turtles, tarpon, barracuda, reef fish).

SHOP INFO: We dove with **Caribbean Sea Sports, CURious 2 DIVE, Go West Diving, Ocean Encounters,** and **Scuba Lodge.** All the shops were excellent, with high standards, which reflects the overall quality of the industry here in Curaçao.

Accommodations

HIGH-END: San Francisco's Painted Ladies on mescaline (or nitrogen narcosis), **Scuba Lodge** is a zesty seaside lodge and dive shop, with an oceanside infinity pool, on-site restaurant, friendly staff, and accommodations ranging from hotel rooms to apartments. They get loads of return visitors. *~$155 USD*

MID-RANGE: All West Apartments & Diving is ideal for divers: Grab tanks, grab your gear, load your truck, and go. Located in Westpunt (about 45 minutes northwest of Willemstad), this small oceanside hotel (12 studios/apartments) is close to Go West Diving. It has a locked storage room for rinsing and drying gear, a filling station for unlimited tank usage, and car/truck rental available with the room rate. *~$115 USD*

BUDGET: Willemstad Resort—what a find! This former hospital building is now a brightly painted resort and an ideal base for independent travelers. We chose a split-level studio, opening onto a shared courtyard, with an upstairs loft bedroom and downstairs kitchenette and sitting area. They've thought of everything: free Wi-Fi, washing machines and drying lines, and on-site bike and car rentals. Easy walking distance to Willemstad. *~$63 USD*

Food & Drink

Restaurant Fort Nassau is a repurposed 18th-century fort that serves up delicious meals under warm lighting in an open-air environment with harbor and city views. (*Tip: Drive; it's a long uphill walk.*)

Restaurant & Café Gouverneur de Rouville was a favorite restaurant. We returned to this 18th-century building, with its views of the Handelskade, many times for the *karni stoba* (a traditional Antillean braised beef dish) for Carrie and the mix grill (Caribbean chicken, beef tenderloin, and spare ribs) for Chris.

La Bohème Curaçao was another regular for us: the best smoothies we've ever tasted (fresh ingredients, no sugar added, some sweet, some sour), *arepas* (filled cornbread), and traditional Chilean stacked sandwiches.

COCOS (KEELING) ISLANDS

The Gem at Journey's End

Cocos (Keeling) Islands looks like a shark's jaw planted in the Indian Ocean, 1,709 miles (2,750 km) northwest of Perth, Western Australia. This external Australian territory comprises 27 islands (two inhabited) encircling a six-mile-wide (10 km), horseshoe-shaped lagoon.

Cocos (Keeling) Islands

AUSTRALIA

The islands are home to one community based on two islands. Around 150 expat Australians live on West Island, which has the airport and, by default, supports most of the industry. Around 450 Cocos Malay people (Muslim, Malay-speaking descendants of the original copra plantation workers) live on Home Island across the lagoon. History established the division; time and isolation forged a bond. The Home and West Islanders respect each other's traditions, celebrate each other's holidays, and know each other's families. It reminded us of a marriage: two individuals sharing a home.

What is there to do here? Snorkel, swim, surf, paddle, and dive in clear, warm water filled with coral gardens and marine life. Kitesurfing takes off with the trade winds, and everyone is invited to join the weekly golf game, which shares its course with the international runway.

Chris, of course, wants us to move to here, and we very nearly stayed. Getting here takes a little time, but we promise—you'll find it a lot harder to leave. ■

Getting around Cocos is sheer joy: Travelers can walk, bike, drive, kayak/stand-up paddleboard/canoe the lagoon, or take the ferry between islands.

When topside, driving, canoeing, and cycling are the best ways to get around, and that's how we explored West Island, the lagoon, and Home Island.

We packed our snorkel gear and a picnic lunch into a rented car to drive around **West Island.** After a quick stop-off at the **West Island jetty** to spot the monster-size green turtles who come here to feed and rest, we drove to the **Big Barge Art Centre.** This cheerful yellow beached boat now houses local art creations, like paintings and jewelry. *(Tip: It's a great spot for picking up unique souvenirs.)*

Next up was **Trannies Beach,** a popular swim spot. After snorkeling with reef fish over beds of staghorn coral, we paused for our picnic lunch and a short stroll through dense palm jungles. These inland forests are a haven for migratory birds (like the drongo cuckoo and frigate birds) and crabs— red hermit crabs, purple land crabs, horn-eyed ghost crabs, and red crabs, found only on Cocos and Christmas Islands. *(Tip: Be crab-aware while cycling and driving—give them a miss.)*

In the afternoon, we took a **Rasa cooking class** at the school on West Island, where kids from the Cocos Malay community taught us how to prepare local dishes in return for the chance to practice their hospitality skills.

We were told the best way to explore the lagoon was on a half-day **motorized outrigger canoe safari with Cocos Islands Adventure Tours.** These outrigger canoes have a three-horsepower motor, which means you don't have to paddle against winds and tides. Starting from West Island, we motored from island to island, stopping for isolated picnics, a hike to Cocos' highest point (a dizzying 30 feet/9 m above sea level), and a drift snorkel that was one of those unforgettable moments, flying over a shallow reef through a cloud of fish, scattering baby blacktip reef sharks, and hunting trevally.

To explore **Home Island,** we loaded our bikes onto the ferry for the short trip across the lagoon from West Island. The **Pulu Cocos Museum** was our first stop**.** *(Tip: Pick up the key from the local shire office; visitors let themselves in and out.)*

The museum is a fascinating walk-through of Cocos' relatively unknown history. Cocos is a tightly woven tangle of the Clunies-Ross dynasty, former owners of the Cocos (Keeling) Islands (a Clunies-Ross has lived on-island ever since 1827), and the people brought here to work the copra plantations. These were mostly enslaved people and indentured servants of Malay descent, but also from China, Indonesia, and Africa. After many years (and some spicy WWI and WWII history—Australia's first naval victory occurred here), the Cocos Malay people voted to integrate with Australia in 1984.

We rode our bikes from one end of the island to the other, past the old settlers' graveyard, through town where we waved at residents who navigate the cobblestone and sand streets in golf carts, and past Oceania House, the stately manor once home to the Clunies-Ross family.

Stunning surface interval: Uninhabited Direction Island is the usual lunch spot while taking a break between dives.

Make a Difference

We can limit our own consumption of single-use plastic and recycle, but real change will only occur once companies are forced to bear the cost of the plastic they're creating by assuming the burden (and paying) for its proper disposal or coming up with sustainable alternatives. This is known as extended producer responsibility (EPR). As of 2021, 20 companies produce 55 percent of the world's single-use plastic. What can you do? Vote with your wallet and at the ballot box (corporations aren't going down without a fight), and advocate for smart, targeted bans that force the introduction of plastic alternatives. Visit **National Geographic's Planet or Plastic?** website to learn more: *nationalgeographic.com/environment/topic/planetorplastic.*

As we waited for the return ferry, we chatted with some Home Islanders, telling them we were here to dive with their sharks. "Ah, we have a good relationship with the sharks," one man told us. "We don't eat them and they don't eat us."

We saw sharks on every dive—blacktip reef, whitetip reef, and gray reef. Although illegal commercial fishing does occur near Cocos, the remoteness of the islands, coupled with regular patrols by the Australian Border Force, discourage many would-be poachers. In May 2021, Australia also announced plans to create a large marine park around Cocos to protect its biodiversity.

Located on the top of a large seamount, diving in Cocos is done by boat, with more than 30 sites to choose from, dependent on weather. Most of the dives are easy reef dives, sloping down to a wall that eventually drops thousands of feet. *(Tip: Due to its remoteness, this is no deco diving—keep an eye on depths.)* Although there is some damage from bleaching and storms, most of the coral is well established and healthy, and there is a ton of marine life to catch your eye. Diving is usually a full-day outing: two dives, with a delicious lunch on pretty-as-a-picture Direction Island for the surface interval.

Two Caves is home to a boat that was purposely sunk after it was caught smuggling people from Sri Lanka to Australia. Batfish are fond of it, as are trevally, barracuda, and zippy gray reef sharks.

Hermit crabs are happy residents of Cocos. You're also likely to spot purple land crabs, horn-eyed ghost crabs, and red crabs.

Over the sloping wall are the namesake two caves, a favorite with whitetip reef sharks.

The **Rose Wall** has beds of beautiful (but storm-damaged) rose-colored, rosette-shaped coral formations, with moray eels poking their noses out of the rosette wheels, and plenty of macro life, turtles, grouper, and, of course, sharks.

From time to time, divers will catch sight of debris, like the two coral-encrusted cannons used for ballast from the days of sailing ships at a site appropriately named **Cannons.**

Sunken boats and cannons are not the only debris you'll see here. Cocos is fighting a war not of its making against rising sea levels, warming

Join the locals for a game of **Scroungers Golf** held every Thursday afternoon. This nine-hole course is played as a team; club rentals/beverage purchases available. No skill (except trash-talking) or experience required.

ocean temperatures, strengthening storms, and knee-deep piles of plastic that arrive with every tide.

At first, Cocos tried to stay on top of the problem. Now they've changed tack. Along with regular beach cleanups where plastic is picked up and sorted to determine where it's coming from (travelers can volunteer—speak to the visitors center), the cluttered beaches are used as a way to have honest conversations with visitors about the stark reality of the problem.

During one cleanup, researchers collected more than 414 million pieces of plastic. On white sand, we waded through plastic bottles (more than one million plastic bottles are bought every minute

around the world), discarded shoes (24.2 billion pairs of shoes were made worldwide in 2018), and toothbrushes (the United States discards an estimated one billion toothbrushes yearly).

Cocos is doing what it can, and they're doing something right. Sixty-three percent of visitors return to this remote and remarkable place. We hope to add to that statistic soon, to thank Cocos for the final gift it gave us, our last dive day on this extraordinary 14-month journey.

At a site called **Cable Bommie,** we not only spotted the striking, endemic Cocos-Keeling angelfish (yellow fading to indigo, with blue rings around the eyes), we also had a visit from four dolphins. We wrapped up the dive with an impressive 18-shark send-off as they patrolled the wall beyond the sloping reef.

We couldn't have asked for a better dive, or a better destination, to end our journey.

Divers of all levels will love Cocos, which has warm water, coral gardens, a healthy population of sharks, and all manner of marine life.

GETTING HERE: There are twice-weekly flights from Perth, Western Australia. Don't wait for deals: The flight is underwritten by the Australian government, and the cost is what it is.

GETTING AROUND: . . . is sheer joy. Walk; rent a bike, car, or scooter; take the ferry between islands.

PACKING TIPS: Relaxed wardrobe for a tropical beach climate with reef-safe sunscreen, reusable water bottle, daypack, and layers. On Home Island, women should cover their shoulders and knees.

WEATHER: Warm weather year-round, rarely dipping below 75°F (24°C), with two (Southern Hemisphere) seasons: the trade winds (June through October) and the doldrums (November through May). During the trade winds, Cocos is a mecca for kiteboarders and can get booked out. There is a cyclone risk during the doldrums, but it's quieter with beautiful weather. Diving is year-round; many activities are tide-dependent.

IN ADDITION: Cocos has limited accommodations and one dive shop; book well in advance.

Diving

OVERVIEW: Stunning diving on a remote Australian island in the Indian Ocean. Cocos has warm, clear water with all manner of marine life, from endemic angelfish to a healthy population of sharks. Divers of all levels will fall in love with this place.

- **Visibility:** From 65 to 100 feet (20 to 30 m)
- **Water Temp:** 77°F (25°C) in winter / 84°F (29°C) in summer
- **Depth Range:** 65 to 131 feet (20 to 40 m)

MARINE LIFE: Coral (gorgonians, table, and leather), sharks (gray reef, whitetip reef, blacktip reef, tiger), dolphins (spinner, common, and bottlenose), manta rays, turtles (green and hawksbill), trevally (black, bluefin, and giant), and clams (giant and electric)

SHOP INFO: Cocos Dive, Cocos' sole operator (West Island–based), is a family-operated business run well by Dieter Gerhard and Karen Willshaw. They take meticulous care of their environment and Dieter doesn't miss a beat. This was the only place we made an exception to our rule about having someone on board the vessel while divers are in the water, due to Dieter's experience and safety protocols. Groups are small, allowing for flexibility. Expect to lend a hand with loading and launching. Courses offered. Contact the shop well in advance of making travel arrangements to make sure diving isn't booked out and they're on-island (they often close in October and November).

Accommodations

HIGH-END: Beachcomber Cottage is a waterfront, four-bedroom house (up to eight guests). It has a kitchen and comes with bikes and water toys. ~$488 USD

MID-RANGE: Cocos Castaway is a handful of super-cute self-contained cottages, some with a shared veranda, others with a private deck. The ocean is a stone's throw in one direction, town in the other, and the hosts are lovely. Bike use included. ~$165 USD

BUDGET: Cocos Beach Resort has 28 rooms available in four configurations, from ocean views to family suites, and is comfortable and centrally located. ~$137 USD

Food & Drink

(Tip: Most places require dinner reservations by signing up on a blackboard outside the restaurant by 4 p.m. and some places rotate openings. Plan in advance.)

By day, **Saltmakers by the Sea** is a lovely little coffee shop, serving smoothies and brunch. At night, it transforms into a restaurant, cooking up Malay chicken rendang and wood-fired pizzas heated up over coconut shells.

Cocos Beach Resort's **Tropika Restaurant** is open seven days for three meals, serving a mix of Western and Cocos Malay cuisine.

Cocos Club is family-friendly. This is the place to have a good feed and cold beer with the locals.

WHAT TO PACK

Packing for any trip (especially a dive trip) is dependent on many factors: climate and conditions, trip duration, planned activities, and more.

Regardless of destination, we always pack the following: hard copies of important documents (spare passport pictures, passport copies, and health insurance information); a hard-copy list of important phone numbers; reusable drinking bottles, shopping bags, cutlery, and straws; a notebook/journal; a pashmina or scarf for warmth and sun protection; and disinfectant wipes (wiping down airplane seat areas is the number one trick for staying healthy in the field). We also pack a power strip, which is incredibly useful for charging multiple devices, especially in accommodations with creatively placed outlets.

As for dive gear, the benefits of traveling with your own equipment is that it's a better fit and therefore more comfortable than rental gear. You also become familiar with how it's supposed to feel, which helps you identify any problems more quickly.

Whether using your own gear or rental equipment, all divers should make sure they understand the safety features (releases, weights, etc.) and should be comfortable with how to use the safety equipment (SMBs, PLBs, etc.).

Our standard travel kit includes:

1 MASK AND SNORKEL: Masks can make or break your dive, so your first investment and the first thing to pack is a mask that fits you well. (For new divers, this is the primary piece of equipment you'll need.)

2 PERSONAL COMPUTER: New divers, this is your second investment. Diving with a computer increases safety margins by removing the guesswork and human error from dive profiles. Read the manual and make sure you know how to use it.

3 SAFETY GEAR: Safety is paramount. The most important item to carry is a brightly colored surface marker buoy (also called an SMB or safety sausage) that can mark your position on a safety stop, in crowded areas, or if you surface at a distance from the boat. A personal locator beacon (or PLB) is also a good investment for divers of any level. In the unlikely event you get separated from the boat, you can send your position to rescuers, which is *crucial* in emergency situations. (If pressed for space, we always pack our masks, computers, SMBs, and PLBs.)

A selection of the gear we carried during our 14 months of fieldwork. Even if pressed for space, we always pack masks, computers, and surface marker buoys (SMBs).

4 EXPOSURE PROTECTION: Wet suits, dry suits, or vests: whatever is appropriate to the conditions. The number one rule about packing is that any item needs to earn its spot in the bag, usually by being versatile. We brought a selection of layers from Enth Degree, technical performance thermal wear for water sports that comes in a useful range: wet suits, vests (hooded and non), etc. Chris found the fleece-lined Aveiro Pant ideal for wearing under his dry suit. I loved the Assana long-sleeved short wet suit, which is a good thermal layer under wet suits, or—when paired with Aveiro Pants—becomes its own full wet suit. Enth Degree also came in useful for other water activities, like kayaking, stand-up paddleboarding, and snorkeling. Gear comes packaged in a reusable dry bag.

5 REGULATORS, BCD, AND FINS

6 CARRY BAG: Mesh gear bags are useful for keeping your gear organized in your suitcase, toting equipment between hotels and dive shops, and for keeping wet gear separate from dry.

7 KNIFE OR CUTTING TOOL: Useful if you get entangled in fishing line or seaweed while diving, or for helping entangled wildlife (exercise caution doing this; injured animals are unpredictable).

8 SAVE-YOUR-DIVE KIT: Miscellaneous repair or spare items for dive equipment, such as O rings, mouthpieces for regulators, silicone grease, and cable ties (these come in very handy).

9 DRY BAG AND FIRST AID KIT: Keep your topside gear dry. Good for storing essentials like phones, wallets, logbooks, and diver ID cards. Also, a travel first aid kit is always useful. (Regular first aid refresher courses never go amiss either.)

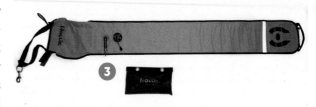

The most important item to carry is a brightly colored surface marker buoy (also called an SMB or safety sausage).

10 REEF-SAFE SUNSCREEN AND LIP BALM: We used Stream2Sea on our trip (and still do). They have great products that work. Stream2Sea's range is free from harmful chemicals, the most tested on the market, and packaged in eco-friendly materials. They also actively support ocean conservation projects. Best stuff out there.

11 FLASHLIGHT: Having a flashlight comes in handy for swim-throughs and nosing around the reef. (It's also an additional safety feature for attention-attracting.) Be aware that new LED-style flashlights are very bright: Try not to shine them directly in animals'—or your dive buddy's—eyes.

12 CAMERA: For capturing moments from your dive. Most divers don't need a professional big rig. We carry Paralenz cameras: user-friendly, flashlight-size cameras designed specifically for divers, with automatic color correction. Paralenz is also taking a strong role in ocean conservation and data collection.

* Pictured: A selection of our own gear carried on the trip. We do not have any sponsorship agreements with any of the brands shown or mentioned in the text. The products were either purchased independently by us, or gear-tested by us, and we are more than happy to recommend any of them.

A CONVERSATION WITH DR. SYLVIA EARLE

DIVING, STEWARDSHIP, AND HOPE

Dr. Sylvia Earle is a legend among ocean lovers. She is an oceanographer, explorer, expedition leader, author, speaker, president and chairman of Mission Blue/the Sylvia Earle Alliance, and a National Geographic Society explorer in residence—and that is a shockingly brief overview of her achievements.

We admire her for another reason: Sylvia is the master of weaving messages of both urgency and hope, born from a soul-deep love of the ocean, scientific knowledge, and a stubborn belief that, as the creators of the problems threatening our world, we are also the world's best hope for solving them.

We sat down to speak with Sylvia about the importance of dive travel, the crisis of complacency, why there is reason to hope, and how each of us can be a better steward of the planet.

Some questions and answers have been edited for brevity and clarity.

MILLER AND TAYLOR (M&T): Let's dive in with one of the most challenging questions to answer: What is it you love about diving and being underwater?

EARLE: I've spent thousands and thousands and thousands of hours underwater, and my best experiences have come by just going underwater and doing what many people do when they go out into a forest and just sit down: I wait for things to happen, the things that you don't see when you're moving along at high speed and trying to cover as much territory as you can on a single dive.

I've been inspected by humpback whales—that was a special moment. They notice you. The same is true with groupers, with snappers, with angelfish. They're curious, collectively, and that's one of the most enduring and engaging things about being in the ocean: You think you're going out there to look at [these creatures], and then [they] come and look at you. It's their curiosity as much as mine that I find irresistible and enchanting.

M&T: You're a big advocate for travel, even though travel does exact a price on the environment. Is experiencing something personally important?

EARLE: A picture is worth a thousand words, but an experience has got to be worth at least a thousand pictures. An expression on the face of the fish that you see in an image is always appealing, but when it's *you* that fish is looking at, it makes all the difference in the world. There's no substitute for being there, to see how we are all embedded in this blue speck in the universe, the interconnectivity between land and sea. There are many incalculable benefits, even though there is a cost.

M&T: The more we learn about the ocean, the more we realize how little we actually know about

"The ocean is where the action is," says Dr. Earle. "97 percent of the Earth's water is in the ocean. It's where 95 percent of the biosphere is."

it. What is something about the ocean you think might surprise people?

EARLE: Most of the action is actually out there in the ocean. Most of life on Earth is aquatic, and most of it lives below where light penetrates. I think generally people don't think about the fact that most of life on Earth lives in the dark all of the time, and it's cold. That's normal. We surface dwellers are in the minority.

This knowledge is now freely available to everyone. We're just beginning to understand the magnitude of our ignorance about the ocean, and our place as a trivial part of what makes life on Earth what it is. We are newcomers on an ancient planet that has taken a very long time to get things just right for us, and we've taken a very short time to disrupt that.

We are losing life and biodiversity at a faster rate than ever before. We don't even know what creatures in the sea we've lost because we've destroyed coral reefs or used bottom trawls that just obliterate everything in a flash, and then they're gone—gone forever. And we don't even know what piece of the system [these creatures] were holding intact.

Think of your car. Or your computer. If I started taking it apart, looking at all the little bits and pieces, and thinking, "Oh, I wonder what this one is for, I don't think it could be very important," and throw it away to simplify things, it wouldn't take long before everything comes to a screeching halt, even if most of the pieces are still there. I unwittingly would have removed something of critical

value. And that's what we're doing to nature. How many critical pieces have we already lost?

There is redundancy and resilience in nature, and often when something goes missing or is depleted, other species will fill in the gaps. But we've lost so much so fast, I think we are in for some real trouble, and the COVID-19 virus was a perfect example. Here we have a wake-up call that no one is immune from the laws of nature. You've got to be nice to nature, or else nature won't be nice to you.

M&T: Which brings us to what you've called our crisis of complacency . . .

EARLE: Complacency and despair are by far our biggest problems. It's a crisis of ignorance. Of greed. It's a crisis of self-importance. Think of the view of Earth from space, that beautiful awareness that Earth is a miracle in a universe of unfriendly options. The Earth doesn't need us, but we don't have an option besides Earth. Our actions are destroying the very systems that keep us alive, and we need to make peace with how fragile, how vulnerable we are.

We might be able to resist extinction if we're smart and use the knowledge that we've got. We still have an opportunity to act, but we can't wait six months to do it.

M&T: Do you still have hope?

EARLE: Yes, I do. I am cautiously optimistic that we're beginning to understand. We are the luckiest generation to ever come along because we know what we couldn't know before. We are the best

"With every drop of water you drink, every breath you take, you're connected to the sea," says Dr. Earle. "No matter where on Earth you live."

> ## *"Each of us has a superpower, and it is up to us to find out what that superpower is, and to use it."*
>
> —Dr. Sylvia Earle

prepared generation. It's us. It's now. We are the cause of these problems. But we are also the best hope for finding a solution, because we have knowledge. We know what to do. We just have to do it.

Burning fossil fuels was a great idea at the time. Plastic was a great idea at the time. But now we know better, we have alternatives, and we find excuses to keep doing the same old thing. That's stupid—knowing what you shouldn't do and doing it anyway.

Laws and governments are important, but just remember that any positive change started because somebody chose to do something. That's how it starts.

M&T: So what can we do then?

EARLE: You look in the mirror. Fortunately, everyone has a unique superpower, something that sets them apart from everybody else. What is it that you love to do or can do well? Polish that something up and make it work for you.

My self-appointed job is to inspire people to explore the ocean for themselves and to use their talents, whatever they are, to make a difference for the natural world. You are obviously using your love and talent for telling stories. You'll get others to say, "I just need to go and see this, I need to find out!"

Divers have a special role because they see what others do not. They're ambassadors. Their job is to

Dr. Sylvia Earle is an oceanographer and National Geographic explorer in residence who has lived underwater on 10 different occasions.

record what's really happening—keep those records, store them, share them—and get others to dive in. My motto is "No child left dry." No adult, either, for that matter.

The most important thing we can all do now, collectively, is protect healthy systems that are in good shape. Don't let them degrade further. Protect with everything you've got and restore what you can. Recovery does happen, but planting trees doesn't make a forest, and planting corals doesn't make a reef—it's a start, but it takes time, and that's why it's important to hold onto what we still have.

Treat the ocean and the natural world as if your life depends on it. Because it does.

MARINE PROTECTED AREAS

Marine Protected Area zones
(more than 5,000 sq km)

- ■ Implemented, highly protected
- ■ Implemented, less protected
- ■ Designated, not implemented
- ■ Proposed, not designated

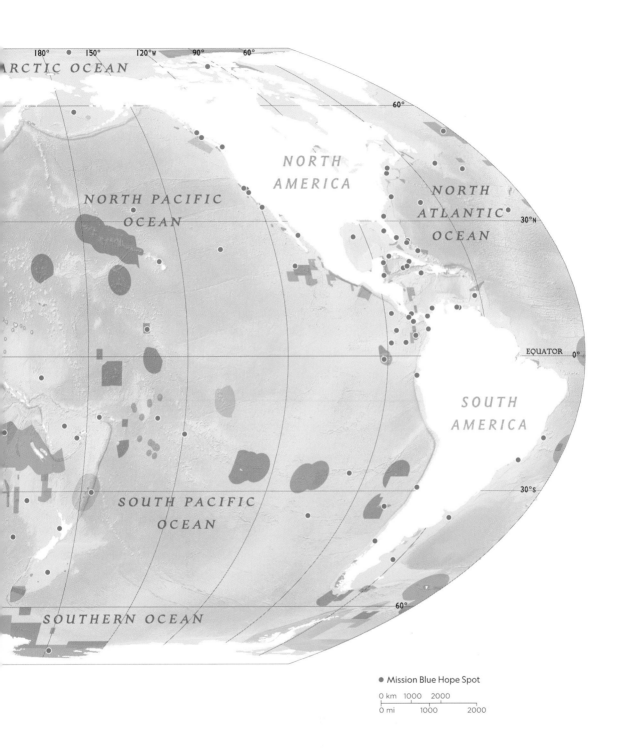

180° 150° 120°W 90° 60°

ARCTIC OCEAN

60°

NORTH
AMERICA

NORTH PACIFIC
OCEAN

NORTH
ATLANTIC
OCEAN

30°N

EQUATOR 0°

SOUTH
AMERICA

30°S

SOUTH PACIFIC
OCEAN

60°

SOUTHERN OCEAN

● Mission Blue Hope Spot

0 km 1000 2000
0 mi   1000   2000

NEW DIVER RESOURCES

All divers, by definition, are explorers: The ocean covers more than 70 percent of our planet's surface, but more than 80 percent of that is still unexplored. The Earth is an ocean planet, and the ocean is our life-support system, responsible for the very air we breathe, yet we know shockingly little about the underwater realm.

When Chris and I began this journey, I was a brand-spanking-new diver, recently certified in Fiji

(page 274). When we got off the road 14 months later, I had completed 66 dives all over the world, from Croatia (page 46) to Cocos (Keeling) Islands (page 310).

I had tried to get certified twice before, assuming that—as a natural water baby—diving would come easily to me. I was wrong. My first Open Water experience (which Chris described as the "worst [he's] ever heard of") shook my confidence to the core. But I am so glad I persevered. Now I can't imagine *not* diving. Even as an avid snorkeler, I had no idea of the ocean's beauty, diversity, fragility, and strange magnificence. Diving made my world bigger.

I mention my experience for two reasons: (1) If you don't take to diving immediately, that doesn't mean diving isn't for you. Be patient, be persistent, and take it slow—the rewards are worth it. (2) The locations we've highlighted as good for new or out-of-practice divers are being recommended by a new diver. When I dove them, I was in your fins, and hopefully that will be a confidence booster.

We traveled to 50 locations in 35 countries over 14 continuous months, spending more than 250 hours underwater to bring you this book.

Here are some tips—gleaned from my own experience, advice Chris (an experienced diver and my favorite dive buddy) gave me, and recommendations from shops and other divers we met along the way.

LEARNING TO DIVE

There are two ways to try scuba diving. A Discover Scuba Dive (also referred to as a DSD, intro dive, resort dive, or trial dive) is a half- or one-day introduction to scuba diving under the guidance of a diving instructor. It usually involves practicing basic skills, followed by a shallow dive. (There is no limit to DSDs; you can do as many of them as you like.)

The second is a dive course (usually called an Open Water course), which is more involved (coursework, skills sessions, and Open Water dives), but at the end of which, you'll be certified to dive anywhere in the world to a certain depth.

Tips:

• Learning to dive in warm, clear water can be a huge advantage. (Poor visibility can be disorienting for new divers, and cold water can make equalizing and drawing deep breaths—critical to remaining calm—more difficult.)

• Mask clearing can be a challenging skill for new divers. Here's a tip that worked for me: Prior to your dive course, practice swimming laps or soak in the tub with a snorkel and mask half-full of water. This will get you used to the feeling of water sloshing around your nose.

TRAVELING AS A DIVER

Dive courses extoll *traveling to new places* and *meeting new people* as two of the key benefits of learning to dive. Although I rolled my eyes during that part of my course, damned if they weren't

If you don't take to diving immediately, that doesn't mean diving isn't for you. Be patient and persistent—the rewards are worth it.

right: Exploring different underwater locations (as diverse and varied as terrestrial ones) and meeting fellow ocean lovers *were* the best parts of our journey.

Tips:

• For a confidence booster, hire a private guide for your first day in a new area. It's more expensive, and you usually have to book in advance, but you'll have an experienced, dedicated diver with you as you settle in. It makes a difference.

• Ask a few key questions:

  • *What depth will we be diving to?*

- *What is the current like?*

- *What is the visibility?*

- *What is the water temperature?*

- *What's the dive plan?* Make sure you understand the dive briefing. (Sometimes accents, language barriers, or wind noise on the boat can make it challenging to hear.) If you have any questions, ask *before* you start gearing up for the dive.

- *Will there be a person on the boat and does the boat stay on-site with the divers?* An answer of no is a cost-cutting measure that cuts your safety margins and raises questions about the shop's professionalism. Be wary.

- *Lastly, do your own assessment.* When you walk into the dive shop, is the gear in good condition and well organized? Do the staff take time to talk to you and answer questions? If you have any concerns, choose another shop and dive another day.

- Log your gear and how you felt (warm or cold, over- or underweighted) in your logbook. This is Chris's favorite tip, especially if you're diving in

Our collective favorite activity is wildlife-watching—both on land and underwater, big or small, like this fireworm in Hvar, Croatia.

different places and/or using rental gear. It will help you build a reference as you gain experience, and you can refer back to it with each new dive and adjust accordingly.

One of the best pieces of advice I received was to learn two new fish (or coral species, etc.) on each dive. If you try to identify every new fish you see, you'll be overwhelmed. Choose two, study them (color/shape/where you spotted them), and look them up after the dive. (Dive guides can be a great help with this; most of them are delightful marine life nerds.) Record your new fish in your logbook—I kept a separate space for my new IDs in each entry. You'll be surprised how quickly your knowledge base grows.

• A well-fitted mask is essential for your dive comfort. It's your most important purchase and should always travel with you. (And it doesn't need to be expensive—my brand-name mask leaked, so I swapped it for a cheap one that fits me much better.)

I traveled with my own dive gear and found it hugely beneficial: I was comfortable, and I knew how it was supposed to feel (which helped me identify any problems). For new divers, it might take time to amass your own kit—not just because of the cost, but because it's worth trying out different styles and brands to see what works. (Closed-versus open-heel fins, for example: Closed are softer on the ankles and more suitable for boat diving; open-heel are better for shore diving.)

Take notes, and keep a list in your logbook, of the personal items you prefer to have with you on a day out diving. (Wind jacket, long-sleeved shirt or scarf for sun protection, lip balm, reef-friendly sunscreen, hat, sunglasses, notebook, reusable water bottle, snack, and, for those of us with long hair, an extra ponytail holder and/or headband, for example.)

"Given that exploration is in our DNA, we would miss so much if our treks were relegated to only dry land," says Brian Skerry.

WHAT SHOPS/FELLOW DIVERS WISH YOU KNEW

A lot of new divers put pressure on themselves not to hold up or inconvenience more experienced divers, but the dive community is overwhelmingly friendly and supportive, and they want you to enjoy your diving. I asked dive professionals and experienced divers about their advice for new divers, and here's what they had to say:

Tips:

• Come prepared. Show up with your certification number, number of dives, date of your last dive, depth you've dived to, an emergency contact number, and a valid dive medical certificate (if required). Also, be healthy and ready to dive: Hangovers, colds, bad sunburn, tummy bugs, and jet lag will affect you more than experienced divers.

• Avoid distractions. Don't bother with an underwater camera if you're a new diver (or if you're an inexperienced diver diving a new site). Focus on your diving first, rather than the distraction of a camera. That can come later, with time, practice,

and more experience underwater to where you're comfortable.

• If you have questions, please ask for help.

• Your gear (even rentals) is your responsibility. If you're setting up your own gear, don't be afraid to ask a guide (or more experienced diver) to check it for you. If the dive shop sets up your gear, double-check it yourself and make sure everything you need is on board before the boat departs. Even experienced divers like Chris make this mistake—on one dive, he got talking to other divers and found out later his fins had been left behind at the shop. Pay attention to your stuff and ask for help when needed: The responsibility of tracking and checking your gear ultimately falls to you.

• It's okay to pause underwater. If you're feeling nervous, let your guide and buddy know *before you gear up for the dive*. Chris and I had a prearranged hand signal I'd use if I was feeling uneasy but otherwise okay. If I used the signal, we'd stop and I'd take a few steadying breaths as he kept an eye on me and our group. Sometimes I'd just need to get my bearings before continuing the dive. "Don't be afraid to take your time, especially in the beginning," Chris told me. "Experienced divers would much rather wait for a few minutes and explore the area around the mooring line while a new diver settles in than get 15 minutes into the dive and have to abort because a new diver's panicking."

• That being said, it's okay to pull the pin on a dive. I aborted two dives I didn't feel comfortable on. On the flip side, there were also times (like in Aliwal

Enjoy the journey—the places you travel to (like Gozo, here), the friends you make, and things you discover. It's the best part of being an explorer.

Shoal, page 286) where I felt ready to push my comfort zone. Trust that you'll know the difference. If it doesn't feel right, your safety comes first.

We hope this book encourages you to go and see leopard sharks in Byron Bay, Australia—and other gems—for yourself. Let's make it game on, not game over.

YOUR RESPONSIBILITIES

• Your dive is your responsibility. Always. Help and support are available, but your safety is your priority: Always dive with a buddy, plan your dive, and dive your plan.

• Have fun. We focus on safety and troubleshooting because it's natural for any new diver to wonder or worry about these things. "Have fun" is hardly a practical tip. However, it's an important one. Learning to drive a car, starting a new job, embarking on a new hobby, traveling solo for the first time— these are all learning processes. It takes time to

become comfortable, and so it is with diving. Enjoy the journey—the places you travel to, the friends you make, and things you discover along the way— both above and below the surface. It's the best part of being an explorer.

• Share what you've experienced. Every dive is a privilege, a gift of a glimpse into an otherworldly realm. And every moment spent in the water is something new, never to be repeated. "Divers have a special role because they see what others do not. They're ambassadors," said Dr. Sylvia Earle. "Their job is to get others to dive in."

DEDICATION

This book is dedicated to the people who made it possible.

To our family and friends, especially the Crocker-O'Malley clan (Shannon, Sean, Margie, Brodie, and the much missed Carol)—thank you for your encouragement and support.

And to our editor, Allyson Johnson. You championed this book from the initial pitch meeting through the final edit and had our backs every step of the way. We couldn't have done this without you.

What an adventure.

ACKNOWLEDGMENTS

We have a global village to thank for this maddening and marvelous project.

To our family and friends: We took all of you with us, everywhere we went. Thank you for the years of encouragement, places to crash, and patience. We couldn't have done this without you. A special thanks to Bill and Marion Miller, Johnathan and Martine Taylor, Ron and Nell Miller, Mary King Miller, Erin and JB Miller, the Brown Family (Zach, Jenny, Cyrus, and Edith), Josh and Sam Taylor, Mark and John Gogoll, Darren Quick, Liz Kevey and Curtis Seagers, John Atkinson and Angela McLean, Hannah Dwyer, Meghan Aftosmis, Janet Crook, Lance Lones, Amanda Walker, and the Cardrona Wedding Crew.

To our Nat Geo family, who brought this book to life: Allyson Johnson, Hilary Black, and Bill O'Donnell championed this book from the very start, and the amazing Dr. Sylvia Earle helped it get the green light. Brian Skerry is a good friend who lent us enormous support. Explorer Dr. Jess Cramp provided inspiration and sage advice. Thank you to Lisa Thomas, Susan Blair, Judith Klein, Michael O'Connor, Nicole Miller Roberts, Elisa Gibson, Sanaa Akkach, and Whitney Tressel.

To our partners who believed in this project: Thank you to Paralenz, Stream2Sea, Australian Underwater Products/Enth Degree, and Katie Thompson and Jennifer Small at PADI. A huge thank you to our agent, Jody Kahn at Brandt & Hochman Literary Agents.

To the crew who helped us get ready for 14 months of fieldwork: Jason Clarke, Aaron Callaghan, Brett Jenkins, James Brewer, Dr. Anna Fenton, and the team at Aspiring Medical in Wanaka, New Zealand (especially Dr. Pip Clearwater, Dr. Jayne Davies, and the fabulous team of nurses)—thank you for keeping us fit, healthy, and (somewhat) sane. And thank you to the Divers Alert Network (DAN) for fielding a few tense calls and providing level-headed advice while we were in the field.

To the people we met on the road: You were the best part of our journey. If we shared a dive, a drink, or a conversation, if we traded travel stories or contact details, thank you for making this experience extraordinary. Special shout-out to Erin Feinblatt, Shaun Ace Wolfe, Andrew Fox, Dr. Andrea Marshall, Clare Thompson, the Raja Crew (Elaine Taylor, Matt Thomson, Tracy and Kevin Plowman), the Lizard Crew (Ashlee and David Jansen, Jimmy McGrath, Davey Jones, and Jasmin O'Brien), and the Boston Sea Rovers. We also worked with remarkable scientists, conservation organizations, dive shops, tourism boards, and businesses—thank you for your help and support, your advice and knowledge, and especially for sharing your love, care, and concern for your corner of the world.

To all the people we have yet to meet: Thank you for fighting the good fight, especially when you feel you're doing it alone. You're not. We met a world full of people fighting with you, and we ended our journey with a feeling of hope. This is only the beginning.

Lastly: Howard Shore—thank you for the *Lord of the Rings* soundtrack, which I listened to more than 150 times while writing this book. And to Rodney Fox, for giving me and Chris some sound advice before we embarked on our trip. "Be present," he told us. "These adventures go by far too quickly." And so they did. Looking forward to the next ones.

ILLUSTRATIONS CREDITS

Cover: Federica Grassi/Getty Images.

Back cover: (UP LE), Moiz Husein Storyteller/Shutterstock; (UP RT), Magnus Larsson; (CTR), falcon0125/Getty Images; (LO LE), Ash Karas Photography; (LO RT), Nick Polanszky/Shutterstock.

2-3, Chris Howarth/Australia/Alamy Stock Photo; 4, SeaTops/robertharding; 7, Steve De Neef/National Geographic Image Collection; 8, Nigel Marsh/Getty Images; 10, Erin Feinblatt; 11, Derrick Thomson/Misool Resort; 12, One of Polynesia's leading photographers, Temoana Poole; 13, Kevin Panizza/Getty Images; 16-7, Michael Amme/laif/Redux; 18, Cristian Umili; 19, Cathrine Stephansen; 20, ProCip/robertharding; 21, Cristian Pacurar/Getty Images; 22-3, Remedios Valls López/age fotostock/Alamy Stock Photo; 24, Eric Martin/Figarophoto/Redux; 25, Brandi Mueller; 26, Stephen Frink/Getty Images; 27, Greens and Blues/Shutterstock; 28, Mathieu Meur/Stocktrek Images/Getty Images; 30, James D. Morgan/Getty Images; 31, NiCK/Getty Images; 32, mikulas1/Getty Images; 33, S. Rohrlach/Getty Images; 34-5, Sue Daly/NPL/Alamy Stock Photo; 36, Venture Design/Getty Images; 37, Krista Rossow/National Geographic Image Collection; 38, Markus Kirchgessner/laif/Redux; 39, apsimo1/Getty Images; 40-1, Ian Trower/robertharding; 42, Liquid Dive Adventures; 43, Anna Flam/Peri-Peri Divers; 44, James R.D. Scott/Getty Images; 45, J.S. Lamy/Shutterstock; 46-7, Gallery Stock; 48, WaterFrame_fur/Alamy Stock Photo; 49, Cedric Angeles/Intersection Photos; 50, Giorgio Filippini/Sime/eStock Photo; 51, Adam Ke/Shutterstock; 52, Orion Media Group/Shutterstock; 54, David Hancock/Alamy Stock Photo; 55, Posnov/Getty Images; 56, Mathieu Meur/Stocktrek Images/Getty Images; 57, Orion Media Group/Shutterstock; 58-9, Andrey Nekrasov/Alamy Stock Photo; 60, Carli Teteris/Stocksy; 61, Gerard Soury/Getty Images; 62, Brandi Mueller; 63, unterwegs/Shutterstock; 64-5, William Torrillo; 66, William Harrigan/Stephen Frink Collection/Alamy Stock Photo; 67, Holger Leue/Getty Images; 68, Stuart Westmorland/DanitaDelimont/Alamy Stock Photo; 69, Deb Liljegren/Getty Images; 70-1, Patrick Endres/Design Pics/National Geographic Image Collection; 72, Dennis MacDonald/robertharding; 73, Blue Marlin Beach Resort; 74, Jenny

Adler/National Geographic Image Collection; 75, VitalyEdush/Getty Images; 76, Brown W. Cannon III/Intersection Photos; 78, Brown W. Cannon III/Alamy Stock Photo; 79, Brown W. Cannon III/Intersection Photos; 80, Mathieu Meur/Stocktrek Images/Getty Images; 81, Brown W. Cannon III/Alamy Stock Photo; 82-3, Jason Edwards/National Geographic Image Collection; 84, Manfred Gottschalk/Getty Images; 85, Mark Gamba/Gallery Stock; 86, Jason Edwards/National Geographic Image Collection; 87, Lewis Burnett/Shutterstock; 88-9, Stefano De Luigi/VII/Redux; 90, Brandi Mueller; 91, Robert Haidinger/Anzenberger/Redux; 92, Stefano De Luigi/VII/Redux; 93, haveseen/Shutterstock; 94-5, Andy Morehouse/Shutterstock; 96, Chris Taylor; 97, Will Burrard-Lucas/NPL/Minden Pictures; 98, Christian Vizl/TandemStock; 99, Gustavo Ferretti/Getty Images; 100, Barry Bland/NPL/Minden Pictures; 102, Vincent Guglielmi/Getty Images; 103, Roberto Rinaldi/NPL/Minden Pictures; 104, a-plus image bank/Alamy Stock Photo; 105, DAAgius/Shutterstock; 106-7, Britt Basel; 108, Douglas Peebles/Alamy Stock Photo; 109, Brandi Mueller; 110, Media Drum World/Alamy Stock Photo; 111, Nigel Marsh/Getty Images; 112-3, Magnus Lundgren/Wild Wonders of China/NPL/Minden Pictures; 114, Magnus Lundgren/Wild Wonders of China/NPL/Minden Pictures; 115, falcon0125/Getty Images; 116, Blue Jean Images/Alamy Stock Photo; 117, unterwegs/Shutterstock; 118-9, Renan Gicquel/Getty Images; 120, Vincent Pommeyrol/Getty Images; 121, Gabriele Croppi/Sime/eStock Photo; 122, Camille Moirenc/hemis.fr/Alamy Stock Photo; 123, kodachrome25/Getty Images; 124, Tui De Roy/Minden Pictures; 126, David Fleetham/Alamy Stock Photo; 127, Olga Kolos/Alamy Stock Photo; 128, Enric Sala/National Geographic Missions Program; 129, Kunhui Chih/Getty Images; 130-1, Jeffrey Greenberg/Universal Images Group via Getty Images; 132, Stephen Frink/Alamy Stock Photo; 133, Jen Grantham/Stocksy; 134, Jörg Modrow/laif/Redux; 135, Aneese/Getty Images; 136-7, Stefan Follows/500px/Getty Images; 138, Nicholas Shallcross/Alamy Stock Photo; 139, Kamalaya Koh Samui; 140, Ephraim Muller/Getty Images; 141, sarahnev/Shutterstock Editorial; 142-3, Rachid Dahnoun/TandemStock; 144, Mathieu Meur/Stocktrek Images/Getty Images; 145, Andrew JK Tan/Getty Images; 146, Tony Myshlyaev/Stocksy; 147, Rich Carey/Shutterstock; 148, Brandi Mueller; 150, Westend61/Getty Images; 151, Brandi Mueller; 152, Brandi Mueller; 153, Kevin Panizza/Getty Images; 154-5, Luciano Lejtman/Getty Images; 156, Erin Feinblatt; 157, Erin Feinblatt; 158, Erin Feinblatt; 159, Michael Zeigler/Getty Images; 160-1, Don Fuchs/robertharding; 162, Ash Karas Photography; 163, Lizard Island; 164, Lizard Island; 165, Andre Erlich/Getty Images; 166, aluxum/Getty Images; 168, Mathieu Rivrin/Getty Images; 169, Gerard Soury/Biosphoto/Minden Pictures; 170, Gaël Modrak/age fotostock; 171, Ivan Smuk/Shutterstock; 172-3, Pete Mesley of Lust4Rust Dive Excursions; 174, Dominique Chapman/Stocksy; 175, Julia Crim/Offset; 176, Dennis Williamson/VISUM/Redux; 177, Jack Burden/Getty Images; 178-9, Matthew Williams-Ellis/robertharding/National Geographic Image Collection; 180, Descend NZ—Milford Sound; 181, Real Journeys; 182, Arno Gasteiger/laif/Redux; 183, apsimo1/Getty Images; 184-5, Alex Lindbloom/Misool Resort; 186, Brandi Mueller; 187, Brandi Mueller; 188, Giordano Cipriani/Sime/eStock Photo; 189, AHDesignConcepts/Getty Images; 190, David Doubilet; 192, Huber/eStock Photo; 193, Te mana o te moana; 194, Ryan Borne for Coral Gardeners; 195, izanbar/Getty Images; 196-7, Moiz Husein Storyteller/Shutterstock; 198, Morten Beier/Stocktrek Images/Getty Images; 199, Beniamino Pisati/Sime/eStock Photo; 200, Chris Taylor; 201, Aquadiver.pl/Shutterstock; 202-3, Christian Berg/laif/Redux; 204, Colin Marshall/

INDEX

Boldface indicates illustrations.

A

Advanced Open Water
  certification
  Ko Samui, Thailand 137
  learning to dive 327
  Malapascua Island, Philippines
    60
  Orkney Islands, United
    Kingdom 229
  Port Lincoln, Australia 247
  Tulum, Mexico 282
Aircraft wrecks
  Curaçao 307
  Espiritu Santo, Vanuatu 301
  Munda and Gizo, Solomon
    Islands 108, 109, **110**
  Saint-Malo, France 169
Alaska: Valdez 292–297
  dive sites 294–295
  harbor **292–293**
  iceberg **296**
  make a difference 296
  marine life 292, **294,** 294–295,
    296, 297
  need to know 297
  Ravencroft Lodge 292, 294, 295,
    295, 297

snorkeling 295
Valdez Museum & Historical
  Archives 296
weather and flight cancellation
  294
wildlife 292, 294
wildlife cruises 296
Alonnisos, Greece 16–21
  Captain Pakis Athanasiou's
    Gorgona Cruises 19–20
  dive sites **18,** 18–19, 21
  exploratory diving 17, 18, 19,
    21
  hiking 20
  island road trip 18
  make a difference 20
  marine life 18, **19,** 20, 21
  Monastery of Kyra Pangia 20
  National Marine Park of
    Alonnisos and Northern
    Sporades 17–19, **19**
  need to know 21
  Old Village 17, 20, **20**
  packing tips 18, 20, 21
  Patitiri 17, 20
  shipwrecks **18,** 18–19
  Steni Vala **16–17**
Andaman Sea see Ko Lanta,
  Thailand
Anders, Bill 6

Andros Island, Bahamas 22–27
  aerial view **22–23**
  dive sites 24–25
  for families 26
  hiking 24
  land animals 24
  make a difference 25
  marine life 24, 27
  need to know 27
  South Andros Blue Hole and
    Nature Trail 24
  Tiamo Resort 22, 24, **24,** 27
  West Side National Park 24
Australia
  Byron Bay **52,** 52–57, **54, 55, 56,**
    331
  Cocos (Keeling) Islands **310–**
    311, 310–315, **312, 313, 314**
  Exmouth **82–83,** 82–87, **84, 85,**
    86
  Lizard Island (Great Barrier
    Reef) **160–161,** 160–165, **162,**
    163, 164
  Lord Howe Island **2–3, 268–269,**
    268–273, **270, 271, 272**
  Port Lincoln **244–245,** 244–249,
    246, 247, 248
  Sydney **28,** 28–33, **30, 31, 32**

B

Bahamas: Andros and Nassau 22–27
  aerial view **22–23**
  dive sites 24–25
  for families 26
  hiking 24
  land animals 24
  make a difference 25
  marine life 24, 27
  need to know 27
  shark diving **25,** 25–26, **26**
  shipwrecks 26, **26**
  South Andros Blue Hole and Nature Trail 24
  Stuart Cove's Dive Bahamas **25,** 25–26, 27
  Tiamo Resort 22, 24, **24,** 27
  West Side National Park 24
Banks (financial institutions) 254
Barragán Paladines, María José 125
Bay of Islands, New Zealand 34–39
  Cape Reinga 36
  dive sites 36–38, 39
  make a difference 38
  Māori history 34, 36, 37, **37,** 38
  marine life **34–35,** 36, 37, 39
  need to know 39
  Paihia 34, 37–38
  Poor Knights Islands Marine Reserve 34, **36,** 36–37
  road trip 34, 36
  Russell (town) 34, 37, **38,** 39
  shipwrecks **34–35,** 38
  Tutukaka 36, 37, 39
  Waitangi Treaty Grounds 34, **37,** 38
Beginner divers
  Andros Island, Bahamas 24, 26, 27
  Belize 73–74
  British Virgin Islands 66
  Curaçao **306,** 307

dive gear 316, 329
Florida Keys, United States 132, 134
Gozo, Malta 105
Grand Cayman, Cayman Islands 98
Hvar, Croatia 49
Kenting National Park, Taiwan 115, 117
Ko Lanta, Thailand 252
Ko Samui, Thailand **136–137,** 138
learning to dive 105, 327
Lizard Island, Australia 163
Lord Howe Island, Australia 270
Marlborough Sounds, New Zealand 175
Moorea, French Polynesia 195
Petit St. Vincent, St. Vincent and the Grenadines 239, **241,** 241–242
Rarotonga, Cook Islands 258
Solomon Islands Discovery Cruises 110
Sydney, Australia **31,** 32
tips from fellow divers 329–330
Tofo Beach, Mozambique 43, 45
Zanzibar, Tanzania 199, 201
Belize 70–75
  Altun Ha (Maya site) 72, **72**
  Belize Barrier Reef 70, 73, 74, 75
  Blue Marlin Beach Resort 73, **73,** 75
  Bocawina Rainforest Resort & Adventures 72, 75
  Cockscomb Basin Wildlife Sanctuary 70
  cultural activities 74
  dangerous dive operators 72
  dive sites 72, 73–74
  Great Blue Hole 72
  guided nature hikes 72–73
  make a difference 74
  marine life **70–71,** 73, 74, **74,** 75

  need to know 75
  Placencia 74
  road trip 72
  South Water Caye **73,** 73–74
  Splash Dive Center 74, 75
  wildlife 72–73
  wish we knew 72
Berents, Penny 162
Bernicot, Titouan 194
Bormes-les-Mimosas, France 118–123
  dive sites 121
  gardens 120
  hatmaking 120
  hiking 120
  make a difference 122
  marine life 120, 121, 123
  Musée Océanographique de Monaco 118, **121,** 122
  need to know 123
  Port-Cros National Park 118, 120, 123
  Sanary-sur-Mer 118, 121–122
  shipwrecks **120,** 121
  snorkeling 120
  village **118–119,** 120
  vineyards 120, **122**
  wish we knew 120
Boso, Sunga 109
British Virgin Islands 64–69
  Baths (rock formations), Virgin Gorda 67, **67**
  Cooper Island Beach Club 66–67, 68, 69
  Cuan Law (liveaboard diving boat) 66, **66,** 68
  for families 68
  land-based activities 66–67
  make a difference 67
  need to know 69
  Sail Caribbean Divers 68, 69
  shipwrecks 66, 67, **68**
  Spring Bay, Virgin Gorda **64–65**
  underwater caves 66

Byron Bay, Australia 52–57
  Aboriginal tours 54
  Byron Bay Wildlife Hospital 56
  Cape Byron Lighthouse 54–55
  dive sites **52,** 53, 55–56, **56,** 57
  Julian Rocks **52,** 53, 55–56, **56, 57**
  make a difference 56
  marine life **52,** 53, 56, **56,** 57, **331**
  Minyon Falls 54, **55**
  need to know 57
  Nightcap National Park 54, **55**
  South West Rocks 54
  surfing **54**
  town center 54

C

California: Laguna Beach **154–155,** 154–159
  dive sites 156–157, **157**
  golfing 157, **158**
  hiking and mountain biking 157
  make a difference 157
  marine life 156, **156,** 157
  marine reserve 156
  need to know 159
  Pacific Marine Mammal Center **156,** 157
  Santa Catalina Island 158
  shops and galleries 157–158
Carbon offsetting 169
Cayman Islands: Grand Cayman 94–99
  Bioluminescence Bay 96–97
  Cayman Islands National Museum 96
  dive sites 98, **98**
  Jean-Michel Cousteau's Ambassadors of the Environment program 97
  kayak tours 96–97
  make a difference 98
  mangroves 97–98
  marine life 98, 99
  mermaid statue **96**
  nearby 96
  need to know 99
  Pedro St. James 96
  Queen Elizabeth II Botanic Park 96, **97**
  Seven Mile Beach **94–95**
  shipwrecks 98, **98**
  wildlife 96, **97**
Charles Darwin Foundation 127
Chile: Easter Island 76–81
  Anakena Beach **79**
  archaeological sites 78–79
  dive sites 79–80
  horseback riding 79
  make a difference 80
  marine life **78,** 79–80, 81
  moai statues **76,** 78, 79, **80**
  need to know 81
  tattoos 78
China, influence in South Pacific 302
Cigarette butts 206
Citizen science efforts 49
Climate change 36–37, 140, 162
Cocos (Keeling) Islands, Australia 310–315
  bicycling 312
  cooking classes 312
  dive sites 313, 314
  Home Island 311, 312–313
  inter-island transportation **310–311**
  marine life 312, 313, **313,** 314, **314,** 315
  need to know 315
  outrigger canoe safari 312
  plastics cleanup 313, 314
  Pulu Cocos Museum 312
  road trip 312
  Scroungers Golf 314
  snorkeling 312
  sunken boats and cannons 313
  Uninhabited Direction Island **312**
  West Island 311, 312
  wildlife 312
Cook, James
  Byron Bay, Australia 53
  dinner service 230
  Hawai'i, United States 150
  Lizard Island, Australia 161, 164, **164**
  Marlborough Sounds, New Zealand 172, 175, **175**
  on sandflies 180
Cook Islands: Rarotonga 256–261
  aerial view **256–257**
  Aitutaki Day Tour 260
  dive sites 258, 261
  food & drink 259, 261
  heritage and culture 256, 259, **259,** 260
  hiking 259–260, **260**
  Koka Lagoon Cruise 260
  make a difference 259
  Marae Moana marine park 258
  marine life 258, **258,** 261
  markets 259
  need to know 261
  snorkeling 260
  Wi-Fi costs 260
Coral Restoration Foundation (CRF) 133
Cousteau, Jacques-Yves 9, 121–122
Cousteau, Jean-Michel 242, 243
Cramp, Jessica 216, 217, 259
Crayweed conservation 31
Croatia: Hvar 46–51
  Blue Cave **50**
  Brač 50
  dive sites **48,** 49–50
  food & drink 48–49, 51
  harbor **46–47**
  Hvar Town 48
  make a difference 49
  Malo Grablje 48–49, 51
  marine life **48,** 49–50, 51, **328**
  marine park (proposed) 49
  nearby 50

need to know 51
Secret Hvar driving tour 48
Stari Grad Plain 46, 48
Stori Komin restaurant, Malo
    Grablje 48–49, 51
Vis island 50, **50**
walking 50, 51
winemaking history 48, **49**
Curaçao 304–309
    airplane wrecks 307
    Curaçao Liqueur Distillery 306
    dive sites 307
    hiking 307
    make a difference 307
    marine life 307, **307**, 308, 309
    need to know 309
    Punda Vibes 308
    shipwrecks **306,** 307
    Substation Curaçao mini-
        submarine 307–308, **308**
    Willemstad **304–305,** 306
    windsurfing 306–307

D

Daga, Brian 109
Darwin, Charles 37, 125, 191
Deep diving
    Alonnisos, Greece 18, 21
    Easter Island, Chile 79–80, 81
    Florida Keys, United States 132,
        132, 134
    Hvar, Croatia **48,** 49, 50, 51
    Kenting National Park, Taiwan
        115
    Ko Lanta, Thailand 253
    Malapascua Island, Philippines
        60
    Munda and Gizo, Solomon
        Islands 108
    Orkney Islands, United
        Kingdom 229
    Outer Banks, North Carolina,
        United States 235
    Petit St. Vincent, St. Vincent
        and the Grenadines 239

Taveuni Island, Fiji 278
Tofo Beach, Mozambique 43
Diving
    birthplace 118, 121–122
    dive gear 316, **317,** 318, **318,** 329
    learning to dive 327
    map of sites 14–15
    responsibilities 330–331
    safety gear 316, **317,** 318, **318**
    tips from dive community 329–
        330
    traveling as a diver 326–331
    what to pack 316–318, **317, 318**
    see also Beginner divers; Deep
        diving; Exploratory diving;
        Open Water certification
Dolphin conservation 38
Dumas, Frédéric 122

E

Earle, Sylvia **321, 323**
    on diving, stewardship, and
        hope 320–323
    on fishing 296
    Mission Blue 200
    on people making a difference
        13, 49
    on Poor Knights Islands, New
        Zealand 34
Easter Island, Chile 76–81
    Anakena Beach **79**
    archaeological sites 78–79
    dive sites 79–80
    horseback riding 79
    make a difference 80
    marine life **78,** 79–80, 81
    moai statues **76,** 78, 79, **80**
    need to know 81
    tattoos 78
Ecuador: Galápagos Islands 124–
129
    Charles Darwin Foundation 125,
        127
    Charles Darwin Research
        Station 126–127, **127**

dive sites 127–128
food & drink 126, 129
Galápagos Marine Reserve 127–
    128
marine life **126,** 127, **128,** 129
need to know 129
Santa Fe Island 126
Tortuga Bay 126
wildlife **124,** 125, 126–127, **127**
Wolf and Darwin Islands 128
Espiritu Santo, Vanuatu 298–303
    Champagne Beach **301,** 302
    dive sites **300,** 300–301
    food & drink 300, 302, 303
    horseback riding 301–302, **302**
    make a difference 302
    marine life 300–301, 303
    Million Dollar Point **300,** 301
    need to know 303
    shipwrecks and aircraft wrecks
        298–299, 299, 300–301
    snorkeling **300,** 301
    World War II equipment **298–
        299, 300,** 301
    WWII History Tour 301
Exmouth, Australia 82–87
    Cape Range National Park 82,
        82–83, 84
    Coral Bay 86
    dive sites 84–85
    Exmouth Navy Pier 84–85, 87
    Jurabi Turtle Centre 85
    marine life 82, 84, **85,** 85–86,
        86, 87
    need to know 87
    Ningaloo Coast 82, 85
    snorkeling with whale sharks
        85, 85–86, 87
    Vlamingh Head Lighthouse
        84
    wildlife 84, 85
Exploratory diving
    Alonnisos, Greece 17, 18, 19, 21
    Easter Island, Chile **78,** 81
    Lord Howe Island, Australia 270

Munda and Gizo, Solomon Islands 108, **109,** 111
Niue 217
Petit St. Vincent, St. Vincent and the Grenadines 242

F

Families
British Virgin Islands 68
Grand Cayman, Cayman Islands 97
Ko Lanta, Thailand 251, 252
Lord Howe Island, Australia 270
Munda and Gizo, Solomon Islands 110
Petit St. Vincent, St. Vincent and the Grenadines 239, 242
Port Lincoln, Australia 246
Raja Ampat, Indonesia 188
Sharks4Kids 26
Fiji: Taveuni Island 274–279
Bouma National Heritage Park 275, 277, **277**
culture 275, 276, 278
dive sites 277–278, **278,** 279
Fiji Time 278
make a difference 277
marine life **274–275,** 277–278, 279
need to know 279
rugby 276, **276**
snorkeling 277
village visits 276
Waitabu Marine Park 276–277
Florida Keys, United States 130–135
African Queen canal cruise 132
Coral Restoration Foundation (CRF) 133
dive sites 132, 134, 135
Fort Jefferson 134
John Pennekamp Coral Reef State Park 130, **130–131,** 132
Key Largo 132, 133

Key West 133–134, **134**
make a difference 133
marine life **132,** 135
Molasses Reef 132
need to know 135
Overseas Highway 132–133, **133**
shipwrecks 132, **132,** 134
Fox, Andrew 244, 247
Fox, Rodney 244, 248
France
Bormes-les-Mimosas **118–119,** 118–123, **120, 121, 122**
Saint-Malo **166,** 166–171, **168, 169, 170**
Frégate, Seychelles **88–89,** 88–93
accommodations **92,** 93
Alphonse Island 92
dive sites **90,** 91–92
hiking 90–91
make a difference 91
marine life 89, 91–92, 93
need to know 93
wildlife 89, 90, 91, **91,** 93
French Polynesia: Moorea 190–195
Coral Gardeners 193, 194, **194**
dive sites 192
dolphin- and whale-watching ecotours 193
hiking 192, **192**
make a difference 193
Maori culture 192–193
marine life 191, 192, 193, 195
need to know 195
Te Mana o Te Moana (sea turtle protection agency) **193,** 193–194
Tuamotus **191,** 194
Friedlander, Alan 217

G

Gagnan, Émile 122
Galápagos Islands, Ecuador 124–129
Charles Darwin Foundation 125, 127

Charles Darwin Research Station 126–127, **127**
dive sites 127–128
food & drink 126, 129
Galápagos Marine Reserve 127–128
marine life **126,** 127, **128,** 129
need to know 129
Santa Fe Island 126
Tortuga Bay 126
wildlife **124,** 125, 126–127, **127**
Wolf and Darwin Islands 128
Gasa, Biuku 110
Gaspar, Cécile **193,** 193–194
Gozo, Malta 100–105
Cittadella 102
climbing 102
dive sites **103,** 103–104
divers **330**
free-diving clinic 103, 104
kayaking 102
Lord Chambray Brewery 102
make a difference 104
marine life **4, 100,** 104
need to know 105
shipwrecks 103
villages 102, **104**
Xewkija Church **102**
Grand Cayman, Cayman Islands 94–99
Bioluminescence Bay 96–97
Cayman Islands National Museum 96
dive sites 98, **98**
Jean-Michel Cousteau's Ambassadors of the Environment program 97
kayak tours 96–97
make a difference 98
mangroves 97–98
marine life 98, 99
mermaid statue **96**
nearby 96

need to know 99
Pedro St. James 96
Queen Elizabeth II Botanic Park 96, **97**
Seven Mile Beach **94–95**
shipwrecks 98, **98**
wildlife 96, **97**
Great Barrier Reef, Australia 161, 162–164, **163,** 165
Great white sharks 244, **244–245,** 246–247, 248, 249
Greece: Alonnisos 16–21
Captain Pakis Athanasiou's Gorgona Cruises 19–20
dive sites **18,** 18–19, 21
exploratory diving 17, 18, 19, 21
hiking 20
island road trip 18
make a difference 20
marine life 18, **19,** 20, 21
Monastery of Kyra Pangia 20
National Marine Park of Alonnisos and Northern Sporades 17–19, **19**
need to know 21
Old Village 17, 20, **20**
packing tips 18, 20, 21
Patitiri 17, 20
shipwrecks **18,** 18–19
Steni Vala **16–17**
Green Fins initiative 61

H

Hassell, Josephus Lambert ("Lambee") 264
Hawai'i, United States 148–153
Big Island 149–151
dive sites **148,** 150–151
helicopter tours 150, **150**
make a difference 151
marine life 150–151, **151,** 152, 153
Mauna Kea Observatory 151–152, **152**

need to know 153
night diving 151, **151,** 152
something special 152
Hector's dolphins 38
Heller, Cara 97
High seas 115
Hodgin, Daniel Boone 294, 295
Hone Heke (Māori leader) 37
Hvar, Croatia 46–51
Blue Cave **50**
Brač 50
dive sites **48,** 49–50
food & drink 48–49, 51
harbor **46–47**
Hvar Town 48
make a difference 49
Malo Grablje 48–49, 51
marine life **48,** 49–50, 51, **328**
marine park (proposed) 49
nearby 50
need to know 51
Secret Hvar driving tour 48
Stari Grad Plain 46, 48
Stori Komin restaurant, Malo Grablje 48–49, 51
Vis island 50, **50**
walking 50, 51
winemaking history 48, **49**

I

Indonesia
Komodo **142–143,** 142–147, **144, 145, 146**
Raja Ampat **11, 184–185,** 184–189, **186, 187, 188**

J

Japan: Okinawa 220–225
dive sites 222–223
karate classes 222
Kerama Islands 223–224
make a difference 224
marine life **222,** 223, **224,** 225
Murasaki Mura 222

Naha 220, **220–221,** 222
need to know 225
Okinawa Prefectural Peace Memorial Museum 224
shore diving **223**
Shuri Castle 220, 222
Sunabe Seawall 222–223
whale-watching **222,** 223–224
Yonaguni Jima 222

K

Keeling (Cocos) Islands, Australia 310–315
bicycling 312
cooking classes 312
dive sites 313, 314
Home Island 311, 312–313
inter-island transportation **310–311**
marine life 312, 313, **313,** 314, **314,** 315
need to know 315
outrigger canoe safari 312
plastics cleanup 313, 314
Pulu Cocos Museum 312
road trip 312
Scroungers Golf 314
snorkeling 312
sunken boats and cannons 313
Uninhabited Direction Island **312**
West Island 311, 312
wildlife 312
Kennedy, John F. 108, 110
Kenting National Park, Taiwan 112–117, **116**
dive sites 115–116
land activities 114–115
make a difference 115
marine life **112–113, 114,** 115, **115,** 117
need to know 117
wildlife 114
Key Largo see Florida Keys, United States

Key West *see* Florida Keys, United
   States
Ko Lanta, Thailand 250–255
   cooking classes **253,** 254
   dive sites **252,** 252–253
   food & drink **250–251,** 254, 255
   Ko Haa marine park **252,** 252–
      253
   land activities 252, **253,** 253–254
   marine life 252, **252,** 253, 255
   Muay Thai boxing academy
      252
   need to know 255
   Old Town **250–251,** 253–254
   Pimalai Resort and Spa 252, **253,**
      254, **254,** 255
   something special 252
Ko Samui, Thailand 136–141
   dive sites 138
   food & drink **140,** 141
   Kamalaya wellness retreat **139,**
      139–140, 141
   make a difference 140
   marine life **136–137,** 138, **138,**
      141
   Muay Thai kickboxing 138–139
   need to know 141
Komodo, Indonesia 142–147
   dive sites 145–146, **146**
   Komodo National Park 142,
      144–145, **145**
   make a difference 146
   marine life **144,** 145–146, 147
   nearby 144
   need to know 147
   wildlife 142, **142–143,** 144–145
Kumana, Eroni 110

L

Laguna Beach, California, United
   States **154–155,** 154–159
   dive sites 156–157, **157**
   golfing 157, **158**
   hiking and mountain biking 157
   make a difference 157
   marine life 156, **156,** 157
   marine reserve 156
   need to know 159
   Pacific Marine Mammal Center
      156, 157
   Santa Catalina Island 158
   shops and galleries 157–158
Lavenan, Solene 168
Lizard Island, Australia 160–165
   Blue Lagoon **160–161**
   dive sites 162–163
   food & drink 162, 165
   Great Barrier Reef 161, 162–164,
      163, 165
   hiking 164, **164**
   Lizard Island Research Station
      161, 162, 164
   make a difference 164
   marine life **162,** 163–164, 165
   need to know 165
   snorkeling 163–164
Lockyer, Megan-Jane 301–302
Lord Howe Island, Australia **2–3,**
   268–273
   Admiralty Islands 270
   bird-watching **270,** 271
   Capella Lodge **268–269,** 273
   dive sites 270–271, **271**
   for families 270
   hiking 271–272, **272**
   Lord Howe Island Museum 272
   make a difference 272
   marine life 268, 270–271, **271,**
      273
   need to know 273
   snorkeling 270
   wildlife 268, **270,** 271–272
Love, Simon 90

M

Madagascar: Nosy Ambariovato
   208–213
   bribes 212
   dive sites 211–212, **212**
   hiking 210
   make a difference 211
   marine life 208, 211, **211, 212,**
      213
   need to know 213
   shipwrecks 211
   snorkeling with whale sharks
      212
   Tsara Komba Luxury Beach &
      Forest Lodge 208, **208–209,**
      210, **210,** 213
   wildlife 208, 210
Malapascua Island, Philippines
   58–63
   bangca (outrigger canoe)
      58–59
   cultural life 58, **60,** 62
   dive sites 60–62
   Gato Island 61, 62
   make a difference 61
   marine life 58, 60–62, **61,** 63
   Monad Shoal 60–61
   nearby 62
   need to know 63
   shark diving 58, 60–62, **61**
   shipwrecks **62**
Malta: Gozo 100–105
   Cittadella 102
   climbing 102
   dive sites **103,** 103–104
   divers **330**
   free-diving clinic 103, 104
   kayaking 102
   Lord Chambray Brewery 102
   make a difference 104
   marine life **4, 100,** 104
   need to know 105
   shipwrecks 103
   villages 102, **104**
   Xewkija Church **102**
Maps
   dive sites 14–15
   Marine Protected Area zones
      324–325
Marine Megafauna Foundation
   (MMF) 42, 43, 44

Marine protected areas map 324–325

Marlborough Sounds, New Zealand 172–177
  dive sites 175–176
  food & drink **174,** 177
  Mail Boat Cruise 174
  marine life **174,** 176, 177
  need to know 177
  Punga People art installation **176**
  Queen Charlotte Sound 172, 175, **175**
  Queen Charlotte Track 172, 174–175
  shipwrecks 172, **172–173,** 175, 176
  Trees That Count 176
  wildlife (birds) 174
Marshall, Andrea 241
Mexico: Tulum 280–285
  bike tours 284, **284**
  cenotes (underwater caves) 280, **282,** 282–283, 284, 285
  dive sites 280, **282,** 282–283, 285
  food & drink 284, 285
  Kin Toh treehouse restaurant 284
  make a difference 283
  marine life 285
  Maya sites 280, **283,** 283–284
  need to know 285
  Sian Ka'an Biosphere Reserve 280, **280–281,** 283
  snorkeling 283
  something special 284
Michener, James A. 300
Milford Sound, New Zealand 178–183
  altitude 180
  day cruises 180, 181
  dive sites **178–179,** 181–182
  make a difference 182
  Māori culture 180, 182

marine life **180,** 181–182, 183
  Milford Track 179, **182**
  need to know 183
  overnight cruises **181,** 182, 183
  Underwater Observatory 181
  wildlife 180
Mission Blue Hope Spots
  about 200
  Andros, Bahamas 22
  Exmouth, Australia 82
  map 324–325
  Mesoamerican Reef system 70, 283
  Raja Ampat, Indonesia 184
  Sydney, Australia 32
MMF (Marine Megafauna Foundation) 42, 43, 44
Monaco 118, **121,** 122
Monk seals 20
Moorea, French Polynesia 190–195
  Coral Gardeners 193, 194, **194**
  dive sites 192
  dolphin- and whale-watching ecotours 193
  hiking 192, **192**
  make a difference 193
  Maori culture 192–193
  marine life 191, 192, 193, 195
  need to know 195
  Te Mana o Te Moana (sea turtle protection agency) **193,** 193–194
  Tuamotus **191,** 194
Mozambique: Tofo Beach 40–45
  Bazaruto Archipelago National Park 42, 43
  beaches **40–41,** 42
  dive sites **43,** 43–44
  food & drink **42,** 44, 45
  Happi (restaurant) **42,** 45
  Liquid Dive Adventures **42,** 45
  make a difference 44
  Marble Arch **43**
  marine life 41, 43, **43,** 44, **44,** 45

Marine Megafauna Foundation (MMF) 42, 43, 44
  mineral extraction 43
  Mozambeat Motel 42, 44, 45
  nearby 42
  need to know 45
  sailing trip 44
  surfing 42
Munda and Gizo, Solomon Islands 106–111
  cultural traditions **106–107**
  Dive Munda 109, 111
  dive sites 108, 109
  for families 110
  Kennedy Island **108,** 110
  make a difference 109
  marine life **8,** 106, 109, **109,** 111
  need to know 111
  shipwrecks and aircraft wrecks 108, 109, **110**
  snorkeling 108
  Solomon Islands National Museum 110
Musée Océanographique de Monaco 118, **121,** 122

N
Napier, Meron 68
Nassau, Bahamas
  for families 26
  need to know 27
  shark diving **25,** 25–26, **26**
  shipwrecks 26, **26**
  Stuart Cove's Dive Bahamas **25,** 25–26, 27
National Geographic
  Planet or Plastic? 313
  Pristine Seas 10, 217, 290
Netherlands see Curaçao; Saba
New Zealand
  Bay of Islands **34–35,** 34–39, **36, 37, 38**
  Marlborough Sounds **172–173,** 172–177, **174, 175, 176**

Milford Sound **178–179,** 178–183, **180, 181, 182**
Rarotonga, Cook Islands **256–257,** 256–261, **258, 259, 260**
Nha Trang, Vietnam 202–207
  dive sites 204–205
  food & drink **202–203,** 205–206, **206,** 207
  Hon Mun Marine Park 204
  make a difference 206
  marine life 204, **204,** 207
  need to know 207
  Po Nagar Cham Towers 205, **205**
  shops 205
  visas 204
Ningaloo Coast *see* Exmouth, Australia
Niue 214–219
  caves and chasms 216–218
  dive sites **216,** 217–218
  driving trips 216–217, 218
  food & drink 216, 219
  Huvalu Forest Conservation Area 215, 216
  Limu Pools **218**
  make a difference 217
  marine life **217,** 217–218, 219
  need to know 219
  Niue Ocean Wide Project (NOW) 217
  snorkeling with humpback whales 218
  Togo Chasm **214,** 216
  wildlife 216
North Carolina: Outer Banks 232–237
  aerial view **232–233**
  Cape Hatteras Lighthouse 234–235, **235**
  dive sites 235
  for families 236
  kite-flying 234
  marine life **236,** 237
  need to know 237

North Carolina Aquarium **234,** 235
shipwrecks 232, 234, 235, **236**
Wright Brothers National Memorial 232, 234
Nosy Ambariovato, Madagascar 208–213
  bribes 212
  dive sites 211–212, **212**
  hiking 210
  make a difference 211
  marine life 208, 211, **211, 212,** 213
  need to know 213
  shipwrecks 211
  snorkeling with whale sharks 212
  Tsara Komba Luxury Beach & Forest Lodge 208, **208–209,** 210, **210,** 213
  wildlife 208, 210

O
OBX *see* Outer Banks, North Carolina, United States
Okinawa, Japan 220–225
  dive sites 222–223
  karate classes 222
  Kerama Islands 223–224
  make a difference 224
  marine life **222,** 223, **224,** 225
  Murasaki Mura 222
  Naha 220, **220–221,** 222
  need to know 225
  Okinawa Prefectural Peace Memorial Museum 224
  shore diving **223**
  Shuri Castle 220, 222
  Sunabe Seawall 222–223
  whale-watching **222,** 223–224
  Yonaguni Jima 222
Open Water certification
  Ko Samui, Thailand 137
  learning to dive 327
  Malapascua Island, Philippines 60

Orkney Islands, United Kingdom 229
Port Lincoln, Australia 247
Tulum, Mexico 282
Orkney Islands, United Kingdom 226–231
  dive sites 228–229
  Highland Park whisky 230
  island-hopping 228
  Mainland (island) 228
  make a difference 230
  marine life **228,** 231
  need to know 231
  Ring of Brodgar **229,** 230
  Scapa Flow 228, 229, 231
  shipwrecks **226–227, 228,** 228–229
  shore diving 228
  Skara Brae 230, **230**
  something special 228
  Stromness Museum 228
Otsubo, Hirokazu 224
Outer Banks, North Carolina, United States 232–237
  aerial view **232–233**
  Cape Hatteras Lighthouse 234–235, **235**
  dive sites 235
  for families 236
  kite-flying 234
  marine life **236,** 237
  need to know 237
  North Carolina Aquarium **234,** 235
  shipwrecks 232, 234, 235, **236**
  Wright Brothers National Memorial 232, 234

P
Packing 316–318
  camera 318
  carry bag 318
  dive gear 316, **317,** 318, **318,** 329
  dry bag and first aid kit 318
  exposure protection 318

flashlight 318
knife or cutting tool 318
mask and snorkel 316, 329
personal computer 316
reef-safe sunscreen and lip balm 318
regulators, BCD, and fins 318
safety gear 316, **317**, 318, **318**
save-your-dive kit 318
Papet, Nathalie 120
Pascua, Isla de *see* Easter Island, Chile
Petit St. Vincent, St. Vincent and the Grenadines 238–243
   Baradal Turtle Sanctuary 241
   beaches 240, **242**
   dive sites 241–242
   exploratory diving 242
   land activities 239, 240
   make a difference 241
   marine life 241, **241**, 242, 243
   Marni Hill 239, 240
   Mayreau 242
   need to know 243
   Petit St. Vincent Private Island Resort **238**, 239–243
   sailing trips **240**, 240–241
   shipwrecks 241
   snorkeling 241
   something special 242
   Tobago Cays Marine Park 240–241
   wildlife 240
Philippines: Malapascua Island 58–63
   bangca (outrigger canoe) **58–59**
   cultural life 58, **60**, 62
   dive sites 60–62
   Gato Island 61, 62
   make a difference 61
   marine life 58, 60–62, **61**, 63
   Monad Shoal 60–61
   nearby 62
   need to know 63

shark diving 58, 60–62, **61**
shipwrecks **62**
Poole, Michael 193
Port Lincoln, Australia 244–249
   make a difference 248
   marine life 244, **244–245, 246,** 246–247, 249
   nearby 246
   need to know 249
   Neptune Islands 247, **247,** 248
   shark-cage diving 244, **244–245,** 246–247, 248, 249
   snorkeling **246**
   town activities 248
   wildlife 247, 248, **248**
Pristine Seas project 10, 217, 290

R
Raja Ampat, Indonesia 184–189
   dive sites 186–188, 189
   for families 188
   guided boat dives 186–187
   lagoons and karst spires **188**
   land activities 187–188
   make a difference 187
   marine life 184, **184–185, 186,** 187, **187,** 189
   Misool Marine Reserve 184, **186**
   Misool Resort **11,** 184, **184–185,** 186, 189
   need to know 189
   snorkeling 184, 186, 189
Rapa Nui *see* Easter Island, Chile
Rarotonga, Cook Islands 256–261
   aerial view **256–257**
   Aitutaki Day Tour 260
   dive sites 258, 261
   food & drink 259, 261
   heritage and culture 256, 259, **259,** 260
   hiking 259–260, **260**
   Koka Lagoon Cruise 260
   make a difference 259
   Marae Moana marine park 258
   marine life 258, **258,** 261

markets 259
need to know 261
snorkeling 260
Wi-Fi costs 260
Reef-World Foundation 61
Reuter, Ludwig von 228

S
Saba 262–267
   dive sites 263, 265–266
   glass-making class 266
   heritage and culture **262**
   hiking 263, 264–265, **265**
   lacemaking 264, **264**
   marine life 265, 266, **266,** 267
   Mount Scenery 265, **265**
   need to know 267
   Saba Conservation Foundation 265
   Saba National Marine Park 265
   something special 266
   villages 263
   wildlife 265
   Windwardside **262,** 263, 264
Saint-Malo, France 166–171
   birding 168–169
   D-Day beaches 170
   dive sites 169, **170**
   fortress **166,** 168
   horse-drawn carriage ride 168
   make a difference 169
   marine life **169, 170,** 171
   Mont-Saint-Michel **168,** 169–170
   need to know 171
   Rance estuary 169
   shipwrecks and aircraft wrecks 169
   wish we knew 170
Sala, Enric 9–10, 116
Seal conservation 20
Seaweed conservation 31
Seru, Viliame 276
Seychelles: Frégate **88–89,** 88–93
   accommodations **92,** 93
   Alphonse Island 92

dive sites **90,** 91–92
hiking 90–91
make a difference 91
marine life 89, 91–92, 93
need to know 93
wildlife 89, 90, 91, **91,** 93
Shark-cage diving: Port Lincoln, Australia 244, **244–245,** 246–247, 248, 249
Shark conservation 25, 26, 248, 259, 277, 296
Shark diving
  benefits 25
  Malapascua Island, Philippines 58, 60–62, **61**
  Nassau, Bahamas **25,** 25–26
  Umkomaas, South Africa 289
  Viti Levu, Fiji 277
Shark Lab 25
Sheffer, Ryan **158**
Shipwrecks
  Alonnisos, Greece **18,** 18–19
  Bay of Islands, New Zealand **34–35,** 38
  Bormes-les-Mimosas, France **120,** 121
  British Virgin Islands 66, 67, **68**
  Curaçao **306,** 307
  Espiritu Santo, Vanuatu **298–299,** 299, 300–301
  Florida Keys, United States 132, **132,** 134
  Gozo, Malta 103
  Grand Cayman, Cayman Islands 98, **98**
  Malapascua Island, Philippines **62**
  Marlborough Sounds, New Zealand 172, **172–173,** 175, 176
  Munda and Gizo, Solomon Islands 108, 109, **110**
  Nassau, Bahamas 26, **26**
  Nosy Ambariovato, Madagascar 211

Orkney Islands, United Kingdom **226–227, 228,** 228–229
Outer Banks, North Carolina, United States 232, 234, 235, **236**
Petit St. Vincent, St. Vincent and the Grenadines 241
Saint-Malo, France 169
Skerry, Brian 6–7, **7, 329**
Solomon Islands: Munda and Gizo 106–111
  cultural traditions **106–107**
  Dive Munda 109, 111
  dive sites 108, 109
  for families 110
  Kennedy Island **108,** 110
  make a difference 109
  marine life **8,** 106, 109, **109,** 111
  need to know 111
  shipwrecks and aircraft wrecks 108, 109, **110**
  snorkeling 108
  Solomon Islands National Museum 110
South Africa: Umkomaas 286–291
  Aliwal Shoal **286,** 287, **288,** 288–289
  annual sardine run 288, 290
  dive sites **286,** 287, 288–289, 291
  landscape **289**
  make a difference 290
  marine life **286,** 287, **288,** 288–289, 291
  need to know 291
  PheZulu Safari Park 290, 291
  safaris 289–290, **290**
  shark diving 289
  wildlife 288, 289–290, **290**
St. Vincent and the Grenadines: Petit St. Vincent 238–243
  Baradal Turtle Sanctuary 241
  beaches 240, **242**
  dive sites 241–242

exploratory diving 242
land activities 239, 240
make a difference 241
marine life 241, **241,** 242, 243
Marni Hill 239, 240
Mayreau 242
need to know 243
Petit St. Vincent Private Island Resort **238,** 239–243
sailing trips **240,** 240–241
shipwrecks 241
snorkeling 241
something special 242
Tobago Cays Marine Park 240–241
wildlife 240
Suyanto, Agus 144
Sydney, Australia 28–33
  Aboriginal Australians 29, 30–31
  Australian Museum 30
  Blue Mountains 32
  Cabbage Tree Bay Aquatic Reserve 31
  dive sites **31,** 31–32
  Harbour Bridge 30, 33
  make a difference 31
  Manly 30–31, **32,** 33
  marine life **28,** 31, 32, 33
  need to know 33
  North Head Sanctuary 30–31
  Opera House 30, **30**
  parks and gardens 30
  snorkeling 31
  surfing 31

T

Tailliez, Philippe 122
Taiwan: Kenting National Park 112–117, **116**
  dive sites 115–116
  land activities 114–115
  make a difference 115
  marine life **112–113, 114,** 115, **115,** 117

need to know 117
wildlife 114
Tanzania: Zanzibar 196–201
   aerial view **196–197**
   ATMs and credit cards 198
   dive sites 199–200
   horseback riding 198–199, **200**
   make a difference 200
   marine life **198,** 200, 201
   Mnemba Island 199–200
   need to know 201
   Nungwi 198–199
   snorkeling 199–200
   Stone Town 196, 198, **199**
Taveuni Island, Fiji 274–279
   Bouma National Heritage Park
      275, 277, **277**
   culture 275, 276, 278
   dive sites 277–278, **278,** 279
   Fiji Time 278
   make a difference 277
   marine life **274–275,** 277–278,
      279
   need to know 279
   rugby 276, **276**
   snorkeling 277
   village visits 276
   Waitabu Marine Park 276–277
Thailand
   Ko Lanta **250–251,** 250–255, **252,
      253, 254**
   Ko Samui **136–137,** 136–141, **138,
      139, 140**
Thresher sharks 58, 60–61
Tofo Beach, Mozambique 40–45
   Bazaruto Archipelago National
      Park 42, 43
   beaches **40–41,** 42
   dive sites **43,** 43–44
   food & drink **42,** 44, 45
   Happi (restaurant) **42,** 45
   Liquid Dive Adventures **42,** 45
   make a difference 44
   Marble Arch **43**
   marine life 41, 43, **43,** 44, **44,** 45

Marine Megafauna Foundation
   (MMF) 42, 43, 44
mineral extraction 43
Mozambeat Motel 42, 44, 45
nearby 42
need to know 45
sailing trip 44
surfing 42
Trash Hero World 146
Trees That Count 176
Tuamotus **191,** 194
Tudor, Berti 48–49
Tuki, Ludovic 80
Tulum, Mexico 280–285
   bike tours 284, **284**
   cenotes (underwater caves)
      280, **282,** 282–283, 284, 285
   dive sites 280, **282,** 282–283,
      285
   food & drink 284, 285
   Kin Toh treehouse restaurant
      284
   make a difference 283
   marine life 285
   Maya sites 280, **283,** 283–284
   need to know 285
   Sian Ka'an Biosphere Reserve
      280, **280–281,** 283
   snorkeling 283
   something special 284

U

Umkomaas, South Africa 286–291
   Aliwal Shoal **286,** 287, **288,** 288–
      289
   annual sardine run 288, 290
   dive sites **286,** 287, 288–289,
      291
   landscape **289**
   make a difference 290
   marine life **286,** 287, **288,** 288–
      289, 291
   need to know 291
   PheZulu Safari Park 290, 291
   safaris 289–290, **290**

shark diving 289
wildlife 288, 289–290, **290**
UNESCO World Heritage sites
   Belize Barrier Reef 70, 73, 74, 75
   Blue Mountains, Australia 32
   Easter Island, Chile 76–81
   Komodo National Park,
      Indonesia 142, 144–145, **145**
   Lord Howe Island, Australia
      268
   Mont-Saint-Michel, France
      168, 169–170
   Ningaloo Coast, Australia 82,
      85
   Okinawa, Jaan 220, 222
   Orkney Islands, United
      Kingdom 227, 230
   Sian Ka'an Biosphere Reserve,
      Mexico 280, **280–281,** 283
   Stari Grad Plain, Croatia 46, 48
   Stone Town, Zanzibar, Tanzania
      196, 198, **199**
   Te Wāhipounamu-South West
      New Zealand 179
   Tubbataha Reefs Natural Park,
      Philippines 62
   Willemstad, Curaçao **304–305,**
      306
United Kingdom: Orkney Islands
   226–231
   dive sites 228–229
   Highland Park whisky 230
   island-hopping 228
   Mainland (island) 228
   make a difference 230
   marine life **228,** 231
   need to know 231
   Ring of Brodgar **229,** 230
   Scapa Flow 228, 229, 231
   shipwrecks **226–227, 228,** 228–
      229
   shore diving 228
   Skara Brae 230, **230**
   something special 228
   Stromness Museum 228

United States
    Florida Keys **130–131,** 130–135,
        132, 133, 134
    Hawai'i **148,** 148–153, **150, 151,**
        152
    Laguna Beach, California **154–**
        155, 154–159, **156, 157, 158**
    Outer Banks, North Carolina
        232–233, 232–237, **234, 235,**
        236
    Valdez, Alaska **292–293,** 292–
        297, **294, 295, 296**

V

Valdez, Alaska, United States
    292–297
    dive sites 294–295
    harbor **292–293**
    iceberg **296**
    make a difference 296
    marine life 292, **294,** 294–295,
        296, 297
    need to know 297
    Ravencroft Lodge 292, 294, 295,
        295, 297
    snorkeling 295
    Valdez Museum & Historical
        Archives 296
    weather and flight cancellation
        294
    wildlife 292, 294
    wildlife cruises 296
Van Bebber, Barbara 308
Vanuatu: Espiritu Santo 298–303
    Champagne Beach **301,** 302
    dive sites **300,** 300–301
    food & drink 300, 302, 303
    horseback riding 301–302, **302**
    make a difference 302
    marine life 300–301, 303
    Million Dollar Point **300,** 301
    need to know 303
    shipwrecks and aircraft wrecks
        298–299, 299, 300–301
    snorkeling **300,** 301

World War II equipment **298–**
    299, 300, 301
WWII History Tour 301
Vietnam: Nha Trang 202–207
    dive sites 204–205
    food & drink **202–203,** 205–
        206, **206,** 207
    Hon Mun Marine Park 204
    make a difference 206
    marine life 204, **204,** 207
    need to know 207
    Po Nagar Cham Towers 205,
        205
    shops 205
    visas 204

W

Whyalla, Australia 246
World Wildlife Fund 151
Wreck diving *see* Aircraft wrecks;
    Shipwrecks

Y

Yonaguni Jima, Japan 222

Z

Zabaneh, Rosalia 73
Zamami Village Whale Watching
    Association 224
Zanzibar, Tanzania 196–201
    aerial view **196–197**
    ATMs and credit cards 198
    dive sites 199–200
    horseback riding 198–199, **200**
    make a difference 200
    marine life **198,** 200, 201
    Mnemba Island 199–200
    need to know 201
    Nungwi 198–199
    snorkeling 199–200
    Stone Town 196, 198, **199**

ABOUT THE
AUTHORS

CHRIS TAYLOR is an experienced diver, with more than 1,000 dives under his weight belt. He has worked in the dive industry throughout Australia and has a particular love for sharks.

Chris and Carrie met in Port Lincoln, Australia (page 244) in 2013. Carrie was on assignment for National Geographic, writing a story about great white sharks. Chris was working as a dive supervisor and shark wrangler for Rodney Fox Great White Shark Expeditions.

When they're not traveling, Carrie and Chris are trying to figure out where to live. (Australia? New Zealand? Niue?)

CARRIE MILLER is a traveler, storyteller, and award-winning writer. She has been writing for National Geographic since 1998. Her first book, *100 Dives of a Lifetime: The World's Ultimate Underwater Destinations,* was published in 2019.

You can follow their work and adventures at Beneath the Surface Media (@beneaththesurfacemedia).

Since 1888, the National Geographic Society has funded more than 14,000 research, conservation, education, and storytelling projects around the world. National Geographic Partners distributes a portion of the funds it receives from your purchase to National Geographic Society to support programs including the conservation of animals and their habitats.

Get closer to National Geographic Explorers and photographers, and connect with our global community. Join us today at nationalgeographic.org/joinus

For rights or permissions inquiries, please contact National Geographic Books Subsidiary Rights: bookrights@natgeo.com

ISBN: 978-1-4262-2092-0

Printed in South Korea

22/SPSK/1

EXPLORATION IS ONLY A DIVE AWAY

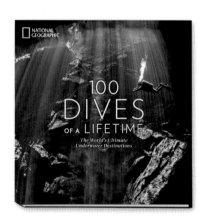

100 DIVES OF A LIFETIME
The World's Ultimate Underwater Destinations

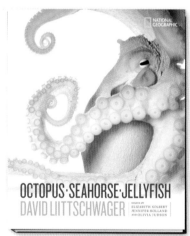

OCTOPUS·SEAHORSE·JELLYFISH
DAVID LIITTSCHWAGER

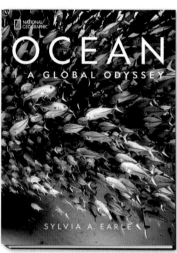

OCEAN
A GLOBAL ODYSSEY
SYLVIA A. EARLE

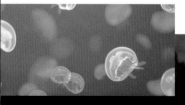

AVAILABLE WHEREVER BOOKS ARE SOLD

 NatGeoBooks    @NatGeoBooks